Windows® 2000 Server For Dummies®

D1370930

Windows 2000 Server Administrative Tools

You can access any of these programs by using the Start⇨Administrative Tools menu or by typing in the name of the launch file in the Run (Start⇨Run) command.

Name	Launch File	Description
Active Directory Domains and Trusts	domain.msc	Used to manage trusts between domains.
Active Directory Sites and Services	dssite.msc	Used to manage sites involved in Active Directory replication.
Active Directory Users and Computers	dsa.msc	Used to manage users, groups, computers, and other objects.
Component Services	comexp.msc	Used to manage COM+ applications.
Computer Management	compmgmt.msc /s	Used to start and stop services, manage disks, and provide access to other computer management tools for local and remote administration.
Configure Your Server	mshta.exe res://srvwiz. dll/default.hta	Used to configure a system for network operations.
Data Sources (ODBC)	odbcad32.exe	Used to manage ODBC drivers and data sources.
DHCP	dhcpmgmt.msc /s	Used to manage DHCP, which assigns TCP/IP settings to clients.
Distributed File System	dfsgui.msc /s	Used to manage DFS, which creates a single shared hierarchy of resources from multiple hosts.
DNS	dnsmgmt.msc /s	Used to manage DNS, which resolves host names into IP addresses.
Event Viewer	eventvwr.msc /s	Used to access various log files under Windows 2000.
Internet Services Manager	mmc.exe H:\W2KSVR\ System32\inetsrv\iis.msc	Used to manage Web and FTP Internet services.
Licensing	llsmgr.exe	Used to manage licenses and client use.
Performance	perfmon.msc /s	Used to monitor the performance of a system or network.
Routing and Remote Access	rrasmgmt.msc /s	Used to manage remote connections and routing activities.
Server Extensions Administrator	fpmmc.msc	Used to manage FrontPage server extensions.
Terminal Services Licensing	licmgr.exe	Used to manage client access to terminal services.

Windows® 2000 Server For Dummies®

Cheat Sheet

Important Windows 2000 TCP/IP Command Line Utilities

Each of these utilities performs some useful function; the "Help String" column shows how to get online help for syntax details on each command.

Name	Help String	Description
Arp	arp /h	Displays and modifies the address translation table maintained by the TCP/IP Address Resolution Protocol.
Ipconfig	ipconfig /?	Displays all current TCP/IP network configuration data.
Nbtstat	nbtstat /h	Displays protocol statistics and current TCP/IP connections using NetBIOS over TCP/IP (NetBT).
Netstart	netstart /?	Displays protocol statistics and current TCP/IP network connections.
Ping	ping	Verifies connections to local or remote computers (PING stands for Packet InterNet Groper; excellent IP troubleshooting tool).
Route	route	Displays and manipulates network routing tables.
Tracert	tracert	Displays the route from your machine to a specified destination.

Important Windows 2000 Net Commands

Each of these command-line utilities performs some useful NetBIOS networking functions. Use Net Help to get general help on this command, or Net Help <command> to get help on a specific Net command.

Name	Description
Net Accounts	Provides a command-line tool to manage user accounts.
Net Computer	Adds or deletes computers in a domain database.
Net Help	Provides access to all Net command help files.
Net Helpmsg	Explains Windows 2000 error messages.
Net Print	Allows you to view or control print jobs.
Net Send	Sends messages to other computers or users on a network.
Net Share	Allows you to display, create, or delete network shares.
Net Use	Allows you to connect or disconnect a computer from a share by name

...For Dummies®: Bestselling Book Series for Beginners

Windows® 2000 Server FOR DUMMIES®

by Ed Tittel,
James Michael Stewart,
Mary Madden

IDG BOOKS WORLDWIDE

IDG Books Worldwide, Inc.
An International Data Group Company

Foster City, CA ◆ Chicago, IL ◆ Indianapolis, IN ◆ New York, NY

Windows® 2000 Server For Dummies®

Published by
IDG Books Worldwide, Inc.
An International Data Group Company
919 E. Hillsdale Blvd.
Suite 400
Foster City, CA 94404
www.idgbooks.com (IDG Books Worldwide Web site)
www.dummies.com (Dummies Press Web site)

Library of Congress Catalog Card No.: 99-66697

ISBN: 0-7645-0341-3

Printed in the United States of America

10 9 8 7 6 5 4 3 2

1O/QS/QS/QQ/IN

Distributed in the United States by IDG Books Worldwide, Inc.

Distributed by CDG Books Canada Inc. for Canada; by Transworld Publishers Limited in the United Kingdom; by IDG Norge Books for Norway; by IDG Sweden Books for Sweden; by IDG Books Australia Publishing Corporation Pty. Ltd. for Australia and New Zealand; by TransQuest Publishers Pte Ltd. for Singapore, Malaysia, Thailand, Indonesia, and Hong Kong; by Gotop Information Inc. for Taiwan; by ICG Muse, Inc. for Japan; by Intersoft for South Africa; by Eyrolles for France; by International Thomson Publishing for Germany, Austria and Switzerland; by Distribuidora Cuspide for Argentina; by LR International for Brazil; by Galileo Libros for Chile; by Ediciones ZETA S.C.R. Ltda. for Peru; by WS Computer Publishing Corporation, Inc., for the Philippines; by Contemporanea de Ediciones for Venezuela; by Express Computer Distributors for the Caribbean and West Indies; by Micronesia Media Distributor, Inc. for Micronesia; by Chips Computadoras S.A. de C.V. for Mexico; by Editorial Norma de Panama S.A. for Panama; by American Bookshops for Finland.

For general information on IDG Books Worldwide's books in the U.S., please call our Consumer Customer Service department at 800-762-2974. For reseller information, including discounts and premium sales, please call our Reseller Customer Service department at 800-434-3422.

For information on where to purchase IDG Books Worldwide's books outside the U.S., please contact our International Sales department at 317-596-5530 or fax 317-596-5692.

For consumer information on foreign language translations, please contact our Customer Service department at 1-800-434-3422, fax 317-596-5692, or e-mail rights@idgbooks.com.

For information on licensing foreign or domestic rights, please phone +1-650-655-3109.

For sales inquiries and special prices for bulk quantities, please contact our Sales department at 650-655-3200 or write to the address above.

For information on using IDG Books Worldwide's books in the classroom or for ordering examination copies, please contact our Educational Sales department at 800-434-2086 or fax 317-596-5499.

For press review copies, author interviews, or other publicity information, please contact our Public Relations department at 650-655-3000 or fax 650-655-3299.

For authorization to photocopy items for corporate, personal, or educational use, please contact Copyright Clearance Center, 222 Rosewood Drive, Danvers, MA 01923, or fax 978-750-4470.

is a registered trademark under exclusive license to IDG Books Worldwide, Inc. from International Data Group, Inc.

About the Authors

Ed Tittel is a grizzled veteran of the publishing game, with several hundred magazine articles and more than 100 books to his credit. Ed has worked on numerous other *For Dummies* books, including *HTML 4 For Dummies,* 2nd Edition (with Natanya Pitts), *Networking with NetWare For Dummies* (with James Gaskin and David Johnson), and books on other topics. Ed presides over a small Austin, TX-based consulting company that specializes in network-oriented training, writing, and consulting. When Ed's not busy writing, he likes to shoot pool, cook, and hang out with his teen-aged Labrador retriever, Blackie. You can reach Ed via e-mail at etittel@lanw.com or through his Web page at www.lanw.com/staff/etbio.htm.

James Michael Stewart is an MCSE and a full-time writer who focuses on Windows NT and Internet topics. Most recently, he has worked on several titles in the Exam Cram and Exam Prep series. Michael has written articles for numerous print and online publications, including *C|Net, Computer Currents, InfoWorld, Windows NT Magazine,* and *Datamation.* He is also a regular speaker at Networld+Interop and TISC. Michael has been with LANWrights, Inc. developing Windows NT and Windows 2000 MCSE-level courseware and training materials for several years. Michael graduated in 1992 from the University of Texas at Austin with a bachelor's degree in Philosophy. Despite his degree, his computer knowledge is self-acquired, based on more than 16 years of hands-on experience. Michael has been active on the Internet for quite some time, where most people know him by his "nom de wire" McIntyre. He spends his spare time learning to do everything, one hobby at a time. You can reach Michael by e-mail at michael@lanw.com or through his Web page at www.lanw.com/jmsbio.htm.

Mary Madden is a freelance writer and consultant in the network and Internet arena. She co-authored *Windows NT Server 4 For Dummies* with Ed Tittel and James Michael Stewart, as well as other books and magazine publications. Mary currently spends most of her time developing her latest Web site for the computing and networking industry at www.ntrc.net. You can contact Mary via e-mail at madden@ctla.org.

ABOUT IDG BOOKS WORLDWIDE

Welcome to the world of IDG Books Worldwide.

IDG Books Worldwide, Inc., is a subsidiary of International Data Group, the world's largest publisher of computer-related information and the leading global provider of information services on information technology. IDG was founded more than 30 years ago by Patrick J. McGovern and now employs more than 9,000 people worldwide. IDG publishes more than 290 computer publications in over 75 countries. More than 90 million people read one or more IDG publications each month.

Launched in 1990, IDG Books Worldwide is today the #1 publisher of best-selling computer books in the United States. We are proud to have received eight awards from the Computer Press Association in recognition of editorial excellence and three from Computer Currents' First Annual Readers' Choice Awards. Our best-selling ...For Dummies® series has more than 50 million copies in print with translations in 31 languages. IDG Books Worldwide, through a joint venture with IDG's Hi-Tech Beijing, became the first U.S. publisher to publish a computer book in the People's Republic of China. In record time, IDG Books Worldwide has become the first choice for millions of readers around the world who want to learn how to better manage their businesses.

Our mission is simple: Every one of our books is designed to bring extra value and skill-building instructions to the reader. Our books are written by experts who understand and care about our readers. The knowledge base of our editorial staff comes from years of experience in publishing, education, and journalism — experience we use to produce books to carry us into the new millennium. In short, we care about books, so we attract the best people. We devote special attention to details such as audience, interior design, use of icons, and illustrations. And because we use an efficient process of authoring, editing, and desktop publishing our books electronically, we can spend more time ensuring superior content and less time on the technicalities of making books.

You can count on our commitment to deliver high-quality books at competitive prices on topics you want to read about. At IDG Books Worldwide, we continue in the IDG tradition of delivering quality for more than 30 years. You'll find no better book on a subject than one from IDG Books Worldwide.

John Kilcullen
Chairman and CEO
IDG Books Worldwide, Inc.

Eighth Annual Computer Press Awards 1992

Ninth Annual Computer Press Awards 1993

Tenth Annual Computer Press Awards 1994

Eleventh Annual Computer Press Awards 1995

IDG is the world's leading IT media, research and exposition company. Founded in 1964, IDG had 1997 revenues of $2.05 billion and has more than 9,000 employees worldwide. IDG offers the widest range of media options that reach IT buyers in 75 countries representing 95% of worldwide IT spending. IDG's diverse product and services portfolio spans six key areas including print publishing, online publishing, expositions and conferences, market research, education and training, and global marketing services. More than 90 million people read one or more of IDG's 290 magazines and newspapers, including IDG's leading global brands — Computerworld, PC World, Network World, Macworld and the Channel World family of publications. IDG Books Worldwide is one of the fastest-growing computer book publishers in the world, with more than 700 titles in 36 languages. The "...For Dummies®" series alone has more than 50 million copies in print. IDG offers online users the largest network of technology-specific Web sites around the world through IDG.net (http://www.idg.net), which comprises more than 225 targeted Web sites in 55 countries worldwide. International Data Corporation (IDC) is the world's largest provider of information technology data, analysis and consulting, with research centers in over 41 countries and more than 400 research analysts worldwide. IDG World Expo is a leading producer of more than 168 globally branded conferences and expositions in 35 countries including E3 (Electronic Entertainment Expo), Macworld Expo, ComNet, Windows World Expo, ICE (Internet Commerce Expo), Agenda, DEMO, and Spotlight. IDG's training subsidiary, ExecuTrain, is the world's largest computer training company, with more than 230 locations worldwide and 785 training courses. IDG Marketing Services helps industry-leading IT companies build international brand recognition by developing global integrated marketing programs via IDG's print, online and exposition products worldwide. Further information about the company can be found at www.idg.com. 1/26/00

Authors' Acknowledgments

As always, there are more people to thank than we can ever mention by name. That's why we mention everybody explicitly that we can think of and apologize in advance for anybody we might have overlooked. Just because we don't mention your name doesn't mean we're not grateful for your help, whomever you may be!

Ed Tittel: Hats off to the fabulous crew of LANWrights for pulling another monster rabbit out of a fairly short hat! To begin with, special thanks to Mary Burmeister for running this project and corralling all this prose into a reasonably coherent and very readable book. Sometimes I wonder how she does it. Thanks also to my co-authors, James Michael Stewart and Mary Madden, for their yeomanly efforts to finish this book. I'd also like to thank my friends and family, especially Dr. Robert R. ("Randolph") Wiggins, for their recent encouragement and moral support.

James Michael Stewart: Thanks to my boss and co-author, Ed Tittel, for including me in this book series. To my parents, Dave and Sue, thanks for your love and consistent support. To Mark, now that you have a job, it gives you a whole new perspective of why people are called sheep! To HERbert, your feline affections, strange as they may be, are priceless. And finally, as always, to Elvis — slowly but surely I'm converting the masses; well, at least they are not laughing at jungle room anymore.

Mary Madden: A big, hearty thanks and hug to Ed Tittel for inviting me to join in on this project and giving me encouragement along the way. Lots of thanks to my co-author Michael Stewart for answering all of my questions — even the dumb ones! Thank you, Mary Burmeister, for ironing out my grammar so it always made sense and also for doing my screenshots (along with having such a cool personality)! Thank you, John Savill — you were so cool and fun to work with on this book! I'd like to thank my colleague, Sherif Ahmed, for helping me research one of my chapters. A big, huge hug to my bestest, bestest friends who have always been there for me in every way — Nancy, Boots, JoAnne, Huggie Bear, Aaron, Sherif, Amal, Cathy, Mark, Nelda, Gloria, Mike, and my mom. And last, but certainly not least, thanks to my fellow Christians at the Cedar Park Church of Christ (www.flash.net/~cofc) for helping me learn that life here on earth is but a temporary journey, and God must always come first in our lives.

All the authors would like to thank the outstanding editorial and contracting staff at IDG Books, including Project Editor Nate Holdread, Technical Reviewer John Savill (who also wrote Chapters 11 and 12 on Active Directory and is one of the few real experts on this subject that we know), Copy Editor Paul Levesque, and the rest of the editorial and production crew listed on the Publisher's Acknowledgments page.

Feel free to contact any or all of us in care of IDG Books Worldwide, 919 East Hillsdale Blvd, Suite 400, Foster City, CA, 94404. Check the "About the Authors" section for our e-mail addresses. Drop us a line sometime!

Publisher's Acknowledgments

We're proud of this book; please register your comments through our IDG Books Worldwide Online Registration Form located at http://my2cents.dummies.com.

Some of the people who helped bring this book to market include the following:

Acquisitions, Editorial, and Media Development

Project Editor: Nate Holdread
    (Previous Edition: Kyle Looper)

Acquisitions Editor: Joyce Pepple

Copy Editor: Paul Levesque

Technical Editor: John Savill

Editorial Manager: Leah P. Cameron

Editorial Assistant: Beth Parlon

Production

Project Coordinator: Maridee V. Ennis

Layout and Graphics: Amy M. Adrian, Karl Brandt, Barry Offringa, Jill Piscitelli, Doug Rollison, Brent Savage, Brian Torwelle. Dan Whetstine, Erin Zeltner

Proofreaders: Laura Albert, Rebecca Senninger, Toni Settle, Charles Spencer

Indexer: Ty Koontz

General and Administrative

IDG Books Worldwide, Inc.: John Kilcullen, CEO

IDG Books Technology Publishing Group: Richard Swadley, Senior Vice President and Publisher; Walter Bruce III, Vice President and Associate Publisher; Joseph Wikert, Associate Publisher; Mary Bednarek, Branded Product Development Director; Mary Corder, Editorial Director; Barry Pruett, Publishing Manager; Michelle Baxter, Publishing Manager

IDG Books Consumer Publishing Group: Roland Elgey, Senior Vice President and Publisher; Kathleen A. Welton, Vice President and Publisher; Kevin Thornton, Acquisitions Manager; Kristin A. Cocks, Editorial Director

IDG Books Internet Publishing Group: Brenda McLaughlin, Senior Vice President and Publisher; Diane Graves Steele, Vice President and Associate Publisher; Sofia Marchant, Online Marketing Manager

IDG Books Production for Dummies Press: Debbie Stailey, Associate Director of Production; Cindy L. Phipps, Manager of Project Coordination, Production Proofreading, and Indexing; Tony Augsburger, Manager of Prepress, Reprints, and Systems; Laura Carpenter, Production Control Manager; Shelley Lea, Supervisor of Graphics and Design; Debbie J. Gates, Production Systems Specialist; Robert Springer, Supervisor of Proofreading; Kathie Schutte, Production Supervisor

Dummies Packaging and Book Design: Patty Page, Manager, Promotions Marketing

◆

The publisher would like to give special thanks to Patrick J. McGovern, without whom this book would not have been possible.

◆

Contents at a Glance

Cartoons at a Glance

By Rich Tennant

page 363

page 7

page 125

page 73

page 249

page 327

Fax: 978-546-7747
E-mail: richtennant@the5thwave.com
World Wide Web: www.the5thwave.com

Table of Contents

· ·

Introduction

*W*elcome to *Windows 2000 Server For Dummies,* the book that helps any-body who's unfamiliar with Windows 2000 Server (or networks in general) find his or her way around a Windows 2000 Server-based network. In a wired world, networks provide the links that tie all users together. Even if you're not using a network already, you will probably use one someday! This book tells you what's going on, in basic, straightforward terms.

Although a few fortunate individuals may be acquainted with Windows 2000 Server and networks already, a lot more of us are not only unfamiliar with networking, but may also be downright scared of it. To those who may be worried about the prospect of facing new and difficult technologies, we say "Don't worry. Be happy." Using a network is not beyond anyone's wits or abilities — it's mostly a matter of using a language that ordinary people can understand.

Ordinary folks are why this book talks about using Windows 2000 Server and networks in simple — and deliberately irreverent — terms. Nothing is too highfalutin to be mocked, nor too arcane to state in plain English. And when we do have to get technical, we'll warn you and make sure to define our terms to boot.

This books aims to help you meet your needs. You'll find everything you need to know about Windows 2000 Server and networking in here, so you'll be able to find your way around — without having to learn lots of jargon or obtain an advanced degree in computer science along the way. We want you to *enjoy* yourself. If networking really is a "big deal," it's important that you be able to get the most out of it. We really want to help!

About This Book

This book is designed so you can pick it up and start reading at any point — like you might read a reference book. In Parts I and II, networking basics are covered: concepts and terminology in Part I, and the design and deployment of network hardware in Part II. In Parts III through V, you'll find ample cover-age of Windows 2000 Server and related networking topics. Part III covers installation and configuration of Windows 2000 Server, whereas Part IV covers its maintenance and management. Part V completes this picture with chapters on a variety of troubleshooting topics.

Each chapter is divided into freestanding sections in which each one relates to the chapter's major theme. For example, the chapter on installing network interface cards, or NICs, contains the following collection of information:

- A description of a NIC and how it works
- The various PC buses for which NICs are available
- How to begin the installation process by documenting your current configuration
- How to insert a NIC into a PC
- How to configure a NIC after it's installed in your PC
- What to do when Plug and Play fails to live up to its promises
- Troubleshooting techniques to try when NIC installation doesn't work on the first (or second . . .) try

You don't have to memorize the contents of this book. Each section supplies just the facts you need to make networking with Windows 2000 Server easy to use. On some occasions, however, you may want to work directly from the book to make sure you keep things straight.

How to Use This Book

This book works like a reference, so start with a topic that interests you. You can use the table of contents to identify general areas of interest or broad topics. The index, however, is your best tool for identifying detailed concepts, related topics, or particular Windows 2000 capabilities, tools, or controls.

After you find what you need, you can close the book and tackle whatever task you've set for yourself — without having to grapple with unrelated details. Of course, if you want additional information about your topic, you can check the cross-references. If you've never worked on a network before, it's a good idea to read Parts I and II in their entirety. Likewise, if you're new to Windows 2000 Server, you might want to read all of Parts III and IV. Otherwise, dig in wherever your fancy moves you!

When you need to type something at the keyboard, you'll see text that looks like this: **TYPE THIS**. You're expected to enter this text at the keyboard, then press the Enter key. Because typing stuff can sometimes be confusing, we always try to describe what it is you're typing and why you need to type it.

This book occasionally suggests that you consult the Windows 2000 Server online help, printed manuals, the *Windows 2000 Server Resource Kit,* and even Microsoft's TechNet CD for additional information. In most cases, though, you find everything you need to know about a particular topic right here — except for some of the bizarre details that abound in Windows 2000 Server.

If there's a topic we don't cover in this book that you need to know more about, we suggest you look for a book on that subject in the *...For Dummies* series, published by IDG Books Worldwide. On the other hand, we also feel obligated to tell you that there's a whole world of Web information about Windows 2000 available on the Internet and that the Microsoft Web site at `www.microsoft.com/windows/server/` is not a bad place to start looking for such information.

Foolish Assumptions

We're going to climb out on a limb and make some potentially foolish assumptions about you, our gentle reader. You have or are thinking about getting a computer, a network, and at least one copy of Windows 2000 Server. You know what you want to do with these things. You might even be able to handle all these things yourself, if somebody could only show you how. Our goal with this book is to decrease your need for such a somebody, but we don't recommend telling him or her that out loud — at least, not until you've finished this book!

How This Book Is Organized

The book is divided into six major parts, each of which consists of three to five chapters. Each chapter covers a major topic, and is divided into sections, which discuss some particular issue or concern related to that topic. That's how things in this book are organized, but how you read it is up to you. Choose a topic, a section, a chapter, or a part — whatever strikes your fancy or suits your needs — and start reading. Any related information is cross-referenced in the text to help guide you through the whole book.

Part I: Laying the Network Foundation

Part I covers basic networking concepts and terminology, including basics of networked communications and what makes networks work — usually, some magical combination of hardware and software. If you're not familiar with networks, this part should come in handy. If you're already a seasoned networker, you can skip this part (and Part II). Look here for discussions about networking terms and concepts, such as client, server, protocol, and topology.

Part II: Hooking Up the Hardware

Part II covers everything you need to know to build or extend a network, or simply to understand what's really happening on an existing network. It starts with coverage of network design and layout principles, and continues on to discuss how to install and configure NICs in a PC. After that, it examines the wiring that links network devices and talks about how multiple networks can interconnect. Part II concludes with a review of all the software components you're likely to encounter on a Windows 2000-based network and why you need them.

Part III: Servers, Start Your Engines!

Part III tackles Windows 2000 Server head on, starting with its installation and configuration. It covers the issues involved in installing and configuring network hardware specifically for Windows 2000 Server. It also covers how to install and manage print servers and services on a Windows 2000-based network, how to handle Transmission Control Protocol/Internet Protocol (TCP/IP) addresses, and how to set up and manage directory services, domains, and trust relationships in a Windows 2000-based environment. Part III is where you figure out how to put the basic pieces of a network together using Windows 2000 Server.

Part IV: Running Your Network

Part IV picks up where Part III leaves off — that is, it talks about living with and managing a Windows 2000-based network after the initial installation and configuration phase is done. It begins with a discussion of how to manage users and groups on a Windows 2000-based network, including profiles and policies, as well as local and global groups. Next, it covers how Windows 2000 controls access to NTFS files and directories, and how to manage network-accessible file system resources called shares.

After a network's users, groups, and data assets are in place, rebuilding such a setup from scratch can be a real pain. That's where a backup comes in really handy, so Part IV covers the ins and outs of backing up and restoring a Windows 2000 Server machine, plus other aspects of fault tolerance. After that, a review of network security principles and practices should help to prepare you to protect your data from accidental loss and from would-be hackers and crackers.

Part V: Troubleshooting Server Snafus

Part V takes a long, hard look at the common causes of trouble on Windows 2000-based networks, and explores those areas that are most likely to fall prey to trouble. It begins with a look at some key Windows 2000 tools for troubleshooting systems then continues on to explore tips, tricks, and techniques for troubleshooting a Windows 2000-based network. Part V concludes by exploring handling problems with Active Directory.

Part VI: The Part of Tens

This part follows the grand tradition of the *...For Dummies* books, all of which include The Part of Tens. Here, you'll find lists of information, tips, tricks, and suggestions, all organized into short and convenient chapters. This supplemental information is designed to be both helpful and informative and is supplied at no extra charge.

Icons Used in This Book

The icons used in this book point you to important (and not so important) topics in the text.

This icon is just what it sounds like. It lets you know when you can go to another part of the book for further, more detailed information on a particular subject.

This icon lets you know that you're about to encounter information that's important to understand if you really want to *get* what's going on with networking or with Windows 2000 Server. It may be painful at times, but you have to slog through it.

Oh gee, we're getting so old that we can't recall what this one means. Maybe you should check one out and see if it's worth watching for!

This icon lets you know that you're about to be swamped in technical details. We include this information because we love it, not because we think you have to master it to use Windows 2000 Server or networks. If you aspire to nerdhood, you probably want to read it; if you're already a nerd, you'll want to write us about stuff we left out or other information we should put in!

This icon signals that helpful advice is at hand. We also use it when we offer insights that we hope make networking or Windows 2000 Server more interesting or easier. For example, whenever we include a shortcut that improves your productivity, it's usually marked with the Tip icon.

 This icon means what it says — you'd better be careful with the information it conveys. Nine times out of ten, it's warning you not to do something that can have nasty or painful consequences, as in accidentally wiping out the contents of an entire hard drive. Whoops!

Where to Go from Here

With this book at your side, you should be ready to wrestle with Windows 2000 Server and the networks it connects to. Find a subject, turn to its page, and you'll be ready to jam. Feel free to mark up this book, fill in the blanks, dog-ear the pages, and do anything else that might make a librarian queasy. The important things are to make good use of it and to enjoy yourself while you're at it.

 Please check out the Web page at www.dummies.com. Be sure to take the opportunity to register your purchase online or to send the authors e-mail with feedback about your reading experience.

Part I
Laying the Network Foundation

The 5th Wave   By Rich Tennant

"I DON'T THINK OUR NEWEST NETWORK CONFIGURATION IS GOING TO WORK. ALL OF OUR TRANSMISSIONS FROM OHIO SEEM TO BE COMING IN OVER MY ELECTRIC PENCIL SHARPENER."

In this part . . .

In this introductory part of the book, we present background material about local area networks, or LANs.
We present the barest essentials: how computers communicate with each other, why communication isn't a bad
thing, and what makes networks work. We also cover vital
concepts, including the rules of communication, called
protocols, that computers use to exchange information,
and the ways in which network wiring can be arranged —
called a *topology*.

Along the way, you discover all kinds of basic network terminology and concepts that you may never have heard of
(but that everyone, including Microsoft, assumes that you
know when you work with Windows 2000 Server).

Each chapter presents its information in small, easy-to-read
sections. If information is really technical (mostly worth
skipping, unless you're a glutton for punishment), it's clearly
marked as such. Even so, we hope you find this information
useful — and maybe even worth a giggle or two.

Chapter 1

Making Networks Make Sense

In This Chapter

▶ Understanding network hardware and software

▶ Recognizing a network's anatomy

▶ Making sure that the network's running

▶ Sharing resources is what networks are for

▶ Following Windows networking trends into the new millennium

*I*f you've ever used a cell phone or watched a TV show, you've used a network, perhaps without even realizing it. Much of the world's modern communications infrastructure, including wired and wireless telephones, cable and broadcast TV, and the Internet, depends on networks.

Windows 2000 Server needs a network, too. Because servers exist to provide file, print, directory, security, and other services to clients across a network, using Windows 2000 Server without a network is like using a telephone that's not plugged into the wall. Although that phone may have some value as abstract art, its real value comes from its ability to connect you with other people or services. The same is true for Windows 2000 Server.

In this chapter, we introduce you to the various components that make up a Windows 2000-based network and briefly discuss how each one works.

What's This about a Network?

A *network* requires that at least two computers are linked in a way that enables them to talk to each other. Most networks use electrical wires of some type to convey signals and data between computers. However, numerous types of networking media, including wireless technologies and fiber-optic cables, also support networked connections. In other words, you can get from "here" to "there" in many ways on modern networks!

A network's key ingredients always include some type of physical connection that allows computers to talk (and listen) to some kind of communications medium. Even if that network medium is wireless, something must connect computers to an antenna or to a similar device that allows those computers to broadcast and receive signals.

But there's more to networking than hardware. Although cables and connections are essential, without software to use these connections, physical components are purely decorative and can serve no useful purpose. In the following sections, you find out a bit more about the hardware and software that are necessary to make networks work.

No hardware means no connections!

First and foremost, networking requires working connections to enable computers to communicate with each other. *Networking hardware* creates connections between computers and a network and defines the medium (or media) that allows information to flow from sender to receiver.

Networking hardware covers a broad range of devices, many of which you may find on your networks. In the first part of this book, we help you understand the roles and functions these devices play on a network.

From the most basic perspective, computers need the following hardware to talk to each other on a typical network:

- ✓ **A network interface card (NIC)** plugs into a computer and attaches to a network cable (or other medium, if something else is used). It turns computer bits into signals on the wire for outgoing stuff, and turns incoming signals into bits for incoming stuff.

- ✓ **Connectors** make it possible to attach a network interface to the network medium. For wireless media, connectors attach antennas or other broadcast devices to interfaces. Connectors bring all the separate pieces of networking hardware together, so to speak.

- ✓ **Cables** convey signals from sender to receiver, using either electrical signals for wire cables or light pulses for fiber-optic cable. In the case of wireless media, the "cables" are the broadcast frequencies used to transmit information between senders and receivers.

- ✓ **Additional network devices** tie bigger, more complex networks together. These devices range from relatively simple *hubs* used to interconnect interfaces on *star-wired networks* (Chapters 4 and 7), *repeaters* used to link individual cable segments (Chapter 7), and *bridges, routers, and gateways* (Chapter 7). Hardware plays an important role in networking. Not only does it attach computers to a network, but it also interconnects multiple networks to manage how and when data flows from one network to another.

A simple view of networking

Networking boils down to three critical requirements:

✔ **Connections** include the necessary hardware to connect a computer to a network, plus cables (called the *network medium*) that ferry messages between computers. The hardware that hooks a computer to a network is called a *network interface.* In most cases, attaching a PC to a network requires inserting an adapter board called a *network interface card,* or *NIC.* Without a physical connection, a computer can't use the network.

✔ **Communications** define rules that computers must follow to exchange and interpret information. Because each computer may run different software, interconnected computers need a shared language to enable them to exchange messages and data. Without shared communications, computers can't exchange data, even though they may share a common network medium.

✔ **Services** are what computers talk about. In other words, services represent what computers do for each other, including sending or receiving files, messages, print jobs, and so on. Unless computers can perform services for each other across a network, a computer can't respond to requests from other computers, nor can it request things from other computers.

Without software, networks don't work

Software lets computers access and use hardware, whether that hardware is used for networking-related functions or for other purposes.

By now, you should understand that hardware provides the necessary connections that make networking possible, and software supports the communications and services needed to access the hardware and the network to which the hardware is attached.

Therefore, many different types of software play a supporting role when networking modern computers. This software includes special-purpose programs called *device drivers,* which allow a computer to address a network interface and exchange data with that interface. The software collection also includes full-blown applications that can access data on a local computer or on a server across the network with equal aplomb. The software also includes a bunch of other stuff that sits between device drivers and applications.

Throughout this book, we show you how to recognize the various pieces of software involved in networking and how to best configure that software to work with Windows 2000 Server on a network.

Investigating Your Network's Facilities

If you tour an average network, you can't help but discover that many different types of equipment and a variety of related software are in use. If you inventory all the components in a network, you can use that data to figure out what's attached to your network and what various devices do for your network.

The infrastructure that makes networking possible is made up of the equipment that hooks computers into a network, the cables or other networking media that ferry information between computers, and the hardware and software used to create and control a network. You might also call the collection of connections, cables, interfaces, and other equipment "glue," because these elements bind computers into a working network.

The three phases of networking

Network software falls into one of three categories: *host/terminal, client/server,* and *peer-to-peer.* Each category reflects a certain type of networked communication.

✔ **Host/terminal networks** are based on an old-fashioned model for networking, even if they don't actually use old-fashioned stuff. In this network's original version, users access information using a device called a *terminal,* which consists of nothing more than a screen, a keyboard, and a network connection. All the software runs on a powerful computer called a *host,* which resides elsewhere on the network. The lowly terminal doesn't do anything more than provide a way for users to access remote data and applications (which is why such devices are also known as *dumb terminals*). In more modern versions, PCs can act like terminals by using *terminal emulation software,* which the PC uses to access a host. The PC still provides some local smarts and access to local word-processing software, spreadsheets, and so on. In fact, Windows 2000 Server supports host/terminal capabilities through a facility called Terminal Server.

✔ A **client/server network** consists of a collection of smart machines. One or more of these machines acts as a *server* and has lots of storage space, a powerful processor, and networking software so it can handle requests for services from other machines. The other machines that interact with the server are called *clients.* Sometimes, client/server networks are also called *server-based networks* to emphasize the server's key role. Windows 2000 Server provides a foundation for the client/server network, which is the subject of this book. However, Novell NetWare and UNIX servers also play similar roles on modern networks.

✔ On a **peer-to-peer network**, any machine that can be a client can also act as a server. Unlike client/server networks, no special-purpose machine acts as a server. On a peer-to-peer network, all machines are more or less alike in capability and in the services they offer. If you use the built-in networking that's included in Windows 2000 Professional, Windows NT Workstation, Windows 98, or Windows 95, you're using this type of networking software.

Workstations for everyone!

One of networking's primary advantages is that a network takes what you do at your desk — and we bet that you usually call it "work" — and lets you do what you do more efficiently by allowing you to interact with remote resources and data. This means that you can access a file on a server as if it's part of your own disk drive, send a job to a printer elsewhere on the network as if it were hooked directly to your machine, and so on. Sharing resources remains the most highly touted benefit of networking, because it connects your desktop computer to file stores, printers, applications, and information resources that would otherwise be inaccessible or too expensive to add to every desktop computer.

The terms *network client, desktop computer,* and *workstation* are all used more or less synonymously in the network world. No matter what you call them, these machines are where users do the bulk of their work (and perhaps some play at odd moments). One of the key goals that drives networking is to inter-connect all the desktops in an organization, whether they run a DOS, Windows, UNIX, or Macintosh operating system, so that they can communicate and share resources. Some of the resources shared by workstations include large disk arrays, expensive color or laser printers, CD-ROM jukeboxes, and high-speed Internet connections (all of which would be too expensive to connect to every desktop machine).

On most networks, the ratio of desktop machines to users is pretty close to one-to-one. In other words, each user has access to a workstation attached to the network, even if that user is not the only person who works on that machine. Because workstations are where requests for services originate, such machines are known as network clients, or more simply, as *clients.*

When you call such a machine a *workstation,* you emphasize its ability to sup-port an individual user more or less independently. When you call such a machine a *client,* you focus on its connection to the network. Whatever you call it, it's a machine that sits on your desk and is connected to a network.

The area of a computer that displays the program icons and the wallpaper is also called the desktop.

A server is always at your service

Networking is about obtaining access to shared services. Because networks are useless unless you can do something with them, access to services is what networking is all about.

On modern networks, servers provide capabilities necessary to obtain access to resources or to get things done. For example, when you send a print job to a networked printer, you can assume that, somewhere in the background, a print server is handling the job. Likewise, when you request a file from a network drive, a file server is probably involved. When you poke around in the network directory — you guessed it! — a directory server is pulling the strings. For every service, some type of server handles and responds to requests. Sometimes, a single server provides many services; at other times, a server provides only a single service.

Computers that provide services to clients are generically called *servers*. A server's job is to listen for requests from clients for whatever service or services it offers, and to satisfy any valid requests for its services. In fact, validating service requests is an important part of what servers do — you wouldn't want just anybody to be able to print the salaries for everybody in your company just because a user asks a print server to do so. You want that server to verify that Bob is *allowed* to access that file before you let him print it! Throughout this book, you find out more about such validations and other key aspects of what it takes for a server to provide services.

The common path of networking

A common pathway must exist between any computer that requests services and any computer whose job it is to satisfy such requests. Just as you need a highway to drive from one city to another, you need a pathway over which your computer can send and receive data. On a network, that's the job of the media that tie all the various pieces together.

Look around and observe the types of cables and connections used on your network. Get a sense of the structure of your network so you can tell which highways the users use — from the side roads that only the folks in the accounting or shipping departments use to the main road that all users use.

When you observe how all the pieces fit together — workstations, servers, and media — you get a reasonably complete view of your network. Figure 1-1 depicts a simple network diagram that shows these purely physical elements of a network. Notice that clients (desktop machines) outnumber servers, and that media tie all the pieces together. Networking follows the laws of supply and demand, so the more clients you have, the more (or bigger) servers you'll need — and the more work will get done!

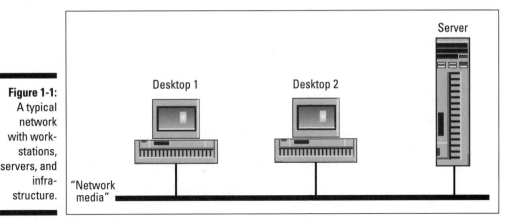

Figure 1-1:
A typical
network
with work-
stations,
servers, and
infra-
structure.

What Is the Sound of a Working Network?

Figuring out whether a network is functioning is both easy and hard, and most observers, including novices and experts alike, agree that telling when a network's *not* working is easier than telling when it is! A client must know how to ask for services from the network and must state precisely what it's requesting. Likewise, a server must know how to recognize and evaluate incoming requests for its services and how to respond appropriately. Only then can a network work correctly.

Understanding how this constant stream of requests and replies works means looking a little deeper into how clients state their requests and how servers satisfy them. In the following sections, we tell you more about the mechanics of this give and take.

Knowing how to ask is where the game begins

Knowing how to ask for network services requires some ability to distinguish between what's available locally on a client machine and what's available remotely from the network. Determining what's local and what's remote is the key to handling network access correctly. This determination depends on specialized software to handle the job in the background, so users don't nec- essarily have to know the difference.

A computer's main control program is called its *operating system,* because it defines the software environment that lets a computer operate and run the applications and system services that get things done on a machine. Most modern operating systems include built-in networking capabilities to augment their control over local resources and devices.

Certain modern operating systems may be called *network operating systems* when they create network server environments. Their built-in networking capabilities include a range of network services as part and parcel of the underlying operating system. Windows 2000 Server certainly fits this bill because it offers a broad range of powerful, flexible networking capabilities.

Right out of the box, Windows 2000 understands the differences between local and remote resources. The same is true for most modern desktop operating systems, including Windows 2000 Professional, Windows NT Workstation, Windows 9x, the Macintosh OS, as well as that old (but still modern) warhorse, UNIX.

In Windows 2000, Windows NT, Windows 9x, Macintosh, and UNIX operating systems, and through add-ons to DOS and Windows 3.x, a special piece of software known as a *redirector* keeps track of what's local and what's remote when users or applications request resources. The redirector takes generic requests for services and sends any that can't be satisfied locally to the appropriate service provider elsewhere on the network (in other words, to the appropriate server). Therefore, if you ask for a file that resides on a server elsewhere on the network, the redirector hands your request off to that machine and makes sure that the results of that request get delivered properly.

What's on today's menu?

For a computer to use network services, the computer must know how to ask for them. That's what a *requester* does. But knowing what to ask for is as important as knowing how to ask. In most cases, applications supply the necessary information about network services that they wish to access, either through information supplied from a requester or through knowledge built directly into an application itself.

E-mail programs and Web browsers represent good examples of applications with sophisticated, built-in networking capabilities. On the other hand, file system access tools, such as Windows Explorer, My Computer, and My Documents, rely on the redirector to furnish them with views of (and access to) shared files and printers elsewhere on the network.

Please note that applications with built-in networking knowledge offer *transparent* access to network services because the applications know how to ask for services and, often, what to ask for on the user's behalf. Programmers design such computer applications to be transparent to keep the applications out of sight and out of mind; therefore, the user remains blissfully unaware of cumbersome networking details and trivia. However, file managers, printer controls, and other tools with access to both local and remote resources require users to be able to tell the difference between what's local and what's remote. In fact, such tools usually force users to request access to remote resources explicitly and directly.

Increasingly, finding out which services a network can provide is becoming more and more implicit, however. This is why all versions of Windows 2000 support a set of directory services to catalog and describe the services that the network can deliver to its users. Likewise, Windows 2000 supports the Distributed File System, known as Dfs, that allows directories on multiple machines all around a network to appear as a single network drive to users. Therefore, the users don't have to know where individual files or folders reside.

Such sophisticated mechanisms make it easier than ever before for users to request and access resources implicitly without having to know how to request those resources or having to determine exactly where they reside. Nevertheless, some explicit knowledge about such things is necessary if you want to make the most of Windows 2000 Server's networking capabilities.

It's All about Sharing Resources

The mechanics of requesting resources depend on having access to the right software tools to determine when network requests are necessary. The software delivers the request to a server whose job is to listen for such requests and to satisfy all the legitimate ones. Ultimately, a server's job is to make resources available to all authorized users. This feature makes sharing possible and helps explain the most powerful benefit of networking — namely, to provide a single, consistent way for multiple users to obtain secure and managed access to files, printers, scanners, data, applications, and more.

The secret to sharing is to find a way to make sure that everyone can obtain access to a shared resource. For example, for access to print services, a temporary storage space must hold incoming print jobs until each one's turn to be printed comes up. Therefore, sharing a printer not only means providing access to the device itself, but it also means keeping track of who's in line, providing a place where pending jobs can reside, and sometimes notifying users when a print job has been successfully completed. All these mechanisms make sharing work easier and explain why servers are so important to any network.

Because servers bring services and data together in a single machine, servers provide a natural point of control and maintenance for the important devices, services, and data on a network, which are, of course, the things that everybody wants to share.

Windows Networking Trends

As we write this chapter, we're absorbing Microsoft's decision to discontinue Windows NT as a brand name. As you know, the latest Windows generation is the Windows 2000 product family. This family embraces several types of servers, including the following:

- ✔ **Windows 2000 Server:** This is the subject of this book.

- ✔ **Windows 2000 Advanced Server:** This is Windows 2000 Server with lots of bells and whistles. This souped-up version allows you to use up to four CPUs (processors) on a single server (which helps improve performance).

- ✔ **Windows 2000 Datacenter Server:** This is a new, high-end Windows operating system that supports even more CPUs than Advanced Server. It has the same features as Advanced Server and more. Windows 2000 Datacenter Server can support more than 10,000 simultaneous users in certain situations.

Although these versions vary, they're more alike than different. Therefore, this book can help you master the basics for any of these types of Windows 2000 products.

Based on the capabilities of Windows 2000, we see the following trends emerging for Windows networking as the next millennium approaches:

- ✔ **Use of Active Directory:** Active Directory is Microsoft's name for the directory services supported by Windows 2000. Active Directory makes it easier for users to identify and access network resources and for applications to use such resources directly and automatically. Currently, you can't see much evidence of this capability, but it will change the way we use Windows — and networks — in the future.

- ✔ **Access to Dynamic Disk Storage:** Windows 2000 supports a variety of sophisticated directory-sharing technologies. Dynamic Disk Storage enables network administrators to define collections of files and directories gathered from multiple servers around a network and present them to users as if the files and directories reside on a single network drive. This makes creating, identifying, and accessing collections of shared files easier.

- ✔ **Consistent naming services:** Part of locating resources on a network is knowing their names (or how to find them). Windows 2000 uses a single enhanced method to translate human-intelligible names for network resources into computer-intelligible network addresses, which makes managing and interacting with network resources far simpler.

✔ **Web-based management console:** In Windows 2000, a single Microsoft Management Console (MMC) plays host to management tools (called MMC snap-ins) for all system services, resources, and facilities. This console makes the Windows 2000 interface simpler and its many capabilities more visually consistent, and therefore easier to learn and manage. In fact, this capability works on any computer with a suitable Web browser (and an administrative password, of course).

As all these new capabilities are used, the trends in Windows networking should be clear:

✔ Easier, more straightforward access to network resources

✔ Simplified administration and management of such resources

✔ More sophisticated tools and technologies to describe, deliver, and control network resources

Get used to it!

Chapter 2

Networking the Client/Server Way

● ●

In This Chapter

▶ Requesting services

▶ Delivering services

▶ Listening in on a client/server conversation

▶ Networking natively means networking nicely

▶ Adding on enhances network capabilities

▶ Understanding the Microsoft network (and its alternatives)

▶ Managing network access

▶ Using the Windows 2000 Server network services

● ●

*F*or most applications, using Windows 2000 Server in a networked environment means buying into the client/server model. To help you understand this networking model, which best explains why it's necessary for Windows 2000 Server to exist, we explore the client/server model in detail in this chapter. Along the way, you discover more about the types of capabilities and services that make client/server networks work and the various ways that clients and servers interact on such networks.

Clients Request Services

In Chapter 1, we explain that clients ask for services and that both hardware and software are necessary to make networking work on any computer. In this chapter, we take a closer look at the various pieces and parts involved in a client/server relationship to help you understand what actually happens when a client requests a service from a server.

At the most basic level, a client must have a network connection available to transmit a request for services. Likewise, the client must have the correct software installed to formulate an intelligible request and pass it to the network, which is where a server can notice and respond to such a request.

Making the connection

To request network services, a client must have the following hardware:

- ✔ **Network interface card (NIC):** A NIC (also called a network adapter and network board) allows a computer to interact with the network. You must configure the NIC properly so it can transmit signals onto the network medium and receive signals from that network medium.

- ✔ **Physical connection:** The link between the computer and its network must work properly. This means that clients can transmit outgoing signals and receive incoming signals through their network connections. Likewise, the network cabling itself — also known as the network medium — must be properly configured and interconnected for signals to travel from sender to receiver.

This takes care of the connections part in a three-part simple model for networking, which requires that connections, communications, and services all be available and working.

Software uses the connection

The software on the client computer handles the communications and services that are necessary for the network to operate. Here's a list of software that you normally find on a networked client computer, starting from the hardware level (or as close as software can get to hardware) and working up to the applications that request network services:

- ✔ **Network driver:** A special-purpose piece of software that enables a computer to send data from the computer's *central processing unit* (CPU) to the NIC when an outgoing message is ready to be sent. The network driver also forwards a request for immediate attention (called an *interrupt*) to the CPU when an incoming message arrives. You might say that the driver allows the PC to communicate with the NIC, which in turn communicates with the network.

- ✔ **Protocol stack:** The protocol stack is a collection of communications software that provides the type of "shared language" (which we describe in Chapter 1) necessary for successful networking. The protocol stack governs which formats network messages can assume, and it defines a set of rules for how to interpret their contents. Two computers must use the same protocol stack to communicate. We cover protocol stacks thoroughly in Chapter 3.

- ✔ **Redirector:** A redirector, or equivalent software, issues requests for remote resources or services to the protocol stack and receives the incoming replies from the protocol stack. With a redirector running in the background, applications don't need to be explicitly network aware, because the redirector handles network connections.

✔ **Network-aware application:** Network-aware applications understand when service requests can be satisfied locally or must be satisfied remotely. In the latter case, a redirector may be present, but it may not necessarily handle certain types of network services (such as e-mail or Web-page access). However, the redirector may handle other types of network services, such as providing access to a file stored elsewhere on the network that's applied as an attachment to an e-mail message. In such a case, the redirector grabs a copy of that file across the network and attaches it to the outgoing e-mail message.

When a client makes a request for a resource or service that requires access to the network, either the application (if it's network aware) or a redirector (if the application isn't network aware) formulates a formal request for a remote service. Satisfying the request may involve the transfer of a small amount of data (as when requesting a listing of a directory on a machine elsewhere on the network). However, it may also involve transferring a large amount of data (as when sending a large file off to be printed or when copying a large file from the client machine to a server).

The request is ferried through the protocol stack that the client and server have in common. For short requests, a handful of short messages travel from the client and are reassembled and handled by the server. For large information transfers, the client breaks up a large file into hundreds or thousands of small information packages, each of which is shipped across the network separately and then reassembled on the receiving end.

The protocol stack tells the driver to send little packages of data (called *frames* or *packets*) from the computer, through the NIC, and across the network to the intended recipient (the server). On the receiving end, the same thing happens in reverse, with a few additional considerations that you find out about in the following section.

Servers Deliver Services

In the preceding section, you found out that clients ask for services and that servers provide them. What handling requests on the server side really means is that a special bit of software, called a *listener process,* runs continuously on the server and listens for requests for a particular service. When a request arrives, the listener process handles it as quickly as possible.

Servers thread through a maze of requests

What usually happens on most server operating systems — including Windows 2000 Server — is that the listener process simply recognizes that a request has arrived. The listener process checks the identity and the associated permissions of the client, and if the client is who it says it is and has the correct permissions for the service, the listener process grants the request for service. It does so by creating a temporary process that exists just long enough to handle whatever service the client requests — after which, the temporary process disappears. For example, a request for a particular file on a server would result in the creation of a temporary process (called an *execution thread* in Windows-speak) that exists just long enough to copy the requested file across the network. As soon as the copy completes, the temporary process goes poof!

Using a listener process to create short-lived execution threads allows a server to handle large numbers of requests, because the listener process never stays busy for long handling individual requests. As soon as the listener process creates a thread to handle one request, it checks for other pending requests and handles them if necessary; otherwise, the listener process goes back to listening for new incoming requests. Typically, a server has one or more listener processes for each service the server supports.

Servers are demand-driven. That is, their job is to respond to requests for services from clients. A server very rarely initiates activity. This "reactive mode" of server operation helps explain why the client/server model is also known as a *request/response* or a *request/reply* architecture, in which clients make requests and servers respond or reply to them.

Other than the necessary listener processes and a set of service applications that actually perform services, servers need the same hardware components that clients do. Servers need one or more NICs with a working connection to the network to allow data to enter and leave the server.

Software is similar on the server side

On the software side, servers also need the following elements so their services can be available across the network:

- ✔ **Network drivers:** Enable the server to communicate with its NIC. This software lurks in the background and exists only to tie the computer to the NIC.
- ✔ **Protocol stacks:** Send and receive messages across the network. This software also lurks in the background and provides a common language shared with clients used to ferry information across the network.

✔ **Service applications:** Respond to requests for service and formulate replies to those requests. This software runs in the foreground and does the useful work. The service application includes the listener process, the temporary execution threads, and some type of configuration or management console so it can be installed, configured, and altered as needed. Typical service applications include directory services (Active Directory), database engines (SQL Server or Oracle), e-mail servers (Exchange), and mainframe gateways (SNA Server).

Most, if not all, software that resides on a server is network aware, because delivering information across a network is a server's primary function.

Decoding a Client/Server Conversation

You may wonder what the steps are in a conversation between a client and server. Examining the exact contents of such a message exchange wouldn't do you much good. However, the following sequence presents a typical request to print a file on a network printer (and, by necessity, through a print server) from a spreadsheet program:

1. **A user requests print services in the spreadsheet program by clicking the printer icon or by choosing File⇨Print.**

   Assume that a network printer is set as the default printer for the designated print job.

2. **The spreadsheet program formats the spreadsheet and then builds an appropriate print file.**

   A print file includes the text and graphics that make up a file's content. It also includes instructions on how (bold, italic, and so forth) and where (top, bottom, left, right) to place the elements to be printed.

3. **The spreadsheet program sends the print file to the printer.**

4. **The local networking software (assume it's a Windows 98 redirector) recognizes that the printer is on the network and sends a print request to print that file to the print server.**

   The redirector accesses name and network address information through a Windows networking service (called the Browse Service, which talks to a browser server on the network) to figure out where to send the print file.

5. **On the server side, the listener process recognizes and checks out the user's print request. We'll assume it's legal, so the listener process creates a temporary execution thread to handle delivery of the incoming print file packets from the client. This temporary thread tells the client to start sending the print file.**

6. Having now obtained permission to start shipping the file, the protocol stack on the client chops the file up into small chunks (called *packets*) that are delivered to the temporary thread on the server.

7. The temporary thread on the server oversees delivery of the file and places it into a temporary holding area (called a *spool file*) where the print server stores all pending print jobs.

   The print server places the job in the *print queue*, which stores the print jobs in the order in which they are received.

8. When the print job reaches the head of the queue, the server creates another temporary thread to ship the job to the printer. In many cases, a different protocol carries data from the server to the printer than the one the client uses to ship data to the server in the first place.

9. In a final (and optional) step, the print server creates another temporary thread to send a message to the client computer stating that the print job is complete. Here, the same protocol used to transport the file from the client to the server is often used to send this message back to the client.

What's worth noting here is that a kind of conversation occurs between client and server. The client initiates this conversation when it asks for permission to print, and then it sends the print job to the print server. The server takes over from there, storing the incoming print file in its spool file, managing the queue, and then printing the file when its turn comes. The conversation ends when the server sends notification of job completion to the client.

Requests for other services, such as access to a database server, an e-mail server, or even a file server, are similar to the previous interchange. In such cases, the conversation usually ends when the server sends a data table, message, or file in reply to the client's initiating requests. This request/reply sequence is really what makes modern networks work.

Clients and Network Access Software

Speaking historically, some of the ugliest problems with PCs have been networking related. Prior to the release of Windows for Workgroups in 1993, Microsoft PC operating systems — primarily, Windows 1.*x*, 2.*x*, and 3.*x*, and all versions of DOS up through Version 6.0 — included no built-in networking facilities.

Therefore, to put PCs on a network, users not only had to deal with installing and configuring NICs and the driver software that makes them work, but they also had to purchase or otherwise obtain networking protocol software and networking services software from other vendors. Because neither those users nor Microsoft provided any of these products themselves, these products were called *third-party components*.

Suffice it to say, networking PCs before the days of built-in networking typically meant adding two or more third-party networking products to the mix of hardware and software components on each machine. Typically, one product was required to supply the protocol stack necessary for networked communications, and one or more other products were needed to access whatever services might use that protocol stack to do things across the network. For example, you would buy a protocol stack, such as TCP/IP (short for *Transmission Control Protocol/Internet Protocol*), for your PC from Chameleon Software, then buy e-mail software from QUALCOMM, and then tie it all together by guess and by gosh.

Starting with Windows for Workgroups, and then picking up in a major way with Windows 95 and Windows NT, Microsoft made networking a lot easier for ordinary mortals. It did so by providing built-in networking components as a part of the operating system. Although this made life hard for third-party vendors who had been making good livings from their protocol stacks and add-on service products, it definitely made using networks vastly simpler. It was especially appealing to users who wanted networking to be something you could "set and forget" rather than "set and regret" or "fret and reset!"

Today, Windows 98, Windows NT, and Windows 2000 include all the elements necessary for networking — from multiple types of protocol stacks to many different types of client and server capabilities. If you base your network entirely on Microsoft technologies or if the majority of your clients and servers use Microsoft technologies, handling networking is just like handling other parts of the Windows operating systems. That is, you still have to know something about what you're doing (which is why you're reading this book, right?), but you don't have to be a rocket scientist to install, configure, and maintain the necessary protocol and service components.

In some compelling cases, however, you may have to mess with third-party networking components, as in days of yore. For example, your network may use a non-Microsoft server, such as NetWare, UNIX, or something else, to provide network services. Or perhaps the collection of built-in services delivered with Windows 98 or Windows 2000 doesn't include something that you need, and you must add it to the mix yourself.

An example of a useful component that you may decide to add for yourself is the *Network File System* (NFS). On UNIX-dominated networks, NFS plays the same role for sharing files that built-in file sharing plays on Microsoft networks. If you want to use this capability on Windows 98 or Windows 2000, you have to buy it from a third-party vendor, such as Sun Microsystems (the inventor of NFS) or Intergraph (the purveyor of the fastest NFS implementation for Windows 2000).

Since 1993, software vendors have come a long way in making their interfaces more Windows-like, making the process of installation and configuration more intuitive for administrators. Today, you can usually find help files and wizards to assist you when installing and configuring third-party compo-nents. Also, many third-party networks function using the Windows native networking facilities with little or no alteration.

The critical issue in choosing between built-in Microsoft networking compo-nents and third-party alternatives (which we cover in detail in Chapters 3 and 8) is the type of functionality your clients need. Certain client capabilities offered by third-party vendors may not work within the native Microsoft framework. If those third-party components don't work with the Microsoft components, you may have to weigh the requirements for this third-party functionality against the complexity of installing and configuring third-party networking software.

If requirements for third-party software are absolute or if their functionality is essential, you have no choice but to bite the bullet and face a possible config-uration nightmare. For example, access to certain driver features in the NetWare client software that aren't supported in the Microsoft counterpart may force you to use Novell software — like it or not. Otherwise, you're better off sticking with native Microsoft client software.

Built-in Functions versus Network Add-ons

You may want to enable clients to access networking services that aren't built into the Microsoft Windows client software. Giving users access to this type of functionality always requires additional software, such as the soft-ware necessary to access NFS. Although Windows 95, Windows 98, Windows NT, and Windows 2000 can all support NFS, that support is not built into those operating systems. Therefore, providing users with access to NFS requires obtaining, installing, and configuring additional software on their computers.

Adding new software to network clients is far less traumatic (and more common) than the situation in the preceding section, where you had to change out the Microsoft client software for Novell client software. This is the case when you install any application on a Windows operating system. The applica-tion must be compatible with that operating system, and you must install and configure it correctly. However, software that uses only existing protocols and drivers on a Windows machine augments the Windows built-in capabilities, rather than replacing (or displacing) them. Therefore, adding compatible prod-ucts, such as QUALCOMM's Eudora e-mail package, Ipswitch's WS_FTP Pro file transfer program, the Netscape Navigator Web browser, and many, many others, to Windows 98 and Windows 2000 is quite easy.

Nevertheless, many network administrators try to avoid adding unnecessary protocols and services to Windows. They do so because each additional protocol and service consumes system resources, such as memory and disk space. Granted, additional protocols and services may not use much memory if they're never or rarely used, but disk space is something services always consume!

One of the most profound ways to improve a Windows 2000 machine's performance is to eliminate unnecessary protocols and services, as well as the *bindings* that tie protocols and services together. By default, Windows 2000 binds all protocols and services, even when those bindings may not be necessary (or wanted). Therefore, a bit of post-installation cleanup can improve performance as well as remove unwanted software connections. This applies to both Windows 2000 Professional and Windows 2000 Server. (Managing bindings is covered further in Chapter 8.)

Adding third-party client applications or services to Windows machines is okay. This is especially true because most such software uses Windows built-in networking capabilities "under the hood."

Managing Network Components

Modern Windows operating systems — by which we mean Windows 95, Windows 98, Windows NT 4.0, and Windows 2000 — include support for two collections of client software for networking.

Both Windows 95 and Windows 98 refer to these collections as the

- ✔ Client for Microsoft Networks
- ✔ Client for NetWare Networks

These two client-software collections appear in Figure 2-1, which shows the Configuration tab of the Windows 98 Network Control Panel. Windows 2000 doesn't use the same terms; instead, in the My Network Places display for a local network it refers to the Microsoft Windows Network and to the Novell NetWare Network. Either way, these operating systems are talking about the same things: two different sets of client software that provide access to two different sets of network resources.

As the name suggests, the Client for Microsoft Networks includes the necessary components for a machine to act as a client on a Microsoft network. Likewise, the Client for NetWare Networks includes similar components needed to act as a NetWare network client. (The same logic applies to the Microsoft Windows Network and the Novell NetWare Network in Windows 2000.) Additional software components come into play on Windows 2000 Server and on client machines that run Windows 2000 Professional, Windows NT Workstation, Windows 98, or Windows 95, all of which we cover in Chapter 8.

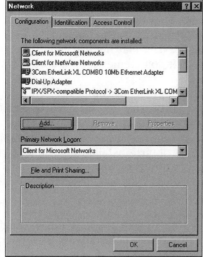

Figure 2-1:
Windows 98
mentions a
Client for
Microsoft
Networks
and a Client
for NetWare
Networks.

You can use the Windows 2000 desktop icon named My Network Places to view information about resources available on your network. By default, this tool displays a list of all the network shares you've created, and the computers they reside on. However, you can instruct it to show all kinds of displays. In Figure 2-2, for example, you see a complete list of all the computers in the same domain as the listing machine.

Figure 2-2:
My Network
Places
shows the
computers
that you've
visited
recently, or
those in
your nearby
network
neighbor-
hood.

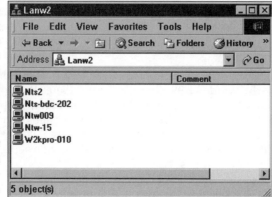

Unmasking the Microsoft network

Even though Windows 2000 differs somewhat from Windows 98 in what it calls its networking software, both of these operating systems contain both Microsoft- and Novell-specific collections of components. In addition, Windows 98 and Windows 2000 share a common terminology when it comes to specific software components. For example, both the Client for Microsoft Network (Windows 98) and the Microsoft Windows Network (Windows 2000) use the same terms when referring to the following collection of software components:

- **MultiProtocol Router (MPR):** The MPR distributes requests for network services to a specific *network provider,* which represents some type of network client environment. (It routes requests for Microsoft services to the Microsoft network provider, and requests for Novell services to the NetWare network provider.) The MPR allows Windows 95, Windows 98, Windows NT, and Windows 2000 to support multiple simultaneous client connections. The MPR also defines a single common interface so applications can access features common to all networks through a single set of interface calls.

- **Microsoft Network Provider:** The Microsoft Network Provider defines an open interface that allows third-party vendors to integrate support for their networks. The Microsoft Network Provider also grants access to (and management of) network resources and components through common utilities, such as the Network Neighborhood and the Network applet in the Control Panel. The Microsoft Network Provider offers a single set of well-defined functions to browse servers, to connect to or disconnect from servers, and to interact with other network resources.

- **Installable File System Manager (IFSMGR):** This file-system access facility integrates multiple file systems through a single interface. The IFSMGR also allows remote file-system access requests to look exactly the same as local file-system access requests in their structure and functions. (They need differ only in how requested objects are addressed.)

- **Client for Microsoft Networks Redirector:** This software component checks all application requests for resources, and hands off any requests for remote resources to the network interface, but passes requests for local resources to the local operating system.

- **NetBIOS interface:** This protocol interface defines a high-level request/response protocol that carries requests for remote resources (and their replies). In particular, the NetBIOS interface uses a special messaging protocol, called *Server Message Block* (SMB), to carry requests from clients to servers and responses to those requests from servers back to their originating clients.

- **Network protocols designed to support Microsoft's Network Driver Interface Specification (NDIS) Version 3.1 or higher:** This refers to the built-in networking protocols for Windows operating systems that we discuss further in Chapter 3.

✔ **A generic NDIS interface:** This programming convention defines a standard code interface to network adapters within Windows 2000, Windows NT 4.0, Windows 95, and Windows 98 operating systems. It allows driver developers to interact with NICs using a well-known, well-documented set of program calls to move data from the computer to the NIC for outgoing messages, and from the NIC back to the computer for incoming messages.

✔ **A specific NDIS adapter driver:** This device driver translates generic network interface formats into formats specific to whatever NIC (or NICs) is installed in a Windows computer. (Note that only Windows 2000 and Windows NT support multiple NICs in a single machine; neither Windows 95 nor Windows 98 offers this capability.)

Figure 2-3 shows this collection of Microsoft Network components and how the various components interact with an application that makes requests and the network that carries those requests to a server, and that delivers the corresponding replies to those requests. Please note that although Windows 95, Windows 98, Windows NT, and Windows 2000 are all similarly constructed and use similar components, details among these individual operating systems vary.

Figure 2-3:
The component structure for the Client for Microsoft Networks/Microsoft Windows Network.

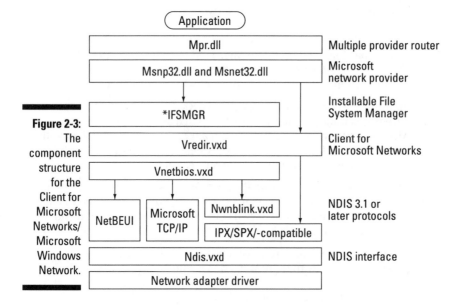

Application	
Mpr.dll	Multiple provider router
Msnp32.dll and Msnet32.dll	Microsoft network provider
*IFSMGR	Installable File System Manager
Vredir.vxd	Client for Microsoft Networks
Vnetbios.vxd	
NetBEUI / Microsoft TCP/IP / Nwnblink.vxd / IPX/SPX/-compatible	NDIS 3.1 or later protocols
Ndis.vxd	NDIS interface
Network adapter driver	

Understanding the Novell network

Even though the component structure for the Client for NetWare Networks is similar to that for the Client for Microsoft Networks (which we cover in the preceding section), their differences lie in specific NetWare-focused components that replace Microsoft counterparts. At many steps along the way, from the application to the NDIS driver, different components specific to NetWare are used instead. The resulting collection of components is as follows:

- ✔ **MultiProtocol Router (MPR):** This software component is common to all network clients for Windows 95, Windows 98, Windows NT, and Windows 2000. As was the case with the Microsoft Network/Microsoft Windows Network, the MPR hands off network service requests to the appropriate network provider.

- ✔ **A NetWare-compatible Network Provider:** This software component provides access to and management of NetWare-accessible network resources and components through common utilities, such as the My Network Places and the Network and Dial-up Connections folder. Like its Microsoft counterpart, the NetWare-compatible Network Provider offers a single set of well-defined functions to browse servers, to connect to or disconnect from servers, and to interact with network resources.

- ✔ **Installable File System Manager (IFSMGR):** This file system access facility integrates multiple file systems through a single interface for consistent local and remote access to NetWare-based file and print resources when the Client for NetWare Networks is at work.

- ✔ **Client for NetWare Networks Redirector:** This software component hands off requests for remote resources to the NetWare network interface and passes requests for local resources to the local operating system.

- ✔ **One of several Network protocols:** Client for NetWare Networks can use either Internet Package Exchange/Sequenced Package Exchange (IPX/SPX) or TCP/IP to access the network.

- ✔ **Generic NDIS interface:** This device driver defines a standard interface to network adapters within Windows 95, Windows 98, Windows NT, and Windows 2000 operating systems. The same interface works for Microsoft and NetWare clients.

- ✔ **A specific NDIS adapter driver:** This device driver translates generic network interface formats into formats specific to whatever NIC (or NICs) is installed in a Windows computer. (Note that only Windows 2000 and Windows NT support multiple NICs in a single machine; neither Windows 95 nor Windows 98 offers this capability.)

Please note the absence of a separate NetBIOS interface in this collection. This omission means that NetWare doesn't use NetBIOS-based names to navigate its networks. (For more information about NetBIOS and NetBIOS names, please consult Chapter 8.)

The Client for NetWare Networks loses none of its NetBIOS capabilities even though there's no separate NetBIOS interface; applications still need NetBIOS support and get it. Notice also that the MPR, the installable file system, the protocols (except for the range of choices), and the NDIS components remain more or less the same for both Microsoft and NetWare clients.

Observing this component-based software structure, you might feel compelled to ask if you can mix and match software components from Novell and Microsoft. Unfortunately, you must go all one way (Microsoft) or the other (Novell) when installing network client software components on a Windows machine. No good comes of trying to meld the two!

You can run both Microsoft and NetWare clients side by side without difficulty, but you can't mix Novell components and Microsoft components willy-nilly on any Windows machine. Therefore, you can use Microsoft software to access both Windows 2000 Servers and NetWare servers, or Novell software to access both Windows 2000 Servers and NetWare servers. But, you can't use Microsoft software to access Windows 2000 Servers and NetWare software to access NetWare servers on the same machine.

Managing Access to Resources

Part of each request that a client makes for a network resource includes the client's own identification. Another part names the resources that the client is requesting from the network. Clients normally use a password to access resources on a peer-to-peer network, which Microsoft calls *share-level access control* (because each password applies to a single shared resource).

In a Microsoft client/server network, the user's level of permissions governs that user's ability to access resources. In Microsoft-speak, *user-level access* means that when a user identifies himself or herself in a request for service, the user's account name helps determine which requests the server can honor and which ones it must deny.

The server checks which resources the user has permission to access, and it also checks whether the operation that the user requests is allowed. For example, Bob may be allowed to read a certain file, but he may not be able to write to or delete that file. If he requests a read operation, the request is permitted, but if he requests a write or delete operation, that request is denied.

Handling requests on a client/server network involves more work than may be immediately apparent, because a *security check* controls access and restrictions. Setting up permissions requires an understanding of which names to attach to resources, to the domains in which they reside, and to the users who state such requests. Much of what you find out in Chapters 8, 11–14, and especially in Chapters 15, 16, and 18 touch on these terms and concepts and explain them to your heart's content.

A Windows Network Services Sampler

In the previous sections, we covered the request/response mechanism that handles all requests for network services and the ways in which responses occur. In this section, we explain what you can do within this structure. The following is an alphabetical list of common services that you're likely to find on a Windows 2000 Server-based network:

- **Alerter:** Provides the ability to send alarms and alerts to specific recipients when events occur in Event Viewer or thresholds are exceeded in Performance Monitor.

- **Computer Browser:** Manages the list of computer and resource names on a specific network, so users can browse a list of what's out there (and available) in Network Neighborhood and other utilities.

- **Messenger:** Provides a way for Windows 2000 Server to deliver on-screen messages to designated recipients in response to explicit commands or to alarms and alerts.

- **Net Logon:** Handles user attempts to log on to the network and ferries information among all *domain controllers* within a single Windows 2000 Server domain.

- **Network DDE:** Allows dynamic updates to occur across a network. *Dynamic Data Exchange* (DDE) refers to a dynamic update technology used to propagate updates from one file or document to another when embedded objects in one document must reflect changes to that object in another document.

- **NTLM Security Support Provider:** Provides a Windows 2000 Server security model that's compatible with LAN Manager (LM). This service handles encryption and delivery of logon requests that can't use more modern Windows security models.

- **Plug and Play:** Makes a Windows 2000 machine Plug and Play-compatible.

- **Print Spooler:** Handles storage of files for pending print jobs; this is the service that manages the scheduling and retention of pending print jobs until their turn to print comes up.

- **Routing and Remote Access Service (RRAS):** Covers a whole range of RRAS services. RRAS provides dial-in/dial-out communications services for up to 256 simultaneous connections on a single Windows 2000 Server, and offers a range of routing services as well.

- **Server:** Acts as the basic listener process for requests for service on a Windows 2000 Server (in fact, stopping the Server service is a good way to temporarily disable network access to a server). Although its name may suggest otherwise, this service is necessary on Windows 2000 Professional machines and Windows 2000 Server machines alike.

✔ **Telephony Service:** Makes it possible for Windows 2000 to use the built-in Windows Telephony Application Programming Interface (TAPI) to access modems, telephones, Integrated Services Digital Network (ISDN), and general Digital Subscriber Line (xDSL) devices through a standard dialer and telephone book interface. It is, therefore, also a key component of the RRAS service.

✔ **Workstation:** Allows a Windows 2000 machine to issue requests for service; namely, this is what supports client-side activity.

To view a comprehensive list of the services available in Windows 2000, check out the Services icon that appears inside the Computer Management tool as part of the System Tools hierarchy.

Although this laundry list doesn't include every service in Windows 2000 Server, it does represent many of the services that you're likely to see running on most computers. Throughout this book, we give you a much better idea of what these and other services can do, as well as how you install, configure, and maintain them.

Chapter 3

Matters of Protocol

● ●

In This Chapter

▶ Describing the roles that protocols play

▶ Managing network access is job one!

▶ Moving data from applications to the network, and vice versa

▶ Ganging up: Protocols never travel alone

▶ Understanding IPX/SPX and NWLink

▶ Introducing TCP/IP: The protocol of the Internet

▶ Mastering miscellany: The "other" protocols

● ●

*I*n this chapter, you examine the communications and messages that move around on networks. Here, we tell you more about what senders send and receivers receive, as you investigate the sets of rules — called *protocols* — that govern how computers exchange information across a network.

In essence, networked communications rely on a shared set of rules for exchanging information and for defining how data looks at the most basic level, such as how to present data digitally (or "What's a one, and what's a zero?"). These rules also dictate the formats for and meanings behind the addresses that indicate where "here" and "there" are on a network, that identify message types and content, and that offer lots of other critical information to boot.

When Computers Communicate

Many of the ways that computers communicate and the ways that humans communicate share common elements. Take a phone call, for example:

✔ Phone calls use highly formulaic introductions to connect the right speakers on each end of the connection. ("Is this the Phlogiston residence? May I speak to Phil, please?") Computers take a similar tack for network communications in that a sender often begins by asking the receiver if a conversation can begin, and only after permission is granted does any actual exchange of data occur.

✔ Taking turns talking on the phone requires careful listening skills and sensitivity to "open spaces" in the other party's talk, so each party can speak when the opportunity arises. Computers have no intuition, so they exchange explicit signals when one party wants to switch from listening to talking. In fact, some communications techniques allow both parties to talk — and listen — at the same time!

✔ Ending a phone conversation can be a matter of mutual agreement, or it can involve well-known signals that one party wants to end the conversation. ("I have to let you go now" is a famous human example.) Computers also exchange signals to indicate that a network conversation is ready to end and conclude by breaking their connection to each other.

✔ Humans possess coping skills to help them recognize unplanned endings to conversations, such as a failed cordless phone battery, driving beyond a cell boundary, or an outright connection failure. They also have the smarts to try again or give up, depending on whether they've satisfied their communication goals. Computers are more simple-minded; they wait until communications resume or a fixed interval of time (called a *time-out period*) elapses before recognizing that a connection is dead and that the conversation is over. Then it's up to the application that initiated the link to decide whether to try again or give up.

Understanding the differences between human communications and computer communications can help you understand networking better. The biggest difference, it seems, is that humans can navigate by the seat of their pants far better than computers can.

The secret's in the interpretation . . .

When humans communicate on the phone, what we say (or hear) is always interpreted and often misunderstood. What you think you said isn't always what another person thinks he or she heard you say. Human communication relies on shared rules and meanings as well as a common frame of reference. Computers rely on these same elements to communicate; but because computers can't make judgment calls or use their intuition, these elements must be spelled out completely. Computers can do only what they're programmed to do.

For computers to exchange data, every element must be explicitly supplied. Computers can't pick up implications and hidden meanings. To communicate, computers have to begin with complete agreement about the following issues (as stated from a computer's point of view):

✔ What's my address? How do I learn my address? How do I learn other computers' addresses?

✔ How do I signal another computer to indicate that I'm ready to send (or receive) a message, that I'm busy, or that I can wait if it's busy?

If you think about the phone system, these issues are the same for humans dialing a telephone and computers dialing a modem. In fact, these questions can be restated as follows:

✔ What's my phone number? How do I learn my phone number? How do I learn the phone numbers for other parties that I wish to reach?

✔ How do I place a call? How do I recognize a busy signal? How do I get the phone to keep dialing if the number I want to reach is busy? (Note also that the phone system handles busy and ring signals, so both computers and humans can tell when a call is going through and when the party they're trying to reach is busy.)

Agreeing on a set of rules

Building a complete and consistent set of rules for computer communications is a time-consuming, nitpicky business that's entirely capable of driving most ordinary people bonkers. In the early days of the computer industry, individual companies or groups would put hordes of programmers to work building computer communications programs to solve specific, isolated problems.

But as time went on, programmers realized that this approach produced lots of unique ways for computers to communicate that worked only within the confines of small, isolated technical communities. After the need to communicate spreads farther, serious incompatibilities prevented such communities from exchanging data unless one community willingly gave up its way of communicating and adopted another's way of communicating.

The U.S. government played a key role in bringing order to this network chaos. When the government tried to get computers from Company A to work with computers from Company Z, it soon realized that it had a monster compatibility problem. A consensus soon emerged that a common set of rules for networking would make communication easier. Likewise, early network pioneers quickly learned that networking was difficult, if not downright impossible, when all players didn't follow the same set of rules.

If this tale had a storybook ending, it would be "Today, there's only one set of networking rules that everyone uses wisely and well." Alas, that's not the case. The degree of networking chaos has decreased significantly, but many sets of mutually incompatible networking protocols are still in use, because hardware and software vendors try to stay on the "bleeding edge" by inventing new rules as they boldly go where no network has gone before.

These fundamental questions must be answered, and they represent just the beginning of a large and complex collection of details that have to be nailed down, codified, and implemented for computers to be able to communicate across a network. The answers to this entire collection of questions are the basis for a set of rules for computer communications; in fact, these rules represent the "rules of the road" — or protocols — for networking.

Following Protocol

The sets of networking rules that we talk about in the previous section are usually called *networking protocols* — but sometimes they're also called *networking standards, standard networking protocols,* and so on. Hopefully, you get the idea that these rules are shared by some group that seeks to communicate amongst themselves and define a common method for computers to communicate with one another. Any particular protocol defines a language, a structure, and a set of rules to support such communications.

Lots of work goes into defining a set of networking protocols, and even more work goes into building software to implement it. This is a huge project, and the amount of work necessary to pull it off explains why users, software developers, and hardware manufacturers all find it convenient to stick to the protocols that best fit their needs.

In diplomacy, protocol establishes a rigid set of procedures and etiquette that representatives from sovereign governments follow to prevent all-out war. For example, protocol helps explain why diplomats refer to screaming matches as "frank and earnest discussions" and to knotty disagreements as "constructive dialogs." Political doubletalk aside, the word *protocol* captures the flavor of rules for network communications quite nicely.

Whales come in pods, protocols in suites

Although this book deals primarily with Windows 2000 Server and the Microsoft protocols, the protocols included in Windows 2000 represent only part of a large body of well-known and well-defined networking protocols. Microsoft does a good job of allowing multiple protocols to run at the same time in Windows 2000, including the Internet standard *Transmission Control Protocol/Internet Protocol* (TCP/IP), Novell's *Internet Package Exchange/ Sequenced Package Exchange* (IPX/SPX), and *NetBIOS* and *NetBEUI* (which were Microsoft's original — and only — protocols to begin with).

Upon examination of any networking implementation, you're likely to observe that protocols rarely, if ever, appear in the singular. Most networking protocols consist of a collection of specific message formats and rules for interaction, each with its own name and functions, rather than a single, monolithic collection of formats and rules. For that reason, protocols may also be called *protocol suites,* not because they like to lounge around on comfortable furniture, but because they travel in packs, like wild dogs.

Making standards happen

One interesting fact about networking rules is that both vendors and standards groups call their protocols *standards.* Some vendors wax eloquently about differences between *de facto* and *de jure* standards. *De facto* means "It's not official, but a lot of people use it, so we can call it a standard if we want to." *De jure* means "It's a standard because the ABC (a standards-setting body) has declared it so and published this 4-foot-high stack of books to prove it!"

Behind the often-heated discussions about what is and isn't a standard lurks a control issue. Purists — including academics, researchers, and techo-weenies — flatly assert that only a standards-setting group can be "objective and fair." Therefore, only such a group can select the very best that technology has to offer by putting it in its standard — making it the best possible standard.

The other heat source comes from the vendors' desperate race to keep up with the marketplace (and customer demands for better, faster, cheaper technology) by struggling to get products finished and out the door. "Of course, we must control our technology," they say. "How else can we keep up?"

The objectivity, fairness, and leading-edge characteristics of most protocol standards may not be open to dispute, but establishing standards involves assembling groups of individuals who must agree on their contents. This takes time. Meanwhile, technology races ahead. (Nothing goes stale faster than leading-edge technology.)

It doesn't matter whether networking protocols are standards or not, whether *de facto* or *de jure.* The markets are where the action is. Vendors must involve themselves in all sides of any debate because they must bet on all the technology horses in any race. Some astute vendors, including Microsoft, publish their "standards" and give customers and industry experts enough documentation to both create workable networks and keep up with the rapid pace of development as well.

Some standards bodies have been wise enough to realize that a standard is viable only when widely used. These groups have allowed hardware and software vendors to deal with the real-world issues involved in getting products to market. The winners in both camps are the most popular protocols. Microsoft's protocol selections for Windows 2000 (and other Windows versions) include the leading standard protocol, TCP/IP, and two widely used vendor protocol suites — IPX/SPX (which originated with Novell's NetWare) and NetBIOS/NetBEUI (which originated at IBM, but was enhanced in cooperation with Microsoft and 3COM in the early 1980s).

Protocols permeate all aspects of networking

If one key concept explains why protocols are necessary, it's that protocols handle the movement of information between the hardware on the network interface and the applications that access the network. The reason why one computer can't talk to another computer without both sharing a common set of protocols is that both the sender and the receiver need to be able to understand the other's operations, data formats, and delivery mechanisms. Without this common frame of reference, networking can't work.

Protocols fill the gap between a network's hardware and its software. The programs that let your computer access the network must use a set of protocols. These protocols ferry data from applications all the way down to hardware, where a protocol says "send this message," to talk to the network. Going the other way, the protocol tells the hardware "give me the message," when the hardware indicates an incoming message has arrived.

Most protocols don't care what type of network they're talking through. In most cases, protocols are unaware of the network technology used, which might be *Ethernet, token ring,* or tutti-frutti. This indifference is possible because the part of the software that provides hardware access resides in a *device driver* for the network interface. The protocols themselves originate from other sources. (In Windows 2000, they reside in software components installed as part of the operating system, unless third-party components have been installed to displace built-in ones.) Therefore, when a protocol "talks to the network interface," it's really talking through a device driver to send data to (or to receive data from) the network.

Specific device drivers tell a protocol exactly how to talk to the network interface (or interfaces) in your machine. If you're lucky, you use a network-ready Intel or Alpha-based PC for Windows 2000 Server (Microsoft supports both Intel Pentium I processors and higher, plus the Compaq/DEC Alpha processors), which includes preinstalled networking abilities. Otherwise, you have to make sure that you install the proper network interface driver when you install Windows 2000 Server so the machine can access the network.

As we explain in Chapter 2, some applications include built-in networking abilities that use a special software interface. Such *network-aware applications* are becoming increasingly common as networks become ubiquitous. Most Microsoft applications include some type of network intelligence, but the amount of such brainpower varies according to each application's focus and capabilities. Other applications may use standard *application programming interfaces* (APIs) and obtain network access anyway, totally unaware that a network is involved. This is where redirectors and other key system elements play a part. Whether applications are network-ready or use external networking facilities, as soon as they access the network, they use protocol software (and device drivers) to accept incoming or send outgoing messages.

The key to network access from applications or the operating system depends on access to a protocol suite. As we explain in Chapter 2, Windows 2000 includes all the components necessary to support network-aware and network-oblivious applications, which makes Windows 2000 Server itself quite network-aware indeed. Even though applications (and the operating system) may make requests for network service, the protocols do the dirty work, packaging messages to be sent across the network and then unpacking incoming messages into a readable form.

On other operating systems, such as Windows 9*x*, UNIX, OS/2, and the Macintosh OS, built-in networking software also handles the network interface and those protocols and services that use it. DOS and older Windows 3.*x* versions, however, use client networking software that Microsoft supplies with Windows 2000 Server (or some other alternative from a third party).

Protocols as Postal Centers

Most of the action that occurs between applications and hardware consists of taking messages, breaking them down, and stuffing them into envelopes as those messages move farther from the application and closer to the hardware. From the other direction — from hardware to application — protocols unpack envelopes and reassemble individual pieces to build complete messages. We hope that the resulting message is meaningful, but remember GIGO, that immutable law of computing — "garbage in, garbage out."

Exploring a post office analogy here may be useful. The post office handles anything that has an address on it and has sufficient postage to pay its way, as long as it conforms to the legal dimensions for a letter or a package. How is a letter delivered? It works something like this:

1. **You address a letter, stick on a stamp, and drop it in a mailbox.**

2. **The mail carrier picks up the letter.**

3. **The mail carrier delivers the letter to the local post office.**

4. **Mail sorters check the zip code and route the letter.**

5. **The letter goes to the post office that serves the destination zip code.**

6. **Mail sorters check the street address and route the letter to the appropriate mail carrier.**

7. **The mail carrier delivers the letter to the address of its recipient.**

At least, that's the way it's *supposed* to work. The basic requirements for successful mail delivery are timely pickup, short transit time, and correct delivery. Factors that affect transit time and delivery are correct identification of and routing to the destination address, plus potential transportation delays between sender and receiver.

The similarity between networking protocols and the postal service lies in the ability to recognize addresses, to route messages from senders to receivers, and to provide delivery. The major difference is that the postal service, unlike networking protocols, doesn't care what's in the envelopes we send as long as they meet size, weight, and materials restrictions. Networking protocols are very unpostman-like in that they care a great deal about what's in the envelopes we send. One of the main jobs of a networking protocol is to divide up the contents of our envelopes and put them into smaller envelopes for delivery.

For example, suppose that you want to copy a 10MB file from your computer to another machine on your network. The file consists of a spreadsheet with some charts and graphics that include a sales forecast for the next quarter, so you want it to arrive quickly and correctly.

To use the post office (or what net-heads call "snail mail"), you would copy the file to a floppy disk and mail it to its recipient. However, that's not fast enough for most computer users. Over the network, it gets there in about 90 seconds (compared to the days it would take via snail mail). As the file moves from your workstation to the other machine, it's chopped into lots of small packages and then reassembled into its original 10MB form upon receipt.

Size restriction — that is, the biggest chunk of data that can move across the network in a single message — is only one reason that network messages are broken up and put into multiple envelopes. Handling addresses is another reason. In the post office example, the post office cares about the destination zip code, whereas the delivering mail carrier cares only about the street address. Likewise, one protocol might care about only the name of the computer to which the file is to be shipped. However, at a lower level, the protocol needs to know where to direct the chunks of data moving from sender to receiver so the file can be correctly reassembled upon delivery.

For senders, the protocol software spends most of its time taking things apart to send them accurately and completely. On the receiving end, the protocol software spends its time stripping off packaging information and putting things back together again. The sender and receiver also exchange information during this process to monitor the accuracy and effectiveness of their communications and to determine if and when delivery is complete. Protocols also keep track of the quality and usability of network links.

In short, a lot more communication and activity is involved in sending and receiving messages across a network than is required to route mail from the sending post office to the receiving one. But, the mail analogy remains a pretty good explanation for how things work in general (ignoring the routine rooting around inside messages done by protocols and not by the post office).

The Dance of the Seven Layers

Network protocols are grouped according to their functions, such as sending and receiving messages from the network interface, talking to the hardware, making it possible for applications to do their things in a network environment, and talking to the software. Protocols are often called *protocol families* or *protocol suites* because they operate in groups.

This group organization involves stacking multiple layers of functionality, where software is associated with each layer. When the software that supports a particular network protocol loads on a computer, it's called a *protocol stack.* All computers on the network load all or part of the stack. They use the same parts of the stack, called *peer protocols,* when they communicate with each other as — you guessed it — *peers.*

The best-known collection of networking layers was developed as part of an open networking systems effort in the 1980s called the *Open Systems Interconnection* (OSI) initiative. This model is known as the *OSI reference model* (also simply called the OSI model), because it defines a common frame of reference for understanding how networks work. Even though the OSI initiative never really achieved widespread adoption, the OSI model remains a standard tool to explain how network communications are structured and how they behave. The OSI model is shown in Figure 3-1.

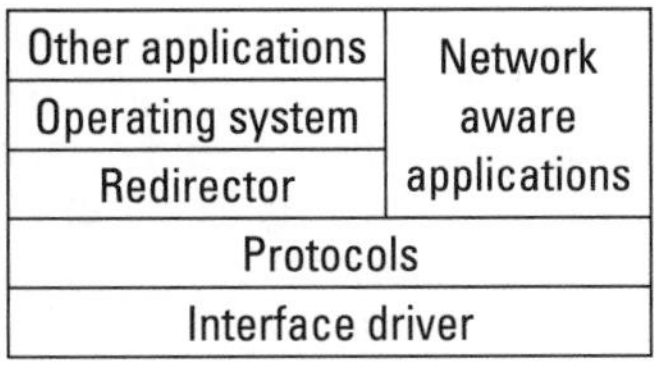

Figure 3-1:
The OSI reference model breaks networking protocols into seven layers.

Other applications	Network aware applications
Operating system	
Redirector	
Protocols	
Interface driver	

The OSI model consists of seven layers, as follows (working from the bottom up):

✔ **Physical layer:** This is the layer where the network hardware operates. Rules for this layer govern the types of *connectors* used, what types of *signaling techniques* carry data across the network, and the types of *cable* or other *networking media* that the physical, tangible part of the network uses. In some sense, this is the only part of the OSI model that you can actually see and touch.

✔ **Data Link layer:** This layer handles communication with the network hardware. For outbound messages, the Data Link layer enables the conversion of the bits that computers use to represent data into equivalent signals needed to move data across the network. For inbound messages, it reverses the process by enabling the conversion of signals into their equivalent bits. The Data Link layer is also where low-level hardware addresses for individual *network interface cards* (NICs) and other devices are handled.

✔ **Network layer:** This layer routes messages between senders and receivers, which means that it also handles translation between human-readable network addresses and computer-readable network addresses (which are not the same as the hardware addresses that the Data Link layer handles). Each message that passes through this layer includes the sender's and the receiver's addresses in order to identify the parties involved. The Network layer moves data from sender to receiver when they aren't both attached to the same cable segment.

✔ **Transport layer:** This layer chops up large messages into so-called *Protocol Data Units* (PDUs), or packets, and sends them across a network. It also puts PDUs back together to reconstitute messages upon receipt. The Transport layer can also include data integrity checks by adding a bit pattern to each message based on a mathematical calculation before sending. This same calculation is repeated by the sender, and the result is compared to the value calculated beforehand. If both values agree, the Transport layer assumes the transmission was accurate and correct; if they don't agree, the Transport layer requests that the PDU be re-sent. This integrity function is optional; therefore, some Transport layer protocols include an integrity check, whereas other such protocols don't.

✔ **Session layer:** This layer sets up ongoing network conversations (called *sessions*) between sender and receiver. This kind of ongoing connection makes it easier for computers to exchange large amounts of data, or to maintain a connection when data moves regularly between both parties to a session. Therefore, the Session layer handles *session setup* (which is just like dialing a phone), *session maintenance* (which is just like having a phone conversation), and *session termination* or *teardown* (which is just like ending a phone conversation and then hanging up the phone).

✔ **Presentation layer:** This layer converts data for network delivery. The assumption that drives this activity is that sender and receiver may not share a common set of data representations. Therefore, the Presentation layer converts data from formats created by the sender into a generic format for network transit, and then converts that generic form into a format specific to the receiver upon delivery. This conversion process allows programmers on both sides of the network connection to assume generic formats for network data, and to handle the details necessary to deliver that data to a specific client more easily.

✔ **Application layer:** This layer's name is something of a misnomer. It doesn't refer to the application or service that seeks to send or receive data across a network. Rather, it refers to an interface between the protocol stack and applications or system services. The Application layer defines the methods by which applications or system services can request network access and by which they can obtain access to incoming data from the network.

Each layer functions more or less independently of the others. But the job of any given layer is to provide services for the layer above it and to deliver data to the layer below. (The lowest level of the OSI model, the Physical layer, simply sends data on to a receiver or to the Data Link layer, depending on whether the communication is coming or going.)

The encoding that a layer does on the sending side is decoded by the same layer on the receiving side. Therefore, the layered OSI model helps emphasize that protocols on the sending end accept data from applications, convert that data into a generic form, manage conversations, prepare data to be sent across the network, address and route data, and then convert that data into signals for transmission across the network.

On the receiving end, that process is reversed: The protocols convert signals into data, figure out where that data is to be delivered, reconstitute incoming messages into their original containers, manage conversations, prepare the data for the client computer, and deliver that data to an application.

Some wags like to claim that there's an eighth layer to the protocol stack, and that it's the most important layer of all. It's called the "Politics and Religion" layer, and it jokingly refers to the organizational beliefs and requirements that drive network use. Even though there is no such layer in the OSI model, you'd be well-advised to keep this layer in mind any time you have to "sell" networking technology to upper management in your organization!

Windows 2000 Protocols (And More)

Just as diplomatic protocols grease the wheels of international relations, network protocols keep the network wheels turning. By getting to know these players, you gain more insight into how your network operates. As an added bonus, you'll also be better equipped to troubleshoot protocol-related problems.

The built-in Microsoft protocols include four protocol suites, plus support for an additional utility that Macintoshes use to attach to Windows 2000. Here are the four core protocols in alphabetical order:

✔ **DLC (Data Link Control):** A printer and host access (terminal emulation) protocol.

✔ **IPX/SPX (Internet Package Exchange/Sequenced Package Exchange):** The NetWare core protocols, developed by Novell in the early 1980s.

✔ **NetBIOS/NetBEUI (Networked Basic Input-Output System/NetBIOS Enhanced User Interface):** NetBIOS is an application programming interface (API), and NetBEUI a fast, efficient, but nonroutable, local-area protocol developed by IBM and refined by Microsoft. These were the original networking components for LAN Manager and Windows NT. NetBIOS also works with IPX/SPX and TCP/IP, so don't assume that NetBIOS requires NetBEUI. (It doesn't.)

✔ **TCP/IP (Transmission Control Protocol/Internet Protocol):** A set of standard protocols and services developed for the U.S. government in the 1970s and 1980s. TCP/IP is now the most widely used networking protocol suite in the world.

Windows 2000 Server also includes built-in support for *AppleTalk,* the networking protocol native to the Macintosh operating system. This add-in module (which isn't installed during Windows 2000 Server's initial setup) lets Mac users access files, printers, and services on a Windows 2000 Server.

You can use any or all of these protocols on your network, which accounts for both the blessings and curses of Windows 2000 networking. In the following sections, we tell you about each of these protocols and give you some guidance about when and why you might want to use one or more of them. Don't worry if the acronyms are unfamiliar or the terminology seems strange; concentrate on finding out how the protocols work to connect programs and services to your network (and your network's users). After you understand these concepts, you'll know all the really important stuff.

Here there be acronyms!

To set up and troubleshoot a Windows 2000-based network, you need to understand what the various protocols do to make educated guesses about the types of problems that each protocol may develop. When working with these protocols, you have to toss around awkward collections of letters (and sometimes numbers) with aplomb.

You should know which acronyms belong together and how the pieces of the various protocol stacks fit together. When things get weird — and we're sorry to report that they sometimes do — you have to know about the Windows 2000 rogue's gallery of protocols so you can run down the possible perpetrators.

Most protocol families are rife with abbreviations and acronyms. Take heart from this fact: Though familiarity may breed contempt, it can also enable you to navigate this complex bowl of alphabet soup!

DLC: Golden oldie

The *Data Link Control* (DLC) protocol is the oldest member in the gang of Windows 2000 protocols. IBM developed DLC to connect *token-ring* based workstations to IBM mainframes and minicomputers. Printer manufacturers adopted this protocol to connect remote (or so-called *network-attached*) printers to network print servers. You probably won't need DLC unless you use some kind of IBM host connection or an older network-attached printer. (Newer network-attached printers usually support TCP/IP print services, which makes sense because most networks use TCP/IP nowadays.)

DLC's primary use is to connect to mainframes and minicomputers through a gateway. A workstation PC (the one on your desk) uses DLC to talk to the gateway, and the gateway translates that into IBM's *Systems Network Architecture* protocols, also known as SNA (if not some other mainframe protocol), to pass on the conversation to a host computer.

Use DLC only if you must, because it's a primitive, nonroutable protocol. (Nonroutable means a router can't forward DLC messages from one network to another.) Its use for network printers and host connections is waning, so you can probably do without it.

IPX/SPX: The original NetWare protocols

Internet Package Exchange (IPX), *Sequenced Package Exchange* (SPX), and *NetWare Core Protocol* (NCP) are the original Novell NetWare protocols. IPX, SPX, and NCP, with more than 48 million users, are among the most widely used networking protocols worldwide. You can use IPX with NetWare for a variety of operating systems, including DOS, Windows 3.*x*, Windows 9*x*, Windows 2000, Macintosh, OS/2, and some varieties of UNIX.

You normally need these protocols only if you use NetWare 4.*x* or older versions on your network. With its latest release of NetWare, Version 5.0, Novell provides native NetWare support for TCP/IP, so we expect IPX/SPX usage to diminish over time. Please note that because Microsoft didn't want to pay Novell to use the IPX/SPX trade name, Microsoft calls IPX/SPX NWLink. (In Windows 9*x*, it's called the "IPX/SPX-compatible Protocol.")

IPX/SPX is a pretty well-behaved protocol with advanced routing capabilities. Therefore, it works on networks of all sizes. But using IPX/SPX typically means a NetWare 4.*x* server (or some older version) is somewhere on your network. You can wean yourself from this protocol over time, or do without it altogether, as your organization follows the inexorable trend toward TCP/IP, the protocol of the Internet (with which IPX/SPX is incompatible).

TCP/IP: The Internet suite

Transmission Control Protocol/Internet Protocol (TCP/IP) grew out of research funded by the Department of Defense (DoD) that began in the 1970s when the feds realized they needed a technology to help them link all their dissimilar computer systems into a single network. These protocols in the TCP/IP suite are sometimes called the *DoD protocols,* because the DoD requires that all computers it purchases be able to use them. Likewise, TCP/IP is known as the *Internet protocol,* because it's the foundation upon which the Internet runs.

TCP/IP is actually an acronym for two members of the protocol suite: the Transmission Control Protocol (TCP) and the Internet Protocol (IP). According to Dr. Vinton Cerf, one of the Internet's founding technologists, more than one million networks are part of the Internet itself, but an equal number (or more) of private networks also use TCP/IP.

With a global community of nearly 100 million users, TCP/IP is the most widely used of all the networking protocols. TCP/IP is also deeply rooted in the UNIX community, because of its inclusion in early-1980s public releases of the free *Berkeley Software Distribution* (BSD) of UNIX and its subsequent inclusion in the official AT&T/Bell Labs offering of UNIX shortly afterward.

Because TCP/IP was designed to allow dissimilar types of computers to inter-connect and communicate, TCP/IP works on more types of hardware than any other networking protocol. Therefore, you shouldn't be surprised that most commercially available operating systems — including Windows, Macintosh, and UNIX — include built-in TCP/IP implementations.

Because TCP/IP is the foundation for the Internet and the most widely used networking protocol, we consider it to be the default choice for most net-works. Although learning and using TCP/IP can be a chore, it provides more functions and capabilities than any other protocol. In fact, Microsoft recom-mends TCP/IP as the best protocol to use with Windows 2000 Server.

NetBIOS/NetBEUI: The original Microsoft duo

IBM developed NetBIOS to enable small groups of PCs to share files and print-ers efficiently. We treat NetBIOS differently than NetBEUI, because NetBIOS represents a widely used *network application programming interface,* but NetBEUI represents a specific set of *protocols.*

In fact, NetBIOS works over TCP/IP (where it's often called NetBT, for NetBIOS over TCP/IP) as well as over IPX/SPX. Because NetBIOS provides access to some key services for Microsoft networks, including name resolution, some version of NetBIOS is almost inevitably found on a Windows 2000-based network. But, because NetBIOS functions over *all* the major Microsoft protocols, that protocol need not necessarily be NetBEUI.

Although Windows NT 4.0, Windows 2000, and Windows 98 include refurbished 32-bit implementations of NetBEUI, and NetBEUI is built into many applications and networking products, NetBEUI has fallen out of use as the size and scope of networks have increased. Here's why: NetBEUI is non-routable, which means it doesn't behave well on large networks. It remains the fastest protocol and the easiest to install for small networks, which probably explains why Microsoft continues to include it with Windows 2000 (and its other modern Windows operating systems). But now, even Microsoft recommends against its use except on the smallest networks.

For networks of ten computers or fewer, NetBEUI may be a good choice, as long as you don't need Internet access. NetBEUI's simplicity, low overhead, and speed make it a good choice for small workgroups without incurring the complexity and management overhead typical for TCP/IP.

Other faces, other protocols

Other, less common protocols may crop up on networks where you work, such as:

- ✔ **AppleTalk:** The name of a set of protocols created by Apple Computer, whose Macintosh computer was one of the first mass-market computers to include built-in networking hardware and software. In most cases, where you have a Macintosh, you have some need for AppleTalk. To offer file and print access to Macintosh clients, Microsoft includes a utility called Windows 2000 Services for Macintosh.

- ✔ **ISO/OSI:** A nifty palindrome that stands for the *International Organization for Standardization's Open Systems Interconnection* protocol suite. OSI has never lived up to its original goal to succeed TCP/IP. Some OSI protocols are in broad use in Europe, where they have established a foothold. OSI is out there in industry, government, academia, and business because many governments, including the U.S. government, require systems to be OSI-compliant.

  Like TCP/IP, OSI is available for a broad range of systems, from PCs to supercomputers. Most protocol stacks resemble the OSI reference model for networking, and this model remains the most enduring legacy of the effort that went into OSI networking in the 1980s. Numerous third-party ISO/OSI implementations are available for Windows 2000, mostly from European companies, but Microsoft itself doesn't include these protocols with the operating system.

✓ **SNA:** This refers to IBM's *Systems Network Architecture,* its basic protocol suite for large-scale networking and mainframe access. Because SNA was a pioneering protocol, companies that invested heavily in mainframe technology also usually invested in SNA. Many SNA networks are still in use, but the number is dropping because SNA is old, cumbersome, and expensive, and because TCP/IP is eating SNA's lunch — even on mainframes. From a Windows 2000 perspective, the Windows 2000 BackOffice component called SNA Server offers a Windows 2000-based SNA gateway to Microsoft network clients.

The networking world includes hundreds of other protocol suites, each with its own collection of acronyms and special capabilities, but you don't need to know most of them. If you haven't seen a protocol that runs on your network in this chapter, you probably know more about it than we do anyway!

Connection types classify protocols

IP, IPX, and NetBEUI are *connectionless* protocols, and SPX and TCP are *connection oriented.* What does this mean? Must you care?

All these protocols operate at lower levels. Earlier in this chapter, we told you that a lower-level protocol's most important job is to break up arbitrarily long messages into digestible chunks when sending data across a network and then to put them back together upon receipt. These chunks (called *packets*) form the basic message units for data moving across a network. These packets are further divided and stuffed into their envelopes by the access method in use. Such envelopes are called *frames.* Look at it this way: Packets move up and down the protocol stack; frames dance across the wires.

Connectionless protocols work the same way as mailing letters through the postal service. You drop the letter into a mailbox and expect the post office to deliver it. You may never know if the letter actually gets there or not — unless it's a bill! IP, IPX, and NetBEUI provide no guarantee of delivery, and frames can arrive in any order.

Connection-oriented protocols, on the other hand, use a handshake to start communications,

where the would-be sender asks the receiver if it can accept input before it starts sending. After transmission is underway, connection-oriented protocols treat each message like a registered letter, where you get a return card to verify its receipt. SPX and TCP packets are sequenced so when they arrive, they can be reassembled in their original order, which makes them more reliable. Connection-oriented protocols can also request redelivery or send error notices when packets are damaged or lost en route from sender to receiver.

IP and other connectionless protocols are typically fast and impose little overhead, but are considered lightweight and unreliable. TCP and other connection-oriented protocols run more slowly than their connectionless counterparts because they keep track of what has been sent and received, and because they monitor status of the connection between sender and receiver. More record-keeping and data-check information is built into each packet, which raises overhead requirements but also increases reliability.

When to Mix Protocols

Sometimes, you may need more than one networking protocol on a computer. This may occasionally require you to go through some interesting contortions, but Windows 2000 Server is accommodating about supporting multiple protocols. In fact, you can run TCP/IP, IPX/SPX (NWLink), and NetBEUI on a single Windows 2000 Server machine on multiple network interface cards without too much hassle. The same is true of Windows 98.

Likewise, Macintoshes can run AppleTalk and TCP/IP together easily, and UNIX can run as many protocol stacks together as you might need to obtain the range of network services necessary. A UNIX machine's protocol collection can include TCP/IP, NetBEUI, OSI, IPX, and more.

Chances are that your biggest problems in using multiple protocol stacks will occur on older PCs running DOS or Windows 3.*x*, where the lack of built-in networking automatically makes installing and using multiple protocols harder to do. Likewise, limited memory management capabilities and lack of support for modern device drivers make hybrid networking a real challenge.

How to See What's Up on Your Server

Windows 2000 Server makes inspecting your system to see which protocols are installed pretty simple. Just launch the Control Panel, then double-click the Network and Dial-Up Connections folder in that window. Next, click on the Advanced Settings entry in the Advanced item from the menu bar, and select the Adapters and Bindings tab in that window. You see the results of these actions in Figure 3-2, which shows that we practice what we preached in this chapter by running only TCP/IP on our network. (Figure 3-2 shows that TCP/IP is bound to all the services that show up for our Local Area Connection.)

In Windows 2000, you can also select Start⇨Settings⇨Network and Dial-up Connection⇨Local Area Connection and under the General tab, you can see the installed components, including protocols.

The only protocols you have to worry about on your network are the ones that show up in this window (or the protocols that you know are supposed to show up but don't, as the case may sometimes be).

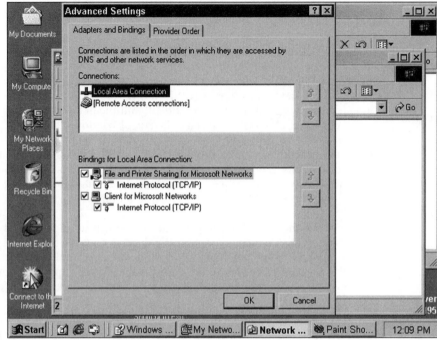

Figure 3-2:
Use the
Advanced
Settings
window in
Network
and Dial-Up
Connections
to check for
installed
protocols.

Chapter 4

My Kingdom for a Topology!

*W*hen mathematicians get together, they enjoy nothing more than making up new terminology to bedevil the rest of us. (Maybe they don't want computer scientists to corner the market on obtuse terminology.) Mathematics is where the networking term *topology* originates; a topology describes the way computers are wired together on a network. Beyond bedevilment, topologies provide a concise and accurate way to describe how a network's various pieces and parts come together. In this chapter, we tell you about various topologies you can mix and match to create networks.

However, topologies don't tell the whole story about network design. You must also consider the specific hardware you use and how that hardware interacts with other hardware — the *hardware implementation,* if you will.

Perhaps jealous of the mathematicians and their coining of cool terms, a group of computer scientists coined the term *network technologies,* sometimes called *networking technologies,* to identify the specific hardware and signaling methods used in a network. Perhaps jealous of *that* group of computer scientists, another group decided that it was more useful to think about the same hardware and signaling methods in terms of *access methods,* a way of thinking that concentrates more on how the hardware gets permission to transmit signals across the network medium.

This chapter also gives you the skinny on specific hardware implementations, network technologies, and access methods that take a topology and make it into a real, working network.

What Is a Topology, Really?

Mathematically speaking, a topology is an arrangement of lines between points in a graph. In a network, the word *topology* refers to the way wires (lines) stretch between computers (nodes in a graph). Therefore, when you hear the word *topology* at a networking conference, what's being talked about is the arrangement of computers in a network.

You can lay out network wiring in many ways. Figure 4-1 shows the two most common layouts — the *star topology* and the *bus topology*. Another common layout, called a *ring topology,* uses a wiring pattern laid out in a circle, where the last computer in the ring links back to the first computer.

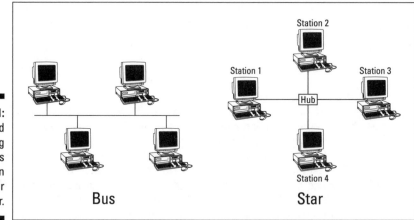

Figure 4-1:
Star and bus wiring layouts often appear together.

Topologies combine in many interesting ways. If you use a bus to link a number of separate stars together, you end up with a *distributed-star network,* also known as a *hybrid network.* Most real networks are hybrids of some type, but most networks work better if you keep things simple.

The star of the network world

A *star topology* consists of separate wires that run from a central point — usually attached to a single device, called a *hub* (hubs are explained later in this section) — to individual devices attached to the other end of each wire. A *bus topology* is a single cable to which all devices on a network (or on some part of a network, as is more often the case) are attached.

If you break a wire in a star topology, only one link is affected, and everything else keeps working. However, if you break a wire on a bus topology, everything connected to that bus loses the ability to access the network.

In a star topology, the hub at the center of the star acts as a relay for computers attached to its arms, like this:

1. The sending computer sends a chunk of data across the wire aimed at some destination computer.

2. The hub sitting between sender and receiver passes the message to the destination computer — if it's attached to the same hub — or to some other hub or network device, if it's not hooked to the same hub.

3. The hub to which the destination computer is attached sends the message to that computer (assuming that both sender and receiver reside within a star topology — however, nothing prevents networking across different topologies, as long as the right types of links exist between them).

On a large network, the middle step might be repeated several times, as data jumps from hub between sender and receiver, or from hub to bus to hub (and so on), until the data eventually reaches its destination computer.

Get on the bus!

In a bus topology, every computer on the same wire sees every message that travels across that wire. If sender and receiver are on the same wire, called a _segment,_ messages travel very quickly. If sender and receiver are not on the same wire, a special message-forwarding computer, called a _bridge_ or a _router,_ passes the message from the sender's wire on toward the receiver's wire by copying the message and retransmitting that message.

Networking devices known as bridges and routers are discussed in detail later in this chapter. For now, think of a _bridge_ as a device that forwards information from one network to another based on _Media Access Control_ (MAC)-level addresses. A _router,_ on the other hand, routes information from one network to another based on network addresses.

Just as you can forward a message through multiple hubs in a star topology, you can forward a message through multiple bridges or routers on a bus topology.

Run rings around your network

The other remaining major topology is called a ring. Real rings are seldom built because they can fail completely if a cable breaks. That's why networking technologies, such as the *Fiber Distributed Data Interface* (FDDI) use true ring topologies that include dual cables and a fault tolerance scheme to allow the network to recover from the break of any single cable.

In fact, most so-called ring topologies are really star- or bus-wired networks that impose a logical ring structure on the physical wiring, whatever its actual topology may be. Therefore, you'll find that network technologies, such as ARCnet (short for *Attached Resource Control Network*), support logical rings atop star- or bus-wired networks, and other technologies such as token ring, support logical rings atop star-wired networks (or distributed star-wired networks). This arrangement appears in Figure 4-2.

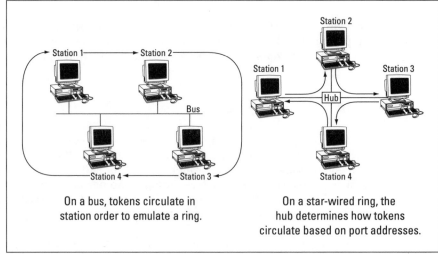

Figure 4-2:
Physical stars or buses can support logical rings.

On a bus, tokens circulate in station order to emulate a ring.

On a star-wired ring, the hub determines how tokens circulate based on port addresses.

Rings are attractive because they keep track of who gets to send a message by circulating an electronic "permission form," also known as a *token,* around and around the network. Only the computer with possession of the token can transmit a message on the network, which completely eliminates any possibility that two computers might try to send a message at the same time. On average, every computer waits about the same amount of time for the token to come around; therefore, each computer has an equal shot at network access over time. This approach allows a network's available bandwidth to be used more fully before the network starts to slow down.

Physical versus logical

Network topologies can be physical or logical. The physical topology of a token ring network is normally a star, but the way data moves from one computer to another is a ring. ARCnet can be a physical bus or star (or some combination of the two), but logically it's a ring. Not even Ethernet is exempt from this confusion. When Ethernet is wired as a bus, it acts like a bus; but when Ethernet is wired as a star, it still acts like a bus.

When thinking about networks, don't confuse a network's topology and the *network technology* in use. The topology identifies the network's wiring scheme, plain and simple. The topology describes how communications move among the computers and other devices on a network. The network technology, sometimes called an *access method,* identifies how the network behaves and what types of interfaces and equipment it requires. Therefore, the network technology also describes the network's physical characteristics in great detail, including

- The network's *electrical characteristics*
- The type of *signaling* the network uses
- The type of *connectors* the network uses
- The types of *interfaces* and how they work together
- The maximum *message size*
- Everything else necessary to build a working environment

Topology deals with network layout; the network technology (or access method) deals with how a network operates. Put another way, a topology names the wiring scheme in use, and the network technology defines what physical components you must buy to make those wires work.

A Network Technology Primer

You can break down all the various network technologies available in today's marketplace according to five categories. Therefore, by answering all five of the following questions, you can distinguish any one type of network technology from another:

- What access method, protocol, and topology does the network use?
- How does the network work?

> ✔ What are the network's technical pros and cons?
>
> ✔ What types of network media does the network support?
>
> ✔ How business-friendly (cost, availability, and so on) is this network?

In the following sections, we examine the pros and cons of various network technologies — just as you must do when you have to apply a certain technology to a particular topology with the goal of best serving the needs of your users.

And the technology contestants are . . .

When you talk about network technologies, you're talking about a specific type of hardware and associated driver software that, when added to a PC, can produce a working network connection. That is, of course, contingent on the right infrastructure — cables, connections, and ancillary equipment (such as bridges or routers) — also being available.

KEY CONCEPT

More than just a simple token . . .

Networks use sets of rules, called *protocols,* to communicate with one another. Some network technologies use *tokens* to control these communications. Other network technologies opt for a free-for-all, in which any computer can send data any time the network's not busy. Networks that send tokens are called *token-passing networks*. They use a token-passing protocol to control network access — that is, they must wait for a usable token to arrive when they wish to send data, and cannot send data whenever they wish.

On the free-for-all side, things are a bit more complicated: Computers must listen to the media to determine if it's in use (indicated by active signals on the media). If a computer wishes to transmit, it stops and listens, like the well-mannered little computer it is, to see if somebody else is talking. If the computer doesn't hear any signals, it can go ahead and transmit right away. When another computer does the same thing at more or less the same time, data from one computer collides with data from another, and both computers must back off and try again.

You want to have something in place to deal with these kinds of collisions. Ethernet implements *Carrier Sense Multiple Access/Collision Detection* (CSMA/CD), whereas ARCnet and token ring implement token-passing protocols. The names that describe how these technologies access network media are called *access methods*. People often confuse topologies with access methods or network technologies, but now that we've got this source of confusion straightened out, the details of the various network technologies described in this chapter should make more sense.

For the purposes of this book, there are two primary network technologies (but that's a tremendous oversimplification, as you'll find out later):

  ✔ Ethernet

  ✔ Token ring

  ✔ Other

Okay, you caught us sneaking in a third, catch-all entry (we almost called it miscellaneous) to give us the opportunity to say something about several of the multitude of other available (but less common) network technologies that we choose not to cover in detail in this book. In fact, recent industry analyses indicate that it's about 75 percent likely that your network uses (or will use) one or both of the two network technologies mentioned in the preceding list. Thus, even though we cover only a small number of technologies in depth, we cover most networks to some degree.

Meet Ethernet, the most popular network technology

Ethernet is the best known, most widely used, versatile, and readily available network technology around. As such things go, Ethernet has been around longer than most, since the mid-to-late 1970s. Ethernet was the brainchild of Xerox's *Palo Alto Research Center* (PARC) and later adopted by Digital, Intel, and Xerox (which is why older 15-pin connectors for thickwire Ethernet are sometimes called DIX connectors). Ethernet has long been a "networking commodity," which means that plenty of vendors play in this market, and that lots of options and choices are available for this technology.

Ethernet uses the CSMA/CD access method. The sidebar titled "Ethernet: Network bumper cars," later in this chapter, explains what this stuff means in everyday English, insofar as the subject allows — which isn't so very far, alas.

The easiest way to describe CSMA/CD is like this: "Listen before sending. Listen while sending. If garbage happens, quit sending and try again later."

Ethernet's strengths and weaknesses

Ethernet's strengths are as follows: It's robust and reliable, and it comes in a broad, affordable range of flavors. Ethernet's weaknesses include the inevitability of collisions and the more difficult troubleshooting techniques that a bus network requires. Ethernet's base speed of 10 Mbps (short for *megabits per second*) is on the slow end for modern networks, but plenty of higher-speed Ethernet versions are now available. (We give you the goods on these in Chapter 7.)

Ethernet: Network bumper cars

The acronym that describes Ethernet's media access method is CSMA/CD, for *Carrier Sense Multiple Access with Collision Detection*. Echoes are the auditory equivalent of a collision, and a collision means that you must repeat a transmission. The following list provides a definition for each term in this access method acronym:

✔ **Carrier Sense:** Everyone attached to the network is always listening to the wire, and no one can send while someone else is sending. When a message moves across the wire, an electrical signal called a *carrier* is used. By listening to the wire, a device knows when it's busy, because it *senses* the presence of the carrier.

✔ **Multiple Access:** Any device attached to the network can send a message whenever it wants, as long as no carrier is sensed at the time. This means that multiple senders can (and sometimes do) begin sending at roughly the same time — when they think things are quiet — and that's why it's called *multiple access*.

✔ **Collision Detection:** If two or more senders begin transmitting at roughly the same time, sooner or later their messages run into each other, causing a *collision*. Collisions are easy to recognize because they produce a garbage signal that is completely unlike a valid transmission. Ethernet hardware includes *collision-detection* circuitry that immediately halts transmission when a collision is observed. When a collision occurs, each sender waits a random time interval before listening to the wire to retry its transmission.

Ethernet does not perform well for high-traffic applications or when real-time delivery is needed (for video and multimedia), nor does it degrade gracefully when high traffic volumes occur. In fact, Ethernet's CSMA/CD access method means that the effective ceiling on its bandwidth is between 56 and 60 percent of total bandwidth (or between 5.6 and 6.0 Mbps on a 10 Mbps Ethernet). That's the level of use beyond which the increasing probability of collisions often results in network slowdowns or failures.

When planning bandwidth consumption for an Ethernet network, use 55 percent of the total bandwidth (5.5 Mbps on a 10 Mbps network, 55 Mbps on a 100 Mbps network, and so on) as the ceiling for usable bandwidth on any network segment. If you plan to consume Ethernet's entire bandwidth when designing a network, you'll be designing a network that's headed for trouble!

However, there's no shortage of bandwidth available to Ethernet customers today. Most newer Ethernet *network interface cards* (NICs) are 10/100 designs, which means that they can sense whether they're used on a 10 Mbps or a 100 Mbps Ethernet network and set their speeds accordingly. Today, Gigabit Ethernet, with an amazing 1,000 Mbps of total theoretical bandwidth, lifts the ceiling on network capacity to new heights but retains compatibility with other Ethernet versions.

All the flavors of Ethernet

Ethernet comes in all the basic flavors. That is, Ethernet runs on any of the major media types — *twisted-pair, coaxial cable* (multiple versions, in fact), and *fiber optic* — and works with both bus and star topologies. One unusual variant — 100BaseVG-AnyLAN — uses a different access method called *demand priority* that gives this implementation interesting abilities. (100BaseVG-AnyLAN is covered in detail in Chapter 7.)

Also, you can easily find Ethernet devices that allow you to mix and match media; so you can use Ethernet to build networks of just about any size and for even the most hostile environments.

In addition, Ethernet technologies support some innovative uses of band-width, so you'll occasionally hear about varieties such as "switched Ethernet" or "full-duplex Ethernet." The former variety depends on a special kind of device (called a switch, naturally) that allows any two nodes to estab-lish a private end-to-end connection. Therefore, switched Ethernet allows pairs of machines to use the entire bandwidth of the network medium. (This is a great way to squeeze extra life out of 10 Mbps Ethernet systems.) Full-duplex Ethernet is limited to 100BaseVG-AnyLAN and uses two pairs of wires so machines can send and receive data at the same time, thereby doubling overall bandwidth.

The business end of Ethernet

Despite its age, Ethernet remains the most widespread and popular network technology. Of the major media types available, twisted-pair leads the pack for new Ethernet installations, but a lot of coaxial cable is still in use. Fiber-based Ethernet is usually limited to networks in campus environments, where long distances and electrical interference issues are greatest. However, it's also used in hostile environments (such as factory floors or engine rooms, where lots of heavy-duty equipment can create major interference) or for high-bandwidth applications, including both 100 Mbps and Gigabit implementations.

The primary reasons for Ethernet's unshaken popularity are as follows:

- **Affordability:** Cabling is cheap and interfaces range from $30 for bottom-end NICs to less than $200 for powerful server NICs. Ethernet is not the cheapest of all the network technologies, but it's darn close!

- **Freedom of choice:** Ethernet supports all types of media, numerous bandwidths, and lots of gear to build hybrid networks. Vendors galore offer Ethernet hardware. For specialized network hardware or media needs, chances are good that some Ethernet variety meets them. If some option isn't available, it's probably on somebody's drawing board.

- **Experience:** Ethernet's longevity means that Ethernet-savvy individuals are easy to find. Also, lots of technical and training material on Ethernet makes expertise relatively easy to build.

✔ **Continuing innovation:** At 10 Mbps, basic Ethernet is no speed demon. However, vendors make high-speed network switches for Ethernet that can deliver the entire 10 Mbps to individual connections, and higher-speed Ethernet varieties are readily available and widely used. As bandwidth needs grow, engineers have found ways to increase Ethernet's abilities to match those needs, as the formalization of Gigabit Ethernet as an IEEE standard (802.3z, in fact) attests.

If you're asked to build a new network and no compelling reasons exist to choose another network technology, choose Ethernet, because of all the reasons previously mentioned!

Taking on token ring

Token ring has gained a substantial foothold in the marketplace, although it hasn't been around in commercial form as long as Ethernet. Token ring is based on technology refined and originally marketed by IBM, so it's most commonly found in environments where IBM is entrenched. When PCs started taking desktop space away from dumb terminals hooked to IBM main-frames, IBM took action. They developed token ring to tie all those new PCs into their mainframe computers.

Token ring uses a token-passing access method in a collection of individual *point-to-point* links between pairs of devices arranged in a circular pattern. Point-to-point means that one device is hooked directly to another. For token ring, point-to-point describes the connection between a computer and a hub, which may in turn, be attached to other hubs or computers. Although the devices used with token ring networks act like hubs, they are more properly known as *multistation access units* (MAUs or MSAUs) or *controlled attachment units* (CAUs). The reason they're not really hubs (and that they're more expensive than most hubs) derives from these devices' abilities to reconfigure themselves on the fly as nodes enter and leave the network. This is more difficult than simply sensing whether a connection is working or not, and requires more expensive hardware to handle the job.

Token ring is mathematically fair to everyone who participates, and it guarantees that the network isn't overwhelmed by traffic. Token ring is said to be fair because it constantly passes the right to transmit around the network. This is done in the form of a special message called a *token*. To send a message, a computer must wait until it obtains possession of the token. The token is not released until the message has been delivered (or until it's obvious that it can't be delivered). Everyone gets the same opportunity at using the token.

The easiest way to think about how token ring works is as follows: To send a message, your system waits for the token. When the token comes by, if it's not already carrying a message, your system tacks your message to the token, and sends the token (and the message) on to its intended recipient. The recipient, upon getting a token addressed to it, copies the attached message and passes the token on around the ring. When the token comes back to your system, it strips off your message and sends the token (now empty of cargo) to the next computer "downstream" on the ring.

Token ring's strengths and weaknesses

Token ring's strengths include equal access for all devices and guaranteed delivery. Token ring works reliably and predictably, even when loaded to capacity. Token ring is available in two speeds: 4 Mbps and 16 Mbps. The older, slower version runs at 4 Mbps. This is 40 percent of the theoretical bandwidth for 10 Mbps Ethernet, but only slightly slower than basic Ethernet's effective speed.

A newer, higher-speed version of token ring runs at 16 Mbps, or 160 percent of basic Ethernet's theoretical bandwidth. It can handle three to four times as much data because it allows simultaneous use of multiple tokens while using 100 percent of total bandwidth. Waiting in the wings is a full-duplex imple-mentation of token ring that works much like switched Ethernet. For higher speeds, a 100 Mbps version of token ring is under construction.

We hear you thinking "If token ring is so great, why buy Ethernet?" Token ring has weaknesses that have less to do with technical considerations and more to do with inflexibility and expense. Token ring's major downside is that it requires the expensive MAUs we discussed in the preceding section. Also, token ring requires that two strands of cable be run from each computer to each hub port. (One for the outbound trip, the other for the return trip.) These requirements add to token ring's expense and reduce the maximum legal distance between computers and hubs. Token ring is also more compli-cated and requires fancier connectors than Ethernet.

Token ring's many flavors

Token-ring implementations for twisted-pair and fiber-optic media are avail-able, but twisted pair is the most common implementation by far and is the most likely medium when tying desktops to hubs. Fiber optic is the cable of choice for spanning longer distances and daisy-chaining MAUs. Only limited amounts of *shielded twisted-pair* (STP) cabling are used on token-ring net-works. Because of individual cable length limitations and maximum ring-size limitations, cabling a token-ring network takes more planning and number crunching than cabling an Ethernet network does.

The business end of token ring

From a cost-benefit perspective, there's not enough benefit in token ring's reliability, fairness, and guaranteed performance to offset its higher costs. Today, token ring costs from 75 to 150 percent more than Ethernet without necessarily providing significant performance or reliability advantages.

Although there are two schools of thought on this issue — "Forget token ring. Ethernet rules." and "We're token-passing fools. What's Ethernet?" — we're not about to climb out on either limb. If someone offers you token ring at a price that's too good to pass up or if that's what circumstances dictate you must use — go ahead and use it. Token ring works just fine. We do not, however, recommend it as a technology of choice for starter networks, because of its expense and complexity.

What other network technologies are there?

If you're thinking "What else is there," you may be wondering why this book omits your network technology of choice. We hate to be the bearer of sad tidings, but if you're not using either Ethernet or token ring, you may be networking too hard (or at least networking the hard way). Sorry!

In fact, hundreds of other types of network technologies are in use today. At least one such technology exists for every letter in the alphabet from A for ARCnet to X for xDSL. If you think that such acronym overkill may end up making your head spin, you're not alone. The proliferation of exotic network technologies can be a problem for Windows 2000 Server, too. A word to the wise: If you're using an exotic network technology, make sure that Windows 2000 Server works with it before you spend any money on the software.

The good news is that Windows 2000 runs over a reasonable subset of network technologies. The bad news is that you'll have to do some research to find out whether what you're using is one of the technologies that Windows 2000 supports. Worse yet, you'll have to work harder to do basic stuff that less exotic network technologies take for granted, and you may have to pass on some sophisticated capabilities as well, such as network-attached printers and other peripheral devices.

Doing without Ethernet or token ring does not necessarily bring with it such harrowing consequences, however. In the following two sections, we do your homework for you and cover a couple of potentially useful network technologies that occur on a reasonably large subset of enterprise networks and are supported by Windows 2000.

Find your way to FDDI

One workhorse network technology found on many networks, especially in campus environments, is called the *Fiber Distributed Data Interface,* or FDDI. FDDI uses a token-passing access method. FDDI cable uses a real ring topology, but consists of two rings. One ring transmits messages clockwise; the other transmits messages counterclockwise. If either ring fails, the other automatically takes over as a backup. Better still, if both rings get cut in the same place — watch out for guys with backhoes on your campus — the two rings automatically splice together to form a ring that's twice the length of the original ring, but still able to function.

FDDI's biggest advantage is reach, now that its 100 Mbps speed is no longer such a big deal. FDDI supports rings as big as 100 kilometers in circumference (that's about 62 miles for non-metric types). FDDI can support as many as 500 active devices on a single ring, which is more than the other network technologies we discuss in detail in this chapter.

On the downside, FDDI requires fiber-optic cables for runs of any length. There's a CDDI (where *C* stands for copper), but it doesn't support cable runs longer than 75 feet, so it's impractical except for workstation connections.

Cost is another negative for FDDI. Fiber-optic cables are more expensive to buy and install than other types of cable, and FDDI NICs cost between $700 and $1,800 each. FDDI looks good primarily for the central line of a campus network (the *backbone*, to use the technical term), and Gigabit Ethernet is not an option (or a requirement).

Accelerating to ATM

A rising star in the area of high-speed networking is ATM, an acronym for *Asynchronous Transfer Mode*. In the last couple of years, several companies have introduced ATM-based *local area network* (LAN) equipment. Long-distance telephone companies already use ATM versions that run at 155 and 622 Mbps, and current ATM specifications support speeds of 1.2 and 2.4 *gigabits per second* (Gbps) as well.

ATM is a fast-switching technology that requires a hub-like switching device and network interfaces for each computer. You can expect to spend at least $2,000 per workstation (including allocated switch and fiber-optic cable costs) to bring ATM to your computers. That probably explains why ATM is far more popular as a backbone technology than for networking computers.

Figure 4-3 gives you the skinny on the comparative speeds of the different network technologies (which will help you a little), but the best way to find out what's what is to go online and seek out the collective wisdom that's so readily available. You can check in on any of Microsoft's Usenet Windows 2000-focused newsgroups through msnews.microsoft.com; use Microsoft's own online service, Microsoft Network (MSN), at home.microsoft.com; or drop in on any of the numerous Windows 2000-focused mailing lists and ask "Does my (fill in the name of your network technology here) work with Windows 2000 Server?" If you don't have access to online information resources, ask around. With so many users worldwide, you shouldn't have to look far to find somebody who can help you.

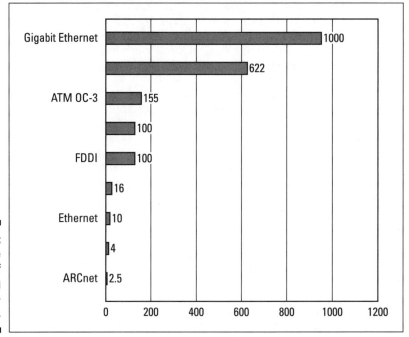

Figure 4-3:
Ranking the
speed of
networking
technolo-
gies.

About Ancillary Equipment

Numerous network devices, besides computers, are sometimes required to help you build networks — especially when networks grow beyond the confines of a simple workgroup. Without dwelling too much on features and more sophisticated functions, here's a list of devices available for most major network technologies (or that incorporate interfaces based on such technologies) that you can use to extend or interconnect existing networks:

 ✔ **Repeater:** A repeater is a simple networking device that copies incoming signals from one connection and then resends them to one or more other connections (called *ports*). The notion behind the name is that this device "repeats" exactly what — and everything that — it "hears." Repeaters can only link media segments that use the same network technology, but those segments can be different media types. Repeaters operate at the *Physical layer* of the *Open Systems Interconnection* (OSI) model. (See Chapter 3 for an explanation of the OSI model.)

Use repeaters when you reach the legal limits for cable lengths that a network technology can support. Repeaters allow you to extend your networks farther than they could otherwise go. Please note that network technologies also have rules about the maximum number of repeaters that occur between any sender and any receiver on a network.

✔ **Bridge:** A bridge is a network device that examines the addresses of incoming network traffic and only copies incoming messages to other network segments if their destinations can be reached through (or on) those segments. The notion behind the name is that these devices act as semi-intelligent links between networks, and they check low-level hardware addresses to decide what may pass from one network segment to another. Bridges operate at the Data Link layer (at the MAC sublayer, in fact) of the OSI model. We explain the OSI model in Chapter 3.

Bridges can not only link media segments for the same network technologies, but so-called "translation bridges" can also interconnect network segments that use different network technologies. (Linking FDDI and Ethernet is a common example.) The protocols on both sides of the device must remain the same, however.

Use bridges when your network includes nonroutable protocols, such as *NetBEUI* or *Data Link Control* (DLC), and such traffic must be forwarded from one network segment to another. Note that some routers (next item) include bridging functions, and that hybrid devices called brouters (item after next) can perform both bridging and routing functions.

✔ **Router:** A router is a sophisticated network device that reads and resolves network addresses from incoming traffic. Routers perform all kinds of interesting functions on such data, including filtering incoming data by address, managing multiple protocols, either blocking or allowing certain types of protocols as well as certain ranges of addresses associated with certain protocols, and more. Routers operate at the Network layer of the OSI model. (See Chapter 3 for details.)

Routers can interconnect dissimilar network technologies and can even reformat data for transmission on an outgoing port whose technology differs from that of the incoming port. The most common example here is when 16 Mbps token ring and Ethernet are linked. Because token ring supports much larger message units than Ethernet, a router may have to break up a single token-ring message into as many as 44 equivalent Ethernet messages.

Routers are what make it possible for two separate networks to function independently yet still exchange information when they must. Routers make phenomena, such as the Internet, possible and have played a critical role in its growth. Use routers when you seek to operate and control your own network(s), but when connectivity to other networks is also required.

✔ **Brouter:** A brouter combines the functions of a bridge and a router. That is, it acts like a bridge for nonroutable protocols and like a router for routable protocols. Brouters are most commonly used on networks that have both kinds of protocols in use. They are also used when a local network requires bridging of nonroutable protocols, but access to the Internet or some other public network requires routing of routable protocols. Brouters operate at both the Data Link and Network layers of the OSI model. (We explain this model in Chapter 3.)

✔ **Gateway:** A gateway is a device that translates application information from one type of environment for some other type of environment. A typical example is an e-mail gateway, which translates between Microsoft Exchange formats and a native Internet e-mail format, known as the *Simple Mail Transfer Protocol* (SMTP), and vice versa.

Other gateways can translate between dissimilar protocol suites, such as *Systems Network Architecture* (SNA) and *Transmission Control Protocol/Internet Protocol* (TCP/IP). Still other gateways support moving data between other dissimilar applications of the same type, such as database management systems or transaction processing systems. Gateways operate primarily at the upper layers of the OSI model (which we explain in Chapter 3) and are concentrated at the Session, Application, and Presentation layers.

As you climb this set of ancillary network devices, their sophistication and abilities increase, whereas their speed and overall handling capacity decline. That's because each step up this ladder involves increased processing and data-handling capabilities, which take time and programming smarts and therefore lowers their overall throughput.

You often find items at the lower end of this ladder — such as repeaters and bridges — sold as simple "black boxes" that are more or less ready to plug in and use. Routers and brouters, on the other hand, are usually special-purpose, high-powered, high-speed computers that accept two or more interface cards (one for each connection that you make to this device).

Windows 2000 includes powerful built-in routing abilities, such as its *Routing and Remote Access Server,* or RRAS. Also, additional software, such as Proxy Server, can be added to Windows 2000 Server to enhance its capabilities. Gateways, on the other hand, usually occupy a general-purpose computer, but they are also normally dedicated to performing only that job.

Mixing and Matching Network Technologies

Networks can easily mix and match topologies within the confines of a single network technology, but interconnecting network technologies requires more sophisticated equipment. Here's a brief rundown of the issues:

✔ **Interconnecting different media within a particular network technology:** Most vendors offer simple devices (that is, repeaters and bridges) to interconnect network segments that use different types of media, such as twisted-pair (10BaseT) and coaxial (10Base2) cable for Ethernet, for example. Windows 2000 Server can handle multiple network interfaces, each with a different media type as well.

- ✔ **Interconnecting different network technologies within a network:** As long as the protocols stay the same, routers or brouters can handle the job, such as interconnecting token ring and Ethernet segments. Likewise, the built-in routing capabilities of Windows 2000 Server allow it to function as router to interconnect different network technologies with ease. It just can't do those things as quickly as special-purpose, high-end routers, such as those from Cisco Systems, Bay Networks, and so forth.

- ✔ **Interconnecting fundamentally different protocols or applications:** Gateways really shine when fundamentally different protocols or applications must exchange data. This exchange involves considerably more effort and intelligence than the lower-level services that bridges and routers provide. However, gateways must also be sensitive to many more nuances and levels of functionality than other devices. This probably explains why they're more prone to problems than other choices as well.

In its TCP/IP settings, Windows 2000 asks for the address of a gateway. In this particular instance, Windows 2000 is using the term "gateway" in a different sense than what we've been discussing here. When configuring its TCP/IP settings, Windows 2000 considers the term "gateway" to be synonymous with the term "router" and, in fact, points to a device that can forward packets not directed to the local cable segment for delivery to the outside world. Be sure to keep this in mind when you configure TCP/IP for Windows 2000!

Part II
Hooking Up the Hardware

The 5th Wave   By Rich Tennant

WE'RE HERE TO SERVICE YOUR LOCAL AREA NETWORK.

In this part . . .

Having covered basic networkng terminology and concepts in Part I, we try to cover something more tangible in Part II — namely, the bits and pieces of equipment and cabling that are necessary to the proper operation of any network.

To begin, you explore the basic principles of network layout and design as you seek to translate neworking concepts into a working network. After that, you tackle the ins and outs of network interface cards, or NICs, as they're more commonly known in the networking trade. With cards in place in your computers, the cables that tie them together come next.

Along the way, you can figure out how to build a new network or extend an old one and how to take stock of an existing network. You also discover how to bring the parts of the network together to create a harmonious whole rather than a hodgepodge of bits and pieces. Your goal is to understand who the players are and how to make them function well as a gung-ho team.

Chapter 5

Network Design Basics

*W*hether you're constructing a complete network or simply renovating an existing network, the basic approach is the same. You begin by planning what you want to implement and then gathering the ingredients necessary to realize your plans. Next, you have to execute those plans according to the blueprint that you devised. The execution of any successful plan involves bringing all the pieces together, applying solid organizational principles to your network, and documenting what you add (and what's already in place) to your network.

Begin at the Beginning: Requirements

Whenever you set forth on a network project, begin by analyzing your requirements. If you're building a network from scratch, this phase can take weeks or even months of effort; if you're simply extending or repairing an existing network, planning may take a day of your time, if not less.

Whatever your project's scope, your plan should contain the following:

✔ **A brief statement of your overall objectives, plus a more lengthy statement of requirements that addresses the following: what applications and services users need to access; estimates of user-to-server bandwidth requirements; and estimates of server-to-server bandwidth requirements (where applicable):** For example: *The new XYZ Inc. network will provide 60 users with access to Windows 2000 file and print services, plus access to a SQL server sales and inventory database. Each user will require no more than 1 Mbps bandwidth, and there are no prime time server-to-server bandwidth requirements, because all backups are scheduled for after-hours and weekends.*

✔ **A complete list of all the elements that you must purchase or otherwise acquire to meet those objectives:** For example: *Three different department servers (Accounting, Manufacturing, and Sales) will act as routers to link two network segments of 10 users each, for a total of 6 user segments based on 10 Mbps Ethernet. The three servers will be connected using a 100 Mpbs Ethernet backbone using 100BaseT. We will purchase 6 16-port 10/100 Ethernet hubs (one per user segment) to leave room for growth, and three two-CPU 500 MHz Intel Zeon Pentium II servers machines, each with 512MB RAM and 24GB of disk space. The Accounting server will have an 80GB DLT tape drive attached so we can back all three servers up across the backbone.*

✔ **A description of the role each element will play on the network, the location of each element on the network, the configuration of each element, and the time during the installation process in which you plan to add each element to the network:** You should use a map or a set of plans to help you place cables, computers, and other components, and a timeline to indicate the order in which you have to install everything. For example: *The Accounting server will handle users from the Accounting and Purchasing departments; the Manufacturing server will handle users from the Manufacturing and Engineering departments; the Sales server will handle users from Administration as well as from the Sales and Marketing departments. All servers, the backbone, and all hubs will be installed when the company is closed between Christmas and New Year's. The network should be operational when normal business operations resume.* A map of this network appears in Figure 5-1.

✔ **A test plan that describes how you plan to test individual elements, individual cable segments, and the entire network to make sure everything functions properly after you finish the installation:** For example: *The three servers will be installed first and tested individually the weekend before the Christmas break. On December 23 and 24, the 100 Mbps backbone will be installed. On December 28, the backbone will be tested. On December 28 and 29, the hubs will be installed and tested. On December 30, workstations on all existing 10 Mbps cable segments will be connected to the new 10/100 hubs and tested individually. From December 31 to January 2, automated testing software will exercise the entire network. On January 3, a network technician will visit our site with Bob, the site administrator, and any last minute changes, repairs, or adjustments will be performed. We believe the network will be ready for use on Monday, January 4.*

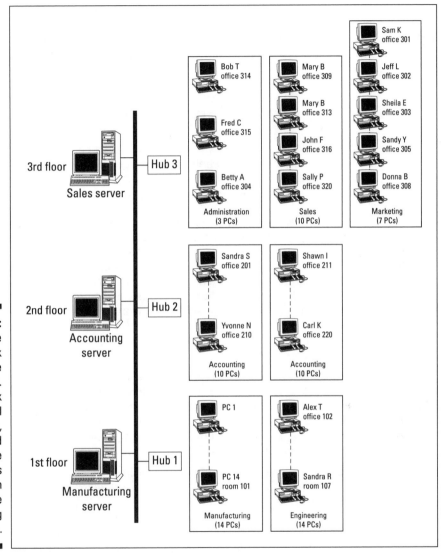

Figure 5-1:
A simple
network
map of the
XYZ Inc.
network
shows all
hubs,
servers, and
cable
segments
overlaid on
a simple
building
floor plan.

This plan helps you to decide where you must place key network elements —
such as servers, hubs, and other network devices. More importantly, the plan
also helps you determine what type of network technology and bandwidth
you need to deploy to meet your objectives. Because most businesses work
on a budget, building a plan also helps you make sure that you won't try to
spend more than you're allowed to spend or incorporate more exotic technologies than you can afford.

Your network implementation plan should also help you evaluate your current network backbone or plan a new one to be able to carry all the traffic that normally comes together on such critical network segments. (We discuss backbones in more detail in Chapter 7.)

Network Design's Barest Basics

The possible implementations from which you can choose when designing a network are innumerable. To help you distinguish among what's improbable, what's possible, what's feasible, and what's recommended, here's a set of guidelines that should be helpful when designing your network:

- **Select a network technology:** When adding to or expanding an existing network, this decision is easy — it simply requires picking something identical to or compatible with whatever you're using. For new networks, you need to analyze what kinds of applications and services users require to select an appropriate network technology. For ordinary office work (e-mail, word processing, spreadsheets, basic database access, and so on) 10 Mbps Ethernet works well; for high-traffic or real-time applications, such as *Computer Aided Design* (CAD), imaging, video conferencing, voice over network, and so on, 100 Mbps to the desktop makes more sense.

- **Stay close to the resources:** When designing a network, the smartest thing you can do is minimize the distance between users and the resources they use most. This applies to printers (so users enjoy easy access to output), servers (so cable runs needn't be too long), and other services (such as fax machines, scanners, copiers, and so on) that users need to access to do their jobs.

- **Build an online work environment:** When designing a network, you also have to take into account current working patterns and arrangements in your offices. If the Accounting and Purchasing departments work together all the time, perhaps they should share a server. This also applies to the type of network you build: For small companies, centralized control and tight security may hamper your workers; in large companies, centralized control and tight security are the norm. You must serve the communities that currently exist in your organization and use the network to help users communicate and be as productive as possible.

- **Arrange servers, hubs, and other key resources:** The places where wiring congregates — namely at punchdown blocks, wiring centers, and equipment rooms (or closets) — sometimes dictate where certain equipment must be placed. Be sure to check the distance between those locations and the areas where workers reside. In most cases, offices are designed to support cabling from a centrally located wiring center or equipment room for groups of offices. If that's not the case in your workspace, you may have to add new equipment rooms and wiring centers or move workers to bring them closer to existing facilities. Either of these solutions takes time and costs serious money, so be sure to get your management involved in deciding which options make the most sense and how your organization will handle these changes.

For more info on wiring equipment, and how to figure out where it's located, please consult *Networking For Dummies,* 4th Edition, by Doug Lowe (IDG Books Worldwide, Inc.). It describes these critical networking components and tells you where to find them in your workplace.

✔ **Build better backbones:** Depending on your network technology choice, you'll probably want to arrange your network to include a special highway for data to travel across when multiple network cables come together. This can happen between servers, as with the XYZ Inc. example that appears at the beginning of this chapter. Such portions of the network are called *backbones.*

A backbone can be something as simple as a so-called *collapsed backbone,* in which a high-speed switch links multiple cable segments and provides a single, high-speed connection between *all* cable segments. A backbone can also be as complex as a *staged backbone,* in which intermediate segments jump from normal 10 Mbps Ethernet to switched Ethernet or 100 Mbps Ethernet at the server (as in the XYZ Inc. example mentioned at the beginning of this chapter). More complex backbones might even include a segment of Gigabit Ethernet on the innermost segment, where traffic is heaviest.

✔ **Plan for growth:** When planning a network, include at least 30 percent spare, unused capacity in your design. This spare capacity should include network ports (unused ports on hubs), unused network cables in offices and cableways, and bandwidth on individual network segments. That way, you can grow within your current environment for a while without having to redesign your network on a regular basis. If your annual growth rate exceeds 30 percent, design at least one year's planned growth into your network — better yet, one year's planned growth *plus* 30 percent.

✔ **Work within the system:** As you discover when you start deploying a network in any organization, networks have a political as well as a technical side. When you plan a network, you should work within your system in at least two ways: First, make sure that management knows about and approves of what you plan. Second, make sure that you handle the work, contracts, purchases, and so on within the rules and regulations of your organization. If you neglect either of these guidelines, the only thing you'll learn how to network is trouble!

✔ **Check your design:** After you put a network design down on paper, review that design against what you know about the network technologies it uses. Be especially careful to check maximum cable lengths, maximum number of devices per segment, and maximum number of cable segments and devices between any two ends of the network against the rules that apply to the technologies you plan to use. You don't want to build a network that tries to break these rules. If you do, your network may not work, or worse, it may work for a while and then quit working as you're adding new users or devices to the network. If you check your work before you build, you won't try to build something that can't work or that's inherently prone to trouble.

✔ **Ask for a sanity check:** Because you've put a network design down on paper and checked your work, you should also solicit input from one or more networking experts. Redesigning a network is always easier while it's still on paper; you don't want to fix a flawed design after you've built a network. The more qualified advice you get before you start building, the better off you'll be in the long run. In fact, this advice is worth paying for, because it can save you a world of hurt (or your job, for that matter).

Although this list of network design principles is not exhaustive, it should lead you down the pathway toward designing a network that works best for your organization. Because these guidelines consider work patterns, politics, and organizational rules, as well as technology, the resulting network should serve your organization well for more than just technical reasons.

Deciding Where Networking Devices Must Go

After your plan is in place, you must purchase the necessary equipment, cables, connectors, and so on and start deploying the components that make a network work. When you start situating key network equipment — including servers, hubs, routers, and so on — you need to make some important decisions about where to put it.

For small organizations of 25 people or less, using separate locked facilities to store hubs and servers may not make sense. Small organizations tend to be more informal and are less likely to have the kind of budget that supports a full-time *information systems* (IS) staff. In these circumstances, you usually want to situate your networking gear along with all your other gear — out in the open with other equipment for easy access to one and all. If you do put the networking gear out in the open, you want to make sure that only users with valid passwords can log onto such equipment. Otherwise, locking it up is highly recommended.

Larger organizations tend to be more concerned about security and control, and, therefore, they usually situate key networking components in locked equipment rooms and in locked wiring closets or wiring centers at various locations around their offices. Because the equipment has to be close to the wiring, it's not uncommon for servers to reside in wiring closets along with punchdown blocks, hubs, and other networking equipment.

Only authorized personnel should be allowed to access these facilities. Likewise, only authorized personnel should be allowed to add users or equipment to the network, usually within a system of regularly scheduled updates or maintenance. In office buildings, for example, this usually means one or two wiring closets or equipment rooms per floor, where only authorized personnel have keys or access codes to get into these rooms.

Pick an approach to situating your servers that makes sense for your organization, and stick with it. If you're going to follow rules for placing equipment, share those rules with employees so they know what's going on. In fact, formulating a security policy for most networks is a smart move, and you should regularly explain that policy to your employees in detail. (For more information on this subject, see Chapter 18.)

Most small- to medium-sized companies — such as the fictitious XYZ Inc. mentioned at this chapter's outset — put their servers into small, locked rooms at each end of the floors they occupy in an office building. This keeps the distances between users' desktops and the wiring centers acceptably low, and puts their servers alongside the punchdown blocks and hubs they use, which helps manage wiring. This approach also provides controlled access to the equipment and software that makes their networks work in a small number of closely managed locations. Finally, it addresses the need for adequate ventilation and power control that hubs and servers require for proper operation, but which many wiring closets do not offer.

Always Check Your Work!

Normally, you install cable and equipment at the same time you build a network. You may run your own cables for your network and perform all equipment installation and configuration yourself, you may contract both the cable and equipment installation out to third parties, or you may pick some point between these two extremes. Whichever way you go, somewhere along the way, you'll be ready to put the finished pieces of your network together.

When it comes to installing cabling, we highly recommend that you employ experienced cable installers with good references. The company that owns or operates your office building may even require a licensed cable installer to perform any such work. Here's why this is a good idea:

✔ Adherence to building and fire codes is mandatory, but it can also be tricky; using an experience professional is a good way to avoid trouble.

✔ Cable placement and routing are sensitive; trained professionals know how to avoid potential trouble spots and will always test their work to make sure that the network will behave properly.

✔ High-speed networks are much more finicky and prone to installation difficulties than lower-speed networks. The faster you want your network to go, the better off you'll be if you leave the cabling to an expert.

We strongly advise that you bring a network up in small, manageable pieces. When installing multiple cable segments, bring up individual segments one at a time and test them to make sure each one works before connecting all of them. Likewise, if you're installing a backbone or a server cluster, test individual components separately before trying them out en masse.

When you install equipment, apply the same principles. After you install and configure a machine, check it by itself to make sure it works before attaching it to the network. This is as appropriate for hubs and routers as it is for server and desktop computers.

Our suggestions on piecewise checking and gradually increasing the complexity of your network come from experience. We found out the hard way that throwing everything together at once can cause problems that are too hard to troubleshoot, because you have to deal with too many unknowns.

At each step toward building or extending a network, check your work. Fix problems as they arise, and you'll make steady progress toward the type of well-run, well-organized network that you want to build!

Don't Take Your Eyes Off the Ball

After you build a network, you may be tempted to rest for a while to enjoy your success. After all, you've earned it, right? However, while you should certainly pat yourself on the back, you should also realize that the real work begins as soon as users start using the network (or a new portion of an existing one). If you're responsible for a network, this not only means keeping things running for the moment, but also keeping them running — and running well — over time.

Whereas the network you build or extend may meet your users' initial needs, any network's ability to meet users' continuing needs diminishes over time. Growth, change in technologies, and new applications and services guarantee that nothing stays the same for long in the workplace — this includes your network as well as the systems and services that the network delivers to your users.

Therefore, you need to conduct regular reviews of how well your network meets users' needs. In small or slow-growing organizations, you may have to review the network only once a year. However, in large or fast-growing organizations, you should review the network on a quarterly basis.

Your network review should include at least these three elements:

- **Traffic analysis and usage review:** You can conduct this yourself by using the built-in Windows 2000 Server tools and facilities (such as Performance Monitor) and third-party software tools. The idea is to take a snapshot of your network during ordinary-load, light-load, and peak-load conditions. If any of these loads encroaches on the boundaries of what the current design can reasonably support, start planning to extend and expand your network again.

  See Chapter 19 for more information on using Performance Monitor.

- **User interviews:** You can do this on a one-on-one basis with selected users in your organization or hold meetings with individual workgroups and departments. The idea is to give employees a chance to share their observations, gripes, and wishes regarding the network with you. This can give you a great opportunity to not only gauge user satisfaction and networking knowledge, but also to determine whether you should give employees additional training on how to use the network more effectively.

- **Management review:** You should also meet with members of management regularly to find out what they're planning and what future information processing needs they're considering. You can also gauge management's impressions of and beliefs about the network as you report to them your findings from the previous two items.

If you perform these reviews and keep in touch with upcoming changes and requirements, you can keep your network and your organization better synchronized than if you neglect them. Planning for change and growth is essential to modern networks, because they've become critical business tools that organizations depend on to get their work done. If you take a proactive approach and plan for the future, you can stay ahead of the curve!

Every Network Map Tells a Story

Earlier in this chapter, we introduce you to most of the basic principles involved in designing and building a network. By now, you have a pretty good idea how networks work. However, as you spend more time around networks, you may realize that what they *do* isn't nearly as important as what you *know* about what they do.

Whether you wrestle with networks only occasionally or full-time, you may discover that there's nothing like a network map to help you find and keep track of things on your network.

It's not a map; it's the whole enchilada!

Calling the collection of data that describes your network a map does not do this concept justice. A network map is certainly more than a mere drawing that shows where network components live on your network — but creating such a drawing is a great way to start building a network map. If you look at the following list of things a network map should contain, you'll see why such a map is more than a mere depiction:

- ✔ A list of all computers on your network, with supporting documentation

- ✔ A list of all network equipment — including servers and hubs, plus any repeaters, routers, and so on — with supporting documentation

- ✔ A list of all printers and other similar equipment on the network, such as scanners, fax machines, and so on, with supporting documentation

- ✔ Lines to indicate where cables run and where junctions, taps, and other media-related elements are located

Capturing data for your network map

Because a network map is so important and such a powerful tool, pause right here and start one immediately. Be prepared to spend some time and energy on this project, because most of the data that makes up a network map is naturally scattered all over the place.

Building a detailed network map is a worthwhile investment. It will pay for itself many times over as you come to depend on it. At worst, you discover more about your network than you ever wanted to know (but not more than you'll ever *need* to know). At best, you get to know your network so well that it will seldom throw you a curve ball — and you may even find some things to tweak and tune while building that map.

Start at the foundation

Obtaining a set of your building's architectural drawings or engineering plans can help a great deal. If you can find any drawings or plans, take them to an architect's supply store and make copies that you can mark up and use as a base map. (Most plans are created using an old-fashioned, ammonia-based copying system called *blue-line*. You can copy even large-sized plans for less than $25 per plan.)

If a professional cabling outfit installed your network, you should be able to get a copy of the cabling plans, which work even better than architectural drawings or engineering plans because they probably already show where the cable is laid and how much of it you've got. This is another good reason why "do it yourself" may not be the best way to cable your network.

If no such plans are available, you can sketch a room-by-room layout on rectangular grid paper (such as an engineering pad) to make it easy to draw to scale. Be sure to mark the location of machines, approximate locations for cable runs, and so on.

Anything on your network should be on the map

Anything that merits attention or costs money is worth recording on your map. You don't need to go into great detail about each and every connector or note the exact length of every cable. (Approximate lengths within a meter or so are useful, however.) Indicate every major cable run, every computer, and every piece of gear attached to the network.

You probably won't have enough room to write all this information on the map itself. Therefore, you should key information to a machine or cable name and record the actual details in a file on your computer. Or, if you prefer to do things your own way, that's fine — just make sure you know how to find what you've recorded. Whatever scheme you adopt, use it religiously. Also, make brief notes about how your scheme works, so somebody else can use your map if you're not available to explain it.

Take stock of your network

The information you gather while producing a network map creates a detailed inventory of what's on your network and where everything is located. Unfortunately, you quickly find out that this is a *lot* of information.

To make keeping an inventory easy for yourself (and anyone who follows in your footsteps), build a template or form that you can fill out for each item on the network. This approach forces you to collect consistent information — and makes delegating information gathering to others easier. Include all of the following information for each computer on the network:

   ✔ **The hardware configuration for each machine:** This should include a list of all interfaces and their settings, information about installed RAM and drives, and the make and model of the keyboard, display, and so on. If you can find out who sold you the equipment, write that down, too.

Keeping track of equipment is typically the accounting department's responsibility. Check with them for a copy of your company's capital assets or a depreciable items inventory (if available). This type of documentation normally includes serial numbers and other identification for hardware on the network. If no one in your company has gathered such information, collect it yourself. It's valuable.

✔ **The software configuration for each machine:** This should include listings of configuration files, operating system data (including version number, most recent Service Pack applied, and so on), as well as a list of programs and versions installed on the machine.

✔ **The network configuration for each machine:** This should include the make and model of each network interface card (NIC), plus a list of driver files with names, version numbers, dates, and sizes. You can capture such data to a file easily on Windows systems by going to Start⇨Settings⇨Control Panel⇨Adminsitrative Tools⇨Computer Management⇨System Tools⇨System Information⇨Hardware Resources; use this as the basis for this inventory.

In addition to information on each computer, your inventory should also include the following data:

✔ **A list of other equipment, such as hubs, routers, printers, and so on:** Include the manufacturer, model, make, and serial number for each piece of equipment. If the equipment includes memory modules, disk drives, or plug-in interface cards, get information about them, too. If the equipment uses software or firmware, record the name, version, release date, and any other information you can garner about such items.

✔ **A list of all the cable segments on the network:** Give each segment a unique name or number, and associate your records with whatever type of identifier you use for those segments. Record the type and make of cable, its length, locations of its ends, and any significant connections or intermediate locations that you may have to visit in the future.

✔ **A list of all the vendors who've worked on your network or its machines:** Include names and phone numbers of contacts at each operation. This can be a valuable resource for technical support and troubleshooting. Over time, you want to add the names and phone numbers of tech support or other individuals at these organizations who prove to be knowledgeable and helpful.

Essentially, the information gathered while creating and maintaining a network map forms a database of everything anyone needs to know about your network. To improve access to and usability of this data, consider storing the text for your network map in an honest-to-gosh database engine. If this is too labor-intensive, a file- or paper-based approach works, but takes more effort to maintain over time. Whichever method of recording data for your map you use, be sure to keep your inventory complete and up-to-date.

Applications such as Visio and HP OpenView can help you create network maps. Search your favorite Web browser's computer or networking section using the keywords "network map" to find other applications and/or companies that can help you with this process.

When the network changes, so does the map!

One thing that you can always be sure of when it comes to networks: They're always changing. Your map is only as good as the information it contains. And the map only remains useful if that information is an accurate reflection of the real network in your organization.

Whenever anything changes on your network, make updating the map and its associated database a priority. Sitting down and checking your map is much less work than walking around and looking at the real objects that the map shows. If the map is current, you can keep on top of things from the comfort of your office. If it's out of date, you'd better start walking!

Chapter 6

Installing Network Interface Cards (NICs)

*B*uckle up, because it's time to hook the network up to your prospective Windows 2000 Server in preparation for putting that sucker to work!

For most PCs, whether they run Windows 2000 Server or some other operating system, the *network interface* (or interfaces, if a machine has more than one network connection) comes in the form of *network interface cards,* known affectionately as NICs.

For the uninitiated, NIC is pronounced "nick" just like what sometimes happens when you shave. NICs provide the essential link between the network medium and a computer that needs to access the network.

In this chapter, you find out about the basic types, functions, and capabilities of NICs, and how to pick the right type to use in your server. Along the way, you have a chance to pick up lots of tips and tricks about setting up these all-important components correctly the first time, every time.

What Makes a NIC Tick?

A typical NIC is an add-in card that's configured to work inside your PC. Its role is to work both sides of the network connection, like this:

- ✔ The NIC plugs into your computer's bus (or a special adapter slot) so it can talk to the CPU (or CPUs), and the CPU can talk to it. This essentially defines a NIC's most important role — namely, its ability to permit a computer to access the network medium and vice versa.

- ✔ A NIC's accommodation for a network connection (where the medium plugs in) requires an external connector to connect the network medium to the NIC in some form or fashion. Some NICs include more than one connector, so if you change your network (or your mind), you don't have to throw out the old NIC and put in a new one.

- ✔ Your network technology determines the details of how a NIC accesses the network medium. There are NICs for Ethernet, token ring, Fiber Distributed Data Interface (FDDI), and so on. NICs don't normally support more than one network technology.

Figure 6-1 shows all the important connections on a NIC, including the bus connector (which makes the NIC and the CPU accessible to one another) and the media interface (which makes the NIC and the networking medium accessible to each other). Media connectors vary with the networking technology and physical media in use. By learning to recognize what you've got, you can select the NIC (or NICs) that's right for your network.

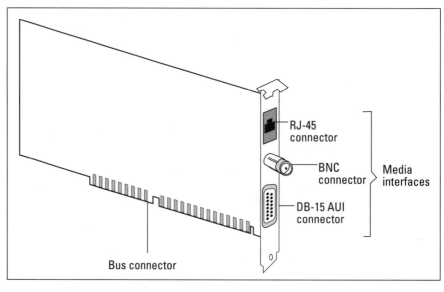

Figure 6-1:
The NIC creates a bridge between your computer and the network.

RJ-45 connector

BNC connector

DB-15 AUI connector

Media interfaces

Bus connector

Figure 6-1 shows a so-called *three-way combo card* for Ethernet, with an RJ-45 connector for *twisted pair* (10BaseT), a BNC connector for *thinwire* (10Base2), and an AUI connector for *thickwire* (10Base5). If this sounds like sheer gibberish, don't worry — you can explore exactly what all this gobbledygook means in Chapter 7.

Not all NICs take the form of adapter cards that plug into a bus inside your computer. Some laptops, portables, and other machines can't accommodate standard internal interfaces like conventional desktop PCs can. Especially on laptops, you must often install PC card adapters (formerly known as PCMCIA, or *Personal Computer Memory Card International Association,* adapters) according to your networking whims.

PC cards look a lot like fat credit cards and are about the same size. You slide them into and out of your computer's PC card slot. Laptops sometimes require a NIC PC card for a network connection in the office and a modem for remote access to network resources when the laptop owner is away from the office. Windows 2000 supports a mechanism known as *hardware profiles* that makes it easy to set up multiple hardware configurations for such machines (for more information, check out Chapter 10).

Find the Newest Bus — and Use It Well!

If your computer is a desktop or server PC, you must match its NIC (or NICs) to an internal bus (or buses) with an open slot (or slots). In this section, we introduce information about a variety of buses that you may find in your PCs, and we offer tips about which ones are better than others.

Because Windows 2000 Server's primary job is handling network service requests, install the fastest, most capable NIC(s) that works on your PC. Then, you can expect the best possible performance for your network clients!

The business end of a NIC plugs into a PC bus and is called an *edge connector.* You can recognize the types of interfaces that your computer includes by looking at a computer's bus slots. Likewise, looking at your NIC can tell you for which type of bus it's made. Figure 6-2 shows the three types of buses covered in this section, with their respective edge connectors.

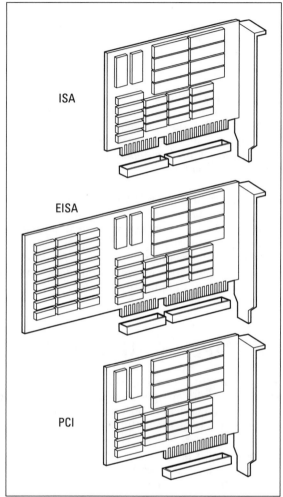

Figure 6-2:
PC buses
and their
connectors
are made to
match up
perfectly.

NICs come in a variety of flavors that generally correspond to PC bus architectures that have found their way into and out of vogue since the 1980s.
Here is a brief list of these architectures:

  ✓ **Industry Standard Architecture (ISA):** ISA is pronounced "ice-ah" and
    describes the bus that most PCs have used since IBM introduced the
    PC/AT in 1985. ISA is still the most common PC bus, so it may be an
    option that you must consider for your Windows 2000 Server machine.
    (But if you can, you should use a faster bus type for better performance.)

  ✓ **Extended ISA (EISA):** EISA is pronounced "eesa." This type of bus is
    fairly difficult to find today. It represented an attempt to extend the
    capabilities of the ISA bus. EISA is *backward compatible* with ISA, which

means that you can plug an ISA card into an EISA slot and it will work even though EISA and ISA cards use slightly different edge connectors (refer to Figure 6-2). Although EISA cards provide better performance than ISA cards and were designed specifically for servers, EISA never really caught on.

✔ **Micro Channel Architecture (MCA):** MCA is a 32-bit bus developed by IBM, with most of the same advantages as EISA: higher speed and a broader, 32-bit data path. If you have a Micro Channel PC, you must buy Micro Channel NICs to go with it, because MCA is a replacement bus, not necessarily an expansion bus. MCA's main advantage is that you can usually plug in a NIC and it handles its own configuration. This convenience does not come cheap, however — MCA NICs cost more than other NICs. MCA buses are rare today except in high-end IBM machines such as *Reduced Instruction Set Computer* (RISC) workstations or AS/400s.

✔ **VESA Local Bus (VLB):** VESA stands for *Video Electronics Standards Association.* VLB is a 32-bit bus technology that runs at speeds up to 66 MHz. A VLB slot uses one 32-bit MCA slot plus another standard ISA, EISA, or MCA slot. This lets manufacturers design NICs that use the local bus or the standard bus at the same time. VLB supports a bus management technique known as *bus mastering,* which enables the board to take control of the bus and frees the CPU to handle other tasks, thereby speeding up overall system performance. Because VLB depends on MCA, VLB is pretty much passé.

✔ **Peripheral Component Interconnect (PCI):** The PCI, developed by Intel, provides a high-speed data path between the CPU and up to ten peripherals while coexisting with ISA or EISA (like other expansion buses). Like VLB, PCI supports bus mastering to free up the CPU. With PCI, you plug ISA and/or EISA boards into their usual slots, and plug high-speed PCI controllers into PCI slots. PCI supports 32- and 64-bit implementations, with clock speeds up to 100 MHz and data transfer rates up to 132 Mbps. It's no wonder that PCI has more or less won the bus wars and that it has become the high-speed local PC bus of choice. PCI offers the best performance for peripheral adapter cards, and when it comes to server NICs, that's the name of the game!

High-speed buses such as EISA and PCI are great, and emerging standards such as *FireWire* (which is Apple's implementation of IEEE 1394) and *Fibre Channel* are even better because high-speed buses meet a server's need for speed in spades. On the other hand, you may not always have the money or open slots to use a high-speed connection, so do the best you can.

For more information on the Institute of Electrical and Electronic Engineers (IEEE) 1394 standard, search your favorite Web browser using the keywords "IEEE 1394" or search the IEEE Web site at `www.ieee.org`.

Because Windows 2000 supports the FireWire and Fibre Channel, high-speed options for networking are broader than for any other Windows server versions. However, we still feel PCI is the best game in town when it comes to providing high performance and advanced features because it's already widely available and supported in Windows 2000. In addition, there are many vendors who offer PCI-based NICs with advanced features suitable for use on Windows 2000 Servers. FireWire and FibreChannel may become better options in the future, but for now the competition out there in the marketplace is not yet fierce enough to bring prices down from their stratospheric levels.

That's why we recommend obtaining the fastest available PCI NIC for your network technology of choice: You can use PCI to make your Windows 2000 Server as fast at networking as it can be, which is highly desirable on a network server of any kind.

Selecting Speedy Server NICs

Certain built-in NIC features affect network performance significantly. Poor NIC performance hurts doubly on a server, because it limits access to its services for everyone. In fact, on networks where all users share a common medium, such as Ethernet, a slow NIC on any computer on a single-cable segment decreases available bandwidth for all network users as long as that slow NIC stays busy.

When selecting a NIC for a Windows 2000 Server computer, start by identifying the network media and the connector that the card must fit. This means recognizing the type of network technology in use and deciding what type of connector the NIC must provide. After covering these basics, you have to consider numerous other NIC options to boost a card's speed and data-handling capabilities. Because server performance is critical, you improve your overall network performance by exploiting speedy NIC options.

Here's a select set of NIC options to look for in any card you wish to use in a Windows 2000 Server machine (you may not be able to find a NIC that supports all of these, but try for as many as you can find — and afford):

✔ **Bus mastering:** Enables a NIC to control a computer's bus so it can initiate and manage data transfers to and from the computer's RAM. Bus mastering allows the CPU to focus on other tasks. It offers the biggest performance boost of any of the items mentioned here, and can increase network performance from 20 to 70 percent. Bus mastering cards cost more than NICs that don't master the bus, but are essential for server use.

✔ **Direct Memory Access (DMA):** Enables NICs to transfer data directly from on-board RAM buffers into a computer's main RAM without requiring the CPU's involvement in the data transfer. DMA can boost NIC performance by as much as 20 to 25 percent.

✔ **On-board coprocessors:** Coprocessors are CPUs built into a NIC itself. They enable NICs to handle data without involving the CPU. Most modern NICs include coprocessors to boost network performance, so it's hard to estimate their overall contribution to performance improvements.

✔ **RAM buffering:** Incorporates additional RAM on a NIC to provide storage space for incoming and outgoing data. Extra buffering boosts network performance because it enables a NIC to process data as fast as possible, without having to pause to empty and refill its buffers.

✔ **Plug and Play compatibility:** One of the best improvements in Windows 2000, compared to earlier versions of Windows NT, is its support for Microsoft's Plug and Play architecture. In English, PnP (as it's usually abbreviated) means that you can insert a device into a PC and it will happily — and correctly — configure itself. Although this confers no performance advantages, we mention it here as an essential feature because it improves *your* performance by speeding installation incredibly. Earlier Windows servers often required incredible contortions to get hardware devices installed and running. As long as a NIC or other device is PnP compatible, it's a snap to install it on Windows 2000!

✔ **Shared adapter memory:** Causes a NIC's buffers to map directly into computer RAM addresses. This fools the computer into thinking that it's writing to its own memory when it's really accessing a NIC's buffers. In other words, the computer treats a NIC's RAM as if it were its own.

✔ **Shared system memory:** Reverses the preceding item, and enables an on-board NIC processor to write to an area in the computer's RAM as if it were NIC buffer space. This enables a NIC to treat computer RAM as its own, and may be preferable to shared adapter memory because it allows a NIC to manage memory and frees the CPU for other tasks.

As network traffic loads go up, the value of these options follows apace. When selecting a NIC for your server, purchase the fastest PnP-compatible NIC you can afford. Invest in a 32-bit, bus-mastering, PnP-compatible NIC that uses either shared adapter or shared system memory and includes added buffer space, and you won't be disappointed.

Preparing to Stick in the NIC

Before you start mucking around inside your PC, be prepared. Messing with your system is one of the few things that can flat-out kill a computer — or you! If you take some preventive steps at the outset, you can ward off all kinds of trouble, and probably get back to work more quickly.

NIC installation maneuvers can turn out one of two ways. With luck, your brand-new NIC will be safely ensconced in your PC, doing exactly what it's supposed to do. Otherwise, it will be back in its original packaging, ready to be exchanged for whatever it is that you now know you *really* need!

Here are some other tips that should improve your installation experience:

✔ **Unplug any PC before you open it:** Electricity is your friend, but there's no reason to get personal with it. *Never, never, never* open a PC that's plugged into a wall socket. This mistake can get you or your machine (or both) fried. This is, technically speaking, not a good thing.

✔ **If you can't go forward, make sure you can go back:** Sometimes, after you install a NIC, you turn on the computer and get a big, fat, resounding nothing! The worst case of all may require sending the computer to a professional for repair. In the not-so-bad (and more common) case, if you take out the new stuff, and reverse any software changes you've made, you're back where you started.

Reverse software changes, you ask? This brings us to a crucial preemptive step that you must always take before fiddling with hardware. *Before* you start messing around, back up any system that will be affected. Backing up confers two vital benefits. First, assuming the worst happens and a DOA computer results, you can install your backup on another similarly configured machine and keep working until the original computer gets back from the shop. Second, if the new installation doesn't work, you can use the backup to restore the machine to the pristine state it presumably enjoyed before you mucked it up.

Before you go the backup route on a machine you've rendered comatose by adding new hardware, try rebooting using the *Last Known Good Configuration* (LKGC) option. This rolls back recent Windows 2000 Registry changes and may let you keep working. However, like our other worst-case scenario, the key to using the LKGC is to have a good Registry configuration available. Make sure that you reboot your machine when your machine appears to be working properly again; that way, the saved version of the Registry should maintain your computer in its working condition.

✔ **Figure out what you're dealing with:** A PC can act like a minefield when you add another interface to an already jam-packed machine. If you don't have an inventory of what's installed and related configuration data, make a list of what's installed and the settings for each item. This makes quick work of installation and may head off configuration anxiety before it can strike. Time may be money, but remember: It always takes longer to do it over than it does to do it right the first time.

One of the many benefits of Windows 2000's built-in PnP support is that it goes through what's called an *enumeration phase* each time the system boots. This phase also occurs when a new hardware device is added to the system or an existing device is removed from the system.

In plain English, this means that Windows 2000 keeps track of what's what, hardware-wise, on a system, and can even keep up with changes that occur while the system is running. This is more meaningful on laptops, where PC cards may come and go while the system is running, than on server machines, where you'd typically have to shut down a system to add or remove an interface card of some kind.

In any event, with the help of Windows 2000, you can now look in the Hardware Resources folder of the Computer Management utility to obtain a current list of devices and related settings on any Windows 2000 machine (use the following menu sequence: Start⇨Settings⇨ Control Panel⇨Adminsitrative Tools⇨Computer Management⇨System Tools⇨System Information⇨Hardware Resources).

✔ **Give yourself room to maneuver:** Clear some work space for yourself. Find some small paper cups or other small containers to hold screws and connectors. If you're really going to take things apart, label what goes where to help eliminate guesswork during reassembly. Also, make sure that you have the right tools for the job. Go to a computer store and get one of those $50 to $100 general-purpose computer toolkits that comes in a nifty zip-up case. (We got a peach of a kit called the JTK-39 ourselves from Jensen Tools at www.jensentools.com/ on the Web.)

You build up static as you walk on carpet or move around in dry conditions. Therefore, always carry NICs in antistatic wrappers. Ground yourself before you reach inside a machine or handle computer hardware. To dissipate static buildup, use antistatic wristbands or heel-caps. Also, keep non-conductive materials (such as polyester clothing and Styrofoam cups) away from electronic components. These materials can generate static charges quickly.

✔ **Learn the lay of your LAN:** You will eventually connect any installed NIC to a network. Part of the configuration drill is knowing the names and addresses of other servers, users, and networks around you. Before you start, read the installation requirements provided by the NIC's manufacturer and go over any of the details that you may need to supply during installation. This heads off any need to stop part way through the process to dig up missing information. Invest the ounce of prevention that helps avoid expensive, time-consuming cures!

Beware the Golden Fingers!

Reading motherboard or adapter manuals from offshore manufacturers gives you a unique opportunity to decipher the bizarre forms that written English can sometimes take in the hands of non-native speakers. For example, one Taiwanese company describes an edge connector (the part of the NIC that plugs into a PC's bus slot) as "golden fingers."

Even if those fingers are brass rather than gold, make sure they're firmly seated and fully connected when you plug a NIC into an empty bus slot. That is, make sure that the edge connector is hidden from view and that the network interface on the side of the card is well positioned in the cutout on the back of your PC case. Don't jam the edge connector into the computer's bus socket; rock it carefully if you must. Too much force can peel the golden fingers away; if that happens, you need a replacement card.

You should also screw the NIC's metal tab into place, using the screw that attached the placeholder before it was removed. Figure 6-3 shows a placeholder and its screw notch.

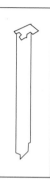

Figure 6-3: Placeholders close off empty slots, and keep dust and dirt out of your PC.

Two things are worth noting about PC placeholders:

✔ Be careful with the little screw that holds the placeholder in position. If you drop a screw, you can usually get it to show itself more readily by picking up the PC case and rocking it back and forth gently. *Never* use a magnetized screwdriver to pick up a screw you've dropped; otherwise, you computer's data may become screwy.

✔ Be sure to put the placeholder in a toolbox or spare-parts drawer so you can find it again later. If you ever have to remove the NIC (or any other card) from your PC, you'll need the placeholder to close the case again. Some cases use odd-sized placeholders, so life will be simpler if you can find the right placeholder when you need it.

Old-Fashioned NIC Configuration

If you're lucky enough that your Windows 2000 Server PC includes only PnP-compatible adapter cards, you can probably skip this section with a certain amount of glee. Your NIC will probably configure itself without any help from you, but if you encounter hardware configuration problems when you try to add your NIC (or some other device) to a Windows 2000 system, you may want to read this material over anyway.

Configuring a non-PnP NIC for Windows 2000 requires making all the right hardware selections and choosing the appropriate software settings. In short, you have to deal with numerous different settings and make sure that the right configuration information is furnished to the NIC's software drivers. Read on for the gory details!

NICcus interruptus

Activity on a network can occur at any time. To receive incoming data and handle outgoing traffic, a NIC must be able to signal the CPU or the bus (for incoming traffic) and vice versa (for outgoing traffic).

The most common way to handle such activity is to reserve an *interrupt request* (IRQ) for a NIC's use. PCs typically support from 15 to 23 IRQs, numbered 0 through 15 or 23, depending on the number of interrupt controllers installed. Interfaces use IRQs to signal activity. Each NIC must have its own unique IRQ value in a range that the card itself can handle.

These variables help explain why mapping a PC's configuration is a good idea. Your mission, whether you like it or not, is to find an IRQ that no other adapter is using and that your new NIC can accept. If such an IRQ is not available, you must alter another card to free up a usable IRQ. For PCI NICs, this exercise is not so difficult because PCI handles IRQs itself.

Setting IRQs usually means making software settings, setting DIP switches (DIP stands for *dual in-line package*), or moving jumpers. The software stuff is self-documenting, but we explain how to use DIP switches and jumpers next.

Flick all DIP switches the right way

Most *DIP switches,* which are really banks of individual switches, indicate which way is on or off. If you can't tell and the manual doesn't help, call the vendor's tech support department right away (or see if it has a Web site). The vendor will know the answer, and this will save you unnecessary and potentially dangerous guesses or experiments. Figure 6-4 shows a typical DIP switch. DIP switches are found on ISA NICs; you won't find them on PCI NICs.

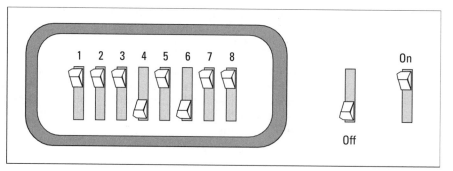

Jumping blocks for fun and networking!

Jumper blocks consist of two rows of adjacent pins, interconnected with teeny-tiny widgets called *jumpers* (see Figure 6-5). Pins are numbered with designations that start with J followed by a number (for example, J6).

Sliding a jumper over both pins turns a jumper on. To turn a numbered pin set off, remove the jumper from both pins and slide it over one of the two pins so it sticks out from the pin block (as in the middle position in Figure 6-5). Often, when you set IRQs with jumpers, you insert one jumper for an entire block of pins. The pin set you jump selects one IRQ. In that case, make sure that the jumper is firmly seated on both pins.

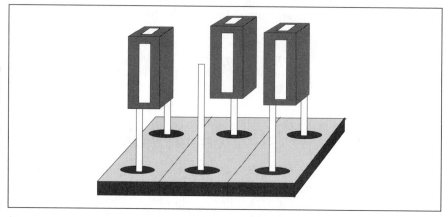

Figure 6-5:
A typical
jumper
block has
multiple
pins, with
individual
jumpers.

Beware de defaults

Before you worry too much about DIP switches or jumpers, check the NIC manual to find out where the factory set the IRQ by default. If the default setting is open, you can stick with that default and do nothing else. Consider it a blessing when this happens!

Sail into the right I/O port

Each card in a system has a unique *input/output* (I/O) port address, with certain addresses reserved for particular interfaces, especially video cards. NICs are choosy and normally get an I/O port address assigned from a range of addresses reserved for their use. This address is generally set by software or by a DIP switch on most NICs because of the broad range of settings possible.

I/O ports let a computer read from or write to memory that belongs to an interface. When an interrupt is signaled, it tells the computer to read from or write to an I/O port. The information written to or read from the I/O port's address is copied across the bus between the NIC and the CPU.

Can we be direct? Setting DMA

Some NICs use a technique called *direct memory access* (DMA) to move information between the NIC and the CPU. This speeds copying information from computer memory to the NIC, and vice versa. This technique has become less necessary (and less common) as computers and equipment have become faster. You probably won't have to mess with this on a newer NIC, but it's a common setting for older ones.

DMA matches two areas of memory: one on the computer and another on the NIC. Writing to the memory area on the computer automatically copies data to the NIC and vice versa. Setting a DMA address means finding an unoccupied DMA memory block to assign to your NIC. Again, your earlier research on what settings are already occupied helps you avoid conflicts. Choose an unoccupied address block and make the right NIC settings to match it. If you encounter a conflict, you have to figure out some way to resolve it. Remember to check your defaults here, too.

MemBase is not a musical instrument

NICs contain their own RAM, called *buffer space,* to provide working room to store information coming on and off the network. This buffer space must be assigned an equivalent region in the PC's memory called the *memory base address,* or MemBase for short.

Just as with IRQs and DMA, this setting must be unique. Watch out for potential address conflicts and steer around them. If software doesn't do the job automatically, you usually use jumpers to set the MemBase on your NIC. Common settings for NICs include C000h, D000h, and D800h.

If a NIC is on the Microsoft *Hardware Compatibility List* (HCL), a possible configuration is probably listed there too, so you won't have to figure everything out without help. Also, be sure to check your NIC's installation software before you install Windows 2000, in case you need to find a driver for the card (as we explain further in the following section).

In the Driver's Seat

After you install NIC hardware, you must deal with device driver software. If your NIC is of recent vintage, the drivers on the disk that's included with the card may actually be worth using.

In that case — which we rank right up there with your chances of winning the lottery — you can load the disk, run an installation program, supply a few values here and there, and be ready to rock and roll. If you're not that lucky, you'll have to chase down drivers on your own.

Our advice: Always determine the latest and greatest drivers for your NICs before you start installing them. Ask for help in the following order:

1. From the company that sold you the NIC.

2. From the vendor that built the card.

3. On the Internet. Use a search engine to search for the NIC by vendor and model. This usually produces usable information, if not usable software.

Bringing the NIC to the Cable

Okay, the software's installed, and the hardware's plugged in. All that's left is hooking the NIC up to the network. For modular technologies, such as twisted-pair Ethernet or token ring, this means inserting the LAN cable's modular connector into a receptacle on the NIC. For other technologies, it means hooking up a T-connector or a transceiver cable from the LAN to your NIC. Whichever option applies, make sure that the connection is tight and that the NIC is seated solidly in its slot. Then, you're ready to fire it up!

When Trouble Shoots at You, Be Ready to Shoot Back!

You've navigated the maze of potential address conflicts and have set your NIC to clear settings. The software's installed, so everything should work, right? Well, it usually does (loud cheers and high fives) but sometimes it doesn't (serious grinding and gnashing of teeth). You learn that things aren't working in one of four ways:

✔ **Your PC doesn't boot:** This one is obvious. When you can't boot, it's time to undo what you just did. First, restore the system to its state before you started messing around. (You *do* have a backup, right?) If that works, you know the NIC's the problem. Get some help from one of our recommended sources. If your system doesn't work when you return to square one, you have bigger problems. Time to visit the repair shop!

✔ **Your PC boots but doesn't load the drivers:** The most common reasons that drivers fail to load are as follows:

   • **Loose connections:** Make sure that the wire is tight and properly seated on the NIC, and that it's plugged into something on the other end.

   • **Installation problems:** Make sure that the drivers are in the right directory, and that this directory is referenced in your bootup file or defined in your PATH statement. Because Windows 2000 actively searches your hard drive for drivers (as long as your NIC is on the HCL), this normally isn't a problem for Windows 2000 machines.

   • **Conflict!** You may have missed something and introduced a conflict. Try all your other stuff; it's a dead giveaway if something else has quit working, too. Time to return to square one and recheck all system settings. Something somewhere is squirrelly, so be extra careful!

   The good news is that such a problem is most likely to result from a loose connection or a configuration boo-boo. If it's not one of those, it may be time for a visit to the repair shop!

✔ **Your PC boots partway but hangs on a blue screen:** Sometimes, Windows 2000 starts booting, but hangs up on a solid blue screen filled with white text that starts with an error code. This condition is known as the "blue screen of death" (a.k.a. BSOD) to Windows aficionados.

If a BSOD appears during installation, it's usually related to some type of hardware driver problem. If it happens right after you install a NIC, but Windows 2000 has booted before, guess what? The NIC driver you just installed isn't working properly and will have to be replaced with one that works. Make sure you've got the latest and greatest driver. If in doubt, send the vendor some e-mail or call tech support. If this problem occurs during an initial installation of Windows 2000, it may not be clear what's causing the problem. If that's the case, consult Chapter 22, which covers installation and configuration tips.

✔ **You try to use the network and it fails to respond:** This is a subtle variant on NIC driver problems and usually results from one or more of the same causes. You're treated to an extra layer of mystery here, because a conflict may result from an application rather than a driver. Or, the network may be stymied by an incorrect NIC setting, an incorrect network configuration, or an invalid login sequence (that is, the software works okay but you're telling it to do the wrong stuff). You must work your way through a careful process of elimination to find an answer. Good luck, and take lots of breaks. Remember that it's okay to ask for help!

After you've made it over any humps and can communicate with the network, you're ready to get to work. Or, if you're a fledgling network administrator, you'll have the pleasure of helping someone else get to work for the first time. Either way, you'll have pushed the networking wave another machine ahead!

Chapter 7

Hooking Up Your Network

. . . .

. . . .

*B*uying computers does not make a network! You have to interconnect computers to enable them to communicate. There are several ways you can set up communications among computers; the one you choose depends on your budget and bandwidth needs. Okay, most of it depends on budget!

Transmission media is a fancy, generic term for cabling and atmospheric transmission. The media provide the means by which computers talk to each other across a network. In fact, computers can communicate through the air-waves using broadcast transmissions, through the wiring in a building, or across a campus. Linking long-haul or Internet connections to local networks means that there's almost no limit to what your network can access!

In this chapter, we examine different methods to interconnect networks using cables and other media. You find out which are appropriate for desktop access and which media work best for server-to-server activity. You also discover more about network anatomy as we tackle two ticklish subjects — namely, backbones and *wide area network* (WAN) links.

Make a Network Medium Happy!

A happy network medium has nothing whatsoever to do with a content TV psychic. Rather, finding the right network medium means implementing network cabling that won't cause bottlenecks. Depending on whether you're building a network from the ground up or starting from scratch, you may need to take a different approach to evaluating cabling options for your network:

✔ If you step into a job where a *local area network* (LAN) is already in place, cabling is probably in place, too. Evaluating the type, capabilities, and usability of an inherited network is almost always a good idea. That way, you can decide whether you can live with what you've got, or whether some change will do the network good. You may learn, for example, that old cabling causes so many difficulties that you're better off replacing or upgrading it. We've actually popped out ceiling tiles and found badly spliced cables hidden from view.

✔ If you're planning a brand-new network, one of your concerns is to determine your cabling needs. Decide which network cabling you're going to use *before* ordering equipment for your network, because you can often order computers and peripherals with the appropriate *network interface cards* (NICs) preinstalled and preconfigured. (Of course, NICs are preinstalled and preconfigured on an existing network, which means your choices have already been made for you.) The more work you save yourself, the better you'll like it!

✔ If a contractor handles your cabling maintenance, don't assume that every old cable gets replaced if it's not completely up to snuff. A contractor may choose to reuse substandard cables to save on material costs. Without proper wiring, your network may be in constant trouble (or it may not even work at all).

If you work with a cable contractor, require that contractor to test each network cable and insist that the contractor provide you with those test results. In fact, many companies hire one contractor to install cables and another to test them. By doing so, they ensure that the common tendency to overlook errors or potential sources of problems on a network can be avoided — plus, it never hurts to get a second opinion.

The most common cabling technology for LANs is *baseband cable,* which is cable set up for baseband transmission. For this reason, we concentrate on baseband cable in this book. Check out the sidebar titled "Use the right pipes in your network's plumbing" for a description of baseband transmission and how it differs from broadband transmission.

If you know what to look for, the name of a particular type of cable can tell you all about its transmission properties. Ethernet cable notation (set down by the *Institute of Electrical and Electronic Engineers,* or IEEE) breaks down as follows:

✔ The speed of the Ethernet in Mbps

✔ The cable's technology — broadband or baseband

✔ The cable's rated distance, in hundreds of meters, or the type of cable — twisted pair or fiber optic

Use the right pipes in your network's plumbing

Wiring on a network is like plumbing in a house. Just as pipes form the pathways through which water flows to and from your plumbing fixtures, a network's wiring provides the pathways through which computers transmit data using electric signals. The amount of data that computers can move through a wiring system at any one time depends on the size of the wires, or pipes, installed. The larger the pipes, the more data computers can send at any one time.

You can think of a network's *bandwidth* as the size of a network's pipes. Bandwidth represents a range of usable frequencies and is measured in hertz (Hz). A higher hertz rating for a network medium means higher available bandwidth. Higher bandwidth translates into bigger pipes to carry data. However, just because you have big pipes, doesn't mean you always get to fill them completely. Therefore, it makes sense to try to measure the actual amount of data (called throughput) flowing through the pipes.

Different types of cabling are rated for different amounts of data flow at different distances. Remember, however, that even if a pipe is big enough to handle all the water you send through it, that pipe can still get clogged. As a result,

although a given amount of data can theoretically flow through a cable, in the real world, you may see less data flow than the maximum bandwidth indicates. Plumbers will tell you that lime and rust deposits can often restrict the water flow in pipes. In keeping with our metaphor, we can say that noise, cross-talk, *electromagnetic interference* (EMI), and other network maladies can often degrade the actual performance of your cable. *Throughput,* commonly measured in *bits per second* (bps), describes the actual amount of data that's flowing through a cable at any one time.

If you take one pipe and divide it into little pipes, you've just reinvented the concept of *broadband transmission* (in which multiple transmissions at different frequencies use the same networking medium simultaneously). If the pipe is kept whole instead of subdivided, you end up with the concept of *baseband transmission* (in which the entire bandwidth is used to carry only one set of frequencies and one transmission at a time).

Whew! Got all that? Maybe it's time to call Roto-Rooter!

For example, 10Base5 is an Ethernet designation that stands for [10 Mbps] [baseband] [5 x 100 meters = 500 meters]. From the name alone, you can tell that the baseband cable is rated to handle up to 10 Mbps on a segment up to 500 meters (1,640 feet) long.

Any time you see a T or an F in such a name, replace that letter with either *twisted-pair* or *fiber-optic,* respectively. For example, *10BaseT* means that this particular baseband Ethernet cable is rated at up to 10 Mbps using twisted-pair cables. Likewise, *10BaseF* means the same thing, except that it uses fiber-optic media instead of twisted-pair.

Cabling is easy, but comes in many varieties

Wiring and cables come in all sizes and shapes. Each type of cable has associated distance limitations. Each type also has different price tags, transmission characteristics, and so forth. The more common types of cable you find on modern networks are twisted-pair, coaxial, and fiber-optic.

Twisted-pair cable: Call it "teepee" for short!

Twisted-pair wiring comes in two flavors: *unshielded twisted pair* (UTP) and *shielded twisted pair* (STP). To explain shielded versus unshielded wiring in the simplest terms possible, STP incorporates a foil or wire braid around its wires, which are twisted together in pairs; UTP doesn't.

UTP

You've probably been exposed to UTP cable if you have any type of phone system in your organization. You may have even seen such cabling inside the walls of your home (if you watched the contractors build it).

A UTP cable consists of pairs of copper wires where a color-coded plastic jacket encases each wire. Individual pairs are twisted together, and the entire cable is wrapped in an outer jacket. Figure 7-1 depicts a cross-section of a typical UTP cable. The number of twists in a cable is important because the twists improve transmission characteristics for the wires involved and improve resistance to interference. This puts a whole new twist on twisted-pair!

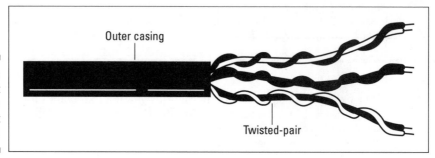

Figure 7-1: Let's twist again, like we did last summer!

Outer casing

Twisted-pair

Notice that the *U* in UTP means *unshielded.* That notation is included because another type of twisted-pair cable is *shielded* — STP (shielded twisted pair). The difference is that STP includes an extra layer of shielding around the twisted wires. Both types of cable are used in modern networks, but UTP is more common because STP is more expensive. You find out more about STP later in this section.

Voice-grade UTP (CAT 1 and 2 — the next paragraph has the skinny on CAT ratings) is the kind of cable installed in most homes and in older phone systems. Voice-grade UTP cable is made to carry voice signals and is quite cheap. Some organizations discover that they have extra phone wires already pulled and terminated in offices, so they try this cable for networking. The problem is that voice-grade UTP is not made to carry data. If you have a small LAN with little traffic, this cable may work. However, if you're building a big network with huge database applications, voice-grade UTP is unacceptable. You need to install UTP cable with a higher CAT rating.

What's a CAT rating? *CAT* stands for *category.* The *Electronic Industries Association* (EIA) places ratings on UTP cable based on how fast such a cable can transmit data. Here's the current roster of CAT ratings that you can find in use in the workplace:

- ✔ **CAT 1 and 2:** Use only for voice and low-speed data.
- ✔ **CAT 3:** Use for data speeds up to 16 Mbps.
- ✔ **CAT 4:** Use for data speeds up to 20 Mbps.
- ✔ **CAT 5:** Use for data speeds up to 100 Mbps.
- ✔ **CAT 5 Enhanced:** Use for data speeds up to 200 Mbps.
- ✔ **CAT 6:** Use for data speeds up to 600 Mbps.

CAT 6 cable is different from its CAT 1–5 counterparts. Each pair is individually wrapped in foil shielding, and then all pairs are enclosed in another layer of foil shielding. This extra shielding helps protect this cable from noise and other disturbances. The only question we have left is "Why is CAT 6 called UTP when the cable is shielded?" But alas, some burning questions must go unanswered!

If you're already using UTP cable on your network and you're not sure how it's rated, call in a cable contractor to test your cables to see what you've got.

If you plan to install CAT 5 cable for your network, make sure that the connectors used from one end of the network to the other are also rated CAT 5. If you follow whatever connection your computer makes on the network through the wall and so on, you find numerous components along the way, including *wall plates, punchdown blocks, patch panels,* and more. All these need to be rated CAT 5 for the network to function properly.

UTP cable is cheaper and more widespread than STP, but it has a few minor foibles that you may not like. Because it's unshielded, UTP is prone to interference from external sources, such as fluorescent lighting. It's not unusual to pop ceiling tiles and find UTP cables strung over light fixtures or near elevators. This placement can lead to network interference; therefore, you should be careful how and where you place your cables.

Another cost factor for twisted-pair cable is that it requires you to connect workstations through a hub. Although you can buy simple eight-port hubs for under $50, the added cost may still become a consideration if you're planning a large network. On the plus side, so-called *smart hubs* can be advantageous on a network because they can actually help you manage your cabling — but those smarts show up on the price tags for such equipment. At the very least, less expensive hubs always have blinking lights that can tell you which ports are active and whether data is transmitting or not.

STP: The shielding improves performance

STP, shielded twisted pair, adds an extra layer of shielding around its twisted pairs. This shielding is a wire mesh or foil layer that sits between individual pairs and the outer jacket. STP can transmit data at speeds of up to 155 Mbps across spans of up to 100 meters (328 feet), but such implementations are atypical (and quite expensive). Normally, you find 4–16 Mbps token ring network implementations based on STP (but sometimes on UTP as well).

The most predictable places to find STP implementations are on older token ring and *LocalTalk* networks, or in older IBM mainframe environments. IBM is token ring's original designer, and it still makes and sells token ring parts. That's why most "Big Blue" shops use token ring networks.

STP cable may require electrical grounding, and it's not much fun to install. STP cable is thick and less flexible, which makes it harder to route and handle than UTP. STP's connectors are bothersome and don't always plug in easily either. STP cable is expensive, so unless you require the higher bandwidth that STP can deliver, you may do better to stick with UTP to simplify your network's installation and to keep costs down.

Coaxial (coax) cable

Coaxial cable, also called *coax*, is another popular transmission medium for networks old and new. Older networks used coaxial cable exclusively before UTP arrived in the mid-1980s. Initially, only thick coaxial cable (which we like to call "frozen yellow garden hose") was available. Thick coax is quite cumbersome to handle and a real pain in the neck to install. Imagine pulling a frozen garden hose through the ceiling and then having to connect transceivers to that cable! Maybe a frozen garden hose is easier, after all. . .

Coaxial cable incorporates two layers of insulation. Beginning in the middle of the cable and spanning outward, the cable has a copper wire surrounded by a foam insulator, which is surrounded by a wire mesh conductor that is then surrounded by an outer jacket of insulation. This jacket, in turn, is surrounded by a plastic casing, called *cladding*. Figure 7-2 shows a cross section of a well-dressed piece of coaxial cable.

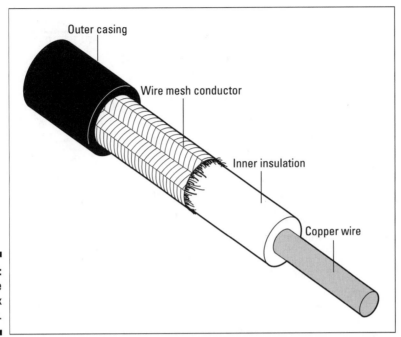

Outer casing

Wire mesh conductor

Inner insulation

Copper wire

Figure 7-2:
An inside
view of coax
cable.

The way you determine cost for the different types of coaxial cable is simple.
The larger a cable's diameter, the more it costs. In this case, bigger is not
necessarily better, but it is more expensive. Table 7-1 shows some coax cable
ratings based on the U.S. military's *Radio Grade* (RG) cable specifications.

Table 7-1	Coax Cable Classifications		
Classification	*Name*	*Ohms*	*Use*
RG-8 and RG-11	Thicknet	50	Thick Ethernet
RG-58	Thinnet	50	Thin Ethernet
RG-59	Broadband	75	Cable television
RG-62	ARCnet	93	ARCnet

When selecting any version of RG-58 for a network, make sure you select one
of the varieties that has a braided wire core, either RG-58A/U or RG-58C/U
(the military equivalent). Although a solid-core variety called RG-58/U is
available, it's not covered in the IEEE specification for 10Base2, and may
occasionally cause problems if used on a 10Base2 network.

10BaseT

10BaseT is a pretty popular version of Ethernet in broad use on today's networks. It's a star topology that uses hubs connected with twisted-pair cable; as it's IEEE name indicates, it's an Ethernet standard rated for a transmission speeds of 10 Mbps. 10BaseT requires at least CAT 3 UTP. You can install CAT 5 for 10BaseT networks to anticipate moving to higher bandwidths like 100BaseT. The following list tells you what you would need to construct a 10BaseT network starting from the device to the computer room:

- **NICs:** Ethernet NICs with RJ-45 connections

- **Cable:** CAT 3-5 UTP from NIC to transceiver (if external transceiver)

- **Transceiver:** Can be external or onboard the NIC

- **Cable:** CAT 3-5 UTP from transceiver (or NIC) to wall

- **Wall plate:** RJ-45 sockets

- **Cabling in wall:** CAT 3-5 UTP

- **Punchdown block:** Incoming UTP wires are brought here and are pressed down into a block of wires using a special tool

- **Cable:** CAT 3-5 UTP from punchdown block to patch panel

- **Cable:** CAT 3-5 UTP patch cable from patch panel to hub

The following are some limitations you need to note when implementing 10BaseT:

- **Distance:** From network device to hub, cable runs can't exceed 100 meters (328 feet).

- **Nodes:** Can't use more than 1,024 nodes on a network without subdividing that network and adding a routing device between the subdivisions.

- **Hubs:** You may not plug more than 12 additional hubs into a main hub to increase the total number of network devices accessible.

You probably noticed that we slipped in some new terms in Table 7-1, such as Thicknet and Thinnet. These are just different classifications for coaxial Ethernet cable, and we describe them in more detail in the following sections, because they're implemented frequently in smaller organizations.

Coax cable cost is directly proportional to its diameter. The thicker the diameter, the more the cable costs; not coincidentally, related equipment costs more, too.

10Base2 (Thinnet)

Thinnet goes by some aliases, such as RG-58, CheaperNet, Thinwire, and 10Base2. Remember that 10Base2 means that this cable is rated at 10 Mbps and can span a distance of 185 meters (okay, so they didn't want to put the notation of 10Base1.85) without any repeating devices. (That's the equivalent of approximately 607 feet for you non-metric types.) It's a thinner type of coax cable (hence the names Thinwire and Thinnet) and is quite popular because it's cheap (hence the name CheaperNet)!

Thinnet is flexible and easy to work with because it's quite thin. You find Thinnet coax in smaller organizations that have only one floor or suite of offices because it's cheaper than CAT 5 UTP and STP, and it doesn't require dedicated connecting devices such as hubs.

Because 10Base2 cable is thicker than UTP, it requires funny-shaped connectors that you've probably seen in Radio Shack but didn't recognize. These connectors are called *British Naval Connectors* (BNCs) or *T-connectors*. The latter name describes this connector's shape, as shown in Figure 7-3. The top part of the "T" interconnects cable segments, and the bottom of the "T" attaches the cable to a computer's NIC. In addition, 10Base2 requires terminating resistors at each end of each cable segment, one end of which is often grounded.

Figure 7-3:
The BNC is also known as a T-connector because of its distinctive shape.

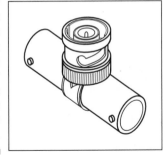

So, how do you connect computers and devices to a network using 10Base2? First, picture a straight line with devices attached to it. 10Base2 is a *bus topology* (see Chapter 4), so it extends in a straight line where each device on the network attaches between two cable segments, as shown in Figure 7-4. Devices attach to the network through the bottom of a T-connector that plugs into the NIC on the back of each computer.

Figure 7-4:
Network attachment between two cable segments.

Install terminating resistors on the unused sides of the T-connectors at each end of a 10Base2 network.

When installing a 10Base2 network, track the number of devices that an individual cable segment supports and how long any such segment of cable becomes. Table 7-2 lays out key information that you need to review before installing a 10Base2 network or when checking out an existing installation.

Table 7-2	10Base2 Limitations	
	Trunk Segment	**Entire Network**
Max length	185 meters (607 feet)	925 meters (3,035 feet)
Max nodes	30	1,024
Min node distance	50 cm (20 inches)	50 cm (20 inches)
Max # repeaters	n/a	4
Max # segments	n/a	5

10Base5 (Thicknet)

10Base5 is a thicker coaxial cable and is, therefore, more expensive than 10Base2. It's also less pliable and subject to more stringent bend radius restrictions. (In English, this means that if you bend it sharply, the cable doesn't work properly.) If you can visualize trying to poke a little hole into a frozen garden hose, you quickly realize that you need some type of special clamping or tapping device to get through the thick outer layers.

To connect network devices to 10Base5 coax, you must have special mechanical devices called *vampire taps* — instead of the T-connectors that 10Base2 uses. The tap clamps onto the coax cable and penetrates through the coax to its inner conductor. You need to use devices called *transceivers* (an abbreviation for transmitter/receiver) to convert a digital signal from the computer into an electrical signal on the wire, and vice versa.

10Base5 uses external transceivers and can support transceiver cables up to 15 meters (50 feet) long, which allows the 10Base5 cable to act as a type of backbone, and the transceiver cables to extend to desktop machines. This makes routing the frozen yellow garden hose quite a bit easier, because it doesn't have to snake its way from computer to computer as do 10Base2 cables.

A typical 10Base5 cable layout is shown in Figure 7-5. This arrangement also explains why 10Base5 cable is used primarily for network backbones or on older networks that haven't changed since their original installations (usually in the 1970s or early 1980s, when this cable represented the only available Ethernet technology).

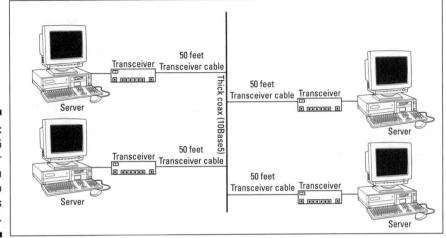

Figure 7-5:
10Base5
transceiver
cables can
span up to
15 meters
(50 feet).

Table 7-3 lists the distance and nodal limitations on 10Base5 networking.

Table 7-3	10Base5 Limitations	
	Trunk Segment	*Entire Network*
Max length	500 meters (1,640 feet)	2,500 meters (8,200 feet)
Max nodes	100	1,024
Min node distance	2.5 meters (8 feet)	2.5 meters (8 feet)
Max # repeaters	n/a	4
Max # segments	n/a	5

Although 10Base5 allows five cable segments to be tied together, it's interesting to note that only three of those cables can contain network devices. This limitation is known as the 5-4-3 rule in Ethernet: On any path from one terminator to another on a network, up to five (5) cable segments may be joined by up to four (4) repeating devices, but only three (3) of those cable segments may be populated with more than two devices.

If you have a small network and a restricted budget, coax can be a good choice, but because of expense factors and ease of installation, Thinwire is invariably a better choice for such installations than Thickwire. You may, however, decide to mix these two cable types if the distance limitations of Thinwire don't allow your cables to span sufficient distance.

Know your network trunks!

A *trunk,* or network segment, consists of an entire cable segment on a network that spans from one repeating device to another, to which individual computers may (or may not) be attached. For 10Base2, a trunk may only span 185 meters (607 feet) and may have no more than 30 devices attached to it. Each device on a 10Base2 trunk must be spaced at least 50 cm (20 inches) from the next device.

You may not use a single unbroken cable segment that's more than 91.5 meters (300 feet) long. That means you must have at least three devices on a segment that spans 185 meters (607 feet). If you ignore these restrictions, your network is likely to experience difficulties. You

can, however, add repeating devices to network trunks and, therefore, extend the length of your network.

Repeating devices take an incoming signal from the network, strip out the noise, amplify the signal, and pass the data onto the next segment of the network. In 10Base2, however, even if you use repeaters, the network's maximum span has physical limitations. The total network span cannot exceed more than 925 meters (3,035 feet), and you cannot (theoretically) place more than 1,024 devices on a single 10Base2 inter-network across all cable segments (practically, experiments indicate that the real limit is more like 900 devices).

You can buy pre-fab cables of different lengths to speed up network installation. Otherwise, you have to purchase special crimping tools and build such cables yourself. If you decide to build your own, spend the extra $200 or so to buy a low-cost cable tester to make sure your cables are put together properly. You can find tools such as cable scanners, *Time Domain Reflectometers* (TDRs), and crimping tools, along with white papers and cabling specs at www.microtest.com — Microtest is the most popular vendor of cabling equipment today.

Fiber-optic cable

Fiber-optic cable is different from twisted-pair and coax cable because it transmits data using light signals instead of electrical impulses. When you look at the layout of the cable, it appears similar to coax, but it has a glass or plastic fiber as its inner conductor instead of a copper wire. Figure 7-6 shows you what the inside of a fiber-optic cable looks like.

In Figure 7-6, notice that the inner glass core is surrounded by a cylinder of glassy material called *cladding.* Surrounding the cladding is a plastic jacket, and the entire cable has another strong jacket around it. The outer jacket is designed to be thick enough to protect the inner fiber from being broken when the cable is handled (with care, that is).

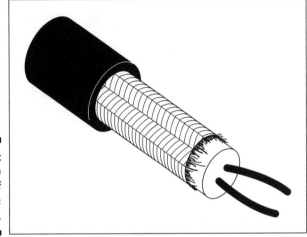

Figure 7-6:
An inside
view of
fiber-optic
cable.

Although it has a higher price tag than electrical cables, fiber-optic cable can also handle greater bandwidth, which means that it can transfer more data over longer distances. Fiber-optic cable is largely immune to *electromagnetic interference* (EMI) and other sources of noise that affect electrically conductive cables. One factor that adds to the expense of fiber-optic cable is the care that's required during installation. A knowledgeable technician must carefully polish each glass fiber with specialized tools and then add special connectors to the cable.

You often find fiber-optic cable installed between buildings in campus environments or between floors in a building. You rarely see fiber pulled to the desktop because of the expense involved — you must use fiber-optic NICs, and two cables must be attached to each workstation because one cable is used to transmit outbound signals, whereas the other one is used to receive inbound signals.

In some locations, such as hospitals, it's necessary to run fiber-optic cable to some desktops because X-ray and MRI equipment can interfere with electrical cables. Also, the bandwidth requirements for medical imaging equipment can be so extreme that conventional electrical cables can't handle the traffic involved. Although the appetite for bandwidth is always increasing, don't expect your desktop to have a "high-fiber diet" any time soon!

For light signals to pass through a fiber-optic cable, a transmitter has to be attached to one end of the cable and a receiver to the other end. This is why two cables are needed to permit any one device to send and receive signals. On the transmitting end, an *injection laser diode* (ILD) or a *light-emitting diode* (LED) sends light pulses down the cable. These light pulses reflect within the glass core and bounce against the mirror-like cladding through the length of the cable until they reach a *photo diode receiver* at the cable's other end. Notice that data flows only in one direction. The receiver converts incoming light pulses into electrical signals and passes the data to the NIC.

Because of the way that light pulses travel through fiber-optic cable, splicing two such cables requires great care so the cable's signal-carrying capabilities are not reduced. Otherwise, a light pulse may arrive at the splice but may not make it through to the other end of the cable. We call this situation a bad splice, but your users will call it much worse names!

Fiber-optic cable is the most expensive type, but it offers the highest bandwidth and the most room for future bandwidth growth.

A final note about cabling

If you're going to install cable yourself instead of hiring a cable contractor, here are a few final notes we'd like to share with you:

- ✔ Obtain a copy of the blueprints for your building or floor and make sure that all the electrical devices and outlets are clearly marked. This map assists you in placing cable away from electrical devices or motors that can interfere with your network. You don't want to install cable near elevator motors, transformers, or other heavy-duty electrical devices (unless you're using fiber-optic cable and even then, you need to protect it from potential sources of damage or wear and tear).

- ✔ Obtain all relevant local, state, and federal building code regulations and make sure that your plans conform to such ordinances. You need to evaluate these requirements before purchasing any cable because some codes require you to purchase *plenum-rated,* fire-retardant cable. Other codes require you to use plenum-rated cable only when you run cable through locations that are likely to catch fire rapidly. In any case, it behooves you to know the rules before you purchase and install a network.

   Plenums are the air handling spaces between the ceiling of one floor and the floor of the floor above where cable is often strung. Fires spread more rapidly in these areas because air carries fire rapidly; therefore, plenum-rated cable is mandated for use in such spaces to keep fire and smoke from spreading through a building.

- ✔ Determine which parts of the network you can build and maintain on your own and which parts you need to subcontract. For example, if you have the time and inclination to build cables and also have the time to troubleshoot the network when those cables don't work, so be it. We recommend that you buy as much prefabricated cable as possible and only make cables when you absolutely must. Why? Because companies that make cables do it all the time, and they are good at it. If you only make cables for your network occasionally, you may introduce problems.

> ✔ Try to hire a contractor to install cable for your LAN. The wiring is your
> network's infrastructure. If it's not installed properly, wiring can cause
> endless network snafus. Wiring contractors should provide you with
> bids, install the cabling, label all cables, test and certify all cables, and
> provide you with final documentation. You're responsible to keep them
> on track. Don't assume that a contractor will follow local ordinances
> unless you make him or her do it. Put all expectations in writing and
> keep tabs on the work.

Raising the Bandwidth Ceiling

As organizations have come to depend on LANs and WANs, they've put more
applications and information on their networks. Speedy retrieval of such
information becomes critical to such organizations. This retrieval is where
the need for additional bandwidth most often manifests itself.

Conventional text-only documents don't normally put much strain on a network. But today, data often takes the form of audio, video, graphics, and
other types of multimedia. Such files or data streams are much larger than
plain-text files and often impose delivery deadlines on networks. If this is
hard to picture, think how frustrating it is when the audio track and the video
track get out of synch on your TV, and then multiply this frustration by several orders of magnitude. Then, think about what delivering time-sensitive
audio, video, or multimedia data across a network really requires. . .

In fact, such complex forms of data can easily consume the full bandwidth of
an ordinary 10 Mbps network while handling only one or two users' needs.
That's why an increasing appetite for higher-bandwidth networks is emerging
in the workplace. Such added bandwidth is increasingly necessary to handle
the more complex types of data traversing the network and to prepare the
infrastructure to deal with emerging applications, such as network teleconfer-
encing, network telephony, collaborative development, and all kinds of other
gee-whiz technologies now under construction.

This is why we feel compelled to tell you about some of the cabling alternatives available for today's networks that might be able to handle tomorrow's
bandwidth needs. Please read the sidebars in this chapter for the full picture
if you really want to understand what's out there!

100 Mbps Ethernet

Two flavors of 100 Mbps Ethernet are available today, each with its own particular access method: CSMA/CD (this means *Carrier Sense Multiple
Access/Collision Detection;* we discuss it in detail in Chapter 4) and *demand
priority* (as described later in this chapter). When proposals for 100 Mbps

were solicited, two factions emerged: one that used the same CSMA/CD access method used in conventional Ethernet (now known as *Fast Ethernet* or *100BaseT*), and another that used a demand priority access method (now known as *100BaseVG-AnyLAN*).

Both factions put proposals forward to implement their approaches. Curiously, both proposals were ultimately accepted as standards, but each one fell under different IEEE committees. Today, the Fast Ethernet standard falls under the 802.3 standards family, but the 100BaseVG-AnyLAN standard falls under the IEEE 802.12 standards family.

100BaseT is similar to 10BaseT except that it runs 10 times faster. When implementing 100BaseT, you need to use equipment designed for 100BaseT throughout your network, but otherwise, designing and building networks is pretty much the same as for 10BaseT. It's even possible to mix and match 10BaseT and 100BaseT technologies on a single network, but you need to include hubs that have 10 Mbps and 100 Mbps capabilities to bring these two worlds together.

100BaseVG-AnyLAN offers the same bandwidth as 100BaseT but uses four pairs of wires instead of two pairs in each cable. Doubling the number of pairs enables a different access method, called *demand priority,* to control access to the network medium. In addition, 100BaseVG-AnyLAN permits devices on the network to receive and transmit at the same time (that's one reason that the number of pairs in the cable is doubled).

100BaseVG-AnyLAN hubs help manage the demand priority scheme and provide arbitration services when multiple requests for network access occur at more or less the same time. When using the CSMA/CD access method, workstations listen before sending, and they transmit as soon as they recognize that the medium is not in use. This arrangement leads to collisions when two or more stations begin to broadcast at more or less the same time, especially as network utilization increases. When a demand priority device wants to transmit data across the network, it signals the hub, and the hub determines when that device may access the network. This setup eliminates collisions and allows networks to function at higher utilization rates than CSMA/CD can support.

On the downside, networking equipment and cabling for 100BaseVG-AnyLAN is more expensive than that for 100BaseT, even though 100BaseVG-AnyLAN offers better performance. Perhaps that's why 100BaseT has proven more popular in the marketplace than 100BaseVG-AnyLAN has.

Gigabit Ethernet

You're probably wondering what you can implement on your network when, even with 100 Mbps technology, you start running out of bandwidth. From there, the next step up is to Gigabit Ethernet. Although Gigabit Ethernet technologies are currently available, they're not yet in broad use. However, because the need for speed will never decrease, we want to give you a taste of this technology so you can salivate over it — even if it's unlikely to show up in your office any time soon.

To begin with, Gigabit Ethernet is not a networking solution for the desktop. (In fact, no conventional PC or other desktop machine can come close to saturating a Gigabit Ethernet network.) Rather, Gigabit Ethernet is used primarily as a backbone technology, especially in large networks where certain pathways need to carry huge amounts of traffic. Ideally, Gigabit Ethernet helps boost server-to-server communications and permits ultra-fast data transfers between switches on a network backbone.

Gigabit Ethernet uses the CSMA/CD access method and the same frame size and formats as conventional Ethernet. Therefore, you can integrate this technology into existing Ethernet networks easily, and you don't need to buy new protocol analyzers, network management software, and so forth.

To jump on the Gigabit Ethernet bandwagon, the devices you need to add to your network include

- ✔ Suitable NICs and connectors for your servers
- ✔ Proper cables (fiber-optic, in most cases; though twisted-pair options are under development)
- ✔ Upgrades to those routers and switches to handle Gigabit Ethernet traffic

In some cases, this emerging standard may require you to replace certain pieces of equipment; but for modern routers and switches, this emerging standard requires only new EPROM chips and upgrades for certain interface cards. Eventually, as the price of the technology drops, you might even consider adding Gigabit Ethernet interfaces into your high-end workstations. This probably won't be necessary for a few more years, however.

The *Gigabit Ethernet Alliance* offers a terrific white paper on this technology. You can download it from: www.gigabit-ethernet.org/. It gives a great overview of Gigabit Ethernet and describes what types of applications demand this kind of network speed.

The Backbone's Connected to. . . Everything Else!

At two points in this chapter, you can read about technologies well suited for *network backbones* — this applies to both 10Base5 and Gigabit Ethernet. If networks have backbones, do they also have hip bones and tailbones? How about it?

Actually, the term *backbone* has a specific meaning in networking. It's a particular cable segment that connects other cable segments, or that provides a high-speed link to accommodate high-volume network traffic on cable segments where large quantities of traffic aggregate. If you think about this situation for a minute and take a quick look at Figure 7-7, you should begin to understand that saying "a cable segment that connects other cable segments" and "a cable segment where large quantities of traffic aggregate" are two ways of saying the same thing.

Simply put, a backbone provides a link to tie many other cables together. As the demand for network bandwidth goes up for individual users, the amount of traffic that backbones must carry multiplies accordingly. Just as a human backbone holds the body together and carries the central nervous system to the brain, a network backbone ties all its pieces together. Backbones also often provide links to outside resources, such as the Internet, or access to massive centralized data collections, such as mainframe databases and their ilk.

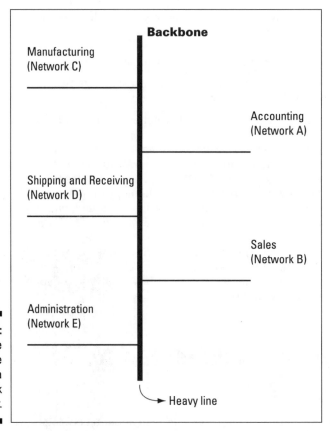

Figure 7-7:
A backbone ties all the pieces of a network together.

When There's More than One Network, It's an Internetwork

Another subtlety of networking has to do with the relationship between individual cable segments and the network that encompasses all of them. For historical reasons too tedious to relate, the term *network* is often used to describe only those devices that attach to a single cable segment.

This limited interpretation of the word *network* made it necessary to invent the term *internetwork.* An internetwork is what happens when some devices (such as repeaters, bridges, routers, and gateways) are attached to two or more cable segments to create a "network of networks." In internetworks, information from one cable segment can flow through one or more of those devices to move from one cable segment to another. The mother of all internetworks, of course, is the worldwide Internet itself, which is a network of more networks than you (or we) want to think about for too long.

 When you're dealing with technical talk about networks, be sure that you understand what the word network means in the context of whatever discussion is underway. In most cases, it doesn't matter that what may commonly be referred to as a network is really an internetwork, but when it does matter, it matters a lot. So pay attention!

Beyond Local Networks

Just as talk about backbones leads to talk about the Internet, talking about networks of networks leads inevitably to talk about *wide area networks,* or WANs. In days of yore, only companies with deep pockets could afford WAN links, because they were too expensive. Today, with high bandwidth connections to *Internet Service Providers* (ISPs) becoming increasingly common, small- to medium-sized outfits now have to worry about linking their internetworks to other networks using a variety of long-haul digital links.

For most Windows 2000 Server-based networks, understanding how to connect to your local ISP is all the WAN linking you'll ever need to do. For most situations, this means T1 or slower technologies. For these circumstances, Windows 2000 Server performs creditably as a router, or works admirably with an external routing device to help you make the outside connections your network needs.

The many flavors of WAN links

WAN links run the gamut of functionality, bandwidth, and associated costs, and include a broad range of technologies. These days, Windows 2000 Server does a good job of supporting all types of WAN links because of its multiprotocol and router support, including:

✓ **Integrated Services Digital Network (ISDN):** This relatively low-speed digital link connects through the telephone system, giving it nearly global reach. Windows 2000 Server includes built-in drivers for a variety of ISDN interfaces and supports a broad range of ISDN-based bandwidths. Normal ISDN connections occur through a so-called *basic rate interface* (BRI) and support one or two 64 Kbps data channels for a maximum bandwidth of 128 Kbps. Monthly costs for a typical ISDN connection vary from a low of $100 a month to as high as $500 a month in some markets. Some ISDN rates accumulate on a per minute basis, so be sure to check with your local telecomm company.

✓ **General Digital Subscriber Line (xDSL):** This term describes a higher-bandwidth technology that also uses conventional phone lines to handle digital data. (There are many types of DSL lines; therefore, the x stands for general.) Windows 2000 Server also includes drivers for a range of xDSL devices, and new xDSL devices are sure to provide drivers for this popular operating system. Most conventional xDSL devices offer bandwidths that range from 256 Kbps to as high as 1.544 Mbps. xDSL costs are still unclear in many markets, but it looks like xDSL will ultimately replace ISDN.

✓ **Cable modems:** Cable modems use CATV coaxial cables to send and receive network data. Although cable modems are not available in all markets, most metropolitan areas serviced by national cable TV companies, such as Time Warner or Cox Communications, now offer cable modem connections. Cable modems usually offer high bandwidth downstream (up to 1.544 Mbps for incoming data) but less bandwidth upstream (up to 512 Kbps for outgoing data). Cable modems are way cheap and can cost as little as $40 a month (but the medium is shared, unlike all the other alternatives mentioned here, so more users means less individual bandwidth).

✓ **T1/E1 or T3/E3:** These terms name the most common high-end digital services for medium-sized companies and larger. T1/T3 describes two classes of digital service available in North America; E1/E3 describes two similar classes of service available in Europe and elsewhere in the world. Bandwidth for T1 is 1.544 Mbps; for T3 it's 45 Mbps; for E1 it's 2.048 Mbps; and for E3 it's 34.368 Mbps. All these services cost at least $1,000 a month and use expensive equipment. T3/E3 costs $20,000 a month or more in most markets.

✓ **Asynchronous Transfer Mode (ATM):** This describes an extremely high-bandwidth technology. It's the WAN technology of choice for phone and other communications companies, and comes in a variety of implementations that range from 155 Mbps to 2.48 Gbps. Windows 2000 Server includes support for lower-speed ATM implementations.

Part III

Servers, Start Your Engines!

The 5th Wave
By Rich Tennant

SURE, HE'S A LITTLE DIFFERENT, BUT HE WORKS HARD AND KEEPS THE SYSTEM FREE OF BUGS,

In this part . . .

When the networking basics are covered, you can jump into the details involved in installing and configuring Windows 2000 Server. That's precisely what this part of the book is all about. It begins with coverage of the Windows 2000 product family (there's more than Server going on here, you know) and continues with detailed coverage of the installation and configuration of the Windows 2000 Server software itself. Connections to the outside world are covered next, in a chapter that explains how to connect your Windows 2000 Server to the Internet, and how to provide dial-in/dial-out access to your users is also covered.

After that, it's on to Active Directory — also known as the "nerve center" of Windows 2000 Server — for a couple of bracing chapters that discuss how to install, configure, and use this powerful new addition to the Windows Server family. From there, it's on to working with printers and print services in the Window 2000 environment. And finally, the chapter ends with a refreshing discussion of TCP/IP addressing and configuration details that anybody who works with Windows 2000 Server should find interesting, if not downright informative.

In short, Part III takes you through just about everything you need to know to install Windows 2000 Server and make it useful on a network for your users. Although some of its more exotic and outlandish services are not covered in this part, what is included will get your network up and running with minimal muss and fuss.

Along the way, you learn how to build a powerful networking environment around Windows 2000 Server, including basic system and network configuration, printing and directory services, and more. You also discover how to use Windows 2000 Server to deliver the goods across a network, be it for file or print services or something a bit more exciting.

Chapter 8

Meet Windows 2000

● ●

In This Chapter

▶ Introducing the Windows NT successor

▶ Understanding Windows 2000 basics

▶ Appreciating the benefits that Windows 2000 can confer

● ●

*F*or a while, Microsoft has been using the slogan "built on Windows NT technology" to help its users understand part of what Windows 2000 (or Windows 2000, Standard Edition in Microsoft-ese) is all about. On the other hand, Microsoft has also been keen on stressing Windows 2000's new features as well — including such catchphrases as "Active Directory," "IntelliMirror," "Plug and Play compatible," and more.

If we ignore the details for a moment, we see that between these two claims lies a fundamental truth about Windows 2000: From a low-level, nuts-and-bolts perspective of basic operating system functions, Windows 2000 is more like Windows NT than it is different from Windows NT. However, in terms of what it looks like (what computer geeks like to call the *Graphical User Interface,* or GUI) and in terms of some of the things it can do (this is where the aforementioned catchphrases come into their own), Windows 2000 is fundamentally different from Windows NT.

"How's that again," you ask? Try to think of Windows 2000 this way: From a low-level, basic functionality operating system perspective, Windows 2000 is very much like (almost identical, in most ways) Windows NT. But, from the perspective of what the software looks like when it's running, how its desktop and utilities are organized, and the kinds of functionality it supports, Windows 2000 is quite different — and in many ways far superior — from Windows NT. If Windows operating systems were automobiles, a pithy way to sum this up would be: "Similar under the hood, but a completely new body, suspension, instrument panel, and interior."

In this chapter, you find out more about what makes Windows 2000 like and unlike Windows NT. You also learn about some of the cool new things that Windows 2000 can do that Windows NT never dreamed of, and about the new lineup of software components that make up the Windows 2000 software family.

The Very Basics of Windows 2000

From a more whimsical perspective, the numeric part of the product's name points to one important difference between Windows 2000 and Windows NT. Right out of the box, Windows 2000 is *Y2K ready.* In English, this means that Windows 2000 won't get discombobulated by the strange behavior of the calendar that occurs in the year 2000, which involves everything from shifting from two-digit dates ("does '02' stand for 1902 or 2002?") to handling the odd fact that every four years there actually is a leap day in that year.

For Windows NT, on the other hand, there's a fair amount of work involved in making that software Y2K ready. In fact, there's a special CD in the Microsoft TechNet Collection in the "Extras" section called "Year 2000 and Other Resources" that was created specifically to help system administrators make Windows NT and other, older Microsoft products Y2K ready.

Beyond the issues associated with the year 2000, there's a lot to like about Windows 2000 in general. Just as Windows NT 4.0 incorporated much of the look and feel of Windows 95, Windows 2000 incorporates much of the look and feel of Windows 98 (particularly if you use Windows 98 with Internet Explorer and Active Desktop). Among other things, this means that Internet-, network-, and desktop-based resources all appear under the Windows Explorer umbrella, and all such resources can be accessed with equal facility in Windows 2000.

Furthermore, in Windows 2000 Server the *Microsoft Management Console* (MMC), which works through Internet Explorer and came on the scene with *Internet Information Server* (IIS) 4.0, becomes the primary user interface for managing a Windows 2000 Server. Although this differs quite a bit from what you may be used to from Windows NT, it provides a more consistent GUI for Windows 2000 and means that any Windows machine with a Web browser can handle at least some Windows 2000 Server management tasks.

System-level changes

At the lowest levels of the operating system — for example, the collection of files used to start up, or boot, Windows 2000 — there's little change from Windows NT to Windows 2000. In fact, files bearing the same names that we called out in the previous edition of this book to build a "generic boot floppy" for Windows NT also work to provide the same function for Windows 2000. (This is covered in Chapter 22 of this book.)

We did *not* say that you could use a generic boot floppy for Windows NT 4.0 to boot Windows 2000, or vice versa. We only said that the files required to create a generic boot floppy for Windows 2000 have the same names as their Windows NT counterparts. Although the names may be the same, the files are different enough that what works for one of these operating systems will emphatically *not* work for the other.

One of Windows 2000's interesting system-level additions is its support for the FAT32 file system — along with the older FAT implementation supported in Windows NT 4.0 — and the NT Filing System (otherwise known as NTFS), originally introduced with the earliest versions of Windows NT. (You can read more about these file systems in Chapter 9.) This enhancement allows more graceful dual-boot configurations for Windows 98 and Windows 2000 than were possible with Windows 98 and Windows NT (which couldn't read FAT32 partitions without extra help). It also supports much larger FAT32 partitions — and much larger files — than is possible with the older FAT implementation.

Another important system-level addition to Windows 2000 (which makes life easier for anyone who must install the software) is its complete support for Microsoft's Plug and Play (usually called PnP) specification. All computer hardware devices require special pieces of software called drivers to permit the computer's CPU to interact with those devices. In most cases, devices with PnP-compliant drivers will configure themselves automatically as a computer starts up and make themselves available for use without requiring human intervention.

In fact, certain PnP devices, such as removable media or PC cards, can be added to or removed from a system while it's running. Such devices are usable while present and vanish when absent, again without requiring any touch of human hands. This is a big plus, when compared to the contortions that adding hardware to or removing hardware from Windows NT systems could sometimes require. The Windows 2000 PnP support is especially tasty for those who — like your humble authors — must run the software on laptops for classroom or presentation use!

Other major system-level changes to Windows 2000, as compared to Windows NT, include its support for Kerberos-based authentication and security mechanisms, and its support for X.509-compliant certificates and certificate services. In short, these mechanisms provide much better ways of identifying who's who on your network and for controlling who gets to access what. For backward compatibility, Windows 2000 still supports old-fashioned LAN Manager authentication, but its strengthened security and access controls are expected to help provide the impetus for organizations to upgrade from Windows NT to Windows 2000. Therefore, you should expect to see Microsoft make much of these features in the months and years to come. In Chapter 18 of this book, you find a detailed discussion of the Windows 2000 security subsystems and features.

New features

One of the most interesting new tricks of Windows 2000 is its so-called "self-repairing" capability. Believe it or not, Windows 2000 is able to detect changes to key software elements, such as Dynamic Link Libraries (DLLs), where specific versions of software elements used may vary from application to application. It can run multiple versions of DLLs in what Microsoft calls *side-by-side* mode, which allows incompatible versions to be used where appropriate.

Certain pundits have said that side-by-side mode lifts Windows 2000 from "DLL hell" (where Windows NT often resided) to "DLL purgatory," but only time will tell if that description sticks. Windows 2000 also monitors changes to key software components, works with an automatic Internet-based system update facility, and can attempt repairs itself when certain known conditions occur. Our experience with self-repair has been that it's not needed often, but it's greatly appreciated when it works like it's supposed to!

If there's one new addition to Windows 2000 that sets it apart from Windows NT, it has to be its support for comprehensive directory services. Under the trade name of Active Directory, Windows 2000 Server delivers the ability to provide centralized control over users, resources, and network regions in ways that Windows NT could only dream about. From a user perspective, Active Directory makes it easier than ever before to identify and access network resources, such as files, directories, printers, applications, and so on. In addition, it's easier to use these resources directly and transparently without having to worry about to which server they belong or where on a network they reside. You have further opportunities to learn more about Active Directory in Chapters 11, 12, and 21 of this book.

You have a chance to inspect a more complete list of other changes, additions, and enhancements to Windows 2000 in the next section. By the time you finish that section, you should have a pretty good idea about the most interesting things that separate Windows 2000 from its predecessor, Windows NT.

Why Use Windows 2000 Server?

Any time a vendor, such as Microsoft, introduces a new version of a popular product, such as Windows NT, it's got to create inducements for users of the previous version to upgrade. Likewise, the company has to attract new buyers to the new version to keep ramping up sales.

Where Windows 2000 Server is concerned, those inducements can be pretty powerful. In addition, Microsoft has been careful to explain that, although Windows 2000 Server functions well in a hybrid environment that also includes Windows NT Servers, Windows 2000 Server functions better when it's the only kind of Windows server in use. In the following sections, you learn about the inducements that Microsoft is pitching to encourage upgrades, attract new users, and spur the migration to networks based entirely on Windows 2000 Servers.

Lowered TCO

Total cost of ownership (TCO) measures what it costs to acquire, install, configure, manage, and maintain a system during its entire productive life. In a magnificent case of making a virtue out of necessity, Microsoft stresses all the ways that Windows 2000 has been engineered to help lower its TCO. In effect, what's happened is that numerous problems with or deficiencies in Windows NT have been remedied in Windows 2000.

Here's what falls under this particular umbrella (much of which is sure to be appreciated by systems administrators and users alike, so we don't mean to suggest that these improvements aren't valuable or significant):

✔ **IntelliMirror management technologies:** IntelliMirror sets up a mechanism to capture updates made to any suitable client machine (which can be on Windows 2000 Server, Windows 2000 Workstation, or Windows 9*x* desktops) and save those updates to a network server. Not only does this allow the original desktop to be rebuilt or repaired on an as-needed basis, but this technology also allows users to rove from desktop to desktop, taking their applications, data, preferences, and desktop settings with them wherever they go. Because it reduces the need to re-create complex configurations and setups, IntelliMirror should greatly help reduce the cost of ownership for maintaining complex modern systems.

✔ **Broad and varied management tools are supported:** Windows 2000 includes an improved and expanded set of built-in remote management tools for networks, desktops, servers, and other key network components. Windows 2000 also works with management agents and software from other vendors, such as Tivoli Systems, Hewlett-Packard, NetIQ, and Microsoft's own Systems Management Server (SMS). Because the Windows 2000 systems can now work with these other vendors, the cost of ownership for maintaining complex modern systems should be significantly reduced.

✔ **Easy to learn and easy to use:** By making Windows 2000 much like Windows 98, Microsoft hopes to leverage that learning curve for those who work with Windows 2000. Even better, Windows 2000 includes numerous wizards and other automation tools that store frequently used fields (such as username and password) and can supply them on demand when input context indicates such data might be helpful. The Windows 2000 desktop is also quite friendly, shows Start menu items based on usage patterns, and is extremely easy to reconfigure and customize. By shortening the learning curve and increasing usability, overall costs of ownership should be reduced at the user level, which is where costs are typically highest.

✔ **Remote computing boosts productivity:** With its inclusion of terminal server technology, plus Web-based remote management and administration tools that can work on any desktop with a suitable Web browser installed, Windows 2000 is easier to set up, configure, and manage than any earlier versions of Windows. This should help manage the cost of ownership for networks; especially for those networks where local expertise may be missing or low, but where global expertise can be applied remotely to handle situations and solve problems that may be beyond the abilities of branch office workers.

✔ **Network-wide availability and access:** The combination of Active Directory — with its globally available window on network resources, access controls, security, and administration — and the Web-based capabilities of Windows 2000's configuration and management tools makes Windows 2000 networks easier to install and maintain for administrators. In addition, it's easier for end users to navigate and use. By lowering the human costs of networking, Windows 2000 therefore promises to significantly lower the costs of ownership and the costs of the equipment and software that make networks work.

In fact, there's even more to Windows 2000's abilities to help control TCO than we could cover in the foregoing bullets. By addressing user concerns stemming from earlier implementations and working to improve Windows 2000's ease of installation, configuration, and everyday use, Microsoft has come up with a truly impressive "benefits package." You should discover that, although such benefits can sometimes seem subtle and elusive, they are quite real when it comes to making the job of a network or systems administrator easier and more straightforward.

Faster and more reliable

This category covers a multitude of Windows 2000 features, all of which contribute either to improved system performance, availability, or reliability. Among the many items that belong to this category, these are the most noteworthy:

✔ **Increased levels of system test:** Microsoft has done more in-house testing — with more hardware configurations — for Windows 2000 than for any preceding version. Likewise, it's released many more beta copies to take advantage of pre-final release user feedback.

✔ **Hardened memory management:** Windows 2000's *Virtual Memory Manager* (VMM) is more robust than earlier versions, and handles illegal memory references from applications, system components, or device drivers better than ever before. In fact, Windows 2000 also includes a signing mechanism for device drivers, so administrators can configure systems to run only those device drivers with valid digital signatures.

✔ **File system enhancements:** By including a disk defragmenter and speeding basic file-system IO operations in the NTFS file system, Windows 2000 can read and write to disk drives faster than earlier versions.

✔ **Fewer reboots and faster restarts:** Windows 2000 only needs to be rebooted after completing about seven system-configuration tasks; Windows NT had to be rebooted after running any of 40-odd system configuration tasks. Also, reduced memory dump requirements, safe mode startup options, a faster CHKDSK utility, and automated system recovery tools make it much easier to restart (or rebuild) Windows 2000 systems.

In the faster and more reliable category, we view Microsoft's efforts to reduce the number of system reboots as the most significant. This helps address one of the most common complaints about Windows NT in general and Windows NT Server in particular.

Exploit the full advantages of Active Directory

It's true that Active Directory can emulate the Windows NT domain model to the point of supporting Windows NT-based backup domain controllers (BDCs) in hybrid Windows 2000 Server/Windows NT Server domains. Active Directory can also support old-style, NetBIOS-based Windows networking client software and LAN Manager-style authentication models.

However, using these features in a hybrid network means that native Windows 2000 Kerberos- and certificate-based security cannot be used to their fullest extent. It also means that the complete structure that a forest of Active Directory directory trees can support will not be available to older clients.

After a network switches all its servers from Windows NT to Window 2000, and clients are upgraded to include Active Directory support, the capabilities of Windows 2000 Server can be much more fully exploited. Administrative controls can be defined for individual machines, groups of machines, single domains, or multiple domains. (In Windows NT, domain administration is more an "all or nothing" proposition.)

In fact, Active Directory-enabled applications can use directory data to find network resources (such as files and printers) without requiring any user direction at all on a "pure Windows 2000" network. Best of all, much more powerful, multi-leveled security controls can be imposed upon resources at the domain, machine, or individual resource level. In addition, Windows 2000 can enforce much more rigorous authentication to make sure that the user ID used to request a resource matches the true identity of the actual requester of that resource.

Microsoft is playing these enhanced capabilities as its trump card to encourage organizations to upgrade wholesale to Windows 2000. The marketplace hasn't yet had time to make its reaction to this strategy known, but the advantages are pretty compelling.

More networking

Windows 2000 supports improved networking access and reliability in a number of ways. Right off the bat, Windows 2000 supports third-party multi-homing solutions that employ multiple NICs, where one or more functions in a *hot-standby capacity*. This means that failure of the primary interface causes failover to a secondary interface, which helps guarantee the continued availability of important network resources in the event of NIC or media failures. Windows 2000 also shares a common driver model with Windows 98, which instantly makes a vast array of high-speed networking technologies and devices available for Windows 2000 to use. This approach also helps assure system administrators that drivers for the latest, fastest, newest networking technologies will be readily available for Windows 2000 when they're released.

Windows 2000 also includes support for high-bandwidth storage area networking technologies, such as Fibre Channel and I20 devices. These technologies allow data to be located almost anywhere on a network, yet be instantly available to whatever server might be called upon either to use that data itself or to provide it to satisfy a client service request.

Improved Internet and network access

Windows 2000 Server includes the latest release of IIS 5.0 (which is now expanded as Internet Information Services, instead of server). This software takes advantage of the improved performance and reliability of Windows 2000 to provide more uptime for Web-based services. In addition, improved support for *Active Server Pages* (ASP) technology makes it easy for Windows 2000 to support powerful, Web-based applications.

Windows 2000 also includes a substantially improved set of application services, including interfaces that already support advanced server functions, such as clustering, load balancing, and transaction processing. In plain English, Windows 2000 makes it easier than ever before to create powerful, reliable applications that share data and code across the network. In fact, all Windows 2000 applications services are Internet-ready, which means they can be deployed with equal success on an in-house LAN, across an intranet or extranet, or across the Internet itself.

Advanced administration tools

Perhaps the most notable change from Windows NT to Windows 2000 affects how systems are administered. Windows 2000 integrates the vast majority of system management tools under the MMC, which brings some much-needed structure and consistency to management applications. The structure of these utilities is different enough that you have a learning curve to climb even if you're already familiar with Windows NT. In fact, Windows 2000 Server feels almost like a brand-new operating system when you're using its management utilities.

However, after that learning curve has been climbed, it's easier to locate and use important system management utilities for everything from services to hardware and software configuration management to networking. If you've ever worked with MMC in IIS 4.0, you have some idea of what to expect. If not, we can only predict that you should be pleasantly surprised.

This does not imply that the hodgepodge of Control Panel utilities has been done away with. In fact, many of your favorites are still there. But, when it comes to managing Active Directory, users, accounts, resources, Web components, and more, you'll find it easy to learn — and like — what's new and different about Windows 2000 as compared to Windows NT.

Chapter 9

Ready . . . , Set . . . , Install!

In This Chapter

▶ Upgrading or installing from scratch?

▶ Knowing if you have the horsepower

▶ Using the Windows 2000 Server installation utilities

▶ Installing Windows 2000 Server, step-by-step

▶ Troubleshooting snafus

▶ Automating installations

*W*indows 2000 Server is relatively easy to install, but it can take up to two hours from start to logon. Many of the delays can be reduced or avoided with just a little planning. By following our suggestions in this chapter, we hope that you can avoid some common installation problems, many of which relate to lack of correct equipment. If you have problems, we provide a troubleshooting section to smooth out any ruffles you encounter along the way.

Installation: Upgrade or New?

Whether you're installing Windows 2000 Server for the first time or you're upgrading from a previous version, planning can help ensure a smooth installation.

Upgrade, as the term implies, means that you currently have an operating system installed on your computer and you wish to install Windows 2000 over the existing operating system while retaining as many settings as possible. Windows 2000 provides upgrade paths from Windows 9*x*, Windows NT Workstation, and Windows NT Server 3.51 and 4.0.

Note that there is also an upgrade path from beta versions of Windows 2000.

If you select to perform an upgrade installation of Windows 2000 Server, we strongly recommend that you begin by backing up all the data on every machine that you plan to upgrade. (We cover backups in Chapter 17.) Although you can upgrade to Windows 2000 without losing current data, hardware and software sometimes have minds of their own and can mess things up. A smidgen of prevention can save you some real heartache!

Installing means you're adding Windows 2000 to a computer that may or may not have an existing operating system. On systems with existing operating systems, you can select to replace the current one or create a multi-boot system. A multi-boot system is a computer hosting two or more operating systems. You're given a choice upon bootup as to which operating system will be loaded. In some multi-boot configurations, data from one operating system will not be accessible from other operating systems (for example, NTFS partitions from Windows 2000 Server cannot be accessed from Windows 95 or Windows 98).

If you're installing Windows 2000 Server for the first time, you need to make some decisions about how you're going to set up the server before you install the software. You have the following three basic ways to install Windows 2000 Server:

- ✔ **CD-ROM:** This type of installation requires that you have a computer with a local CD-ROM drive installed. CD-ROM installations do not require a network interface card (NIC), but if you plan on connecting the system to a network, it's best to have the NIC in place during installation. We focus on this type of installation in this chapter.

- ✔ **Across the network:** This type of installation requires network access and that the CD-ROM files be available on the network. Network access can be gained either from an existing operating system or via a boot floppy.

- ✔ **Automated:** This type of installation requires you to input installation information into a data file that you can then merge into a script file for execution.

Preparing for the battle

We offer the following pre-installation list to help you gather the information and equipment that you need for your setup. Windows 2000's Setup program doesn't require all the items that we list in the following sections during installation, but we like to have everything handy whenever we perform an installation so we don't need to run around looking for things during the process.

Manuals

The following is a list of books that you may want to have within arm's reach (although, of course, this book is the most important):

- ✔ **Windows 2000 manuals:** The manuals you receive with Windows 2000. In some cases they are in print form, in others they are only available in electronic form either from the distribution CD or online at the Microsoft Web area, which is `www.microsoft.com/windows/`.

- ✔ **Computer hardware manuals:** The manuals for the base machine and all additional components or peripherals on which you plan to install Windows 2000. You especially want to have the manuals for your NIC(s) and video cards.

- ✔ **DOS manuals:** You need these if you don't know how to create a DOS partition using the FDISK utility. (A DOS partition is where you will load DOS drivers and other information.)

- ✔ **Modem manual (optional):** Grab this manual only if you plan to install one or more modems on this server.

Software

Make sure that you have the following software handy so you don't find yourself hunting around halfway through the installation:

- ✔ **Windows 2000 Server CD-ROM:** This disc is the CD-ROM that ships with Windows 2000 Server. You also need the CD key number from the yellow sticker on the back of the jewel case.

- ✔ **Windows 2000 Server Service Pack CD-ROM or downloaded file:** Don't expect a Service Pack for Windows 2000 for at least three months after it's officially released, but, rest assured, there will be enough bugs or errors that a Service Pack will be necessary. When this occurs, you can follow our advice and instruction on the Service Packs. Until then, you can skip the Service Pack section later in this chapter.

- ✔ **DOS disks:** The latest version of DOS (probably 6.22), including the FDISK utility, that you need to create a small FAT partition.

- ✔ **NIC driver:** Windows 2000 Setup should find the NIC in the server, but keep a floppy with the necessary drivers handy in case it doesn't.

- ✔ **Small Computer System Interface (SCSI) drivers:** Windows 2000 Setup should recognize all SCSI devices if they're listed in the Hardware Compatibility List (HCL). Again, keep the drivers handy just in case.

Hardware

Of course, setting up Windows 2000 Server also requires some hardware, particularly the following:

- ✔ **Computer:** You must have this item to install Windows 2000 Server! Make sure that it complies with the HCL. Remember that you'll need at least a Pentium 166 MHz CPU, but we don't think you'll be satisfied with anything slower than 233 MHz. You also want to have a mouse attached to the computer — it just makes life easier!

- ✔ **RAM:** The more memory that you can afford, the better. We like at least 128MB. If you can afford it, you'll get better results with 256MB.

- ✔ **CD-ROM drive:** If you're installing Windows 2000 Server from a CD-ROM, you need this item installed. Later model computers allow this drive to participate in the boot sequence, and this allows you to start your Windows 2000 installation directly from the CD.

- ✔ **Hard disk:** You should have at least 4GB of disk storage space.

- ✔ **Modem:** If this server connects to the Internet or provides access to remote users, a modem (either internal or external) is one way to provide this connection. We prefer at least a 56 Kbps modem.

- ✔ **Video:** VGA or higher resolution video adapter and monitor.

- ✔ **Cables:** Depending on the components you install, you may need modem cables, telephone cables, power cords, monitor cables, and more.

Information

You need to make several choices as you go through the setup routine. You're better off if you already have an idea of what you're going to answer before you begin the install. Consider the items in the following list:

- ✔ **SETUP.TXT file:** The Windows 2000 Server installation CD provides this file, which you find in the \setuptxt subdirectory, for some last-minute information and installation details gathered too late to include in the printed manuals. Check there for a lot of good information.

- ✔ **FAT/NTFS:** *NTFS Version 5* is the Windows 2000 native file system and is much more secure than the File Allocation Table (FAT) file system. We recommend that you create only a small FAT partition (200MB) using the DOS FDISK utility and format the remainder of your hard disk as NTFS. Doing so allows you to load drivers and other components onto your system for emergency use if the system crashes. You can partition the hard disk with the operating system of your choice; we find DOS efficient for what we need to do while troubleshooting.

- ✔ **Licensing:** You need to know how you purchased your Windows 2000 and client licenses, because the Windows 2000 Setup program asks you whether you want per-seat or per-server licensing.

- **Computer name:** Each computer needs a unique name that you can identify easily on the network.

- **Workgroup/domain name:** If this is the first domain controller installed in a network, you must create a domain name. If this computer joins a current domain where a domain controller already exists, you're better off connecting this computer to a network with access to that domain. If you're installing Windows 2000 into a workgroup, you need the workgroup name. Remember it's an either-or setting, but you can always change your mind later.

- **Protocols:** Determine which protocols this computer uses (or will use) to communicate. If you're planning to use the Transmission Control Protocol/Internet Protocol (TCP/IP), see Chapter 14 for more details. Decide whether you must configure TCP/IP manually or automatically through a Dynamic Host Configuration Protocol (DHCP) server. If this server connects to the Internet, make sure that you have a valid IP address.

- **Remote connectivity options:** Determine if the server connects (or will connect) to the Internet or host a Web server. If so, you can install Internet Information Services (IIS) to provide Web services and Remote Access Services (RAS) for the connectivity. RAS can also enable your users or customers to dial into the network. You can always install RAS and IIS later. In either case, you need a working Internet connection.

- **Server roles:** The game has changed in regard to the roles servers can play when maintaining a domain. The function of your server may affect how you install Windows 2000 Server, but it's no longer a life-threatening decision because it's not configured until after initial installation is complete. We've moved this discussion into later chapters to help explain it, so see Chapters 11 and 12 for more details.

Got Enough Horsepower?

Before you install Windows 2000 Server (whether just upgrading or performing a new installation), you need to know Microsoft's minimum hardware requirements. If your server doesn't match these requirements at the barest minimum, your installation can halt midway and leave you stuck. Microsoft goes easy on its minimum requirements, so we provide some more realistic numbers to match real-world needs. If you follow Microsoft's numbers, you can expect to end up with a "doo-dah" server that lacks the "zip-a-dee" part. Table 9-1 shows a comparison between Microsoft's numbers and our real-world numbers.

Table 9-1	Minimum Requirements: Microsoft versus Dummies	
Item	*Microsoft Says*	*Real World Says*
Processor	Pentium 166 MHz	Pentium 233 MHz or better
RAM	128MB	256MB or better
Monitor	VGA	SVGA or better
NIC	None*	One (at least 32 bit)
CD-ROM	None	12X or better
Hard disk	850MB+**	1GB or better***
Floppy disk	3.5"	3.5" high density

*Note: A NIC is required for direct network access. If a NIC is not present at the time of installation, one can be easily installed later.

**Note: 850MB is only the minimum required for a system meeting minimum requirements. An additional 2MB should be added for every additional MB of RAM above 65MB. Also, some non-default components may require additional space. Both FAT system partitions and installations over a network require an additional 100-200MB of free drive space. Upgrades may also require additional space to accommodate temporary files as data is moved into Active Directory.

***Note: 1GB is only what's recommended to install just the Windows 2000 Server operating system. You must factor in items such as application software that you add to this Windows 2000 Server. For most small- to medium- sized offices, plan to start out with 4GB hard disk space, but chunk out 1GB of this for the Windows 2000 Server operating system. The system partition has an 8GB maximum.

You can squeak by with Microsoft's minimums, but many of your server's capabilities end up terribly slow or intractable. For example, even though DOS supports low-resolution monitors, you want to use a higher-resolution monitor (SVGA or better) because of the Windows 2000 Server graphical user interface (GUI). More is better in many cases (disk space, RAM, processor power, and so on). Buy as much as your budget allows so you don't need to upgrade too soon.

Take a trip to Microsoft's Web site, particularly the Windows 2000 Server pages at www.microsoft.com/windows/. There you can find white papers and Frequently Asked Questions (FAQs) that answer common questions to many issues, such as licensing, minimum requirements, upgrades, and more. If you don't find enough answers there, head to www.ntfaq.com for a searchable Windows NT FAQ site — it hosts a separate section for Windows 2000 information.

Another important item to check is whether your server appears on Microsoft's HCL. Microsoft's test lab spends its time testing products for compatibility with Windows 2000. Obtaining Microsoft lab certification means that an organization can display Microsoft's logo on its product or products. Similarly, Microsoft places listings for certified products in its HCL.

Windows 2000 utilities aplenty

Utilities abound for Windows 2000 because of its popularity. No single operating system can do everything that users want. Programmers and others adept at computing typically develop small scripts or programs to perform functions that the basic operating system doesn't include. You can find many of these utilities, especially installation tools, on the Internet at popular Windows 2000/NT Web sites, such as http:// windowsnt.miningco.com or www.bhs. com.

In some cases, the same tool used on Windows 9x or Windows NT will work on Windows 2000 Server. However, be forewarned that this is not always the case. You should test applications on Windows 2000 before you actually use them in situations where data loss is possible.

Microsoft sells a Windows 2000 Resource Kit. You can purchase this kit on the Internet or at a bookstore. The package includes utilities for installation, file management, troubleshooting, and planning purposes. The following list of installation tools gives a good notion of what comes with this kit:

- **ADSIEDIT:** This is an Active Directory low-level editor and a Microsoft Management Console (MMC) snap-in. It simplifies the creating, editing, and removing of Directory Service objects and attributes.

- **BROWSTAT:** A character-based diagnostic tool used to investigate the browser server status in domains and workgroups.

- **LDP:** A tool used to connect, bind, search, modify, add, and delete entries in any *Lightweight Directory Access Protocol* (LDAP)-compatible directory, such as Active Directory.

- **NETDIAG:** A network diagnostic tool to locate connectivity problems.

- **DXDIAG:** A tool used to display data about components and drivers of the Microsoft DirectX *application programming interface* (API) present on the system.

- **NLTEST:** A tool used to perform various administrative tasks, such as synchronizing account databases, listing domain controllers, forcing a shutdown, and observing trust status.

- **DSKPROBE:** A sector editor used to directly edit, save, and copy data on physical hard drives that may not be accessible any other way. It can be used to repair the Master Boot Record (MBR) and partition sectors.

- **PPTPCLNT and PPTPSRV:** Utilities used to verify *Point-to-Point Tunneling Protocol* (PPTP) activity.

- **MEMSNAP:** A tool used to take a snapshot of current memory resources to identify which process are using which sections of memory.

Selecting a network server from the ones listed in the HCL helps ensure the smoothest installation possible, because you know Microsoft has already tested and certified that product. Certifying products for the HCL is an ongoing task at Microsoft, and the company maintains an updated HCL on its Web site (www.microsoft.com/hcl/default.asp) for all of its current operating system releases. A text file of the HCL is also available from ftp.microsoft. com/services/whql/win2000hcl.txt.

If you're unsure about the compatibility of an entire system or a specific component, you can either look it up on the HCL or employ a Microsoft *Windows Hardware Quality Labs* (WHQL) Hardware Compatibility Test CD. This test CD is used to inspect the compatibility of each component of a system with a particular operating system. This test CD is a major advance over the *Hardware Query Tool* (HQT) for Windows NT 4.0, which went out of date a month after it was released. The CD can be ordered for a single release or as a four-update subscription from www.microsoft.com/hwtest/sysdocs/.

Step-by-Step: Installing Windows 2000

In this section, we walk you through an entire Windows 2000 Server installation — screen by screen. We don't have enough space in this book to present screens for every possible type of installation, so in this section, we provide instructions on how to install Windows 2000 Server from a CD-ROM, employing the four boot floppies and accepting the default options. We divide this coverage into sections to make it easier to read and digest.

Server: Are you ready?

The first major task in getting the software onto a Windows 2000 Server is to make the server ready for the process. Generally, these are the issues you must resolve before traveling into the Windows 2000 Server installation process, so follow these steps:

1. **Ensure that all hardware is HCL compatible.**

   Whereas it's possible to install Windows 2000 onto a system with some components not on the HCL, it's not always an easy task. In short, if it's not HCL compatible, you don't want to keep it in your system.

2. **Create a 200MB DOS partition using the DOS FDISK utility.**

   Note that creating a DOS FAT partition is not strictly required to install Windows 2000. However, we've found, through many bad experiences, that the ability to boot to DOS can help resolve problems or configure devices in ways not possible directly through Windows 2000 Server. If you desire, you can skip this step.

3. **Install the NIC in the server.**

   Don't close the server's case — you may need to adjust that card's settings. Fortunately, Windows 2000 supports Plug and Play, so most card changes can be made on the fly — that is, unless you've got a card so old it still uses dual in-line package (DIP) switches or jumpers.

4. **(Optional.) Install the modem into the server if you need an internal modem and want to connect this server to external sources such as the Internet.**

Windows 2000 Setup: DOS portion

There are several different ways to launch the installation of Windows 2000 Server:

- ✔ **Floppy boot disks:** Windows 2000 ships with four boot diskettes and a CD. You start the installation of Windows 2000 with the three installation disks, and then you're prompted for the CD. The installation floppies load CD-ROM drivers; therefore, when you're asked to insert the CD, hopefully the Windows 2000 drivers will recognize your drive. If not, you have to load the CD drivers for your drive model manually.

- ✔ **CD-ROM boot installation:** If your computer allows the CD-ROM drive to participate in the boot sequence, you can boot the Windows 2000 installation program from the CD and omit the use of the floppies.

- ✔ **CD-ROM from operating system installation:** If the operating system already on your computer gives you access to the CD-ROM drive, you can launch the Windows 2000 setup without the boot floppies. (See the "Installing Directly from the CD-ROM" section later in this chapter for details.)

- ✔ **Across the network installation:** You can perform this if the Windows 2000 installation files are available on some other computer on the network. The files can be on a shared CD-ROM drive or a copy of the contents of the distribution CD can be on a network share. See the "Installing Across a Network" section later in this chapter for details.

- ✔ **Remote Installation:** Microsoft has created a new Remote operating system (OS) Installation procedure that enables network administrators to push a Windows 2000 installation out to network clients.

If you've lost your four setup disks, you can rebuild them by obtaining four blank formatted floppies and executing MAKEBOOT (16-bit tool) or MAKEBT32 (32-bit tool) from the \BOOTDISK directory on the CD. This launches a creation routine that creates the floppies for you. Just follow the simple prompts, and you'll soon be ready to go!

The following steps begin the Windows 2000 installation process from a CD-ROM, employing the four boot floppies and accepting the default options. The entire installation is actually comprised of two distinct sections, a DOS, text-only portion and a GUI portion. We discuss these sections separately and in order. Ready, set, here are the DOS-based steps:

1. Insert the Windows 2000 Server CD-ROM into the CD-ROM drive.

2. Insert the Setup Boot Disk 1 floppy into the floppy drive and reboot the computer.

3. After data is copied from the first disk, you're prompted to insert the second disk. The prompt that appears is similar to the following:

```
Please insert the disk labeled
Windows 2000 Server Setup Disk #2
into Drive A:
* Press ENTER when ready.
```

   Remove Disk #1, insert Disk #2 and then press Enter. Repeat this for Disks #3 and #4.

4. After data from Disk #4 is read, the Windows 2000 Server Setup routine prompts you with:

```
Welcome to Setup.
This portion of the Setup program prepares Microsoft (R)
        Windows 2000 (TM) to run on your computer.
* To set up Windows 2000 now, press ENTER.
* To repair a Windows 2000 installation, press R.
* To quit Setup without installing Windows 2000, press F3.
```

5. Press Enter to continue.

6. Setup scans your local hard drives and then presents you with the license agreement. Use the Page Down key to read the license agreement. When you're done, press F8 to indicate that you agree with its stipulations.

7. Setup scans your system for previous operating systems. If any are found, you're presented with an option to repair or continue a fresh install. We assume you're not repairing an installation at this point. Press Esc to continue.

8. Setup now prompts you to select the drive and partition where Windows 2000 Server will be installed. Use the arrow keys to select a partition hosted by a physical hard drive.

   • If you want to use all of the free space on a drive for the Windows 2000 boot partition, press Enter after selecting the location.

   • If you want to use only a portion of the free space on a drive for the Windows 2000 boot partition, press C. Next, you're prompted for the size of the partition to create. Type a value between one and the maximum space available on the drive and press Enter. The newly created partition appears on the list of drives and partitions as "New (Unformatted)." Select this new partition, and then press Enter.

- If you need to delete existing partitions, select the partition and then press D. You're then prompted to confirm partition deletion by pressing L. After you press L, the partition is destroyed.

Usually, you want to select the first drive on the system and the first free partition for the Windows 2000 boot drive. Also, you should create a partition of at least 1GB to host Windows 2000.

9. **After Setup asks for the file system with which you want to format the selected partition, select NTFS (the default) and then press Enter to continue.**

Setup spends a considerable amount of time formatting the drive, especially if the partition is larger than 1GB. After formatting is complete, setup inspects your hard drives, builds a file list, then copies lots and lots and lots and lots and lots of files from the CD to the newly formatted drive. This would be a great time to stretch, change your oil, get coffee, or learn how to cross stitch.

10. **After the copy operation is complete, you see the following message:**

```
The MS-DOS based portion of Setup is complete.
Setup will now restart your computer. After your computer
         restarts, Windows 2000 Setup will continue.
If there is a floppy disk in Drive A:, remove it now.
Press ENTER to restart your computer and continue Windows
         2000 Setup.
```

Eject the floppy and press Enter.

After the reboot, Windows 2000 Setup enters the GUI mode.

Windows 2000 Setup: GUI portion

After you complete the DOS portion of the setup, the GUI wizard loads and provides you with a guided installation from this point forward. Follow these steps:

Note that you should use caution when working through the GUI wizard. Often, after you click the Next button to continue, the system takes several seconds (sometimes up to a minute) to change the display. DO NOT TRY TO CLICK THE NEXT BUTTON AGAIN — even if you suspect that you missed the button by accident. If you click the Next button twice, you will skip screens, and the Back button does not always work; in some places it is even grayed out. If, after you wait two to five minutes, the system does not change the display, try clicking Next again.

11. **On the GUI wizard welcome screen, click the Next button to continue.**

Setup now performs a system-wide component inspection. It looks for any and all devices, including legacy and Plug and Play devices. This may take several minutes.

12. **Setup then offers you the opportunity to customize regional and keyboard settings. If you're in the United States, the defaults are correct. If not, make the necessary changes. Click Next to continue.**

13. **Setup prompts for your name as well as your organization's name. Type the necessary information into the appropriate fields. (If you're using the server for personal use, you can leave the organization's name blank.) Click Next to continue.**

14. **Setup asks you to select the type of licensing you're using: per server or per seat.**

   Check your purchase order to verify which license you purchased before marking this selection. *Per-seat licensing* is typically used on enterprise networks and *per-server licensing* on small networks. Remember that you can change from per-server licensing to per-seat licensing only once, so you must consider this installation option carefully before continuing.

   If you're not sure which option to choose, select Per Server.

   Mark either Per-Seat Licensing or Per-Server Licensing and then click the Next button to continue.

15. **Setup prompts you for a computer name and the administrative user account password.**

   Type the appropriate computer name and administrative user account password into the appropriate fields and then press Enter to continue.

   If your organization employs a naming convention, make sure the computer name you select complies with this policy.

   The administrator account password should be a non-blank, complex password of at least six characters, preferably with upper- and lower-case characters and at least one number or non-alphanumeric character. Well, that is if you don't want someone to figure it out easily.

16. **Setup displays a list of alternate components you can select to install along with the basic and default components. We're assuming that you always accept the defaults when offered options such as this.**

   If you select or deselect any components from this list, you may alter the Setup procedure. In such cases, you may need to provide additional configuration settings that you may not be prepared for. We recommend leaving well enough alone

   Click Next to continue.

17. **If a modem was detected in your computer, Setup prompts you for dialing information. In most cases, you only need to provide an area code. Enter the correct dialing information and click Next to continue.**

18. **Setup prompts you for the date, time, and time zone.**

   Enter the correct date, time and time zone information according to your present location and then click Next to continue.

19. Setup proceeds to load drivers for the detected network components. As part of this process, Setup asks you whether you want to accept the default settings or customize the settings for your network.

    - The typical settings set TCP/IP to use DHCP, a dynamic configuration service. If your network offers this service and this system is required to employ it, you can select to accept the typical settings.

    - If you need to specify an IP address, subnet mask, and default gateway, you need to select custom settings.

    After you select either typical settings or customized settings, click Next to continue.

20. If you select custom settings, Setup displays the name of the detected NIC and lists three network services: Client for Microsoft Networks, File and Printer Sharing for Microsoft Networks, and Internet Protocol (TCP/IP).

    Select Internet Protocol (TCP/IP) and then click the Properties button.

21. This displays the Internet Protocol (TCP/IP) Properties dialog box. Select the Use The Following IP Address button.

22. Fill in the fields for IP address, subnet mask, and default gateway. Click OK when finished.

23. Click Next to continue.

24. Setup prompts you for the name of the workgroup or domain this system will join.

    - If you select workgroup, type the appropriate name in the field.

    - If you select domain, type the appropriate name in the field.

    Click Next to continue.

25. If you selected domain, you're prompted for an administrator-level user account and password.

    Enter the appropriate information in the domain fields (if needed) and then click OK.

26. Setup copies and configures system components and then fine-tunes the Start menu and Registry.

    While this goes on, you get to wait. Keep waiting, and waiting, and waiting. (As if you have nothing better to do.)

    After Setup indicates that its work is done, click the Finish button to reboot your system into Windows 2000 Server for the first time.

27. The Welcome splash screen appears after reboot. Press Ctrl+Alt+Del to call up the logon dialog box.

28. When the logon dialog box appears, type your password for the Administrator account in the logon dialog box. Click OK to log in.

After several moments, the Windows 2000 Server desktop appears as a sure sign that you've successfully installed Windows 2000 Server! (Just to keep you on your toes, Windows 2000 Server automatically launches the Configure Your Server Wizard in preparation for your next set of tasks. Jump to Chapter 11 to learn more about the Configure Your Server Wizard.)

 Copying the \i386 subdirectory from your Windows 2000 Server CD-ROM to your newly installed server makes drivers and other resources immediately available to you if you want to add services and resources later on. If you don't take this recommended step, you must insert the CD-ROM every time you want to add resources or services to that machine.

Installing Directly from the CD-ROM

If you're lucky, you can install directly from the CD-ROM without having to deal with all the floppies. In fact, in some cases, installing directly from the CD-ROM is even easier than the across-the-network or automated methods. If your computer already has an existing operating system with access to the CD-ROM drive, such as DOS, Windows 3.1, Windows for Workgroups, Windows 9x, Windows NT Workstation 4.0, or Windows NT Server 4.0, you can launch the Windows 2000 Server Setup without the floppies.

To install directly from the CD-ROM drive, you need to issue one of the following from a command prompt or a Run dialog box:

✔ If you're using a 16-bit operating system, such as DOS, Windows 3.1, or Windows for Workgroups, you need to use this command:

```
<CD-ROM drive letter>:\i386\winnt
```

✔ If you're using a 32-bit operating system, such as Windows 9x or Windows NT, and you don't have autorun enabled, you need to use this command:

```
<CD-ROM drive letter>:\i386\winnt32
```

If you try to run the wrong setup program, the tool will tell you. So, just run the other one.

Manually launching setup from DOS, Windows 3.x, or Windows for Workgroups requires you to follow these steps:

1. **A DOS text-only display appears, asking for confirmation of the location of the distribution files. Make sure that this is the correct path to the i386 directory on the distribution CD-ROM. Then press Enter.**

   Setup copies files from the CD to your hard drive.

2. **After Setup informs you that all files have been copied, press Enter to reboot and continue.**

   After the machine has rebooted, the setup resumes at Step 5 of the "Windows 2000 Setup: DOS portion" section earlier in this chapter.

If you insert the Windows 2000 Server CD into a CD-ROM drive under an operating system with autorun enabled (for example, Windows 9*x* or Windows NT), the Windows 2000 Server splash screen appears and asks whether you want to upgrade to Windows 2000. By clicking Yes, you don't need to manually locate and execute WINNT/WINNT32.

Launching Setup from Windows 9*x* or Windows NT requires you to follow these steps:

1. **Select Upgrade or Install on the Welcome to the Windows 2000 Setup Wizard screen. Click Next.**

2. **Read the license agreement. Select "I accept this agreement" and then click Next.**

3. **In the Select Special Options screen, click the Advanced Options button.**

   Alter the "Windows installation folder" if the default is not satisfactory. If you want to install Windows 2000 onto a partition other than the one currently hosting an operating system, select the check box beside "I want to choose the installation partition during Setup."

4. **Click OK.**

5. **Click the Next button to continue.**

   Setup copies files from the CD to your hard drive. It then offers a 10-second delay before automatically rebooting your computer.

   After the machine has rebooted, the setup resumes at Step 5 of the "Windows 2000 Setup: DOS portion" section earlier in this chapter.

Installing Across a Network

Installing Windows 2000 Server across a network is almost exactly the same as performing the installation from a local CD-ROM. Both methods require network access (duh!) and you have to manually launch the WINNT or WINNT32 setup tools.

Manually launching setup from DOS, Windows 3.*x*, or Windows for Workgroups over a network requires little change to the process described in the previous section. However, from these operating systems, you need to map a local drive letter to the network share. Be sure this mapped letter is used to tell setup where the distribution files live. Setup automatically copies all of the data files it needs before rebooting.

Manually launching setup from Windows 9x or Windows NT over a network requires an additional checkbox. In the Advanced Option screen (you know, the one that appears when you press the Advanced Options button on the Select Special Options screen during the installation process), be sure to select "Copy all Setup files from the Setup CD to the hard drive."

Remote Installation

Microsoft has created a new Remote operating system (OS) Installation procedure that enables network administrators to push a Windows 2000 installation out to network clients. This means that Windows 2000 can be deployed on a network without requiring the administrator to go to each and every client to launch the setup.

Needless to say, this process, although simplifying multiple client installations overall, is not necessarily a simple activity. It requires the installation and configuration of several key services, namely Domain Name Service (DNS), DHCP, and Active Directory, in addition to the Remote Installation Services (RIS) itself.

The clients that will have the Windows 2000 installation pushed to them must either have an existing operating system connected to the network or be booted with a special network client boot disk.

If you want to explore the Remote OS Installation procedure further, we highly recommend that you obtain the Remote OS Installation document that is found on TechNet (`technet.microsoft.com/cdonline/Content/Complete/boes/bo/win2ksrv/technote/rmosinst.htm`). You can also find more information on remote installations in the Windows 2000 Resource Kit.

Post-Installation Stress Disorder

After you finish the basic installation, you've simply defined a basic server. You need to dress it up with things such as users, groups, domain controllers, Active Directory, applications, services, and printers, as we describe in Chapters 11 through 18. But, before you get excited and flip to those chapters, there are two more issues we'd like to mention.

Windows 2000 Service Packs

A service pack is a release of updates and patches for a software product. Microsoft is famous for releasing service packs to repair its software. This reveals the fact that Microsoft is concerned enough about its user community to maintain a product, but not concerned enough to get it right the first time. Be that as it may, Windows 2000 will probably have a service pack released sometime near the middle of the year 2000. Keep an eye out for that.

Microsoft has integrated two new capabilities into Windows 2000 to ease the burden of maintaining an up-to-date version. First, it's added the Windows Update tool, which can be configured to regularly check for new updates and prompt you whether to download and install them. Second, Microsoft has promised a method of slipstreaming a service pack into an installation while the initial setup is being performed. In other words, service packs can be applied to a distribution point so new clients automatically get installations with the service pack applied. How this occurs has not been revealed yet, but you'll probably find details about it on the Windows Update site (follow the Start⇨Windows Update command to reach it) or on the Windows 2000 Web site. (It's a link from `www.microsoft.com/windows/`.)

Microsoft also claims that Windows 2000 service packs will not entangle you in the catch-22 problem of installing files from the original distribution CD after a service pack is applied. In other words, adding new services will not require the reapplication of service packs, and the application of service packs will not require the reinstalling of services from the distribution CD.

Recently, Microsoft has started advertising the releases of its service packs, thus making it much easier for the typical user to locate, download, and apply these jewels. You'll usually find a link on the product-specific Web page off the main Windows page at `www.microsoft.com/windows/`.

Emergency Repair Disk

The Emergency Repair Disk (ERD) was a godsend tool for Windows NT 4.0 systems because it could be used to repair startup files and some portions of the Registry. However, the current status of Windows 2000 does not include a true ERD anymore. The ERD for Windows 2000 now only contains copies of the AUTOEXEC.NT, CONFIG.NT, and SETUP.LOG files. In addition, an ERD is not created during installation anymore; it can only be created through the Backup tool. (Start⇨Programs⇨Accessories⇨System Tools⇨Backup. It's the Emergency Repair Disk button on the Welcome tab.)

A new feature, *Automated System Recovery* (ASR), is partially designed to replace the function of the previous ERD repair process. ASR automatically repairs boot problems on the fly. However, it's limited to accessing the files from the `\repair` directory under the system root and the distribution files from the CD. In most cases, if the ASR alters any file modified since it was created during installation, you'll lose something — either drive configuration, system settings, user accounts, or something equally valuable. Yeah, we agree. The outlook here is bleak at best.

What this means is that if your boot partition is inaccessible, you cannot repair your system. You can manually copy the \repair directory to an alternate location (local drive, network share, or floppy), but a method to use these files is no longer present. It seems that Microsoft has decided that you're not smart enough to repair a failing system. Therefore, your only option is to reinstall. ARGH!

The only method offered to you to retain the system state is the backup. So, if you have a failing system, you need to perform a complete (or nearly complete) system restoration from backup media. We hope you have backup software that operates from DOS or a boot disk, because you'll probably need this capability when the system will not boot. (Remember, if you can't get into Windows 2000, you can't use the built-in Backup tool to restore data!)

Oops, My Installation Didn't Take

In most cases, as long as your hardware is on the HCL, installation will be a breeze. (Well, how about a long, continuous gust?) However, installation problems can occur. Here are some common problems and how you can resolve them:

- **CD-ROM problems:** The entire Windows 2000 installation ships on a CD-ROM, so if you can't read the CD, you can't install Windows 2000 (unless you're installing over a network, but even then, the distribution files have to come from a CD at some point). CD-ROMs are similar to music records in that one little scratch or speck of dust on the surface can cause problems. On the other hand, the CD may be okay, but the drive may not be functioning correctly or Windows 2000 may not recognize the drive. We hope that your drive appears on the HCL. To determine whether the drive or the CD isn't functioning, take the CD to another CD-ROM drive and see whether you can read it there. After you determine which element is the culprit, you can replace either one and retry your installation.

- **Hardware problems:** If Windows 2000 Setup doesn't recognize a server's hardware, it's likely to stop. Make sure that the machine's hardware appears in the HCL and that you configured all devices correctly. If you have more than one SCSI device, for example, make sure that they are chained correctly.

- **Blue screen of death:** Sometimes, Setup simply crashes and gives you a blue screen; other times, it gives you a display of error codes that only a propeller head could understand. By itself, the blue screen simply means that you must reboot. If you get a fancy stop screen, however, you can look at the first few lines to determine the error code. Using this number, you can look up the error message in the error-message manual. Stops typically occur if a driver problem occurs; if you look beyond the first few lines of the error-message screen, it tells you which drivers were loaded at the time the crash occurred. A good idea is to write the first few lines of the stop screen down before attempting to reboot.

✔ **Connectivity problems:** Installing a machine into an existing domain requires that the new system be able to communicate with a domain controller to create a domain computer account. If communication is not possible for any reason (wrong NIC, wrong driver, bad or missing cable, domain controller offline, too much network traffic, etc.), you will not be able to join the domain. In some cases, you can resolve the problem by quickly replacing a cable or allowing the system to try the connection a second or third time. In other cases, you can delay confronting the problem by joining a workgroup instead. Then, you can resolve any problems (such as NIC, driver, and configuration problems) with a functioning system.

✔ **Dependency problems:** Some services in Windows 2000 depend on other services loading correctly. If service A doesn't load, service B doesn't work, and you get error messages if service B is set to automatically start at bootup. If a NIC isn't installed correctly, for example, all services that use that NIC fail to start as well. Your first order of business, therefore, is to get the NIC to function correctly. If you get this far in the installation process, you can view the error logs (Start➪ Programs➪Administrative Tools➪Event Viewer) to see which service did not start and then work your way from there.

✔ **Script file errors:** The Windows 2000 automated installation program is not forgiving if you mistype a script. If a script stops midway and the Windows 2000 Setup program asks you for manual input, you entered something incorrectly. Check the input file to look for transposed letters or anything else that may be out of place. Scripts expect to feed the computer exactly what you put in the script file. If you don't enter the right information, Setup doesn't receive the information it expects.

✔ **SETUP.TXT file:** If you encounter driver problems or other problems missing from the preceding list, obtain and read this file to see whether some late-breaking news that Microsoft couldn't get into the manuals may have affected your installation. The file resides in the \setuptxt subdirectory.

About Automated Installation

Windows 2000 includes an unattended installation feature that enables you to install Windows 2000 without keyboard interaction. You need only to start the process and walk away. Unattended installation uses a script file that pipes in information and keyboard strokes from a data file that you compose in advance. If you already know all the answers to the questions that the install program asks, you can answer these questions and place them in a data file. You can use more than one data file for different types of installations.

Unattended installation is great for organizations that install Windows 2000 over and over again on machines with the same hardware configurations. Large enterprise networks that include remote offices can also take advantage of unattended installation, because home office administrators can customize script files and transmit them to remote offices. The caveat here is that you must test the script files for accuracy thoroughly in the central office; otherwise, the folks in the remote office may soon be screaming for help!

Details on creating the automation scripts are contained in the Windows 2000 Resource Kit.

Chapter 10

Configuring Connections to the Universe

*E*ven after you complete the installation of Windows 2000 Server, you're still faced with a number of decisions you have to make before you can safely say "mission accomplished." What role will the server play in the network? Will it host multiple network interfaces? Will you need remote access? In this chapter, we look into the answers to these questions and show you the steps you can take to implement your decisions.

Before you get too excited, we'd like to warn you that certain topics brought up in this chapter are just flat-out complicated. We try to give a general overview of each topic, but, in some cases, these issues are just beyond the scope of this book. When this happens, we refer you to other resources and materials where you can find meaningful, reliable coverage of the topics.

Meeting the Configure Your Server Wizard

In this section, we take you through the steps you need to take to get your Windows 2000 Server up and running. Starting at square one, you see that the first time you log on to Windows 2000 Server after completing the initial installation, you're confronted with the Configure Your Server Wizard (see Figure 10-1). This wizard appears by default when you log on unless you've unchecked the Show this Screen at Startup checkbox; however, you can always access it again by choosing Start⇨Programs⇨Administrative Tools⇨Configure Your Server.

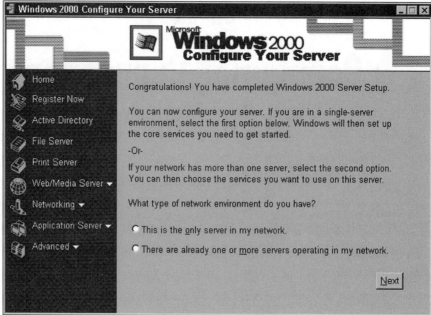

Figure 10-1:
The
Configure
Your Server
Wizard.

The Configure Your Server Wizard has nine menu options down its left side:

- ✔ **Home:** Use this option to define the network environment. You can let Windows 2000 Server know whether your system is the only server on the network or whether other servers are already present on the network.

- ✔ **Register Now:** Use this option to register your copy of Windows 2000 with Microsoft. This lets Microsoft know who you are so it can offer you a wider range of technical support (or so it claims).

- ✔ **Active Directory:** Use this option to install and configure Active Directory. Because Active Directory is such a new concept, we've devoted two chapters to explain it. See Chapters 11 and 12 for details.

- ✔ **File Server:** Use this option to set up and manage shared folders. We give you the details on shared folders in Chapter 16.

- ✔ **Print Server:** Use this option to configure and manage shared printers. We fill you in on the rewards and challenges of shared printers in Chapter 13.

- ✔ **Web/Media Server:** Use this option to configure Web and Streaming Media servers. (See the "Getting the word out" section later in this chapter for details.)

- ✔ **Networking:** Use this option to install and configure *Dynamic Host Control Protocol* (DHCP), *Domain Name Service* (DNS), *Remote Access*, and *Routing*.

✔ **Application Server:** Use this option to configure the server to host network applications, such as *Terminal Services, database servers,* and *e-mail servers.* These are fairly advanced topics; therefore, you should consult the Windows 2000 Resource Kit for more details.

✔ **Advanced:** Use this option to install and manage advanced components for Windows 2000, including *Message Queuing,* support tools, and optional components. These are fairly advanced topics; therefore, you should consult the Windows 2000 Resource Kit for more details.

Going home

The first bit of information you need to feed your Windows 2000 Server system to get it up and running is whether it's the first server on your network. If it's the first server, the Configure Your Server Wizard helps you install the core services required to maintain a *domain*. If it's not the first server in a network, you have the option of setting up the server as another domain controller or as just a member server.

For now, we assume that your server is the first server on the network. To set up your server, follow these steps:

1. **On the Configure Your Server Wizard, select the Home option from the menu list on the left side.**

   The Configure Your Server Wizard appears automatically the first time you log on to your Windows 2000 Server.

2. **Select the option that says this is the only server on my network and then click the Next button to continue.**

3. **The wizard informs you that this server will be configured as a domain controller. Several core services will be installed, including Active Directory, DHCP, and DNS.**

   Click the Next button to continue.

4. **Enter a domain name and your Internet domain name and then click the Next button to continue.**

   The domain name can be anything, as long as it abides by the NetBIOS naming restrictions and it conforms to your organization's naming convention policy. The Internet domain name would be the .com, .org, .edu, or .whatever you registered through Network Solutions (the company with which you must register all domain names). If this network is not the host of your organization's Internet services, you should just type **local** for the domain name. The wizard automatically shows you the Active Directory and DNS name equivalents based on your inputs. (For more information on the intricacies of domain names, see Chapter 12.)

5. **After digesting this information, Windows 2000 Server informs you that the computer will be restarted. After the reboot, you can configure the installed services using the ever-helpful Configure Your Server Wizard, which will appear (again).**

Click the Next button to reboot.

During the reboot, the wizard performs several configurations and service installs. You may be prompted for the Windows 2000 Server CD. If so, place it in the CD-ROM drive and click the OK button. It's very important that you do not interfere or interact with the system during this process. So, let go of the mouse and step away from the computer, or the bunny gets it!

6. **After the reboot, you're informed that you need to assign a static IP address for this server, authorize DHCP, and restart the computer again.**

If you've already assigned a static IP address, you can skip this task. Otherwise, follow the step-by-step instructions given by the wizard. To authorize DHCP, follow the step-by-step instructions given by the wizard. If you don't want to use DHCP, you can skip this task. You can always authorize it later if you want to start using it. (See Chapter 14 for more information on DHCP.)

7. **Click the OK button to inform the wizard you've performed the tasks (or at least performed the ones you wanted to).**

You'll need to manually reboot for any changes to take effect. (Yeah, rebooting again. Don't you just love it?)

If your server is not the first server on the network, you can spell out a more specific network role for it to play. By choosing the option that says there are already one or more servers operating in my network in the Home option of the Configure Your Server Wizard, you can bypass the default configurations made to the first server in a network.

At this point, you can decide which network or application components you want to install on the new server. The second, third, and fourth servers installed on a network can each have a different network role, including serving as one of the following:

- A domain controller hosting Active Directory
- A network management server hosting DHCP, DNS, *Windows Internet Name Service* (WINS), and/or Routing and Remote Access
- A file or print server
- A Web, media, or application server

We cover Active Directory in Chapters 11 and 12, file servers in Chapter 16, and print servers in Chapter 13. All you need to know about these Configure Your Server options appears in these chapters.

A Windows 2000 Server is just a stand-alone system acting like a measly workstation until you employ the configurations offered through the Configure Your Server Wizard. After you do that, it can take on almost any role you choose. Unlike Windows NT, where you have either primary or backup domain controllers, all domain controllers on Windows 2000 Server are essentially the same. Each and every domain controller shares the responsibility of maintaining the domain, updating changes to the Active Directory, and distributing authentication and communication load.

Getting the word out

Windows 2000 includes *Internet Information Services* (IIS) 5.0 and supports *Windows Media Services*. IIS allows you to host Web and *File Transfer Protocol* (FTP) sites to intranet and/or Internet users. Media Services has been designed to allow you to create stunning multimedia presentations combining audio, video, slides, interactive media, and more — all delivered by means of streaming connection.

You can use the Web/Media Server item on the Configure Your Server Wizard to jump directly to the administrative tools for IIS 5.0 and Media Services. You can also access the *Internet Services Manager* (also known as the IIS MMC snap-in), shown in Figure 10-2, by going to Start➪Programs➪Administrative Tools➪Internet Services Manager. The Media Services administration tool will probably be included in the Administrative Tools menu when Media Services is added to Windows 2000.

Because IIS 5.0 is its own application, its features are far beyond the scope of this book. If you really want to set up this service on your server, see the Windows 2000 Resource Kit or TechNet. For the detailed lowdown on IIS 5.0, check out the soon-to-be-released *IIS 5.0 For Dummies*.

Organizing the neighborhood

The Networking option on the Configure Your Server Wizard offers you quick access to the configuration tools used to manage *DHCP, DNS, Remote Access,* and *Routing.*

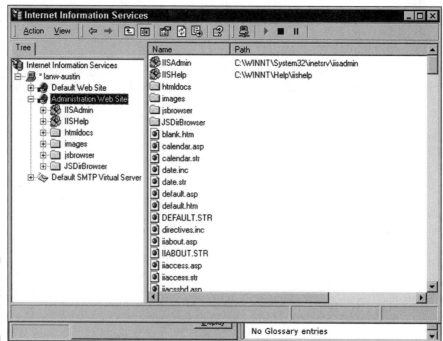

Figure 10-2:
The Internet
Services
Manager.

DHCP, or *Dynamic Host Control Protocol,* is a method of automatically configuring the *Transmission Control Protocol/Internet Protocol* (TCP/IP) settings of clients and non-critical servers upon bootup. DNS, or *Domain Name Service,* is a method of resolving host names into IP addresses. We cover both DHCP and DNS in Chapter 14.

DHCP and DNS certainly qualify as neat stuff — but before you get all excited, DHCP and DNS are fairly complex topics that are not covered in detail in this book. Please look in the Windows 2000 Resource Kit for complete instructions on configuration and management of these services.

Routing and Remote Access is the service that combines two functions: routing and remote access (duh!). Routing is the ability to direct network communications either within a local area network (LAN) or — with the help of a remote access link — across a wide area network (WAN). Remote Access is the ability to establish network connections over either telephone or *Integrated Services Digital Network* (ISDN) lines. Windows 2000 Server can act as a client to connect to remote systems or it can act as a server to accept inbound calls. Both the Remote Access and Routing selections under the Networking option on the Configure Your Server Wizard offer a link to the Routing and Remote Access management console (see Figure 10-3). With this console, you can install and configure Routing and Remote Access. Here are the basic steps to enable this service:

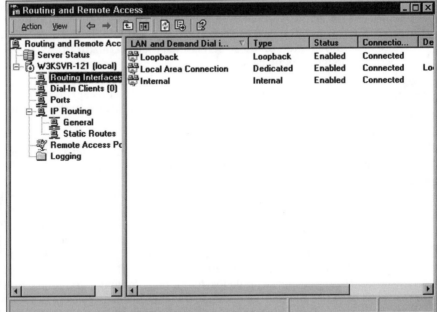

Figure 10-3:
The Routing
and Remote
Access
management
console.

1. **Open the Routing and Remote Access management console (Start⇨ Programs⇨Administrative Tools⇨Routing and Remote Access).**

2. **Click on the Routing and Remote Access item in the left pane so it displays the list of servers on the network.**

3. **Right-click over your server and select Configure and Enable Routing and Remote Access.**

   This reveals the Routing and Remote Access Server Setup Wizard.

4. **Click the Next button to continue.**

5. **The wizard then provides a selection list of common configurations and the option to manually define settings.**

   These options available in the Common Configurations windows are as follows:

   - Internet connection server

   - Remote access server

   - Virtual private network (VPN) server

   - Network router

   - Manually configured server

   Select the option that best matches your needs or select manual to customize a configuration. Click the Next button to continue.

6. **Each of the four common configuration suggestions will prompt you for further details to fine tune the system. Just follow the prompts through the rest of the wizard to complete the configuration. For more information on these selections, please consult the Windows 2000 Server Resource Kit.**

Keep in mind that to enable routing, you need at least two network interfaces. These can either be NICs or specialized connections to the Internet or even modems.

Although it looks like everything has been enabled, we recommend you reboot before you make any further modifications.

After the reboot, Routing and Remote Access is installed and functioning. All it needs now is additional interfaces and a bit of configuration. The new Routing and Remote Access interface is a *Graphical User Interface* (GUI), which — compared to the previous command-line, text-only control and display — is a great improvement. Furthermore, this management tool allows you to install routing protocols, monitor interfaces and ports, watch dial-up clients, define access policies, and modify logging parameters. You'll never want to use the ROUTE command again! However, routing is not a subject for the timid. For this reason, we recommend that you consult the Windows 2000 Resource Kit for more information. Needless to say, we don't want to leave you completely in the dark either, so we do list a few more features of Remote Access in the "Other frills" section a little later in the chapter.

Remote Connections

Remote communications consist of two distinct elements: the client and the server. Windows 2000 Server can either establish a connection to a remote system (as a dial-up client) or accept connections from remote clients (as a dial-up host). For more information on using Windows 2000 Server as a dial-up host, please see the Windows 2000 Resource Kit.

Getting connected

Using Windows 2000 Server as a dial-up client is not terribly difficult. In most cases, you dial out to an *Internet Service Provider* (ISP) to make an Internet connection. We can take you step-by-step through the process of establishing such a connection if you have the following pieces of information at hand:

- Phone number of the ISP
- Logon name
- Logon password

For this type of connection, we assume that you have a modem and not an ISDN line or other connection device. If you don't have a modem, you definitely need one. You can install a modem using the Add/Remove Hardware applet from the Control Panel. If you follow the prompts, you'll be amazed at how simple it is.

We also assume that your ISP has a simple logon procedure. If you require special characters prefixed to your logon name, must traverse a logon menu, or must execute a logon script, you need to consult with the ISP directly for instructions on how to configure Windows 2000 to properly establish a connection. Fortunately, most ISPs have a simple logon. Here's how to get things rolling:

You should have a modem installed before you follow these steps.

1. **Open Network and Dial-up Connections (see Figure 10-4) from Start⇨Settings.**

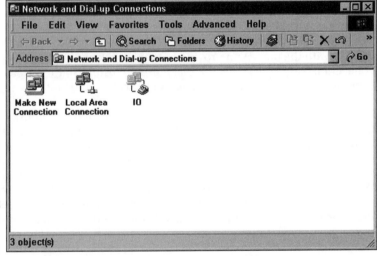

Figure 10-4:
The Network and Dial-up Connections management console.

2. **Double-click on the Make New Connections Wizard.**

3. **Click the Next button to continue.**

4. **Select the Dial-up to the Internet radio button and click the Next button to continue.**

   This launches the Internet Connection Wizard.

5. **Select the option that allows you to set up an Internet connection manually.**

6. **Click the Next button to continue.**

7. **Select the option that allows you to connect through a phone line and modem, and then click Next.**

8. **If a modem is not already installed, the wizard asks if you want Windows 2000 to automatically detect your modem or if you want to choose your modem from a list. Allow the automatic detection by clicking Next. After the modem is found and installed, click Finish.**

9. **Provide the dial-up ISP phone number in the field provided, and then click the Next button to continue.**

10. **Provide the logon username and associated password in the fields provided, and then click the Next button to continue.**

11. **Define a name for this connection, and then click the Next button to continue.**

12. **When prompted whether to configure your Internet mail account, select No, and then click the Next button to continue.**

13. **Deselect the Connect Immediately checkbox, and then click the Finish button.**

That's it! An icon now appears in the Network and Dial-up Connections window with the name you provided. Double-click on this icon to open the connection dialog box. Click the Dial button to establish the connection. After a few noisy moments, you'll establish a connection and you're ready to surf!

You can view the status of the connection by placing your mouse cursor over the connection icon (the one with the two overlapping computers) in the icon tray. You can also double-click on the icon to open a dialog box with more information.

You can change the parameters of the dial-up connection by right-clicking on the icon in the Network and Dial-up Connections window and selecting Properties from the pop-up menu. In this dialog box, you can change every aspect of the connection.

To end the connection, right-click over the connection icon in the icon tray and select Disconnect from the pop-up menu — or double-click on the connection icon to call up the Details box and then click the Disconnect button.

Other frills

Remote Access under Windows 2000 has several enhancements over the same service from Windows NT. Fortunately, it has retained nearly all of its old capabilities and functions, so you can rest assured that if you could accomplish something using Windows NT 4.0 RAS, you can do it better by using Windows 2000 Remote Access.

These features include but are not limited to:

- ✔ *Point-to-Point Protocol* (PPP) for dial-out and dial-in connections. *Serial Line Internet Protocol* (SLIP) is still retained for outbound connections to non-PPP systems

- ✔ Multilink PPP for aggregating similar connections into a single pipeline

- ✔ *Point-to-Point Tunneling Protocol* (PPTP) for link establishment over the Internet for secure communications

- ✔ Authentication encryption to secure logon passwords

- ✔ New security features: IPSec and L2TP (see the Windows 2000 Resource Kit or TechNet for more information)

- ✔ Support for smart cards (which are small cards that are added to the system to store security information)

- ✔ Full *Remote Authentication Dial-in User Service* (RADIUS) support

- ✔ Shared connections (a single computer sharing its connection with other network clients)

For an in-depth discussion of Remote Access, check out the Windows 2000 Resource Kit.

Chapter 11

Doing the Directory Thing

● ●

In This Chapter

▶ Understanding a directory service

▶ Introducing the Windows 2000 Active Directory

▶ Planning for Active Directory

▶ Installing Active Directory

▶ Coping with multiple domains

● ●

*I*n this chapter, we look at the single biggest change in Windows 2000: the implementation of a directory service known as Active Directory. You find out what a directory service is and why you want one, as well as how to plan for and install Windows 2000's exciting new Active Directory. It may not be the greatest thing since sliced bread, but it's at least as good as saltine crackers!

Many of you are already familiar with Windows NT's reliance on NetBIOS-based domains. You may even be confident about their usage and implementation. But, as the old Microsoft saying goes: "It's time to relearn everything you already know."

What Is a Directory Service?

You may not know it, but you use directory services all the time. When you get hungry and crave pizza, you open your telephone directory and look under P for this peerless paragon of sustenance. That telephone book is a kind of directory service — namely, it contains the information you need, along with a way to locate the information you require. (In this case, it's in alphabetical order.) A computerized directory service works pretty much the same way: It contains information about numerous aspects of your company, organizes that information, and provides one or more tools to help you explore the information it contains.

Windows 2000 is not the first operating system to offer a directory service. Novell's NetWare has included its *Novell Directory Services* (NDS) since 1993, starting with NetWare 4. In fact, a version of NDS is also available for Windows NT. However, Windows 2000 marks the first version of a Windows operating system that includes a built-in directory service — Active Directory. Microsoft bases the entire Windows 2000 domain structure around its directory services, rather than simply offering them as an add-on to previous domain implementations.

When it comes to its names, Microsoft has an obsession with the word *active*. There's Active Desktop, Active X, and now, Active Directory, but it's accurate. After all, Active Directory *is* active (when it's used correctly).

Meet Active Directory

To do its job properly, a directory service must meet three primary requirements:

- ✔ It must include a structure to organize and store directory data.
- ✔ It must provide a means to query and manage directory data.
- ✔ It must supply a method to locate directory data and the network and server resources that might correspond to such data. (For example, if the directory data includes a pointer to a file and a printer, the directory service must know where they reside and how to access them.)

Windows 2000's Active Directory fulfills all these requirements using various technologies. For more information about Active Directory, pick up a copy of *Active Directory For Dummies* by Marcia Loughry (IDG Books Worldwide Inc.).

Organizing and storing data

The structure is implemented using the *ISO X.500 protocol*. (ISO stands for *International Organization for Standardization*.) The hierarchical structure of an X.500 directory is shown in Figure 11-1. This is a common standard used in nearly all directory services, including not only Microsoft's Active Directory, but also Novell Directory Services (NDS), Netscape products, and other implementations. X.500 has proven to be useful for this application because it organizes data in a hierarchy that breaks an organization's directory information into a variety of useful containers, such as countries, organizational units, subunits, and resources. Our example in Figure 11-1 organizes the directory down to the user objects.

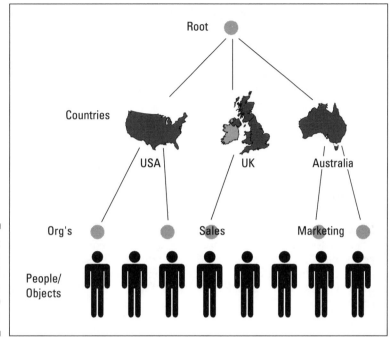

Figure 11-1:
The
hierarchical
structure
of an X.500
directory.

Today, two X.500 standards are commonly used every day: These are known as the 1988 and 1993 X.500 standards. The 1993 version includes a number of advances over the older 1988 version. Happily, the 1993 version is the standard upon which Windows 2000 built Active Directory.

Managing data

A special-purpose TCP/IP-based protocol known as the *Lightweight Directory Access Protocol* (LDAP) provides the second ingredient for the Active Directory service. As the latter part of its name suggests, LDAP is designed specifically to retrieve and access directory data. (The *Lightweight* part of its name stems from the fact that it's a stripped-down version of an older, more cumbersome X.500 DAP.)

This terminology may seem familiar to those of you who are acquainted with Microsoft Exchange Server's directory service because Windows 2000's Active Directory service shares a common heritage (and common technology) with the Exchange Server directory service. In fact, an Exchange connector is supplied with Windows 2000 Server to link the two directory services and to replicate data between them. Not surprisingly, this software component is called the Active Directory Connector.

Locating data and resources

If Windows 2000 directory data is structured using the X.500 protocol and this data is accessed using LDAP, there still must be a way to locate directory data. Time for the missing third ingredient! How does Active Directory meet the third and final requirement for a working directory service? We're glad you asked. Active Directory relies on the well-known and widely used Internet standard called the *Domain Name Service* (DNS) as its locator service.

Of Domains and Controllers

Behind every great domain is a great domain controller (so the Aretha Franklin song goes), but before you look at how Windows 2000 uses domain controllers, a quick recap of the Windows NT 4.0 usage is in order. Just be aware that the Windows 2000 way of doing the domain controller thing is quite different from the Windows NT 4.0 way — mainly because of Active Directory.

In the beginning . . .

In Windows NT 4.0, 15-character NetBIOS names represent domains. (In such names, in fact, the sixteenth character is an invisible special character ⟨1C⟩ that denotes the name applied to a domain.) Such domains revolve around a shared user/group/policy database, stored in writable format on a single, primary server known as the *primary domain controller* (PDC).

Any model that depends on a single domain controller introduces a single point of failure. Because access to the domain database is required to access a domain's resources, Microsoft added a second type of server to this mix, known as a *backup domain controller* (BDC), to improve availability and reliability of the domain database. A BDC, however, stores a read-only version of the domain database, sometimes called the *Security Accounts Manager* (SAM) database. Users can access the BDC to log on to a domain and to investigate user, group, or account information, but changes to the database can only be applied to the PDC.

In this kind of domain environment, the PDC must periodically update the SAM database on all BDCs in its domain to keep them synchronized. Should a PDC ever fail, a BDC can be promoted to become the PDC and write-enable its copy of the SAM database. However, there's an unbreakable master-slave relationship between PDCs and BDCs, because changes to the SAM database must be applied to the PDC and copied from the PDC to all BDCs. Therefore, if the PDC ever goes down, no changes can be applied to the SAM database unless the PDC is brought back up, or a BDC is promoted to become the new PDC instead. Phew! Got all that?

Although this sounds like a form of subjugation, a master-slave relationship is computerese for "everything that changes on the master is copied to all slaves" and "only a master can accept changes, and copies all changes to its slaves."

Windows 2000 no longer uses NetBIOS to name its domains; instead, it uses Domain Name Service (DNS) domain names. (See Chapter 14 for more information on DNS domain names.) Therefore, rather than the familiar "Dummies" domain, you might have `sales.dummies.com` as a legal domain name. Likewise, the concept of a SAM is no longer used in a Windows 2000 domain. All information about users, passwords, and groups is stored in Active Directory. Therefore, instead of servers that can read from or write to the SAM, servers must supply the LDAP service that's needed to interface with Active Directory.

On a Windows 2000 network, the servers that host the LDAP service are the domain controllers. As in Windows NT-based networks, these servers are responsible for authentication and other domain activities. In Windows 2000-based networks, however, servers use Active Directory to provide the services that their older counterparts delivered using the SAM database.

Wherefore art thou, BDC/PDC?

The concept of PDCs and BDCs has been removed from Windows 2000. In this Brave New World, all domain controllers are equal (though some are, indeed, more equal than others). How is this equality maintained? A process known as *multi-master replication* ensures that when changes occur on any domain controller in a domain, these changes are replicated to all other controllers in that domain. Therefore, instead of the older master-slave relationship between PDC and BDCs, you have a peer-to-peer relationship among all domain controllers in a Windows 2000 domain (and beyond) where trust relationships exist. (A *trust relationship* is a special inter-domain access arrangement that you define when users in one domain require access to resources in another domain.)

Obviously, you won't be able to upgrade all your domain controllers from Windows NT 4.0 to Windows 2000 in one fell swoop; therefore, Windows 2000 Server allows you to operate your domains in a *mixed* mode. This allows Windows NT 4.0 BDCs (but not PDCs) to participate in a Windows 2000 domain. The idea is that you begin by upgrading PDCs and then proceed to upgrade BDCs until all domain controllers have been converted.

For a Windows NT 4.0 BDC to function properly, it needs to obtain updates from a PDC. Therefore, in mixed mode domains, a single Windows 2000 domain controller impersonates a Windows NT 4.0 PDC, which allows changes to be replicated to any Windows NT 4.0 BDCs in that domain.

In mixed-mode domain operation, clients can use NetBIOS names to access old-style domain services, or they can use Active Directory to access Windows 2000 domain services. To find a Windows 2000 domain controller, clients must query a DNS server for a service record that takes the general form `_ldap._tcp.<domain name>`, where `_ldap._tcp.dummies.com` represents the domain controllers for the `dummies.com` domain, for example.

Windows 2000 domain controllers do not have to run the DNS service; the only requirement is that the DNS servers used support the service record type so those domain controllers can be located.

What Makes Active Directory Tick?

Putting things in a technobabble nutshell, Active Directory is implemented using a X.500 structure for directory data, an LDAP interface to access directory data, and Dynamic DNS as a locator mechanism for directory data. So, now that you know all this stuff about Active Directory, what does it give you? The following list recounts some of Active Directory's main features and advantages:

- ✔ **Security:** Information is stored in a secure form. Each object in the Active Directory has an *Access Control List* (ACL) that contains a list of resources that may access it and what access privileges are granted to each such resource.

- ✔ **Query capabilities:** Active Directory generates a *global catalog* to provide a flexible mechanism for handling queries. Any client that supports Active Directory can query this catalog to request directory data.

- ✔ **Replication:** Replication of the directory to all domain controllers in a domain means easier access, higher availability, and improved fault tolerance.

- ✔ **Extensible:** Active Directory is *extensible*, which means that new object types can be added to a directory or existing objects *extended.* For example, you could easily add a salary attribute or an employee ID to the user object.

- ✔ **Multiple protocols:** Communication between directory servers or across directories from multiple vendors can use numerous networking protocols because of Active Directory's X.500 foundation. These protocols currently include LDAP Versions 2 and 3 and the *Hypertext Transfer Protocol* (HTTP). Third parties can extend this capability to include other protocols as well, if needed.

✔ **Partitioning:** In an Active Directory environment, information may be partitioned by domain to avoid the need to replicate large amounts of directory data. Each such domain is called a *tree* because of the way that X.500 structures directory data into an interlinked hierarchy with a single root; in a large and complex network, a collection of domains forms a group of trees which is — you guessed it — called a *forest!*

When you partition Active Directory data into different trees, it does not mean that Active Directory cannot be queried for information from other domains. *Global catalogs* contain a subset of information about every object in an entire domain forest, which allows such searches to be performed on the entire forest through the agencies of your friendly local domain controller.

What replication means

In a Windows 2000 domain, all domain controllers are equal. Therefore, if you apply changes to any domain controller, the complete domain directories of all other domain controllers must be updated (through a process called *multi-master replication)* to record those changes.

Here's how this works: Each object in Active Directory on each domain controller has an attribute known as an *Update Sequence Number,* or USN (so does each domain controller as well). Every time a change is applied to Active Directory data, the server where the change is applied has its USN incremented by one, along with the USN for each object that is changed. These changes must then be replicated to all domain controllers in the domain. Here, the USN provides the key to multi-master replication.

USN increments are *atomic operations;* in English, this means that the increment to the USN's value (and the actual change to directory data) occur at the same time. If one part fails, the whole change fails; therefore, it's not possible to change any Active Directory object without its USN being incremented. Thus, no changes will ever be lost. Each domain controller keeps track of the highest USNs for the other domain controllers with which it replicates. This allows the domain controller to calculate which changes must be replicated during each replication cycle. In the simplest terms, the highest-numbered USN always wins!

At the start of each replication cycle, each domain controller checks its USN table and queries all other domain controllers with which it replicates for their latest USNs. As an example, Table 11-1 represents the USN table for Server A.

Table 11-1	Server A's USN Table
Domain Controller	*USN*
DC B	54
DC C	23
DC D	53

Server A then queries the domain controllers for their current USNs and gets the results shown in Table 11-2.

Table 11-2	Current USNs for Other Domain Controllers
Domain Controller	*USN*
DC B	58
DC C	23
DC D	64

From this data, Server A can calculate the changes it needs from each server, as shown in Table 11-3.

Table 11-3	The Changes Server A Needs from Each Server
Domain Controller	*USN*
DC B	55, 56, 57, 58
DC C	Up-to-date
DC D	54-64

It would then query each server for the updates it needs.

Because objects also have properties, they also have *Property Version Numbers* (PVNs). Every property of an object has a PVN, and each time a property is modified, its PVN is incremented by one. (Sound familiar?) These PVNs are used to detect collisions, which happen when multiple changes to the same property of an object occur. If a collision occurs, the change with the highest PVN takes precedence.

If those PVNs match, a *time stamp* is used to resolve any such conflicts. Time stamps are a great second line of defense in avoiding collisions, because they explicitly mark when each change to the directory data has been made, thus enabling the system to determine whether one change does in fact take precedence over another. Don't forget, however, that time stamps can only do their job correctly if the domain controllers on your network are closely synchronized with one another. So, take a tip from the old war movies and synchronize your domain controllers!

In the highly unlikely event that the PVNs match *and* the time stamp is the same, a binary buffer comparison is carried out so the larger buffer size takes precedence. PVNs are only incremented on original writes and not on replication writes (unlike USNs). PVNs are not server specific but travel with the object's properties.

A propagation-dampening scheme is also used to stop changes from being repeatedly sent to other servers. The propagation-dampening scheme used by Windows 2000 prevents logical loops in the Active Directory structure from causing endless proliferation of updates and prevents redundant transmission of updates to already current servers. Consequently, each server keeps a table of up-to-date vectors that represents the highest originating writes received from each domain controller. These vectors take the following form:

```
<change data>,<name of domain controller that made the
        original change>,<USN for the change>
```

For example:

```
<object savillj, property Password xxx>,Titanic,54
```

represents a change to the `savillj` object's password value on the domain controller named `Titanic` with a USN of 54.

Domain controllers send this information with their USNs so they can calculate if they have already made the change that another domain controller is trying to replicate.

The grand schema things

Every object in a domain has a *schema,* which is a blueprint or diagram of the object's characteristics. In other words, when objects are created, there are certain attributes automatically applied to them. For example, a user object has attributes such as name, address, and phone number. The collection of these attributes and their definitions is called the schema. You might think of an object's schema as a laundry list of its attributes or a checklist of its capabilities. The default schema supplies definitions for users, computers, domains, and more. You can have only one schema per domain per object because you cannot have multiple definitions for the same object.

The default schema definition is defined in the SCHEMA.INI file, which also contains the initial structure for the NTDS.DIT file that stores Active Directory data. The SCHEMA.INI file is located in the `%systemroot%\ntds` directory, it's an ASCII file, and it can be viewed on-screen or printed.

By default, the Active Directory schema cannot be edited. If you want to make that schema extensible, you must first edit the Registry to indicate that the schema is editable. After you edit the Registry, the schema is extensible, which means you can add your own attributes or even define completely new object types. For example, you could easily add a salary attribute or an employee ID to the user object.

An entire enterprise forest (a collection of Active Directory trees into a single organizational container) shares a single schema; therefore, if you change that schema, it affects every domain controller in every linked domain. Therefore, you had better be sure that any changes you make are both correct and desirable. The schema should only be changed by experienced programmers or schema administrators. For more information on extending the schema, search the Microsoft Web site (`www.microsoft.com`) for "Active Directory Programmer's Guide."

You should only extend the schema if the object does not have an attribute that you need. To add an attribute to the schema, complete the following steps:

This activity should be performed by only a schema administrator or a programmer.

1. **Start the Registry editor by going to Start⇨Run and typing REGEDT32.EXE.**

2. **Go to HKEY_LOCAL_MACHINE\SYSTEM\CurrentControlSet\ Services\NTDS\Parameters.**

3. **Choose Edit⇨Add Value and create a new value entry named "Schema Update Allowed" (of type REG_DWORD).**

4. **Set the value of the new value key to 1.**

5. **Click OK.**

6. **Close the Registry editor.**

Global catalogs

The global catalog contains an entry for every object in the enterprise forest (which is a collection of trees that do not explicitly share a single, contiguous namespace), but it contains only a limited number of properties for each object. The entire forest shares a global catalog. Multiple servers hold copies of the entire catalog.

Searches across the entire enterprise forest can only be applied to those object properties that actually appear in the global catalog. Searches in a user's domain tree can be for any property when you perform a so-called *deep search* on properties not in the global catalog. Only directory services (or domain controllers) can be configured to hold a copy of the global catalog.

Do not configure too many global catalogs for each domain, because the replication needed to maintain such catalogs wastes network bandwidth. One global catalog server per domain in each physical location is sufficient. Windows 2000 Server sets servers as global catalogs as necessary; therefore, you shouldn't need to modify its default selections unless users complain about slow response times for directory queries.

Because full searches involve querying an entire domain tree rather than the global catalog, grouping an enterprise into a single tree improves search times because it allows you to query items for the entire enterprise that aren't in the global catalog. Setting up your enterprise as a single domain tree produces a larger search space and gives users access to the entire directory database in a single deep search (rather than requiring a deep search for each tree in the forest).

Planning for Active Directory

If you're running some version of Windows NT, you may have multiple domains with several trust relationships between individual pairs of domains. Theoretically, you could just upgrade each domain, keep existing trust relationships, and make no changes. However, if you did that, you'd lose the advantages of Active Directory.

Before you upgrade a single domain controller, you should create a plan for your domain. Then, you should use this plan to govern the order and method for your migration from Windows NT domains to Windows 2000 Active Directory.

What's in a namespace?

A namespace is a logically bounded region that contains names based on a standardized convention to symbolically represent objects or information. Specific rules guide the construction of names within a namespace and how a name can be applied to an object. Many namespaces are hierarchical in nature, such as DNS or Active Directory. Other namespaces, such as NetBIOS, are flat and unstructured.

In Windows 2000, domains use full-blown DNS names rather than NetBIOS names. This creates interdomain parent-child relationships — where one domain may be created as a child of another — that Windows NT could not support. For example, `sales.dummies.com` is a child of the `dummies.com` domain. (A child domain always contains the full parent name within its own.)

It's important to remember that parent-child relationships can be created only from within a parent domain using the domain controller creation wizard; the parent domain must exist before you create a child of that parent. Therefore, the order in which you create or upgrade your domains is crucial!

In the next section, you find out more reasons why it's important to create your domains in a certain order. But even before you concern yourself with site issues, you need to be aware that you should always create an enterprise root domain before creating any other domain. For example, if you begin by creating the `dummies.com` root domain, the `sales.dummies.com` domain and all other dependent domains can then be created as children of the `dummies.com` root domain. This structure helps when searching other domains and enables the possibility of moving domains around in future versions of Windows 2000.

Making sites happen

Sites in Active Directory are used to group servers into containers that mirror the physical layout of your network. This organization allows you to configure replication between domain controllers. A number of TCP/IP subnets can also be mapped to sites, which allows new servers to join the correct site automatically, depending on their IP address. This addressing scheme also makes it easy for clients to find the domain controller closest to them.

When you create the first domain controller, a default site called Default-First-Site is created, and the domain controller is assigned to that site. Subsequent domain controllers are added to this site, but they can be moved. You can also rename this site to any name you prefer.

Sites are administered and created using the Active Directory Sites and Services Microsoft Management Console (MMC) snap-in. To create a new site, perform the following actions:

1. **Start the Active Directory Sites and Services MMC snap-in (Start⇨ Programs⇨Administrative Tools⇨Active Directory Sites and Services).**

2. **Right-click on the Sites branch and select New Site from the displayed context menu.**

3. **In the New Object - Site dialog box, enter a name for the site, for example, NewYork.**

   The name must be 63 characters or less and cannot contain '.' or space characters. You must also select a site link (by default, there's only one DEFAULTIPSITELINK or type IP).

4. **Select a site link to contain the new site. Click OK.**

5. **Read the confirmation creation dialog box and click OK.**

Now that the site is created, you can assign various IP subnets to it. To do so, follow these steps:

1. **Start the Active Directory Sites and Services MMC snap-in (Start⇨ Programs⇨Administrative Tools⇨Active Directory Sites and Services).**

2. **Expand the Sites branch.**

3. **Right click on Subnets and select New Subnet.**

4. **In the New Object - Subnet dialog box, enter the name of subnet in the form `<network>/<bits masked>`. For example, 200.200.201.0/24 is network 200.200.201.0 with subnet mask 255.255.255.0. Select the Site with which to associate the subnet, for example, New York.**

5. **Click OK.**

You now have a subnet linked to a site. You can assign multiple subnets to a site if you want. For more information on subnets, see Chapter 14 and for even more detailed information, search the Windows 2000 Help menu for subnets.

Oh, you organizational unit (OU), you

The *organizational unit* (OU) is a key component of the X.500 protocol. As the name suggests, organizational units contain objects in a domain that are organized into logical containers, thus allowing finer segregation and control within a domain. Organizational unit containers can contain other organizational units, groups, users, and computers.

OUs can be nested to create a hierarchy to closely match the structure of your business or organization. Using OUs, you can eliminate the need for the cumbersome domain models developed for Windows NT Server-based domains (the master domain model, for example, in which several resource domains use accounts from a central user domain). Using Active Directory, you can create one large domain and group resources and users into multiple, distinct OUs.

The biggest advantage of OUs is that they allow you to delegate authority. You can assign certain users or groups administrative control of an OU, which allows them to change passwords and create accounts in that OU but does not grant them control over the rest of the domain. This capability is a major improvement over Windows NT domain administration, which was an "all or nothing" situation.

Installing Active Directory

In previous versions of Windows NT, you set up each server's type during installation. The server's function could be in one of the following roles:

- ✔ Stand-alone/member server
- ✔ PDC
- ✔ BDC

With the exception of PDC/BDC swapping, a server's role could not be changed without reinstalling the software. For example, it wasn't possible to change a member server to a domain controller without reinstalling Windows NT.

Windows 2000 has left all that behind by allowing you to install all servers as normal servers. You can use a wizard (covered in the following section) to convert normal servers to domain controllers, or domain controllers to normal servers. This facility also gives you the ability to "move" domain controllers from one domain to another by demoting a domain controller to a member server and then promoting it to a domain controller in a different domain. In the Windows NT environment, demoting and promoting domain controllers also typically requires reinstalling the operating system or jumping through some pretty major hoops!

Promoting domain controllers

Windows 2000 allows you to convert servers from normal servers to domain controllers and vice versa. To do this, you use the Active Directory Installation Wizard, which you execute by opening the DCPROMO.EXE file. There's no shortcut to DCPROMO in the Administrative folders. You have to run it directly from a Command Prompt or Run command. To upgrade a stand-alone/member server to a domain controller, perform the following actions:

1. **Click Start⇨Run.**

2. **In the displayed Run dialog box, type DCPROMO to open the Active Directory Installation Wizard.**

   Before you attempt to run DCPROMO.EXE (which opens the Active Directory Installation Wizard), you must ensure that the Windows 2000 domain you're going to create has a DNS zone configured. The DNS zone supports service records and is enabled for dynamic updates. Without this information, the wizard can't do its job.

3. **Click Next in the introduction screen of the Active Directory Installation Wizard.**

4. **Two choices appear:**

   • New Domain

   • Replica Domain Controller in Existing Domain

   There's no concept of a BDC in Windows 2000 Server. All domain controllers are more or less equal.

   For this example, select New Domain and click Next.

5. **Windows 2000 introduces a new concept called *trees*, which enables the creation of child domains.**

   If you're starting a new top-level domain, select Create New Domain Tree. To create a child domain, select Create New Child Domain.

   Click Next to continue.

6. **If you elected to create a new domain tree, you're asked if you want to Create a New Forest of Domain Trees or Put This New Domain Tree in an Existing Forest.**

   Forests allow you to "join" a number of separate domain trees and create a transitive trust relationship between them. If this is your first Windows 2000 domain tree, you should create a new forest.

   Click Next to continue.

7. **You're asked for the DNS name of your domain.**

   For example, `savilltech.com` is a valid domain name. It's important this matches information configured on the DNS server.

   Enter the DNS name and click Next.

8. **You're asked for a NetBIOS domain name, which, by default, is the left-most part of the DNS domain name (up to the first 15 characters), for example, `savilltech`. (This can be changed.) Click Next to continue.**

9. **Next, provide a storage area for the Active Directory and the Active Directory log. Accept the defaults and click Next.**

10. **Finally, select an area on an NTFS 5.0 partition for the system volume (SYSVOL) for storage of the server's public files, which are `%systemroot%\SYSVOL` by default. Click Next.**

    The share system volume (SYSVOL), which stores logon/logoff scripts, must reside on a NTFS 5.0 volume because it uses the *File Replication Service* to replicate its content to other domain controllers.

11. **You're given an option to weaken security for 4.0 RAS servers, which you probably don't want to do. Make your selection and click Next.**

12. **A summary screen appears. Click Next to start the upgrade.**

    The wizard sets security and creates the directory server schema container. Information from the default directory service file and the old SAM is then read in if the machine is an upgraded PDC.

13. **Click Finish and reboot the machine.**

You now have a Windows 2000 domain controller. Additional domain controllers can be added by performing the preceding steps and selecting Replica Domain Controller in Existing Domain in Step 2. The Wizard would then ask you the name of the domain to replicate.

If you upgrade an existing domain controller to Windows 2000, the DCPROMO program runs after installation is complete and omits the option to change the NetBIOS name, but you will be able to choose a new DNS domain name.

Active Directory's database and shared system volume

Although you should think of the Active Directory as an information "bubble," it is stored in file form on each domain controller in the file named `%systemroot%\NTDS\ntds.dit`. This file is always open and cannot be backed up using a simple file copy operation. However, like old methods for backing up the SAM in Windows NT 4.0, the new NTBACKUP program included with Windows 2000 includes an option to take a snapshot of the Active Directory and back up that information. There's even a special *directory restoration mode* you must boot into to restore an Active Directory backup! (Chapter 17 covers backups in detail.)

The *share system volume,* or SYSVOL, is the replication root for each domain. Its contents are replicated to each domain controller within the domain by using the File Replication Service. The SYSVOL must reside on an NTFS 5.0 volume, because that's a File Replication Service requirement.

SYSVOL is also a share that points (by default) to `%systemroot%\SYSVOL\sysvol`, which contains domain-specific areas, such as logon scripts. For example, the logon share NETLOGON for domain `savilltech.com` points to `%systemroot%\SYSVOL\sysvol\savilltech.com\SCRIPTS`. You can simply copy files used for logon or logoff to this directory and the change will be replicated to all other domain controllers in the next replication interval (which is set to 15 minutes, by default).

Modes of domain operation

Windows 2000 Server domains operate in two modes: mixed and native. *Mixed mode domains* allow Windows NT 4.0 BDCs to participate in a Windows 2000 domain.

In *native mode,* only Windows 2000-based domain controllers can participate in the domain, and Windows NT 4.0-based BDCs are no longer able to act as domain controllers.

The switch from mixed to native mode cannot be reversed, so do not change this mode until all domain controllers are converted to Windows 2000. Also, be sure there are no plans to add any Windows NT 4.0-based BDCs after this switch occurs.

In addition, the switch to native mode allows the use of the new *universal groups,* which, unlike global groups, can be nested inside one another. Older NetBIOS-based clients will still be able to log on using the NetBIOS domain name even in native mode.

To change all domain controllers to Windows 2000 domains, perform the following steps:

1. **Start the Active Directory Domains and Trusts MMC snap-in (Start⇨ Programs⇨Administrative Tools⇨Active Directory Domains and Trusts).**

2. **Right-click on the domain you want to convert to native mode and select Properties to open the Properties dialog box for that domain.**

3. **Select the General tab.**

4. **Click the Change Mode button.**

5. **A dialog box appears and asks you if you're sure you want to change the domain to Native Mode. Click Yes to accept the confirmation.**

6. **Click Apply in the Properties dialog box of the domain you just changed to Native Mode.**

7. **A success message is displayed. Click OK.**

8. **Reboot the machine (although we've been told that a reboot is not necessary).**

You also need to check all other domain controllers in the domain. When the domain operation mode says Native Mode (instead of Mixed Mode), reboot the domain controller, which can take as long as 15 minutes (or more, if network access to other domain controllers fails for some reason).

If a domain controller cannot be contacted when you make the change (for example, if it's located at a remote site and only connects to the main site periodically), the remote domain controller will switch its mode the next time replication occurs.

When Domains Multiply

In this section, you look at new methods available in Windows 2000 to interconnect domains. In Windows NT 4.0 domains, you're limited to simple unidirectional or bidirectional trust relationships to interconnect two domains explicitly at a time. Windows 2000 has many more sophisticated, more functional models to create relationships and connections among its domains.

Trust relationships across domains

Windows NT 4.0 trust relationships are not transitive. For example, if domain A trusts domain B, and domain C trusts domain B, domain C does not automatically trust domain A (see Figure 11-2).

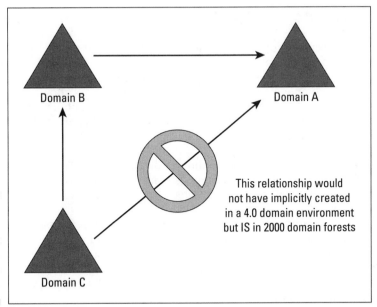

Figure 11-2:
An example
of a trust
relationship
in Windows
NT 4.0.

Domain B

Domain A

This relationship would
not have implicitly created
in a 4.0 domain environment
but IS in 2000 domain forests

Domain C

This lack of transitivity is no longer the case with the trust relationships used to connect members of a tree/forest in Windows 2000. Trust relationships used in a Windows 2000 tree are two-way, transitive trusts. This means that any domain in a tree implicitly trusts every other domain in its tree and forest. This removes the need for time-consuming administration of individual trusts between pairs of domains, because such trusts are created automatically whenever a new domain joins a tree.

The security of Windows 2000 trusts is maintained by employing Kerberos. Kerberos Version 5.0 is the primary security protocol for Windows 2000, but it's not a Microsoft protocol. Kerberos is a security system developed at the Massachusetts Institute of Technology (MIT). It verifies both the identity of the user and the integrity of all session data while that user is logged in. Kerberos services are installed on each domain controller, and a Kerberos client is installed on each Windows 2000 workstation and server. A user's initial Kerberos authentication provides that user with a single logon to enterprise resources. For more information about Kerberos, see the Internet Engineering Task Force's (IETF's) Requests for Comments (RFCs) 1510 and 1964. These documents are available on the Web from www.rfc-editor.org.

Building trees

In Windows 2000, one domain can be a child of another domain. For example, `legal.savilltech.com` is a child of `savilltech.com` (which is the root domain name and therefore the name of the tree). A child domain always contains the complete domain name of the parent in it. As shown in Figure 11-3, `dev.savillCORP.com` cannot be a child of `savilltech.com` because the domain names do not match. A child domain and its parent share a two-way, transitive trust.

When a domain is the child of another domain, a domain tree is formed. A domain tree must have a contiguous namespace (which means all namespaces share a common root, i.e., have the same parent).

Because the domains are DNS names and they inherit the parent part of the name, if a part of the tree is renamed, all of its children will implicitly also be renamed. For example, if `parent ntfaq.com` of `sales.ntfaq.com` is renamed to `backoffice.com`, the child is automatically renamed to `sales.backoffice.com`. (Actually, Windows 2000 lacks this facility at present, but it will appear in future versions.)

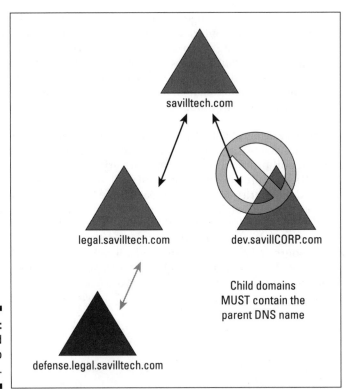

savilltech.com

legal.savilltech.com

dev.savillCORP.com

Child domains
MUST contain the
parent DNS name

defense.legal.savilltech.com

Figure 11-3:
Parent/child
relationship
example.

Domain trees can currently only be created during the server-to-domain-controller-promotion process with DCPROMO.EXE — this, too, may change in the future.

There are a number of advantages in placing domains in a tree. The first and most useful is that all members of a tree have Kerberos transitive trusts with their parent and all its children. These transitive trusts also mean that any user or group in a domain tree can be granted access to any object in the entire tree. In addition, a single network logon can be used at any workstation in the domain tree.

Understanding forests

You may have a number of separate domain trees in your organization with which you would like to share resources. You can share resources between domain trees by joining those trees to form a forest.

A *forest* is a collection of trees that does not explicitly share a single, contiguous namespace (however, each tree still has to be contiguous). Creating a forest may be useful if your company has multiple root DNS addresses.

For example, in Figure 11-4, the two root domains are joined via transitive, two-way Kerberos trusts (like the trust created between a child and its parent). Forests always contain the entire domain tree of each domain, and you can not create a forest that contains only parts of a domain tree.

Forests are created during the server-to-domain-controller-promotion process with DCPROMO and cannot currently be created at any other time. (This will change in the next version.)

You're not limited to only two domain trees in a forest; you can add as many trees as you want, and all domains within the forest will be able to grant access to objects for any user within the forest. Again, this cuts back the need to manage trust relationships manually. The advantages of creating forests are as follows:

- ✔ All trees have a common global catalog containing specific information about every object in the forest.

- ✔ The trees all contain a common schema. Microsoft has not yet confirmed what will happen if two trees have different schemas before they are joined. We assume the changes will be merged.

- ✔ Searches in a forest perform deep searches of the entire tree of the domain from which the request is initiated and use the global catalog entries for the rest of the forest.

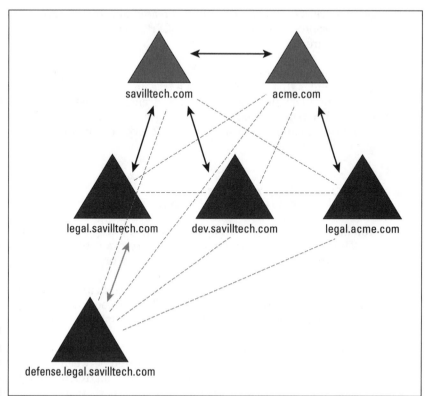

You may, of course, choose not to join trees into forests. Instead, you may create normal trusts between individual elements of the trees.

Because of the shared schema among forests, many organizations have two forests to enable the testing of schema modifications before implementing them on a live forest.

Chapter 12

Working with Active Directory, Domains, and Trusts

*A*ccess to Active Directory's sheer power is useless to you unless you can manipulate and configure its content. Only then will you be able to get the most out of its powerful (but cryptic) environment. In this chapter, you take a long hard look at Active Directory. Before you enter into this staring contest with your computer screen, however, we want to show you how manipulating and configuring content is tied to manipulating and configuring domains. That's right; you get to tackle domains one more time. So once more unto the breach, dear friend, so you too can become a master of your own domain.

For details on domain controllers and their changing role in Windows 2000, see Chapter 11. We suggest picking up a copy of *Active Directory For Dummies* by Marcia Loughry.

Master of Your Domain

Unlike previous versions of Windows NT, domain controller roles are no longer defined during the installation of Windows 2000 but rather by running the DCPROMO wizard. (For more information about the DCPROMO wizard, see Chapter 11.) Windows 2000 does borrow the concept of a *primary domain controller* (PDC) from Windows NT when it feels it needs to, but it has completely jettisoned Windows NT's concept of a *backup domain controller* (BDC). In Windows 2000, all domain controllers are equal and share peer-to-peer relationships, rather than acting either as a master (PDC) or a slave (BDC) in a master/slave relationship.

To support older Windows NT Server 4.0 and 3.51 BDCs in a mixed-mode environment, one of the Windows 2000 domain controllers has to emulate the actions of a Windows NT Server 4.0 PDC. Then, it has to replicate changes to those old-fashioned BDCs so they can make the necessary changes, for example, password modifications.

Having all these peers around can cause problems if you don't watch out. (Ever hear the expression, "Too many cooks spoil the broth"?) Windows 2000 utilizes five special roles designed to keep all these peers in line. One role was specifically designed to support any Windows NT vintage clients and domain controllers. The other four roles work to eliminate the risk of multiple domain controllers making changes to the same object and losing attribute modifications.

These roles are called *Flexible Single Master of Operations* (FSMO) roles, where each of the five roles manages a particular aspect of a domain/forest. Their *flexibility* comes from the fact that these roles can be moved between domain controllers, although it does take a bit of effort on your part to actually move them around. (They must be moved manually in the same way that a BDC had to be manually promoted to a PDC in previous versions of Windows NT.)

You assign the FSMO roles using the NTDSUTIL utility. For more information on the NTDSUTIL utility, see the Windows 2000 Server help files or the Resource Kit.

The following bulleted list gives you an idea how these five roles work with domains within Active Directory:

- **Schema master:** At the heart of Active Directory, the schema is a blueprint for all objects and containers. Because the schema has to be the same throughout an entire forest, only one machine can authorize modifications to the schema. Therefore, the schema master role is used to assign modification rights to one machine per forest. (See Chapter 11 for a more detailed definition of the schema.)

- **Domain naming master:** To add a domain to a forest, its name has to be verifiably unique. The domain naming master of the forest oversees the domain name operation and ensures that only verifiably unique names are assigned. There's only one domain naming master per forest.

- **Relative ID (RID) master:** Any domain controller can create new objects (such as user, group, and computer accounts). However, after creating 512 user objects, the domain controller must contact the domain's Relative ID master for another 512 Relative IDs. (The domain controller actually contacts the RID master when it has less than 100 RIDs left. This means that the RID master can be unavailable for short periods of time without causing object creation problems.) This ensures that each object has a unique RID. There can only be one RID master per domain.

✔ **PDC emulator:** For backward compatibility reasons, one domain controller in each Windows 2000 domain must emulate a PDC for the benefit of any Windows NT 4.0 and 3.5 domain controllers and clients that may be present. One PDC emulator is assigned per forest.

✔ **Infrastructure master:** When a user and group are in different domains, there can be a lag between changes to the user profile (a user name, for example) and its display in the group. The infrastructure master of the group's domain is responsible for fixing the group-to-user reference to reflect the rename. The infrastructure master performs its fix-ups locally and relies on replication to bring all other replicas of the domain up to date. (For more information on replication, see the section "When replication happens," later in this chapter.)

Trusts Are Good for Windows NT 4.0 and Active Directory Domains

In the good old days before the need for FSMO roles, you had one main domain controller (a "primary" domain controller, or PDC) that could make changes to the *Security Accounts Manager (SAM)* database. Those changes were then replicated to other "backup" domain controllers (BDCs). In this model, the SAM database was simply a file stored on each PDC that contained information about the domain's security objects, such as users and groups. To support authentication across domains (and thus hinder unauthorized access to the network), you created one-way trust relationships between domains that would allow users and groups from the trusted domain to be assigned access to resources in the trusting domain.

The whole concept of trusting and trusted is relatively confusing, so we're going to try to shed some light on the subject. Just imagine a trust between two domains: A and B. Domain A trusts domain B, so domain B is the trusted domain and domain A is the trusting domain. Because domain A trusts domain B to correctly authenticate its users, users from domain B can be assigned access to resources in domain A. (You could create a bi-directional trust relationship, where domain A trusts domain B with its resources and domain B trusts domain A with *its* resources. However, what you really have with a bi-directional trust is two uni-directional trusts that have been joined.)

Before you get the idea that we're all one happy, trusting family, don't forget that Windows NT 4.0-based trusts are not transitive; therefore, if domain C trusts domain B, and domain B trusts domain A, domain C does not implicitly trust domain A. For domain A to trust domain C, you must establish an explicit trust relationship between domain A and domain C. Got all that? Remember it; we'll come back to it later.

Although Windows 2000 does make use of the spanking new Active Directory to keep domains in line, things are not that different from the Windows NT model when it comes to trust relationships. Windows 2000 domain controllers still store the directory service information in a file (NTDS.DIT), and trust relationships are still needed to authenticate across multiple domains. Admittedly, Windows 2000 now automatically creates trust relationships between all domains in a forest, but the real change from the older model to the Active Directory approach lies in how modifications are made and replicated to the domain database.

How domain controllers work together

In the days of Windows NT, domains had it easy. You made changes at only one domain controller and then the changes were copied at regular intervals to any other controllers for the domain.

Now, with Windows 2000, you can make changes at any domain controller and remain confident that Windows 2000's left hand will always know what its right hand is doing. How does this work, you ask? The answer, dear friend, is *multi-master replication.*

With multi-master replication, any domain controller can make changes to the Active Directory database. Then, those changes are replicated to all other domain controllers in that domain.

When replication happens

Replication between domain controllers in a Windows NT 4.0 domain is configured using a couple of Registry settings — that's it — fairly useless really. Windows 2000 is *much* cooler!

A *site* is a collection of machines and domain controllers connected via fast network and grouped by IP subnets. What do sites have to do with replication, you ask? Well, everything. They allow us to define different replication schedules depending on the domain controllers' site membership.

There are essentially two types of replication: *intra-site replication* (between domain controllers in the same site) and *inter-site replication* (between domain controllers in different sites).

Intra-site replication

Within a domain, there are sets of replication partners and the changes are then replicated to all the domain controllers within a set by a process called *propagation.* (Propagation is simply the transmission of changes between one domain controller and another so that after the process completes, each domain controller in a set has an exact copy of the Active Directory data.) Replication is initiated at a defined regular interval (five minutes, by default) and urgent replication using notification can be initiated for any of the following:

✔ **Replication of a newly locked out account:** Prevents users from moving to another part of a domain to log in with a user account that has been locked out on a domain controller.

✔ **Modification of a trust account:** Enables all members of a domain to take advantage of a new trust with another domain.

Obviously, there are some problems with this replication methodology. In the good ole days (in other words, with Windows NT 4.0), you changed your password at the PDC to avoid the problem of the new setting not being replicated for a long time. With Windows 2000, the password changes are initially changed at the PDC FSMO and, in the event of password failure, the PDC FSMO is consulted in case the password has been recently changed but has not yet been replicated.

Inter-site replication

Inter-site replication is where Windows 2000 really shines. You can configure a timetable of how often to replicate for every hour of every day. All you need to do is go through the Active Directory Sites and Services MMC snap-in (Start➪Programs➪Administrative Tools➪Active Directory Sites and Services). Go to the Inter-Site Transport branch and select IP. Select a site link in the right-hand pane (for example, a remote domain), right-click, and choose Properties. Make sure the Link Properties General tab is selected and click Change Schedule. (See Figure 12-1.)

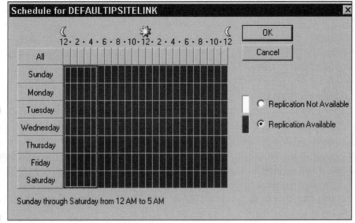

Figure 12-1:
The dialog box used to change replication times.

In Figure 12-1, replication is set to occur from 12 a.m. to 5 a.m. Sunday through Saturday. You can change this to any schedule you like. For example, you can set it to only replicate on Sundays from 6 p.m. to 7 p.m.

You can have different replication schedules for every pair of sites, so depending on the network connectivity and geographical location, different schedules may be appropriate. For example, if a slow WAN link exists between two sites, a replication with less frequent updates may be necessary to prevent bandwidth consumption.

There's one other area of replication that crosses domains: Global Catalog information. The Global Catalog contains a subset of information for every object in a domain; however, Windows 2000 performs all the calculations needed to optimize this replication, so mere mortals like us don't need to worry about it.

Know your database limits

In Windows 2000, there's really no limit to the number of objects per domain — you're organization will never get that big! Windows NT 4.0 domains are limited to around 40,000 objects per domain. This forces some companies to require multiple master domains joined by bi-directional trust relationships.

Windows 2000, on the other hand, extends this to around 10,000,000 objects per domain. Compaq has performed tests and created 16,000,000 user objects in a single domain with no significant performance problems. However, it had some *very* powerful hardware — probably much more powerful than your home PC, or even your company's primary server!

Obviously, these objects have to be replicated at some point. However, Windows 2000 uses *property* rather than *object* replication, which means that only the property change is replicated, not the entire object. In other words, if you change just one property of an object (a user's phone number, for example) only the property change (the new phone number) is replicated and not the entire user object.

Your database size is really governed by your domain controller hardware and the physical network infrastructure. However, if you have enough money to invest in the proper hardware, we doubt you would need more than a single domain (unless your company is really big). There will of course be other reasons for needing multiple domains and forests, such as needing different schemas. (See Chapter 11 for a more definition on the schema.)

Obviously, backup may govern database size because a huge directory database is no good if it takes days to back it up.

1205 Thurs

~ w/ Bentley

10 458 2947

a Anyone? (Controlling
l Directories)

ve sufficient tools available to manipulate and manage Active
ower won't do you much good. Fortunately, not only does
come with a complete set of ready-made tools, but you can
r own tools and scripts using the *Active Directory Scripting*
), if you're so inclined.

ctory management console

thing else in Windows 2000, management of Active Directory is
l using a Microsoft Management Console (MMC) snap-in. The
snap-in you ii use most often is the Active Directory Users and Computers
snap-in (shown in Figure 12-2), which is what you use to create, manage, and
delete everything from users to computers. It includes some of the features
of the old User and Server Manager from Windows NT.

To access the Active Directory Users and Computers snap-in, choose
Start⇨Programs⇨Administrative Tools⇨Active Directory Users and
Computers. When you first start the Active Directory Users and Computers
snap-in, you see your domain name (represented as a DNS domain name) at
the top of the directory. You'll also notice several containers (also known to
you as folders). Some of these containers are built in organizational units, or
OUs (which contain objects in a domain that are organized into logical containers, thus allowing finer segregation and control within a domain). The
containers that appear in a typical installation include:

- **Built-in:** By default, this contains the details of the old Windows NT 4.0
  groups, such as Administrators and Backup Operators.

- **Computers:** This contains the computer accounts that used to be managed using Windows NT's Server Manager. Computer objects in other
  organizational units are not listed in this container.

- **Domain Controllers:** This is a built-in organizational unit that contains
  all domain controllers.

- **Users:** This is the default store for all domain users. Again, users in other
  organizational units are not listed.

In a fully functional domain, you'll find various organizational units, depending on the services you have installed and the organizational units you
create.

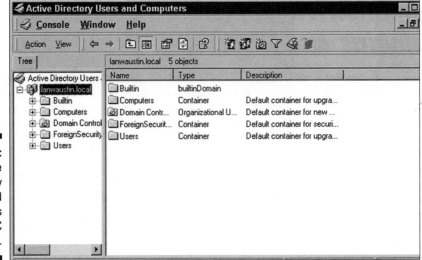

Figure 12-2:
The Active
Directory
Users and
Computers
MMC
snap-in.

Everything is *context menu driven* in Windows 2000. This means that if you right-click on an object or container, a menu specific to that object or container is displayed. This is much better that hunting through huge standard menus for options relevant to the chosen object.

Creating directory objects

There are tons of different objects in Windows 2000, such as computer, user, group, shared folder objects, and more. In this section, we're only going to concentrate on the creation of the first two (computer and user objects) because the others are fairly intuitive and don't support many configuration options.

In a Windows NT 4.0 domain, it never took too much advanced planning to create new user or computer objects. You just did it. In Windows 2000, you can't be quite so spontaneous. You first need to think about where you want to create such an object. Placement is important because, although you can still move objects around, it's much easier for you in the long run if you create an object in the correct location from the get-go. However, because you may not always have the time to plan ahead and do it right the first time, you can always move the object later if you have to (just don't say we didn't warn you).

Use OUs to help you organize your data into logical containers. You can create an OU for the various departments in your organization (for example, one for accounting, engineering, personnel, etc.), then you can put all user and computer objects in that department in that OU. In addition, you can lighten your administrative load by assigning a person in each department the rights necessary to manage his or her OU and that OU only. Pretty nifty, huh?

You can create a user object in one of two places: in the default User/Computer container or in some organizational unit you or someone else has already created. If you delegate the ability to create objects, you can set it up so the delegated users will only be able to create objects in one location.

To create a user object, perform the following steps:

1. **Start the Active Directory Users and Computers MMC snap-in (Start➪Programs➪Administrative Tools➪Active Directory Users and Computers).**

2. **In Active Directory Users and Computers, right-click on the container (such as Users) in which you want to create the user object and select New➪User from the pop-up menu.**

3. **The first page of the User creation wizard is displayed (as shown in Figure 12-3). Enter the user's name and a logon name, and then click Next.**

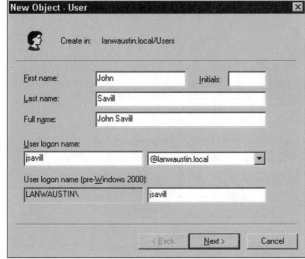

Figure 12-3:
The first page of the user creation dialog box.

4. **The next page of the wizard allows you to set the new password and the following options:**

   • User must change password at next logon

   • User cannot change password

   • Password never expires

   • Account is disabled

   Make the appropriate selections and click Next.

5. **A summary of the proposed addition is displayed. Click Finish.**

That's it; you've created a new user. You're probably thinking, "What about all the other user attributes, such as security features?" Well, you no longer define those settings during the creation of the user. After you create the user object, you right-click on it and select Properties. The Properties dialog box for the user appears (as shown in Figure 12-4).

Notice the arrows that appear at the top right of the Properties dialog box. To navigate through the tabs, use these arrows. Each tab pertains to various aspects of the user object selected. These tabs vary, depending on the Windows 2000 subsystems in use, on other back office applications, and even on what third-party software you have installed.

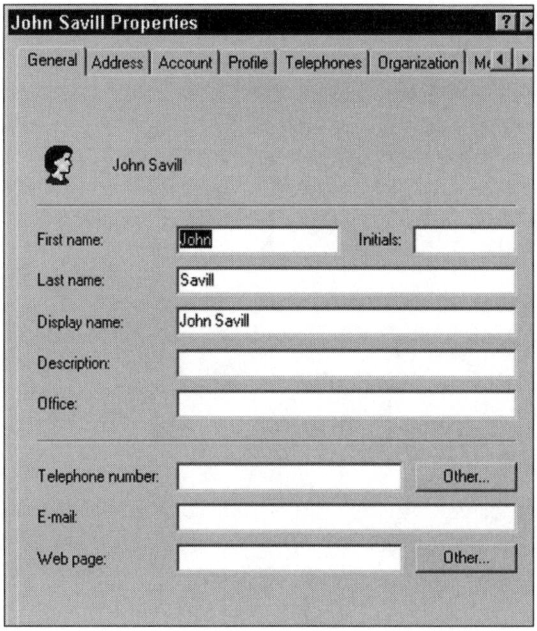

Figure 12-4:
The John
Savill user
object.

Computer account creation is much simpler and doesn't bombard you with quite so many tabs. Again, in Active Directory Users and Computers, right-click on the container in which you want to create the new computer (such as computers) and select New⇨Computer. The dialog box in Figure 12-5 appears. You only have to give a computer name and select who can add the computer to the domain.

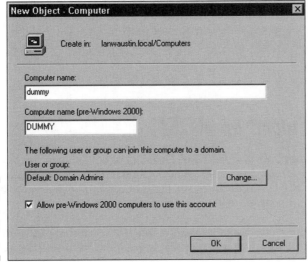

Figure 12-5:
A new computer named dummy.

Finding directory objects

Finding objects is one of Active Directory's greatest pluses. Using the Global Catalog, you can find an object anywhere in an enterprise forest by querying Active Directory.

You can search for anything — a user, a computer, even a printer — and you can search for many attributes. (The attributes presented vary depending on the type of object you're searching for.) For example, you can ask Active Directory to find the closest color-capable, double-sided printer at your site. You don't even have to tell Active Directory where you are. It figures that out automatically.

On a Windows 2000 Server computer, there's a Search component that you can access from the Start menu (Start⇨Search). Under this menu, there are a number of options you can use to search for users, folders, and printers. The available options are as follows:

- ✔ For Files or Folders
- ✔ On the Internet
- ✔ For Printers
- ✔ For People

For example, if you want to search for a color printer, you would select Start⇨Search⇨For Printers. There are three available tabs: Printers, Features, and Advanced. You would choose the Advanced tab because it allows you to specify that you're searching for a color printer. After you enter all your details, click Find Now and your results will appear. In a large enterprise, many listings that meet your requirements may appear, so always try to be as specific and detailed as possible when performing a search.

A final word on ADSI

Active Directory Scripting Interface (ADSI for short) allows you to manipulate the directory service from a script. You can use Java, Visual Basic, C, or C++ scripts. With ADSI you can write scripts that automatically create users, including setup scripts, profiles, details, and more.

If you need to manage a medium/large domain, you should learn ADSI now because in the long run it will save you a great deal of time and aggravation.

Microsoft has some great information on ADSI. Search the Microsoft Web site at `www.microsoft.com/Windows/server/` for **ADSI**, and you'll find loads of information (more than you would want!). Also check the Windows 2000 Resource Kit for details.

Permission to Proceed? Handling Directory Permissions

The old concept "you're the administrator, administrate no longer" does have some truth to it in Windows 2000 Server. Although some tasks still require a full-fledged domain administrator, the common management of a domain may be more easily accomplished when you grant different sets of users permissions to manage different sets of users/user properties. In English, this means you can delegate responsibility for managing low-level users to slightly higher-level users, and so on, until you, as the administrator, only need to get involved to manage more weighty constructs, such as domain forests and trees or intra-site access.

About Active Directory permissions

If you're familiar with the Windows NT security model, you probably know all about *Access Control Lists* (ACLs). ACLs allow a set of permissions to be applied to a file, directory, share, or printer (and more), thus controlling which users can access and modify these particular objects.

Windows 2000 takes this to the next level by assigning an ACL to every single attribute of every single object. This means that you can control user access to such a fine degree that you can micromanage your users into the nearest insane asylum. You could insist, for example, that "User group Personnel Admin may change the address, phone number, and e-mail attributes of all users but nothing else."

Assigning permissions

There are a number of ways you can assign permissions to Active Directory objects. Here, we show an extreme case, so everything else should look like a piece of cake!

Remember the Active Directory Users and Computers MMC snap-in? Well, earlier in this chapter in the "The directory management console" section, you saw a nice, basic view of this utility. However, it has other options that are only shown when it's in Advanced Features mode. To turn on Advanced Features, start the Active Directory Users and Computers MMC snap-in (Start⇨Programs⇨Administrative Tools⇨Active Directory Users and Computers), then select View⇨Advanced Features.

Some new branches are added to the basic domain root: LostAndFound, ForeignSecurityPrincipals, and System. We don't care about that though; we're interested in the new tab added to the objects — the Security tab.

In Active Directory Users and Computers, find a user, any user, right-click on the object and select Properties. Use the right arrow on the user's properties dialog box to locate the Security tab, and then click the Advanced button. You are shown a list of permission entries that consist of a type (Allow/Deny), a user or group, and the permission and its scope.

If you select one of these Permission Entries or add a new one and click View/Edit, you see a list of permissions (as shown in Figure 12-6) and an Allow and Deny checkbox for every property. Notice the size of that scroll bar. Ouch!

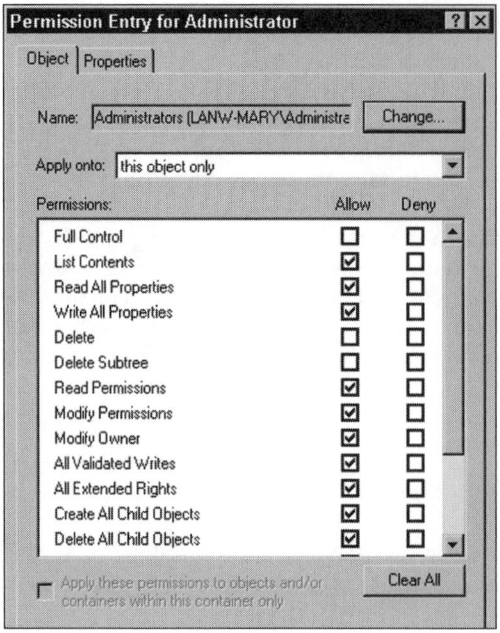

Permission Entry for Administrator ☐ ?✕

Object | Properties

Name: [Administrators (LANW-MARY\Administra] [Change...]

Apply onto: [this object only] ▼

Permissions: Allow   Deny

	Allow	Deny
Full Control	☐	☐
List Contents	☑	☐
Read All Properties	☑	☐
Write All Properties	☑	☐
Delete	☐	☐
Delete Subtree	☐	☐
Read Permissions	☑	☐
Modify Permissions	☑	☐
Modify Owner	☑	☐
All Validated Writes	☑	☐
All Extended Rights	☑	☐
Create All Child Objects	☑	☐
Delete All Child Objects	☑	☐

☐ Apply these permissions to objects and/or
   containers within this container only

[Clear All]

Figure 12-6:
The permis-
sions entry
for adminis-
trator.

Obviously, assigning permissions explicitly to every object takes forever.
Thankfully, Active Directory uses an inheritance model so you only need to
make changes at the root and the changes propagate down from there. The
following section spells out how this works.

Permissions inheritance

There are two types of permissions: explicit and inherited. *Explicit* permissions are assigned directly to an object, and *inherited* permissions are
propagated to an object from its parent (and so on). By default, any object in
a container inherits permissions from its container.

There may be times when you don't want permissions to be inherited. For
example, when you're working with a directory structure where different permissions are defined on each contained object, such as with a multi-user File
Transfer Protocol (FTP) site or a shared folder that contains user home
directories. The default setting in Active Directory specifies that permissions
are inherited, but this default behavior can be changed.

Remember the Advanced Features view for Active Directory Users and
Computers? Well, you need it again. When you turn on the Advanced
Features from the View menu and check out the Security properties of a user

(right-click on the user, select Properties, then select the Security tab), notice the small box that says "Allow inheritable permissions from parent to propagate to this object." This box was easy to miss, wasn't it?

The Allow Inheritable Permissions from Parent to Propagate to This Object box is checked by default; however, if you uncheck it, any changes made to the parent container no longer propagate to the objects it contains. You have disabled inheritance for the object.

If you do disable inheritance, you're given the following options:

✔ Copy previously inherited permissions to this object

✔ Remove inherited permissions

✔ Cancel the inheritance (disable)

Of course, you can re-enable this later if you want. It's not a one-way operation, so don't panic!

Delegating administrative control

Delegating administration over certain elements of your domain is one of the great things about Active Directory — no more administrator or non-administrator. Different people or groups can be delegated control over certain aspects of a domain's organizational unit. The following steps can be employed to delegate administration on objects:

1. **Right-click on a container (an organizational unit or domain) in the Active Directory Users and Computers MMC snap-in, and select Delegate Control.**

2. **The Delegation of Control Wizard starts up and the welcome screen is displayed. Click Next to start delegating!**

3. **On the next screen of the wizard, you need to select the group of users to whom you wish to delegate control. This is done by clicking the Add button and browsing the users/groups.**

   Make your selections (hold down Ctrl to select multiple users at the same time) and click Add. Then click OK.

   The users are now displayed in the selected user's area. The people you have selected are the ones who can perform the tasks you're about to choose.

4. **Click Next.**

5. **A list of common tasks is displayed for which you can delegate control (reset passwords and modify group membership, for example). You can also choose to create a custom task to delegate. If you choose this option, follow the steps presented by the wizard.**

   Make your selections and click Next.

6. **A summary screen is displayed (as shown in Figure 12-7), giving you the option to change your mind.**

   If you're happy with the changes you have made, click Finish.

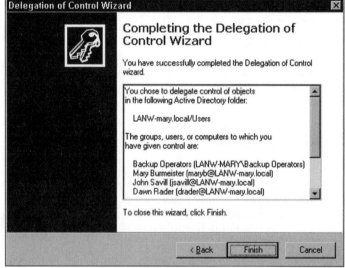

Figure 12-7:
The sum-
mary screen
of the
Delegation
of Control
Wizard.

That's it; a couple of clicks of a mouse and you've delegated control of a container to a specific person or groups of persons.

Managing Trusts

In Windows NT 4.0, trust management was a big problem in a large enterprise. However, in Windows 2000, it's simple if you use the tree and forest concepts, because two-way transitive trust relationships are automatically created between parent and child domains.

Two-way transitive trusts are created automatically when you run DCPROMO; however, the old Windows NT 4 style trusts can still be created for domains that are not part of the same enterprise forest.

Establishing trusts

Old style trusts are created using Active Directory Domains and Trusts, which is accessed by choosing Start⇨Programs⇨Administrative Tool⇨Active Directory Domains and Trusts. Right-click on the domain of your choice in the Active Directory Domains and Trusts interface and select Properties (see Figure 12-8). Select the Trusts tab to create *one-way trusts*. (One-way trusts are not transitive in nature and work exactly the same as the old Windows NT 4.0 trusts.) You can delete a trust by selecting the trust and choosing Remove.

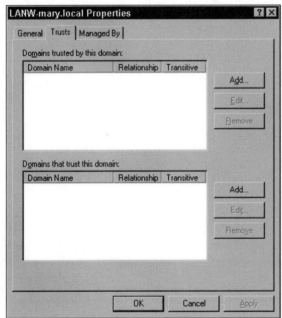

Figure 12-8:
Trusts for a
domain.

If you open the door to trusts, who gets to come through?

In a forest, when you open the trust door, anyone gets to come in. All trusts are transitive, so anyone in any domain in the forest can be granted permission to any resource.

For older style trust relationships that were created (as under Windows NT 4.0), the trust is not transitive. Only users in the two domains for which the trust is defined can be assigned access to resources and only in the direction of the trust.

There's no need to panic, though, because obviously users can't access resources without permission. Therefore, although they *can* be given access, they won't be able to gain access until specifically given permission to do so.

Chapter 13

Printing on the Network

● ●

In This Chapter

▶ Printing the Windows 2000 way

▶ Meeting the Printers folder

▶ Adding a (networked) print device

▶ Sharing print device access

▶ Managing Windows 2000-based print devices

▶ Teeing off with the right print device driver

▶ Preventing print device problems

● ●

*N*ext to not being able to access network resources, nothing freaks out users more than not being able to print their work. We bet you can't find a network administrator who can say that he or she hasn't struggled with print devices (such as laser printers) at one time or another. We think that Microsoft designed Windows 2000 with a good model for printing and, in this chapter, you find out the specifics on setting up print devices on your network and avoiding some common printing problems.

Throughout this chapter, we use the Microsoft terminology "print device" and "printer," which may be confusing in the real world. Microsoft defines "print device" as the physical printer, such as an HP LaserJet 4Si, and it defines a "printer" as the software on the server where you configure settings for the physical print device. We use Microsoft's terms in this chapter to be technically accurate. However, if this is your first time working with Windows 2000, this terminology may be confusing.

Windows 2000 Has a Print Model

When a user prints, the print data follows a particular path from the user to the print device. In Windows 2000 Server, the basic pieces of this print scheme are as follows:

✓ **Print users:** Print users are the people who want to send print jobs to a print device located either on the network or Internet, or attached to their workstation. To actually print, users must have a *print device driver* (called a *print driver* in non-Microsoftspeak) installed on their workstation. The only exception to this rule occurs when printing on a Windows 2000 network from a workstation with the Windows NT Workstation or Windows 2000 operating system. In these special cases, print users don't need drivers at their workstations because they can use the drivers installed on the Windows NT and 2000 servers. That is, for all Windows NT and 2000 workstations on the network, you install one print device driver on the server and you're done. The servers and clients do the rest for you — how nice!

✓ **Graphics Device Interface (GDI):** The already expanded GDI is a software program that finds the appropriate print device driver and works with the driver to render the print information into the appropriate printer language. After the information is rendered, the GDI sends it to the client-side spooler. (A Windows client application would call the GDI the *print process.*)

✓ **Print device driver:** This software piece is either provided by the manufacturer (for the latest version) or by Microsoft (not always the latest) and corresponds directly to a make and model of a print device. It's the interface between the software application and the print device. Again, this is called a *print driver* in non-Microsoftspeak. You may also hear it referred to as a *printer driver.*

✓ **Printers:** This is also called a *logical printer*, and it's not the physical piece of machinery you sometimes want to kick, but rather the bundle of settings you need to make the print device run. It exists as the software on the server that you use to configure settings for the physical print device.

✓ **Print jobs:** Print jobs are file(s) you want to print. Print jobs are formatted at the workstation by the GDI and a print device driver and submitted for output on a local or networked print device. If the print device is local (attached to the workstation), the output is printed right there and then. If a network print device and print server are involved, the output is sent (spooled) to a queue on the print server until a print device is available to service the request.

✓ **Print servers:** Print servers are computers that manage the network print devices attached to them. A print server can be any computer located on a network (or Internet) that has a print device attached and runs some flavor of a Microsoft operating system, such as Windows 2000, Windows NT Server, Windows NT Workstation, or Windows 9*x*. (Even a user workstation can function as a print server — although we don't like this approach because it typically brings too much traffic to the user's workstation.) When a user submits a print job, the print server stores the job in a queue for the print device and then polls the print device to check for its availability. If the print device is available, the print server pulls the next job out of the queue and sends it to the print device.

Any network administrator or user with appropriate access rights can manage print servers from anywhere on the network. By default, in Windows 2000, all members of the group Everyone can *print* to a device, but only those members specifically given rights can *manage* the device.

✔ **Print queues:** A print queue is a location on the hard disk where spooled files wait in line for their turn to be printed. Each print device has at least one corresponding print queue (though additional queues are possible), and as users submit print jobs, the jobs go into the queue to wait to be printed. You define a queue for a print device when you add the print device to the Printers folder and assign it a name. Print jobs enter the queues on a first-come, first-serve basis.

Only someone with the appropriate access rights to manage queues (Administrators, Print Operators, and Server Operators) can alter the print order in a print queue. You can assign users on your network the permission to manage the print queues for you. Windows 2000 has a built-in group called Print Operators, and you can add users to this group to give them the proper access rights for the task by choosing Start⇨Programs⇨Adminstrative Tools⇨Active Directory Users and Computers, selecting a domain, and opening the Buitin folder.

Giving some users print-queue management rights rather than other users could be seen as "playing politics" if you don't exercise great caution in making the assignments. Some folks may accuse others of playing favorites when print jobs are rearranged in the queue. We've seen this happen a lot. Try to pick people who are neutral, and your life will be easier!

✔ **Print devices:** Print devices are physical devices or physical printers, such as HP Laser printers. You can walk up to them and touch them. Print devices can be attached locally to a workstation or server, or directly to the network. In the real world, this is what we normal people call a printer!

Physical print devices

We call print devices *physical print devices* because you can walk up to these devices and touch them. Print devices come in different categories, including laser, plotter, ink jet, and bubble jet print devices. You can attach a physical print device locally to a workstation, server, print server, or directly to the network (as shown in Figure 13-1).

A print server is just a network-attached workstation that services print jobs — so, technically, we could lump workstations and print servers in the same category. We list them separately in this case because we want to distinguish between a workstation where a user sits and a dedicated print server workstation located on the network.

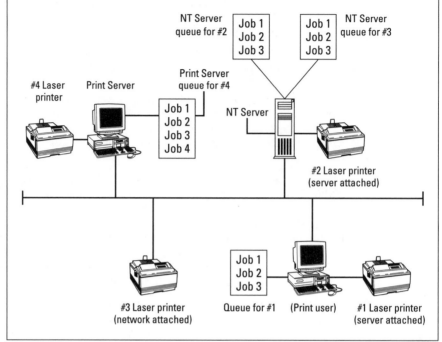

Figure 13-1:
A network
showing
different
methods to
connect
print
devices on a
network.

Logical assignments

A *logical printer assignment* isn't a print device — it exists intangibly, only in the form of a Windows 2000 definition. It's sort of like a name that Windows 2000 uses to identify a physical print device (or a group of physical print devices, as you see later in this section). Each time you define a print device and its properties in Windows 2000, the operating system assigns a logical printer definition to the physical print device so it knows to which physical print device you want to send your jobs.

When you first install a print device, a one-to-one correlation exists between the physical print device and the logical definition. However, you can expand the use of logical printer assignments to allow for one logical printer assignment to serve as the definition for several physical print devices. This use is known as *print device pooling,* and you set it up through print device properties by adding ports to the print device's definition.

You don't need to be too concerned about defining logical printers unless you intend to pool the print devices. This happens whenever you attach a print device to the server (as explained later in the section "Attaching print devices to servers"). Just understand that Windows 2000 correlates a logical printer definition to one or more physical print devices attached to your network.

For example, you're likely to have several print devices connected to your network, and all or many of them may be the same type, such as HP4MV. If you don't define a logical printer definition for Windows 2000, how does it know to which HP4MV print device to send your jobs? You could be running all around the building looking for your expense report! Defining a logical printer definition keeps order in your world. You could name one logical printer *2FLWest,* and you would know that your report is sent to the HP4MV on the second floor of the west wing of your building.

Another bit of magic that logical assignments can help you with is balancing print jobs. Suppose that you have three physical laser print devices (A, B, and C) located on your network in close proximity. If a user chooses to send a print job to printer A, which is printing a large print job, a lot of time and resources are wasted because printers B and C are sitting idle.

You can help your users in this regard by setting up one logical printer defini-tion and assigning it several different physical print devices to which to print. Therefore, your users print to the one logical assignment, which then figures out which physical print device is available. This takes the decision making and worrying from the user and transfers it to the operating system. The only caveat here is avoiding too much distance between print devices. Try to make sure that all physical print devices in the logical printer definition are in the same general area so your users don't have to run around the building looking for their printouts.

When setting up logical assignments to service more than one physical print device, the physical print devices must be identical. The only changes you can make are to properties, such as the bin number and paper size of each print device.

Conversely, you can assign several printer assignments to service one physi-cal print device. You want to do this if users are printing special items, such as envelopes. Define one printer assignment to print to the envelope bin on the physical print device and define another printer assignment to print letter-size paper on the same print device.

If you name the logical assignments something descriptive, the users will know where the print device is and what type of function it performs. For example, naming two logical assignments *2FLWestEnv* and *2FLWest* tells the user that 2FLWestEnv is on the second floor of the west wing and it prints envelopes, whereas the other is a normal print device on the second floor of the west wing. Both printer assignments actually service the same physical print device, but they may print to different bins on the print device, or one may pause the print device between pages, and so on. Here, you don't need to do anything other than define separate print devices that all print to the same port.

Server-Side Installation

Before you set up clients to print on your network, first make sure to go to the server and install all the print device definitions, drivers, and hardware, and then go to the client side. Doing so ensures that when you finally get to the user's workstation, you can submit a test print job right away because all the components are in place. If you start at the user's side first, you have to go back later to test.

Meet the Printers folder

Nearly everything you want to do with print devices can be found on the server in the Control Panel's Printers folder. (This information is more quickly available by choosing Start⇨Settings⇨Printers.) We say *nearly* everything because the print device drivers are stored outside of the print devices folder. (Most of the drivers are found on the Windows 2000 Server CD-ROM.)

When you install Windows 2000 Server for the first time, the Printers folder contains only an Add Printer icon, which is designed to help you install a physical print device (or logical printer definition). Each time you install a new print device by clicking the Add Printer icon (we cover the installation later in this chapter), Windows 2000 assigns it a separate folder in the Printers folder, as shown in Figure 13-2.

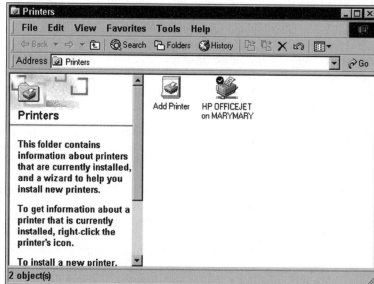

Figure 13-2:
The Windows 2000 Printers folder showing an installed print device plus the Add Printer icon.

When you click the Add Printer icon, the Add Printer Wizard appears, bringing with it a set of default policies that it uses to guide you through the process of adding each new print device to the Printers folder.

After you've installed the print devices you want, you can still make changes to print devices by visiting the Printers folder. Right-click the print device you added and select Properties from the pull-down list that appears. A window with numerous tabs appears. You make all of the changes to the particular print device in this Properties dialog box, so take some time to familiarize yourself with the available settings.

Adding a (networked) printer

In an ideal world, your network and users would allow you to set up one type of print device in one manner (all laser print devices of the same make and model with network interface cards, or NICs, and so on); however, in the real world, things don't pan out like that. Therefore, the engineers at Microsoft designed Windows 2000 Server to provide you with four different ways to attach print devices to your network:

- Print server
- Windows 2000 Server
- Workstation
- Networked (as shown earlier in Figure 13-1)

In the following sections, we show you the four different approaches to installing print devices on your network. Although all of the approaches are different, three of the four installations are very similar; they're just performed on different machines. For example, the steps for installing print devices attached to networks and for installing print devices attached to workstations are very similar. Both machines have print devices connected to their local ports, and they both share print devices on the network.

Attaching print devices to servers

You may find a need to attach a print device directly to your server. We don't recommend that you use this method unless your organization can't afford to spare a machine for you to use as a dedicated print server. Why? Because any time you attach a device to a file server, you run the risk that it may get hosed and crash the server. We've seen this happen often, so we advise against attaching a print device to your server whenever possible. If you're on a tight budget, however, you may need to use this configuration.

To attach a print device to a Windows 2000 Server, you need a print device, a Windows 2000 Server computer, a cable, the Windows 2000 Server installation CD (if you didn't copy it to your server's hard disk), and any print device drivers you want automatically downloaded to the clients.

Connect the print device directly to one of the ports on the server (for example, LPT1) and install the print device on this machine in its Printers folder by choosing Start⇨Settings⇨Printers. Then, follow these steps:

1. **Double-click the Add Printer icon, which invokes the Add Printer Setup Wizard, and click Next.**

2. **Select Local Printer, mark Automatically Detect My Printer, and click Next.**

   The New Printer Detection window of the wizard appears and searches for and installs attached Plug and Play print devices. If the print device is not Plug and Play, you must follow the rest of the steps in this section.

3. **Mark Use the Following Port, select the port to which you attached this print device (such as LPT1), and click Next.**

4. **After you click Next, a Window appears that allows you to choose the manufacturer and model of the print device.**

   In the Manufacturers section of the window, highlight the print device manufacturer; in the Printers section of the window, highlight the model of the print device. Click Next.

   If you don't see your print device listed here, it means you have to provide the Add Printer Setup Wizard with the driver. Click the Have Disk button and point the wizard to the location and path where the driver resides.

5. **In the Name Your Printer window of the wizard, Setup suggests a name for this print device. Accept this name or type a new name for this print device and then click Next.**

6. **In the Printer Sharing window of the wizard, type a share name for this print device if you want to share it. If you don't want to share it, choose the Do Not Share This Printer option. Click Next.**

   The share name is the name that your users will see when they print to this print device, so make it meaningful (for example, 2ndFLWestEnv).

7. **In the Location and Comment window of the wizard, type a location and description for this printer.**

   Your users can use this information when determining to which print device they wish to print. The more information you give here, the less your head will hurt later!

8. **Choose whether you want to print a test page (always a great idea) and then decide if you want to install drivers for the other client operating systems that will access the print device. Click Next.**

   Setup copies files from the Windows 2000 installation CD to the Windows 2000 Server computer's hard disk. Also, if you chose to share the print device in Step 6, you need to have the operating system print drivers handy to install (see Step 8), so Windows 2000 Server can automatically download the drivers to the client.

9. **If you chose to install additional drivers in Step 8, Setup begins copying drivers for this print device and, if need be, pauses to ask you for the location and path of the appropriate printer drivers. Type the path information and click OK.**

   You can go to the Printer's Properties under the Sharing tab to modify any drivers you've installed. See the section "Managing Windows 2000-Based Printers," later in this chapter, for further information.

10. **If you chose not to print a test page and not to install additional drivers, Setup presents you with a summary page of your choices. Click Finish if your choices were correct. Otherwise, use the Back and Next buttons to correct the information.**

If you're familiar with setting up print devices on Windows 9*x* and Windows NT, you probably whipped through the previous steps quickly because the print device setups are similar. At this point, you have set up the following:

- ✔ **One basic logical printer assignment that points to one physical print device on a Windows 2000 Server:** We say basic because you haven't customized any options, such as paper bins, dots per inch, and separator pages, for this print device yet. You probably weren't aware that as you defined this physical print device, you also assigned it a logical printer assignment. Remember that there's a one-to-one correlation between the two each time you install a physical device and define it unless you add more physical devices.

- ✔ **A print queue for this print device:** Even though you weren't aware that you did this, Windows 2000 does this for you when you define the print device. To view the queue, double-click the print device icon. You won't see anything in the queue just yet.

- ✔ **Shared access to this print device by everyone on the network:** When you define a share name on the network for a print device, Windows 2000, by default, assigns the Everyone group access to this print device. You have to change this default policy if you don't want "everyone" to have access to this print device. If you have Active Directory installed, the print device is published to the Directory.

You can have multiple logical printer assignments pointing to one physical print device. If you want to assign another logical printer assignment that services this physical print device, you repeat the previous steps but assign a new computer and share name. You can assign different properties to this physical print device for each logical printer definition. Each logical printer assignment you define here requires 30 to 40KB of space in the Registry.

Attaching print devices to print servers

In the preceding section, we show you how to hook up a print device to a Windows 2000 Server computer so your Windows 2000 Server functions as a print server on your network in addition to its other duties. To help manage the load on the Windows 2000 Server, you can offload this printing task to another computer on your network and have *it* function as your print server.

The print server is just another computer on your network with a print device attached to it that you set up to manage print spooling, print queues, and print jobs. We like this method because it frees up the Windows 2000 Server to perform other tasks. When your clients print to the print server, they bypass the Windows 2000 Server and send print jobs directly to the print server.

You can install any Microsoft operating system that you like on the computer that will be your print server. We recommend at least Windows 9*x*, but we prefer a Windows NT/2000 workstation because you can download the print drivers directly to the client workstations from the print server automatically with no intervention on your part. This means that you don't have to install drivers manually on each of the client workstations.

After you've installed an operating system on your soon-to-be print server, repeat Steps 1 through 10 from the "Attaching print devices to servers" section if you're using a Windows NT/2000 Workstation as the operating system. If you're using Windows 9*x*, repeat the same steps but exclude the downloadable print device drivers from Steps 8 and 9. Instead, you have to go to each client and install the corresponding print device drivers.

Attaching networked print devices to print servers

Some print devices, such as HP laser print devices, are neat because after you plug a NIC into them, they're almost ready to be placed anywhere on your network where there's an electrical outlet and an available network connection. Almost, but not quite! You still need to make all the physical connections and assign an IP address to the printer. After you do that, perform the following steps to add the networked print device to the print server:

1. **Click Printers.**

   The Printers window appears.

2. **Double-click the Add Printer icon to invoke the Add Printer Wizard, and then click Next.**

   The Add Printer Wizard appears.

3. **On the Local or Network Printer window, click Local Printer, and unmark the Automatically Detect My Printer checkbox. Then click Next.**

   The next screen of the Add Printer Wizard appears.

4. **On the Select the Printer Port window, mark Create a New Port and under Type, select Standard TCP/IP Port from the drop-down list. Click Next.**

   The Welcome to the Add Standard TCP/IP Printer Port Wizard screen appears.

5. **Click Next.**

   The Add Port screen appears.

6. **On the Add Port screen, enter the IP address of the networked print device and give the port a name. The wizard will fill in a name for you, but you can change it if you like. Click Next.**

7. **If your print device is properly configured and set up, and you've entered the proper information in the wizard, the wizard locates your device on the network and displays information for it. Click the Finish button to complete.**

When installing a printer on a Windows 2000 Server with Active Directory installed, the Add Printer Wizard shares the print device and publishes it in the Directory — unless you change the policy rules. For more information on the Active Directory, please read Chapter 11.

Attaching print devices to a workstation

Some users may have print devices on their desks that you want to make available to other users on the network. Attaching a print device to a workstation is the method that's the least desirable because it involves users going to another user's workstation to pick up their print jobs. This can cause a disruption in workflow to the user who's unfortunate enough to have the print device on his or her desk. However, in smaller organizations where budgets are tight, this method is used.

You need to go to the user's workstation desktop and share that print device on the network. You can restrict access to that share so the entire organization isn't allowed to print there. Where do you find all this? In the Printers folder (Start⇨Settings⇨Printers for Windows 95/98 users) on the user's desktop, of course! Right-click the Add Printer icon if no print device is installed and choose the print device to be a local print device connected to LPT1 and assign it a name. If a print device is already defined, right-click the print device icon and select Properties to give this print device a share name. After you share the print device on the network, other users can see it.

This method causes the user's workstation to manage the printing process. You can define this workstation-attached print device on your Windows 2000 Server so your Windows 2000 Server will manage the print process instead. Here's how:

1. **Go to the user's computer desktop and define a share for this print device, but limit access to the username of "JoePrinter."**

   See the following section, "Sharing Printer Access," to find out how to define a share.

2. **Mosey back over to the Windows 2000 Server.**

3. **Add a user named "JoePrinter" in Users and Computers (Start⇨Programs⇨Administrative Tools⇨Users and Computers. If Active Directory is installed, it says Active Directory Users and Computers.)**

4. **Double-click Add Printer in the Printers folder.**

5. **Follow the same steps as in the "Attaching print devices to servers" section earlier in this chapter, except for the following changes:**

   • Click the Add Printer icon and choose the networked print device instead of the locally attached print device (My Computer).

   • Select the radio button that says Type The Printer Name or Click Next to Browse for the Printer. Either type the share name or use the Browse option to select and choose the share name you gave the print device on the client's desktop.

   • Give this print device a new share name that the rest of the users on the network will see.

We don't recommend that you use this method unless your organization is tight on money. It can cause aggravation for the user who has to share the print device with other people on the network and can disrupt that user's work environment. Use this method only if your budget doesn't allow one of the other methods.

Sharing Printer Access

After you've installed a print device on your network (as we explain in the preceding sections), the next step is to create a share on the network for that print device. (See Chapter 16 for more details on Windows 2000 network shares.) Until you share a print device, your users can't see it on the network. To share a print device, open the Printers folder (Start⇨Settings⇨Printers). Right-click the print device you want to share and select Sharing from the menu options to open the Sharing tab. Select the Share As radio button and type a descriptive share name (for example, 2ndFlWest). If you want this print device listed in the Active Directory, mark the List in the Directory box. Click OK and you're done!

When you share a print device, it's available to everyone on the network by default. You must specifically restrict groups or users from accessing the print device if that's what you want.

If you have MS-DOS-based clients on your network, make sure that your share names for print devices are only eight characters long.

Bringing Printers and Clients Together

The final step in setting up networked printing involves setting up the print devices on the client side. Fortunately, not much is required in this process. Everything you need will be on the Windows 2000 Server, the print server, or in the user's Printers folder on his or her desktop, depending on which operating system he or she uses.

If the client operating system is a Windows 2000/NT Workstation, you only need to add the print device in the Printers folder (Add Printer) and select Networked Print Device. The reason is that the print device is actually attached to another computer somewhere on the network, not local to this workstation. For the port, use the Browse option and find the share name of the print device to which you want to print. That's it!

Remember that Windows 2000 Server and Windows 2000/NT Workstations work together so the server can provide the print drivers dynamically for Windows 2000/NT Workstation clients.

If your clients have Windows 9x and your clients are printing to a Windows 2000 Server (and you've installed the various client operating system drivers at the server), you simply add the print device in the Printers folder (Add Printer) and select it as a networked print device. When you select the port as the share name of the networked print device, Windows 2000 Server automatically downloads the drivers.

Managing Windows 2000-Based Printers

You can view and perform some management of your print servers, queues, and print devices from anywhere on the network, including your Windows 2000 Server. Therefore, you can view what's going on with all of the print devices on your network from one location. The only thing you can't do remotely is install something on the print device itself, such as memory or cables. But you knew that already! The following list includes some issues to keep in mind as you manage print devices:

✔ **Disk space on server:** If you set up spooling on your network, you need to keep a close eye on the hard disk space of the print servers. The spooling process involves sending files from the print user to the print server. Remember that the print server can also be your Windows 2000 Server. In either case, if your network has a high volume of print activity, it's possible to fill up a hard disk quickly with the spooling process.

After files are spooled to the print server, they remain on the hard disk in the queue until an available print device is ready. If there's a problem with the print device, jobs can get backed up quickly. Remember that queues take up space on the hard disk, so if the queues back up, more and more space is needed. Be careful that you don't run low on disk space!

✔ **Memory in the print device:** Anytime your users print graphics on the network, memory becomes an issue on the print devices. Large graphics files require more memory to print. You can find out how much memory is in a print device by performing a self-test on the print device. Some organizations don't have a large budget for adding extra memory to all of their networked print devices, so they select one or more in strategic locations and then define logical print device setups that point to the loaded print devices.

✔ **Configuring the Printer's Properties:** You can access the Printer's Properties menu by right-clicking on a print device's icon in the Printers folder. (Figure 13-3 shows the various settings you can alter for any print device on your network.) We go through each of the tabs here to help you understand which print device properties you can change:

• *General:* Here's where you add information about this print device, such as comments, location, whether to use a banner page, and more. We recommend that you add some general comments about the print device and its location. In medium- to large-sized operations, adding a separator page so print jobs are more easily distinguished from each another is a good idea. The current print driver information is also found here. Change this only if you're going to install a new driver.

- **Ports:** This is where you tell the system to which port your print device is attached. If it's a network-attached print device, you define it here using the *Media Access Control* (MAC) address; if it's a *Transmission Control Protocol/Internet Protocol* (TCP/IP) print device, you define it here using the IP address.

- **Scheduling:** You may opt to have print jobs run at night for this print device. This is where you can schedule the print device's availability, priority, and spooling options.

- **Sharing:** If you want users on the network to see this print device, you define the share name here (and make it meaningful). You can also tell Windows 2000 to allow this device to show up in the Directory. This is also the location where you tell Windows 2000 which client operating systems you have on your network to which you want print drivers automatically downloaded.

- **Security:** This is where you set up auditing of your print devices, which enables you to gather information should something go wrong with a print device. You may want to use the Security tab for charge-back purposes on a departmental basis (where you audit the usage and charge users or departments for that use), or you can use it to limit this print device's availability. You can also define who is allowed to manage this print device.

- **Device Settings:** This is where you define specific properties of the print device, such as paper size, dots per inch, paper bin, and more.

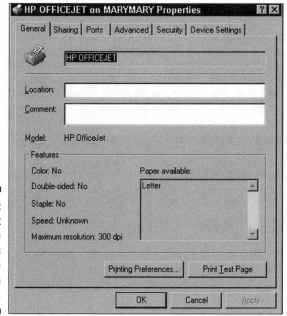

Figure 13-3:
View of print device Properties tabs within the Printers folder.

Preventing Printer Problems

Printing problems on a network can wreak havoc. Here are a few pointers we can pass along to help you head off this type of trouble before it starts. If you do experience problems, See Chapter 22 for some troubleshooting help.

- ✔ **Purchase HCL-compatible devices:** Only purchase network print devices listed in the *Hardware Compatibility List* (HCL). Otherwise, you don't know if the print device will work on the network, and you may spend hours trying to get the print device to work. And always remember to check Microsoft's site for the latest version of the HCL.

- ✔ **Get the latest print device drivers:** Make sure that you obtain the latest print device driver associated with each print device on your network. Newer drivers fix bugs found in older drivers. If you use an older driver, you sometimes end up troubleshooting a known bug and one that is already fixed in the newer driver.

- ✔ **Purchase a name brand:** We hope that your organization can afford to purchase name brand print devices, such as Hewlett-Packard and Epson, for your network. We find that the biggest printing problems on networks stem from cheaper models. Even if you're able to hook these cheaper print devices up, sometimes it takes so long to get all the pieces working that you may have done better to have invested in more popular brand name print devices.

- ✔ **Purchase from one manufacturer:** We like to stick with one type (brand name) of print device where possible. Notice we said brand and not model. We realize that some organizations need to print in both black and white and color; however, if you can purchase all of your print devices from one manufacturer (for example, Hewlett-Packard), your life, and your users' lives, will be easier. If you have all Hewlett-Packard laser print devices on your network, don't buy another manufacturer's laser print device just because it's on sale that day at your local computer superstore. You can save time by working with one vendor and its equipment and drivers, rather then having to hunt all over the Internet for various manufacturers' Web sites. Allow your users to become familiar with the one brand, and they won't have to relearn new equipment all the time.

- ✔ **Buy enough memory:** The influx in graphics software has placed a strain on memory usage in print devices to produce the desired output. Don't wait until print jobs start fouling up before adding more memory. If your budget is too low to do this up front, find a local vendor that stocks memory for your computer and keep its telephone number handy.

✔ **Join a Windows 2000-related Internet mailing list:** You can find some very valuable information on these. Remember, though, that some mailing lists are very active, so if you sign up, be prepared to receive at least 50 e-mails per day in some cases.

✔ **Look for Windows 2000/NT Frequently Asked Questions (FAQs) on the Internet:** There are a few good sites where you can find Windows 2000/NT-related information and FAQs: `www.ntfaq.com` and `www.bhs.com` are two of the more familiar locations. You can also go to one of the main search engines like `www.search.com` and type **2000 FAQ**. Sometimes, just looking at these FAQs provides insight into problems, questions, and answers that others have pioneered.

Chapter 14

IP Addressing: Zero to Insane in Two Seconds Flat

. . . .

In This Chapter

▶ Working with TCP/IP and NetBIOS names

▶ Understanding IP addressing, nets, and subnets

▶ Obtaining Internet-ready IP addresses

▶ Using private IP addresses

▶ Using proxy servers and address translation

▶ Working with DHCP

▶ Knowing when to use WINS

▶ Working with DNS

. . . .

*T*he *Transmission Control Protocol/Internet Protocol* (TCP/IP) drives the Internet and makes it accessible around the world. TCP/IP, however, is a lot more than just a collection of protocols: Many elements in the TCP/IP marry protocols to related services to provide more complete capabilities. Important examples include dynamic address allocation and management, known as the *Dynamic Host Configuration Protocol* (DHCP), plus domain name to address resolution services, known as *Domain Name Service* (DNS). You find out about TCP/IP names, addresses, and related standard services in this chapter, as well as some other related services hosted by and unique to Windows 2000.

Resolving a Name: TCP/IP and NetBIOS

Whenever you issue a command in Windows 2000, you're expected to use the proper syntax. Otherwise, your efforts might not produce the desired results. For example, when you issue a NET USE command from a command prompt, you must enter the server name and a share name, as well as the drive you wish to map. Therefore, a simple command like NET USE G: \\LANWRIGHTS\ APPS associates the drive letter G: with a share named APPS on the LAN-WRIGHTS server. If you use the TCP/IP protocol to convey the data involved, the protocol doesn't know how to interpret the name LANWRIGHTS as the server. Instead, it understands *Internet Protocol* (IP) addresses, such as 172.16.1.7.

If you use TCP/IP on your network, you need some way to convert IP addresses into names, and vice versa. Just as the United Nations requires translators so everyone can communicate, so does Windows 2000, which is why understanding naming conventions and name-to-address resolution is such an important part of working with TCP/IP on Windows 2000.

NetBIOS names

If you're like most folks, you freeze like a deer in the headlights when you hear the word NetBIOS. Don't worry. Only a small number of people really understand NetBIOS in detail, but figuring out what you need to know without stressing out is easy.

A NetBIOS name is often called a computer name. When you install Windows 2000 onto a network, each computer that runs Windows 2000 requires a unique computer name. This allows all NetBIOS-based utilities to identify each machine by its name. Any time you enter a command that includes a computer name, Windows 2000 knows which computer you're talking about.

If you try to give two devices the same name, you run into trouble — like trying to use the same Social Security number for two people. Each time a computer joins the network, it registers its name with a browser service that keeps track of such things. When the second computer with the same name tries to register, it's rejected because that name is already "taken." In fact, that machine will be unable to join the network until its name is changed to something unique.

When creating NetBIOS names, you need to work within their limitations, which are:

- NetBIOS names must be between 1 and 15 characters long. (If you have DOS or Windows 3.*x* machines on your network, they can't recognize NetBIOS names with more than 8 characters.)

- NetBIOS names may not contain any of the following characters: " (double quotation mark), / (right slash), \ (left slash), [(left square bracket),] (right square bracket), : (colon), ; (semicolon), | (vertical slash), = (equal sign), + (plus sign), * (asterisk), ? (question mark), < (left angle bracket), and > (right angle bracket). Dollar signs are not recommended because they have a special meaning. (A NetBIOS name that ends in $ does not display in a browse list.)

✔ Don't use lengthy names or put spaces in names. Windows 2000 doesn't care if you use longer names or include embedded spaces, but other networking clients or systems may not be able to handle such uses.

✔ Pick names that make sense to users and are short and to the point. Don't name machines after their users or locations, especially if users come and go regularly, or if machines move around a lot. When it comes to servers, name them to indicate organizational role or affiliation (for example, Sales, Accounting, or Engineering).

What's in a NetBIOS name, you ask? A NetBIOS name should have a short, clear indication of what's being named so users can recognize what they see. At best, this type of naming convention will make sense without requiring further explanation. At the very least, you can do what we do and put a sticker with the machine's name on each monitor for self-identification purposes. You can view a list of your network's NetBIOS names by double-clicking the My Network Places icon on your server's desktop and double-clicking Computers Near Me. See Figure 14-1 for a sample list of NetBIOS names (taken from our own network).

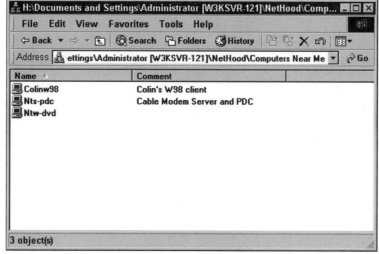

Figure 14-1:
NetBIOS
computer
names on
our network.

TCP/IP names and addresses

TCP/IP uses a different scheme for names than NetBIOS does. TCP/IP uses 32-bit numbers to construct IP addresses (for example, 172.16.1.11). Each host or node on a TCP/IP network must have a unique IP address.

IP addresses are not meaningful to most humans and are difficult to remember. Therefore, it's helpful to have some way to convert IP addresses into meaningful names. On a Windows 2000 network, you use computer names (also known as NetBIOS names). The Internet community uses a different naming convention called domain names. Translation methods, such as *Windows Internet Name Service* (WINS) and *Domain Name Service* (DNS) maintain databases for converting an IP address to a computer name (WINS) or a domain name (DNS).

If you've ever used a Web browser on the Internet, you know that you can type a *Uniform Resource Locator* (URL), such as 206.224.65.194/ or www.lanw.com/, to obtain access to a Web page. You can do so because the Internet uses DNS to resolve IP addresses to domain names and vice versa. If you type the IP address, the Web browser jumps straight to the named address; if you type a domain name, your request goes through a DNS server that resolves the name to an IP address, and then the browser jumps to the named address.

In the IP world, the naming scheme you can use is limited if you plan to connect your network directly to the Internet. Network Solutions (www. networksolutions.com), a partner of the *Internet Network Information Center,* or InterNIC (www.internic.net), is in charge of approving and maintaining the database of "legal" Internet domain names. You can request any domain name you want, but if someone else is using it or has a legitimate claim to a trade or brand name, you won't be able to use it. For example, you probably won't be able to use mcdonalds.com or cocacola.com as domain names; likewise, if somebody else has already registered xyzcorp.com, you wouldn't be able to use that name, even if your company is named XYZ Corporation.

The format for a typical IP name is host.domainname.suffix. The domain name is something you can't guarantee, but typically represents your organization. The suffix sometimes identifies the country of origin (for example, .ca is Canada, .de is Germany) or the type of organization (.gov is government, .edu is education, .com is a commercial business, .org is a nonprofit organization, and so forth).

Some domain names are more complex; they can take a form such as host.subdomain.domainname.suffix, as in jello.eng.sun.com, where the host name is jello, the subdomain is eng (for engineering), and the domain name is sun (the domain name for Sun Microsystems, Inc.), which is a commercial (.com) entity. The only parts of the name under control of Network Solutions/InterNIC are the domain name and the suffix — every domain name must be unique in its entirety to be properly recognized.

Names that include the host part, the domain name, and the suffix (plus any other subdomain information that may apply) are called *Fully Qualified Domain Names* (FQDNs). To be valid, any FQDN must have a corresponding entry in some DNS server's database that allows it to be translated into a unique numeric TCP/IP address. For example, your authors' Web server is named www.lanw.com, which resolves into a numeric address of 206.224.65.194.

As long as you're completely isolated from the Internet and intend to stay that way, you can assign any names and IP addresses you like on your network. However, if you ever connect your network to the Internet, you'll have to go back and change everything! If your network will be — or simply *might ever be* — connected to the Internet, you have one of two options for assigning addresses:

> ✔ **You can obtain and install valid public IP addresses and domain names now.**
>
> You can obtain these directly from Network Solutions/InterNIC at some difficulty and expense, or you can pay your Internet Service Provider (ISP) to do this for you. We recommend the latter course. When you obtain a range of IP addresses for your network — remember, each computer needs its own unique address, and some computers or devices need multiple addresses (one for each interface) — make sure you get enough to leave some room to grow.
>
> ✔ **You can (and should) obtain a valid domain name from Network Solutions/InterNIC, but you can use any of a range of reserved IP addresses, called private IP addresses, to number your networks.**
>
> These addresses may not be used directly on the Internet, but have been set aside for private use. When used in concert with a type of software called *Network Address Translation* (or NAT for short), this approach requires you to obtain only a small number of public IP addresses but still allows Internet access for every computer on your network. This topic is discussed in more detail later in this chapter in the section "Address translation: The new magic."

To find out more about the process of obtaining a domain name, visit the Network Solution's Web site at www.networksolutions.com. The form for researching (determining if a FQDN is already in use) and registering (applying for a new FQDN) domain names is on the main page. You'll find details on name registration services as well as on the directory and database services that support the Internet's distributed collection of DNS servers.

Calling Every Node

A unique numeric identification tag, called an *IP address*, is assigned to each interface on a TCP/IP network. Every IP address within a TCP/IP network must be unique. Each device on a TCP/IP network is known as a *host*. Each host has at least one network interface with an assigned IP address. However, a host can have multiple *network interface cards* (NICs), and even multiple IP addresses assigned to each NIC.

To network ID or host ID, that is the question

An IP address consists of two components: a *network ID* and a *host ID*. The network ID identifies the network segment to which the host belongs. The host ID identifies an individual host on some specific network segment. A host can only communicate directly with other hosts on the same network segment. A network segment is a logical division of a network into unique numeric network IDs called *subnets*. A host must use a router to communicate with hosts on other subnets.

A *router* moves packets from one subnet to another. A router reads the network ID for a packet's destination address and determines whether that packet should remain on the current subnet or be routed to a different subnet. When a router delivers a packet to the correct subnet, the router then uses the host ID portion of the destination address to deliver the packet to its final destination.

A typical IP address looks like 207.46.131.137 (which matches the domain name www.microsoft.com). This numeric IP address format is known as *dotted-decimal notation*. However, computers "see" IP addresses as binary numbers. This same IP address is 11001111 00101110 10000011 10001001 in binary form and is written in collections of eight bits called *octets*. Each octet is converted to a decimal number and then separated by periods to form the dotted-decimal notation format shown at the beginning of this paragraph. The decimal version of IP addresses is more human-friendly than the binary version. As you may already know, domain names and NetBIOS names are still more friendly because they use symbolic names that make sense to humans.

An IP address requires 32 binary digits and defines a 32-bit address space that supports nearly 4.3 billion unique addresses. Although this seems like a lot of addresses, the number of available IP addresses is quickly dwindling. Consequently, several plans exist to expand or change the IP addressing scheme to make many more addresses available. For more information on such plans, please search for IPng Transition in your favorite search engine.

IP designers carved the entire galaxy of IP addresses into classes to meet different addressing needs. Today, there are five IP address classes labeled by the letters A through E. Classes A, B, and C are assigned to organizations to allow their networks to connect to the Internet, and Classes D and E are reserved for special uses.

The first three classes of addresses differ by how their network IDs are defined:

- ✔ Class A addresses use the first octet for the network ID.
- ✔ Class B uses the first two octets.
- ✔ Class C uses the first three.

Class A addresses support a relatively small number of networks, each with a huge number of possible hosts. Class C addresses support a large number of networks, each with a relatively small number of hosts, as shown in Table 14-1 (Class B falls in the middle). Therefore, branches of the military, government agencies, and large corporations are likely to need Class A addresses; medium-sized organizations and companies would need Class B addresses; and small companies and organizations would need Class C addresses.

When it comes to recognizing address classes A through C, the network ID for Class A addresses always starts its first octet with a zero. Each Class B network ID always starts with 10, whereas Class C network IDs always start with 110. Consequently, you can determine address classes by examining an address, either in binary or decimal form. (See Tables 14-1 and 14-2.)

Table 14-1	Address Classes and Corresponding Network and Host IDs			
Class	**High-Order Bits**	**First Octet Range**	**#Networks**	**#Hosts**
Class A	0xxxxxxx	1-126.x.y.z	126	16,777,214
Class B	10xxxxxx	128-191.x.y.z	16,384	65,534
Class C	110xxxxx	192-223.x.y.z	2,097,152	254

Table 14-2	Division of IP Address Component Octets According to Class		
Class	**IP Address**	**Network ID**	**Host ID**
A	10.1.1.10	10	1.1.10
B	172.16.1.10	172.16	1.10
C	192.168.1.10	192.168.1	10

Note that the network ID 127 is missing from Table 14-1, which is because it's a *loopback address*. Loopback addresses are used when testing IP transmission — they transmit to themselves.

No valid IP address may include an octet that consists entirely of ones or zeros (0 or 255 in decimal), because these addresses are reserved for broadcast addresses (255) and subnet identification (0).

Subnetting: Quiet time for IP addresses

Subnets represent divisions of a single TCP/IP network address into logical subsets. The motivation for subnetting is twofold. First, subnetting reduces the amount of overall traffic on any network segment by collecting systems that communicate often into groups. Second, subnetting makes it easier for networks to grow and expand, and it adds an extra layer of security controls. Subnets work by "stealing" bits from the host part of an IP address and using those bits to subdivide a single IP network address into two or more subnets.

Network administrators typically use *subnet masks* to divide IP address blocks into smaller subnetworks. A subnet mask is a special bit pattern that "takes over" part of the host ID portion of an IP address, and that permits a larger network to be subdivided into two or more subnetworks, each with its own unique network address. The base subnet masks for Class A, B, and C networks are 255.0.0.0, 255.255.0.0, and 255.255.255.0 respectively. By adding extra bits set to 1 in the space occupied by the 0 that appears next to the rightmost 255 in any such number, additional subnet masks may be created. This transformation is illustrated in Table 14-3, which shows some typical values for usable subnet masks.

Routers move packets among subnets and networks

Only *routers* can transfer packets from one subnet to another, or from one network ID to another, in the TCP/IP world. Routers are specialized devices that include high-end, high-speed devices from companies such as Cisco Systems or Bay Networks. However, any computer with two or more NICs installed (where each NIC resides on a different subnet) can be a router provided that the computer can forward packets from one NIC to another (and thus, from one subnet to another). Right out of the box, in fact, Windows 2000 includes the software and built-in capabilities to function as a router. Computer nerds like to call such machines *multi-homed computers* because the machines are "at home" on two or more subnets.

Table 14-3	Subnet Masks and Results		
Binary Mask	Decimal Equivalent	Number of New Subnets	Number of Hosts
00000000	A: 255.0.0.0 B: 255.255.0.0 C: 255.255.255.0	A: 16,777,214 B: 65,534 C: 254	1
10000000	A: 255.128.0.0 B: 255.255.128.0 C: 255.255.255.128	A: Not valid B: Not valid C: Not valid	Not valid
11000000	A: 255.192.0.0 B: 255.255.192.0 C: 255.255.255.192	A: 4,194,302 B: 16,382 C: 62	2
11100000	A: 255.224.0.0 B: 255.255.224.0 C: 255.255.255.224	A: 2,097,150 B: 8,190 C: 30	6
11110000	A: 255.240.0.0 B: 255.255.240.0 C: 255.255.255.240	A: 1,048,574 B: 4,094 C: 14	14
11111000	A: 255.248.0.0 B: 255.255.248.0 C: 255.255.255.248	A: 524,286 B: 2,046 C: 6	30
11111100	A: 255.252.0.0 B: 255.255.252.0 C: 255.255.255.252	A: 262,142 B: 1,022 C: 2	62
11111110	A: 255.254.0.0 B: 255.255.254.0 C: 255.255.255.254	A: 131,070 B: 510 C: Not valid	126

Because routers are required to communicate across IP subnets, some router's IP address on each subnet must be known to every client on that subnet. This address is called the *default gateway,* because it's where all out-of-subnet transmissions are directed by default. (It's the gateway to the world outside each local subnet, in other words.) If no default gateway is defined, clients can't communicate outside their subnet.

Putting your shingle out: Obtaining Internet IP addresses

Deploying your own network or using a stand-alone system with Network Address Translation (NAT) to connect to the Internet requires that you obtain one or more valid IP addresses. For some uses, you may simply contract with an ISP to use a dial-up connection. Each time you connect, you're assigned an IP address automatically from a pool of available addresses. After you disconnect from the ISP, that IP address is returned to the pool for reuse. This works equally well for stand-alone machines and for the servers that might dial into an ISP to provide an on-demand connection for users who have private IP addresses but can attach to the Internet using NAT software.

One way to attach an entire network to the Internet is to lease a block, or subnet, of IP addresses from an ISP. However, leasing IP addresses can be expensive and can limit your growth. Also, many ISPs can no longer lease large blocks of IP addresses so you may have to limit Internet access to specific machines or subnets.

For more information about taking this approach, you need to contact your ISP to find out what it can offer by way of available addresses and contiguous subnets. For some uses, public IP addresses are required because security needs dictate a true "end-to-end" connection between clients and servers across the Internet. In plain English, a true end-to-end connection means that the IP address that a client advertises to the Internet is the same one it uses in reality. In the section "Address translation: The new magic," you discover an alternate approach where the IP address advertised to the Internet is different from the private IP address that a client uses on its home subnet.

For some applications, particularly where secure IP-based protocols such as *IP Secure* (IPSec) or particular *Secure Sockets Layer* (SSL) implementations are required, network address translation techniques may not work! Make sure you understand your application requirements in detail before you decide whether to lease public IP addresses or use private IP addresses with network address translation.

Address translation: The new magic

If you don't want to pay to lease a range of IP addresses, and your application requirements allow you to use private IP addresses, you can employ the IP addresses reserved for private use in RFC 1918 on your networks. When used in combination with network address translation software to connect to an ISP, a single public IP address (or one for each Internet connection) is all you need to service an entire network.

RFC 1918 (which can be found at `www.faqs.org/rfcs/rfc1918.html`) defines special IP addresses for use on private intranets. These addresses, which appear in Table 14-4, will not be routed on the Internet by design. This approach actually provides improved security for your network as a fringe benefit, because it means that any impostor who wants to break into your network cannot easily masquerade as a local workstation. (Doing so would require routing a private IP address packet across the Internet.) Because all of these addresses are up for grabs, you can use the address class that makes sense for your organization (and for Class B and Class C addresses, you can use as many as you need within the legal range of such addresses).

Table 14-4	Private IP Address Ranges from RFC 1918	
Class	*Address Range*	*# Networks*
A	10.0.0.0 - 10.255.255.255	1
B	172.16.0.0 - 172.31.255.255	16
C	192.168.0.0 - 192.168.255.255	254

Therefore, using address translation software to offer Internet access reduces your costs and allows nearly unlimited growth. If you think private IP addresses combined with NAT software makes sense for your situation, consult with your ISP for specific details and recommendations on how to use this technology on your network.

You've probably heard the terms *firewall* and *proxy* thrown about often when reading or talking about Internet access. Firewalls and proxy servers are network tools that are little more than special-purpose routers. A firewall may be used to filter traffic — both inbound and outbound.

Firewall filters can be based on source or destination address, a specific protocol, or port address, or even on patterns that appear in the content of a data packet. A proxy server is an enhanced firewall, and its primary purpose is to manage communications between an in-house network and external networks such as the Internet. Proxies hide the identity of internal clients and can keep local copies of resources that are accessed frequently (this is called *caching,* and it improves response time for users).

You can check out several great online resources for firewalls, but online information on proxies is limited to product documentation. In addition to consulting the Windows 2000 Resource Kit and TechNet (`www.microsoft.com/technet/default.asp`), here are several online resources you might want to check to discover more about these technologies:

- ✔ **Zeuros Firewall Resource:** www.zeuros.co.uk/
- ✔ **Great Circle Associates:** www.greatcircle.com/
- ✔ **4 Firewalls:** www.4firewalls.com/
- ✔ **Microsoft's Proxy Server 2.0 (for Windows NT 4.0):** www.microsoft.com/proxy/ (version 3.0 for Windows 2000 should be released soon)
- ✔ **Aventail VPN:** www.aventail.com/
- ✔ **Netscape's Proxy Server:** www.netscape.com/
- ✔ **Ositis Software's WinProxy:** www.ositis.com/
- ✔ **Deerfield Communication's WinGate Pro:** www.deerfield.com/

For example, your authors use Ositis Software's WinProxy product, which acts as a proxy and provides NAT services, to link their networks to an ISP across an *Integrated Services Digital Network* (ISDN) connection. We allow the ISP to assign us an IP address each time we log onto its host for an Internet connection. This doesn't matter because the NAT service translates between whatever address it assigns us and the internal address each machine uses on the other side of the WinProxy software. We only pay for the temporary use of a single IP address, but we can handle up to eight connections to the Internet at a time!

Forcing IP down 2000's Throat

Configuring TCP/IP on Windows 2000 can range from simple to complex. We review the simple process and discuss a few advanced items, but for complex configurations, you should consult a reference such as the Windows 2000 Resource Kit or TechNet.

Three basic items are always required for configuring TCP/IP:

- ✔ IP address
- ✔ Subnet mask
- ✔ Default gateway

With just these three items, you can connect a client or server to a network. The protocol is configured on the Internet Protocol (TCP/IP) Properties dialog box (see Figure 14-2). To access this dialog box, follow these steps:

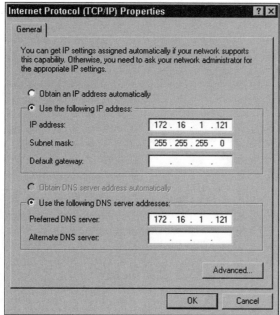

Figure 14-2:
The Internet
Protocol
(TCP/IP)
Properties
dialog box.

1. **Select Start⇨Settings⇨Network and Dial-up Connections.**

2. **Right-click on Local Area Connection, and select Properties from the pop-up menu.**

   This opens the Local Area Connection Properties dialog box.

3. **Select Internet Protocol (TCP/IP) from the list of installed components, then click Properties.**

   This opens the Internet Protocol (TCP/IP) Properties dialog box.

If TCP/IP is not already installed, follow these steps:

1. **Click Install on the Local Area Connection Properties dialog box.**

2. **In the Select Network Component Type dialog box, select Protocol, and then click Add.**

3. **In the Select Network Protocol dialog box, select Internet Protocol (TCP/IP). Click OK. You may be prompted for a path to the distribution CD.**

4. **Provide the configuration details as discussed later in this section.**

The Internet Protocol (TCP/IP) Properties dialog box offers fields for defining the three IP configuration basics. Notice there's a selection to obtain an IP address automatically. This setting configures the system to request IP configuration from a Dynamic Host Configuration Protocol (DHCP) server.

Because most servers don't work well using dynamic IP addresses, you may want to define a static IP address for your Windows 2000 Server instead of using DHCP. You will either obtain a public IP address from your ISP, or use a private IP address from one of the reserved address ranges defined in RFC 1918.

You must also calculate a subnet mask for your network (that is, as long as you are not using DHCP). Here again, you may obtain this from your ISP if you're using public IP addresses, or calculate your own if you're using private IP addresses. In most cases where private IP addresses are used, the default subnet mask for the address class should work without alteration or additional calculations.

Finally, you must also provide a default gateway address for your server. (Unless you just don't want this system to communicate with other hosts outside of its subnet.) The default gateway should be the address of the router on the local subnet to which the server is attached that can forward outbound traffic to other network segments. On networks using public IP addresses, this is probably a router, firewall, or proxy server that connects the local subnet to other subnets, or the Internet. On networks using private IP addresses, this is usually the machine on which the proxy and NAT software resides, which mediates between the local subnet and an Internet connection.

The Internet Protocol (TCP/IP) Properties dialog box also offers fields to configure Domain Name Service (DNS). Well, for the most part, you can leave these blank . . . at least for now. We talk more about DNS in the "DNS Does the Trick" section later in this chapter.

After you define an IP address, a subnet mask, and a default gateway, click OK, then close all the windows you've opened and reboot. That's all there is to basic TCP/IP configuration on Windows 2000!

More complex configurations become necessary when your network is larger, and therefore, more complicated. To deal with such complexity, you have to do some "advanced" work. Click the Advanced button on the Internet Protocol (TCP/IP) Properties dialog box to reveal the Advanced TCP/IP Settings dialog box, complete with its four tabs. The tabs (along with brief descriptions) are:

> ✔ **IP Settings:** This tab allows you to define multiple IP address/subnet mask combinations for a single NIC. You can also define additional default gateways, as well as an interface metric, which is used by routers (or the routing service of Windows 2000) to determine to which path to send data — the path with the lowest metric is used first.

✔ **DNS:** This tab allows you to define additional DNS servers — the one or two you defined on the Internet Protocol (TCP/IP) Properties dialog box appears here as well, so don't get confused. In addition, you can specify how to search or resolve issues based on DNS server, DNS domain, and DNS parent domains. The two checkboxes at the bottom of the DNS tab allow you to use dynamic registration to automatically add your server's IP address and domain name to your local DNS. For more information about DNS, please consult the "DNS Does the Trick" section later in this chapter.

✔ **WINS:** This tab is where IP addresses for *Windows Internet Name Service* (WINS) servers are defined. WINS servers resolve NetBIOS names into IP addresses. WINS is convenient for Windows 2000 networks with multiple servers and network segments. This tab also offers you control over how/if NetBIOS operates over TCP/IP. For more information about WINS, please consult the "Everybody WINS Sometime" section later in this chapter.

✔ **Options:** This tab is where you can define alternate settings associated with TCP/IP. This tab offers access to IP Security and TCP/IP Filtering by default, but the layout of the interface seems to hint that other optional features or services may be configured here if they are installed later. IP Security allows you to set TCP/IP based communications to require or accept Kerberos security, which is a security system developed at the Massachusetts Institute of Technology (MIT). TCP/IP Filtering allows you to define TCP, User Datagram Protocol (UDP), and Protocol ports that will be allowed to function. In other words, it blocks all traffic except the traffic for the ports that you choose to allow in. This interface is rather limited because it doesn't tell you which ports you need to allow in. We recommend deploying a proxy or firewall to perform TCP/IP filtering, because a proxy or firewall is more user-friendly and tells you which ports you need.

Everybody WINS Sometime

In a Microsoft Windows network, TCP/IP hosts can be called by NetBIOS names instead of IP addresses or domain names. Because NetBIOS names are more or less unique to Microsoft Networks, there's no current standard for associating NetBIOS names with IP addresses. On a Microsoft Network that uses TCP/IP as its only networking protocol, it's essential to be able to resolve NetBIOS names to IP addresses. This is where *Windows Internet Name Service* (WINS) comes in.

A glimpse at WINS

Because resolving NetBIOS names to IP addresses is the key to providing access to many of Windows 2000's built-in services and facilities, Microsoft provides two methods to handle this process:

- **LMHOSTS:** You can use a file named LMHOSTS to create a static table that associates specific NetBIOS names with specific IP addresses. (LM stands for LAN Manager, and points to the network operating system that preceded Windows NT in the Microsoft product world.) Such a file must be present on every machine to provide the necessary name to address resolution capabilities.

  For small, simple networks, using LMHOSTS files is an acceptable method. On large, complex networks, the busy work involved in maintaining a large number of such files can quickly get out of hand.

- **WINS:** Larger, more complex networks are where WINS comes into play. WINS runs on Windows 2000 Server machines as a service that automatically discovers NetBIOS names and manages a dynamic database that associates NetBIOS names with TCP/IP addresses. As networks grow in size, multiple WINS servers sometimes become necessary to help speed up the time it takes to handle name resolution requests.

  A single WINS server can handle an entire network. However, on networks that include multiple sites or thousands of users, multiple WINS servers can distribute the load involved in providing name resolution, and speed users' access to NetBIOS-based resources.

WINS has several advantages over LMHOSTS files. For one thing, it's built on a dynamic database, which means that as networks change and names and addresses come and go, the database changes as the WINS server detects new name and address relationships, or finds old names with new addresses. WINS can be especially important on networks where DHCP is used, if clients also share files or printers on their machines. Also, WINS is something like a Spanish-English dictionary that's constantly updated as new words are added. For example, you give it a Spanish word, and out pops an English word that means the same thing!

WINS servers

A WINS server maintains a database that maps computer names to their respective IP addresses and vice versa. Rather than sending broadcasts for address information, which eats excess network bandwidth, a workstation that needs a NetBIOS name resolved makes a request directly to a designated WINS server (that's the real purpose of the WINS tab in the Advanced TCP/IP Settings dialog box, in fact).

This approach lets workstations take advantage of a well-defined service and obtain address information quickly and efficiently. Also, when workstations with NetBIOS names log onto the network, they provide information about themselves and their resources to the WINS server. Then, any changes will automatically appear in the WINS server's database.

Although WINS is much simpler than DNS, it's still not an easy process. You need to install WINS as a network service component through the Network and Dial-up Connections interfaces. However, we recommend seeking guidance from the Windows 2000 Resource Kit before starting on that journey.

WINS clients

When configuring workstations or servers (at least, those servers that don't play host to the WINS server software) on your network, you'll provide an IP address for one or more WINS servers on your network. When those machines boot, they provide the WINS server with their computer names, share names, and IP addresses. The WINS server handles everything else. If a workstation needs an IP address that corresponds to a NetBIOS name, it asks the WINS server to supply that information.

NetBIOS over TCP/IP

The bane of many security consultants, NetBIOS over TCP/IP is a piggyback *application programming interface* (API) employed by Windows 2000 for all of its internal and server-to-server communications. Within a secured environment, such as behind firewalls and proxies, NetBIOS over TCP/IP is a benefit because it supports many of the user-friendly features of Windows 2000 networking. But, without adequate security, it's a gaping hole that devious individuals can exploit to overtake your network or stand-alone system. The WINS tab offers you the ability to disable NetBIOS over TCP/IP on the current system (meaning NetBIOS will not be transmitted over network links from this computer) or to allow it to mimic its DHCP server (if the DHCP server disabled NetBIOS, this system will as well).

DNS Does the Trick

One way to simplify TCP/IP host identification is to use *Fully Qualified Domain Names* (FQDNs) instead of IP addresses. An FQDN is the type of name used to identify resources on the Internet to make access easier for humans (such as www.microsoft.com). Resolving domain names and FQDNs to IP addresses is a crucial service on TCP/IP networks in general and especially on the Internet, where hundreds of millions of names and addresses can be found. This is where the Domain Name Service — sometimes called the Domain Naming Service or Domain Name System, but always abbreviated as DNS — comes into play.

As with NetBIOS names and IP addresses, the association between FQDNs and IP addresses can also be maintained in two ways:

- **HOSTS file:** You can create a HOSTS file on each system. The HOSTS file maintains a local table that associates specific FQDNs with specific IP addresses. Whenever such associations change, the HOSTS file must be updated manually and copied to all machines on a network.

  HOSTS files are not suited for interaction with large IP-based networks, especially the Internet. This explains why HOSTS files are mostly historical relics of an earlier, simpler era of IP networking. Except as a fallback in case access to DNS fails, nobody uses HOSTS files anymore.

- **DNS:** Access to a DNS server allows network machines to request name resolution services from that server instead of maintaining name-to-address associations themselves. Although DNS servers must be configured manually, a DNS server can handle the name resolution needs of an entire network with ease. DNS servers can also communicate with one another, so a name resolution request that the local server cannot handle can be passed up the FQDN name hierarchy until it reaches a server that can resolve the name into an address, or indicate that the name is invalid.

The Internet includes tens of thousands of DNS servers. ISPs manage many of these DNS servers; others fall under the control of special top-level domain authorities. To stake out an Internet presence, you must obtain a unique FQDN through the InterNIC (or let your ISP do it for you). After you obtain this name, it is associated with a special root IP address in some DNS server (probably at your ISP, unless you decide to set up a DNS server of your own).

Windows 2000 supports a new twist on DNS called Dynamic DNS. It has added automatic registration of domain name and IP address to the previously manual-only service. This can reduce administrative overhead if employed properly on servers hosting network applications. You can access the simple configuration checkbox using the Advanced button when configuring TCP/IP.

Whether to DNS

Unless you manage a large, complex network, chances are better than average that you will work with somebody else's DNS server — probably, your ISP's — rather than managing your own. However, if you have a large network with over 1,000 computers, or your network spans multiple sites using private wide-area links, a DNS server may be just the thing to help you stake out the right type of Internet presence.

One unique feature of Windows 2000 is that it automatically installs three services on the first server of a domain: Active Directory, DHCP, and DNS. Although you don't actually have to employ DHCP and DNS, they're still installed by default. Installing these services is therefore a breeze (so much so that the Configure Your Server wizard does it for you automatically). The real headaches come when you try to configure DNS (or DHCP for that matter).

The deans of DNS

If you think you may be interested in setting up a DNS server, you need to consult a technical resource, such as the Windows 2000 Resource Kit or TechNet. We also highly recommend *DNS on Windows NT,* a book by Paul Albitz, Matt Larson, and Cricket Liu (O'Reilly & Associates, Sebastopol, CA, 1998, ISBN 1-56592-511-4) as the ultimate resource for using Windows NT as a DNS Server. Albitz and Liu also wrote a general book called *DNS and BIND,* now in its third edition (O'Reilly & Associates, Sebastopol, CA, 1998, ISBN 1-56592-512-2) that is widely regarded as the best general reference on DNS. Both of these books should be updated soon to encompass new material for Windows 2000.

DHCP: IP Addressing Automation

DHCP, the *Dynamic Host Configuration Protocol,* is used to dynamically assign IP addresses and other configuration settings to systems as they boot, which allows clients to be automatically configured at startup, thus reducing installation administration. DHCP also allows a large group of clients to share a smaller pool of IP addresses, if only a fraction of those clients need to be connected to the Internet at any given time.

What is DHCP?

DHCP is a service that Windows 2000 Server can deliver. In other words, a Windows 2000 Server can run DHCP server software to manage IP addresses and configuration information for just about any type of TCP/IP client.

DHCP manages IP address distribution using leases. When a new system configured to use DHCP comes online and requests configuration data, an IP address is leased to that system (by default, each lease lasts three days).

When the duration of the lease is half-expired, that client can request a lease renewal for another three days. If that request is denied or goes unanswered, the renewal request is repeated when 87.5 percent and 100 percent of the lease duration has expired. If a lease expires and is not renewed, that client can't access the network until it obtains a new IP address lease. You can initiate manual lease renewals or releases by executing `ipconfig /renew` or `ipconfig /release` at the Windows 2000 Command Prompt.

You can view the current state of IP configuration using the `ipconfig` command. Issuing the command `ipconfig /all|more` at the Command Prompt displays all of a machine's IP configuration information one screen at a time.

Is DHCP in your future?

We can think of two profound reasons why DHCP is a real godsend to Windows 2000 administrators who need to use it:

1. DHCP enables you to manage an entire collection of IP addresses in one place, on a single server, with little effort beyond the initial configuration of the address pool (the range of addresses DHCP will be called upon to manage). In the old days (before DHCP), managing IP addresses usually required walking from machine to machine on a far too frequent basis.

2. DHCP automates delivery of IP addresses and configuration information (including subnet mask and the default gateway addresses) to end-user machines. This makes it astonishingly easy to set up IP clients and to handle configuration changes when they must occur.

   To configure IP on a new client, all an end user (or you) must do in Windows 2000, Windows NT, or Windows 9x is click the single radio button on the IP Properties window that says "Obtain an IP address automatically." DHCP does the rest!

   When configuration changes occur, these changes are automatically introduced when IP leases are renewed. You can even cancel all existing leases and force clients to renew their leases whenever major renumbering or configuration changes require immediate updates to their IP configurations.

The ultimate reason for using DHCP is because it makes your job much easier. DHCP is recommended for all networks that use TCP/IP with ten or more clients. The first Windows 2000 Server in a domain has DHCP automatically installed, but you still need to enable and configure it properly before it will do you any good. So, if you think you may be interested in setting up a DHCP server, you need to consult a technical resource, such as the Windows 2000 Resource Kit or TechNet, for all the details of installation and configuration.

Ironing Out the Problems

Problems that occur on TCP/IP networks are almost always associated with incorrect configurations. The wrong IP address, subnet mask, default gateway, DNS, WINS, or DHCP server can bring a system, if not a whole network, to its knees. Therefore, you need to take extra caution to double-check your settings and changes before putting them into effect.

If you connect to an ISP, you should contact the ISP's technical support personnel early on to eliminate as much "wheel-spinning" as possible. You may discover the problem is not on your end, but theirs. If so, your only recourse is to wait it out, then complain. If problems occur too often for your comfort at an ISP, take your business elsewhere.

Windows 2000 includes a few TCP/IP tools that you can employ to help track down problems. We already mentioned `ipconfig`, so here are the others:

- ✔ **PING:** This tool tests the communication path between your system and another remote system. If a ping returns, you know the link is traversal and the remote system is online. If the ping times out, either the link is down or the remote system is offline.

- ✔ **TRACERT:** This tool reveals the hops (systems encountered) between your system and a remote system. The results inform you if your trace route packets are getting through and at what system a failure is occurring.

- ✔ **ROUTE:** This tool is used to view and modify the routing table of a multi-homed system.

- ✔ **NETSTAT:** This tool displays information about the status of the current TCP/IP connections.

- ✔ **TELNET:** This tool is used to establish a text-based terminal emulation with a remote system. Telnet gives you access to remote systems as if you were sitting at its keyboard. Windows 2000 Server does not include an inbound Telnet server.

Complete details on these tools are included in the Windows 2000 help files, the Windows 2000 Server Resource Kit, and TechNet.

Enough TCP/IP to Choke a Hippo

If this chapter has whetted your whistle for TCP/IP, there are lots of great resources where you can obtain more details and information:

- Bisaillon, Teresa and Brad Werner. *TCP/IP with Windows NT Illustrated.* McGraw-Hill, 1998. ISBN: 0079136486.

- Stevens, W. Richard. *TCP/IP Illustrated Volumes 1,2 & 3.* Addison-Wesley, 1994. ISBN: 0-201-63346-9, 0-201-63354-X, 0-201-63495-3.

- Comer, Douglas E. *Internetworking with TCP/IP, Vol. I-III.* Prentice Hall, 1995, 1996, 1997. ISBN: 0-13-216987-8, 0-13-973843-6, 0-13-848714-6.

- Wilensky, Marshall and Candace Leiden. *TCP/IP For Dummies,* 3rd Edition. IDG Books Worldwide, Inc., 1999. ISBN: 0-7645-0473-8.

Part IV
Running Your Network

The 5th Wave   By Rich Tennant

"If it works, it works. I've just never seen network cabling connected with Chinese handcuffs before."

In this part . . .

After Windows 2000 Server is up and running, the real fun — namely, maintaining the server and network you've just so laboriously constructed — begins. Or at least, so goes the conventional wisdom on this subject. In a very real sense, therefore, Part IV begins where Part III leaves off.

First, you begin with managing the users (and their groupings) who will be working on your network and using your server. Then, it's on to a crucial discussion of how to set up and handle NTFS and share permissions, with a heaping order of file systems and related topics. After you've got the data and users to protect, backing up your system is no longer an option — it's a downright necessity — so it's the next topic on our systems management agenda. Part IV closes out with an exercise in "positive paranoia" wherein you learn about computer and network security in a discussion that covers the bases from physical security all the way up to how to build a solid password.

Therefore, Part IV covers all the important topics related to managing a Windows 2000 Server-based network to prepare you to live with one of your very own (or to work on somebody else's). Use these chapters to help establish a regular round of systematic maintenance at regular intervals — not only will your users thank you, but you'll probably save yourself some time and effort, too!

Remember this: Maintenance activities and costs usually represent 90 percent of any computer system's life cycle. That's why establishing a solid maintenance routine and sticking to it religiously are the keys to running a successful network. Do yourself a favor and DON'T learn this lesson the hard way. . . .

Chapter 15

Managing Users with Active Directory Users and Computers

● ●

● ●

*U*ser accounts are an indispensable element in the Windows 2000 Server environment. User accounts are the central management and control tools used by the operating system to authenticate users, provide access, and enforce control. If you don't have a defined user account on a Windows 2000 Server stand-alone system or a Windows 2000 Server hosted network, you can't gain access. This chapter looks at managing user accounts and policies through the Active Directory Users and Computers console.

Users Have Properties

Computers are typically used by more than one person. Even systems that workers use exclusively on their desktops allow system administrators to log on. The computer distinguishes between one person and another by employing a security device — the *user account object*. Each user on a computer or a network has a unique user account that contains details about the user, his or her rights and restrictions to access resources, and more.

A Windows 2000 Server-based user account contains, is linked to, or is associated with the following items:

- ✔ **Password security:** User accounts are protected by a password so only the authorized person can gain access to the system.

- ✔ **Permissions:** Permissions are the access privileges granted to a user account. These include group memberships and user-specific settings to access resources.

- ✔ **Identification:** User accounts identify a person to the computer system and/or a network.

- ✔ **User rights:** A user right is a high-level privilege that can be granted to users or groups to define or limit their actions on a computer system.

- ✔ **Roaming:** You can define user accounts so a person can log on to a system by any means, including local logon, *Remote Access Service* (RAS), or over a gateway.

- ✔ **Environment layout:** Profiles are user-specific and store information about the layout, desktop, and user environment in general. You can define profiles so they follow the user no matter where he or she gains access.

- ✔ **Auditing:** Windows 2000 Server can track access and usage by user accounts.

Access to Windows 2000 Server requires that users successfully authenticate themselves with their user accounts, which means that, when a user sits down at a Windows 2000 system, he or she must press Ctrl+Alt+Del to start the logon process. Then, the user must provide a valid username and password. After the system verifies this information, the user is granted access. After a user completes his or her computing task, he or she can log out and leave the system available for the next user to log on.

When Windows 2000 Server is installed, two user accounts are automatically created. One of these accounts, the Administrator account, is the account used to initially configure the system and to create other user accounts. The second account, the Guest account, is a quick method to grant low-level access to any user.

Administrators rule!

The Administrator account is the primary means by which you initially configure Windows 2000. It's also the most powerful account in the Windows 2000 environment; therefore, you should make sure that the password for the Administrator account is complex and secret. The Administrator account has unrestricted access to everything within Windows 2000, including managing user accounts, manipulating shares, and granting access privileges.

The Administrator account boasts the following features:

- ✔ You can't delete it.
- ✔ You can't lock it out or disable it.
- ✔ You can rename it (right-click on the account and choose Rename from the pop-up menu that appears).
- ✔ Although you can define a blank password, some services don't function properly if you do; therefore, you should provide a valid, complex password for this account.

Renaming this account is a good idea. Would-be hackers (that is, people who want to gain unauthorized access to your system) need only two items of information to gain access to your system: a user account name and password. Unless you rename this account, they already have half the information they need to gain access to the most powerful account on your system.

Guests can wear out their welcome

The Guest account is the second default account created by Windows 2000. You can use this account as a temporary public-access method. It has minimal access rights and restricted privileges to resources.

The Guest account boasts the following features:

- ✔ You can't delete it.
- ✔ You can disable it and lock it out.
- ✔ It can have a blank password. (It has a blank password by default.)
- ✔ You can rename it.
- ✔ Changes to the environment aren't retained by this user account. (That is, the user profile is mandatory because user changes to the environment are not retained.)

The Guest account can be a security hole, so plugging it is important. We suggest that you keep this account disabled, or rename it and assign it a valid password.

Creating New Users

Creating new users is a common and simple task. You use the Active Directory Users and Computers console (see Figure 15-1) on Windows 2000 Server to create and manage user accounts and groups. You can also define account policies, set user rights, configure auditing, and establish trust relationships (some of which is discussed later in this chapter).

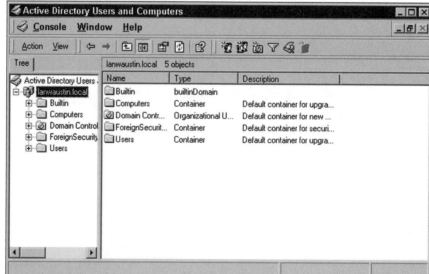

Figure 15-1:
Active
Directory
Users and
Computers.

Creating users isn't difficult, but you need to pay attention to lots of details. First, we walk you through creating a quick-and-dirty user account. Then, we talk about all the fine tuning you can perform on this account.

To get to Active Directory Users and Computers, choose Start⇨Programs⇨ Administrative Tools⇨Active Directory Users and Computers. Double-click on the domain or organizational unit to which you want to assign this new account. You'll see all of the default settings for this domain or organizational unit, including users. If you're assigning the user to the Users container, when you click it, initially, you see the Administrator and Guest accounts, plus other accounts that Windows 2000 Server set up, depending on the services you installed. You can create a new user from scratch by highlighting the container or unit, then selecting Action⇨New⇨User from the toolbar. (You can also right-click on the container or unit and select New⇨User from the pop-up menu.) This reveals the Create New Object - User dialog box/wizard. (See Figure 15-2.)

An organizational unit is an Active Directory container that holds other organizational units, computers, users, and/or groups. For more information on organizational units, see Chapter 11.

When you create a user object from scratch, you should pay attention to every detail of that account. The following steps guide you through the process:

1. **The New Object - User setup wizard presents you with your first screen and asks you to fill out the following information:**

   • **First name:** Hopefully this is obvious, but if not, type the user's first name.

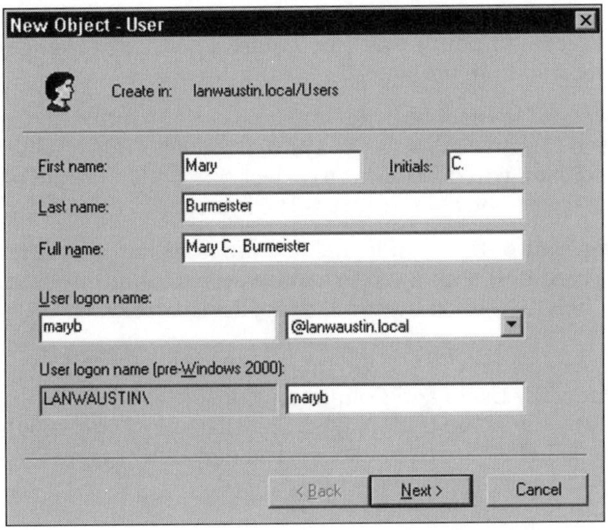

Figure 15-2:
New Object
- User
dialog
box/wizard.

- **Last name:** Type the user's last name.

- **Initials:** Type the user's middle initial, if applicable.

- **Full name:** Although this is not as obvious, this is how the name will be displayed on the system. Notice that the setup wizard has entered the name for you. You can replace what's filled in for you and arrange the display of the full name any way you like. Usually, the first name is displayed, then the last name.

- **User logon name:** Type the information you want the user to use to validate him or herself to the network. You should create a company standard such as last name first initial or something similar. (See the "What's in a name?" sidebar later in this chapter.)

- **Downlevel logon name:** This is the name given to the user for pre-Windows 2000 systems. Notice that the wizard fills in this information for you. You won't need to change this unless you're a tech head.

2. **Click the Next button to continue setting up this new user account object.**

   In the next screen, you enter information about the password. Type a password for this account, and then confirm that password to the system by retyping it. Next, configure the password settings using the options described in the following list:

   - **User Must Change Password at Next Logon checkbox:** Forces users to change their passwords.

   - **User Cannot Change Password checkbox:** Prevents users from changing their passwords.

- **Password Never Expires checkbox:** Exempts this account from the account policy that can require a password change after a specified time period.

- **Account is Disabled checkbox:** Ensures that this account can't be used to gain access to the system. Chances are, if you're creating a new user, you don't want to select this option because you want the user to be able to access the system.

3. **Click the Next button when you're done marking your selections. You're presented with a confirmation screen about the choices you've made. Click the Finish button if everything is correct.**

You've just created a new user account object, and you'll see that object in the Active Directory Users and Computers console window. In Step 1, we mention the way the name is displayed, and that's how you should see the object's name listed. If you right-click on the new object and then click on Properties, you'll see the following tabs:

- General
- Address
- Account
- Profile
- Telephones
- Organization
- Member Of
- Dial-in

This is where you can go through and enter more information about the new user account object, such as the groups to which it belongs. You may see other tabs, depending on the services installed on your Windows 2000 Server.

In the following sections, we go through the default tabs individually, so you can know what to fill in and why.

General

When you click the General tab, you can type more information about this account, such as description (additional location information, what the account is used for, or whatever you want), office, telephone, Web page, and e-mail address. The more information you can provide at this time, the more you'll be relieved later down the road when you might need this information. The description information shows up in the Active Directory Users and Computers console if you have the detail view selected (View⇨Detail).

What's in a name?

Windows 2000 Server actually uses a SID, or Security Identifier, to recognize and track user accounts. Windows 2000 Server doesn't actually use or even care about the human-friendly name assigned to a user account. But, because you're human, you should employ human-friendly names whenever possible. This not only lessens stress and makes user management easier, but it also improves your odds at winning the lottery.

What we're trying to say is that you should employ a naming convention. A *naming convention* is just a predetermined method for creating names for users, computers, resources, and other objects. The two key features of a naming convention are its ability to always create new names and that the names created provide descriptive information about the named object.

Small networks rarely need complex or even predefined naming conventions. However, when the number of named items on your network exceeds about 100 or so, you may find it increasingly difficult to remember who or what "jackal," "herbie," and "8675309" actually are. Therefore, starting a small network with a naming convention can ease the growth process later.

Windows 2000 Server doesn't impose or suggest a naming scheme. It just lets you define names as you please. If you decide to use a naming convention, you need to be diligent in enforcing and employing that scheme.

The naming convention you choose or create doesn't matter ultimately, as long as it always provides new names and those names indicate information about the objects they label. Here are some general naming-convention rules:

- The names need to be consistent across all element types (user names, computer names, share names, directory names, and so on).

- The names should be easy to understand. (If they're too complex or difficult, they won't be used.)

- The name should somehow identify the type of object.

You can create new names by mimicking the structure of existing names. Here are some examples of partial naming conventions that you can customize for your system:

- Create user names by combining the first and last name of a user (for example, JohnSmith and Jsmith).

- Create user names by combining the last name of a user and a department code (for example, SmithAcct and SmithSales5). With Active Directory, this type of schema is less needed because it typically reflects the organizational area.

- Create computer names by combining the user name, a computer type code, and room number (for example, SmithW98 and JS102).

- Create group names by combining resource descriptor, location, project, or department names (for example, Tower12, Planning2, and Conference12).

- Create share or directory names by combining the content or purpose descriptor with a group or project name (for example, Documents, SalesDocs, and AcctSheets).

- Create printer names by combining the model type, location, department, and group names (for example, HP5Sales, CLJRm202, and HP4Acct).

As you can see, each of these suggested partial naming schemes always creates new names and provides enough information about the named object to determine where it is and whether it's a user account, computer, share, or printer.

Address

Click the Address tab to type information about this user's physical mailing address. Although this information is not required, it's good to have handy.

Account

Click the Account tab to reveal the logon name, downlevel name, password information, logon hours, and account expiration information. Most of the options in this tab are self-explanatory — except the logon hours and expiration information, which are described as follows:

✔ **Logon hours:** Click the Logon Hours button to reveal the Logon Hours dialog box (see Figure 15-3). In this dialog box, you can define the hours during which a user can gain entry to the system. If this user account attempts to log on during off hours, the logon fails. If the user is already online when the hours expire, the user remains online but can't establish any new network connections (that is, the user can't send a document to a printer or open a new file). You define hours by selecting the day/hour sections and marking the Logon Permitted or Logon Denied radio button. This option is mostly used for contractors that are allowed to use the system only during regular working hours.

✔ **Account expiration:** Mark the Account Expires End Of radio button to define when (if ever) the account expires. This is useful for contract or temporary employees that have been granted access to the system for a specified period of time.

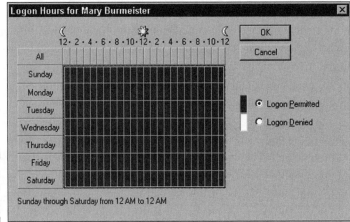

Figure 15-3:
Logon Hours
dialog box.

Profile

Click the Profile tab in the Properties dialog box to reveal current information about this user account's profile (see Figure 15-4). In this dialog box, you can define the following:

- ✔ **User profile path:** The location where the roaming profile (which makes a user's working environment available to them on any workstation on the network) for this user is stored. (See the "Give Your Users Nice Profiles" section later in this chapter.)

- ✔ **Logon script name:** The filename of the script file to be executed at logon. Logon scripts are usually batch files that define paths, set environmental variables, map drives, or execute applications. You typically only use logon scripts in Windows 2000 for compatibility purposes with older servers or DOS applications or to automatically configure settings for NetWare server access.

- ✔ **Home directory:** The default storage location for this profile as a local path or as a mapped drive letter to a network drive.

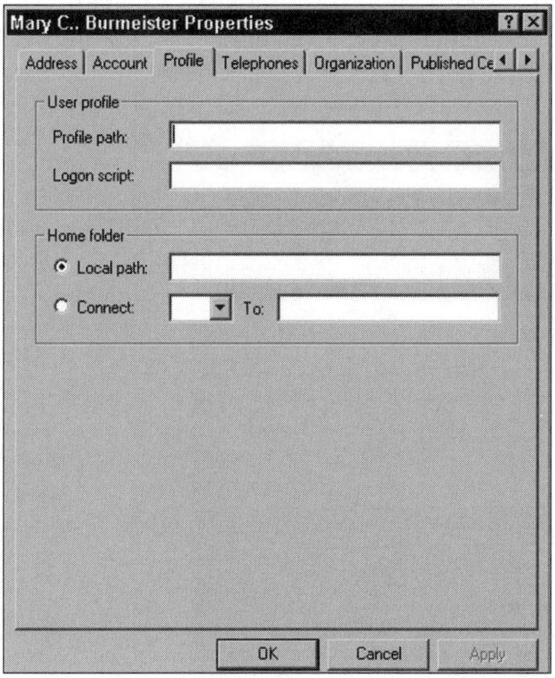

Figure 15-4:
User Profile
dialog box.

Telephones

Click the Telephones tab in the Properties dialog box to enter every imaginable phone number a person can have these days, such as pager, fax, mobile, and so on. There's even a Comments section where you can add whatever you want.

Organization

Click the Organization tab in the Properties dialog box to enter any information about this user's title within the organization, plus any direct reports. If your organization is prone to restructuring, you may opt to leave this tab blank.

Member Of

Clicking the Member Of tab in the Properties dialog box reveals information about this account's group membership status. This is where you can add/remove a user account object to/from a group (see Figure 15-5). If you want to add this object to another group, click the Add button and select the group. As we discuss later in this chapter, group membership determines the resources to which you grant a user account access.

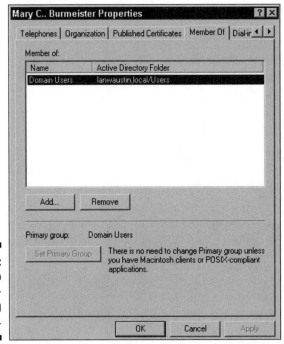

Figure 15-5:
The Group
Member-
ships dialog
box.

Dial-in information

Click the Dial-in tab in the Properties dialog box to enable or disable this account from dialing into the network. This is also where you can set any *Callback* options. Callback means that, as a user dials into the network, the server dials back a preset telephone number to verify that the user is in fact the person he or she says he or she is. This number can be preset ahead of time or set by the user. This is often used in security situations; however, dial back doesn't work particularly well in situations where a user is on the road and staying in different hotels, which all have different telephone numbers. Use this option with caution.

Getting Pushy with Users

At some point during your management lifetime, you may need to disable, rename, or delete user accounts. You can do all this using Active Directory Users and Computers.

Disabling a user account is when you "turn off" the account so it can't be used to gain entry to the system. To disable an account, highlight the user account and select Disable Account from the Action menu. When you create a user using the setup wizard (see the "Creating New Users" section earlier in this chapter), you can choose the Account Disabled checkbox, and the user account is disabled until you enable it.

Renaming a user account changes the human-friendly name of the account. Just select the user account and select Rename from the Action menu. A dialog box prompts you for the new name. A name change doesn't change the Security Identifier (SID) of the account, just the username.

Deleting a user account completely removes the user account from the system. Highlight the user account you want to delete and select Delete from the Action menu. You're prompted to confirm the deletion. When you delete an account, it's gone for good. The SID used by the deleted account is never reused. Creating a new account with exactly the same configuration as the deleted account still results in a different account.

When users leave your organization, you need to decide if you want to retain their old user accounts to use for their replacements. This is your best option because it retains all the department and group settings, but it does mean that you have to change all the personal information so it relates to the new user.

What About Groups?

A *group* is a collection of users who need similar levels of access to a resource. Groups are the primary means by which Windows 2000 grants users access to resources. Groups simplify the administration process by reducing the number of relationships that you have to manage. Instead of managing how each individual user relates to each resource, you only need to manage how the smaller number of groups relate to resources and to which groups each user belongs. This reduces the workload by 40 to 90 percent. Windows 2000 Server has a Best Practices section under its Help guide that encourages you to use groups in as many situations as you can.

A group is nothing more than a named collection of users. Three scopes of groups exist: global, domain local, and universal. *Global groups* exist on a domain level. They are present on every computer throughout a domain and are managed by any Active Directory for Users and Computers tool hosted by Windows 2000 Server. *Domain local groups* exist only within a single computer. They aren't present throughout a domain. *Universal groups* extend beyond the domain to all domains in the current forest.

The three group scopes simplify the user-to-resource relationship. Although it may seem a bit complicated for a small network, using groups greatly reduces the management overhead for medium and large networks. You can use groups like this:

- ✔ Local groups are assigned access levels to resources.
- ✔ Users are assigned membership to a global group or universal group.
- ✔ A global or universal group is assigned as a member of a local group.

Therefore, users are granted access to resources by means of their global or universal group membership and, in turn, that group's membership to a local group has access to the resource. Whew, now it's time for a drink!

Here are a few important items to keep in mind about groups:

- ✔ A user can be a member of multiple global or universal groups.
- ✔ A global or universal group can be a member of multiple local groups.
- ✔ A resource can have multiple local groups assigned access to it. Using multiple local groups, you can define multiple levels of access to a resource from Read/Print to Change/Manage to Full Control.

Although you can assign a user direct membership to a local group or even direct access to a resource, doing so subverts the neat little scheme that Microsoft developed to simplify your life. So, just follow this prescription and you'll be vacationing on the beach in no time.

Whereas any other group can be a member of a local group, a local group cannot be a member of any other group.

You manage groups on Windows 2000 Server using Active Directory Users and Computers. To create a new group using Active Directory Users and Computers, follow these steps:

1. **Click the domain to which you want to add the group; then from the Action menu, choose New⇨Group.**

2. **In the New Object - Group dialog box, type the new group name.**

   The Group Name for pre-Windows 2000 machines is filled in automatically.

3. **In the New Object - Group dialog box, select the Group Scope: Domain Local, Global, or Universal.**

   Universal is something new in Windows 2000. Universal is a powerful group because it extends to all domains in the current forest.

4. **Select the Group Type: Security or Distribution.**

   You'll almost never use the distribution group setting because it does not contain the *access control list* (ACL) information necessary for security purposes. Instead, the distribution group setting is used mainly for things such as e-mail operations where you would want to send an e-mail to a collective group of users but would not need any security attached to it. We recommend always using the Security type.

5. **Click OK.**

After the group object is created, you double-click on the object to add more attributes to it. You see several new tabs called General, Members, Member Of, and Managed By. These tabs are fairly self-explanatory, but here's a little bit about them:

 ✔ **General:** This tab contains the same information that you filled in when you created the group, such as Group Name, Description, E-mail, Group Scope, and Group Type.

 ✔ **Members:** This tab shows the users that are members of the group and this is where you add users to the group.

 ✔ **Member Of:** This tab is where you can add this group to other groups.

 ✔ **Managed By:** This tab allows you to specify who manages the group. You can provide information about this user such as name, address, phone number, and so on.

You don't have to create your own groups: Windows 2000 Server has several built-in local groups that you can use. The following lists them in alphabetical order (the default members are in parentheses):

> ✔ Account Operators
>
> ✔ Administrators (Administrator, Domain Admin, Enterprise Admin)
>
> ✔ Backup Operators
>
> ✔ Guest (Domain Guests, Guests)
>
> ✔ Print Operators
>
> ✔ Replicator
>
> ✔ Server Operators
>
> ✔ Users (Domain Users, Authenticated Users)

Note that your screen may show that these built-in groups have more members than we've listed, depending on which services are installed on your server. For example, if you've installed Internet Information Services (IIS), you'll see more members in the built-in guest account.

These groups have both predefined built-in abilities and default user rights. You can modify the user rights of these groups (see this chapter's section titled "Users Have Properties"), but not the built-in abilities. Figure 15-6 displays the abilities of these accounts.

Windows 2000 Server includes these three default global groups as well (default members are in parentheses):

> ✔ Domain Admins (Administrator)
>
> ✔ Domain Users (Administrator)
>
> ✔ Domain Guests (Guest)

Windows 2000 has three more groups that it classifies as special identities: Everyone, Network, and Interactive. These are built-in groups that you cannot modify directly, but you can indirectly. For example, the Everyone group may reflect a membership of 20 users until you add another user. The user is automatically added to the Everyone group with no intervention by you. Therefore, although you did not specifically make the new user a member of the Everyone group, you did affect its members. Guests are also added to the Everyone group, so be careful and modify the Guest account to restrict access to the network. (See the "Guests can wear out their welcome" section earlier in this chapter for more information.)

The Network group is for those users who use the network as a means to access resources. When you give users access to resources across the network, they are automatically added to the Network group.

As you may have guessed by now, the other group, Interactive, represents those users who access resources by logging on locally.

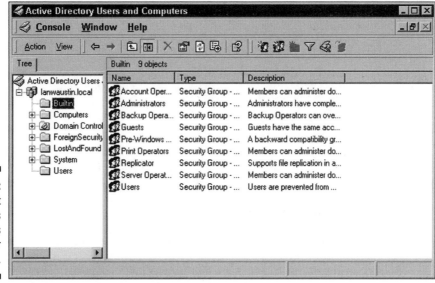

Figure 15-6:
The default
properties
of Windows
2000 Server
groups.

Again, you can't change who is a member of these groups in a direct sense. However, when you set permissions to resources, these groups will appear and you should modify the access levels of these groups to specific resources. For example, when giving users access to the root level of a volume, you can restrict access to the Everyone group so those users have only Read permissions.

You should create groups that make sense to your organizational pattern, method of operations, or just common sense. Groups should be meaningful, and their names should reflect their purposes. Naming a group Sales isn't very useful, but a name such as SalesPrintOnly is very informative. You should create groups so users are divided by purpose, access levels, tasks, departments, or anything else you consider important. Remember that groups exist for your benefit, so try to get the most out of them.

Give Your Users Nice Profiles

A *user profile* is the collection of desktop, environment, network, and other settings that define and control the look, feel, and operation of the workstation. Windows 2000 records profile information automatically for each user. However, unless you make them roaming profiles (which you find out about later in this chapter), these profiles are only accessible locally. A user profile records lots of information about the user's environment and activities, including the following:

- ✔ Start menu configuration

- ✔ Screensaver and wallpaper settings

- ✔ List of recently accessed documents

- ✔ Favorites list from Internet Explorer

- ✔ Network mapped drives

- ✔ Installed network printers

- ✔ Desktop layout

In addition, a profile includes a compressed copy of the HKEY_CURRENT_USER Registry key in a file named NTUSER.DAT. To find definitions for all the various Registry keys, access the Windows 2000 Resource Kit Registry Tools Utility and access REGENTRY.HLP.

You can turn profiles into *roaming profiles*. (Note that a nonroaming profile is called a *local profile*.) A roaming profile is a profile that's stored on a network accessible drive; therefore, no matter which workstation is used to gain access, the user's profile is available. As a result, the user's working environment follows him or her from one computer to the next. (You can also set it so the user cannot customize his/her roaming profile, which is called a Mandatory User Profile. See the last paragraph of this section for details.) To create and enable a roaming profile for a specific user, follow these steps:

1. **On the domain controller, create and share a directory named Users (or whatever name you like best).**

2. **On the workstation where the existing local profile resides, choose System from the Control Panel.**

3. **Select the User Profiles tab.**

4. **Select the profile that you want to make into a roaming profile.**

5. **Click the Copy To button.**

6. **Define a network accessible path for the new storage location for the profile in the dialog box that appears.**

    For example, `controller\users\<username>`, where `domain controller` is the name of the domain controller, `users` is the share name, and `username` is the name of the user who belongs to the profile.

7. **On the domain controller (or any Windows 2000 Server in the domain), launch the Active Directory Users and Computers.**

    To do this, choose Start➪Programs➪Administrative Directory Users and Computers.

8. **Right-click on the user object you just copied to the domain controller. Select Properties from the pop-up menu, and then click on the Profile tab.**

9. **In the User Profile section, type the same path from Step 6 (that is,** `controller\users\<username>`**) into the Profile Path field.**

10. **Click OK.**

The profile for the selected user is now a roaming profile. After a user has a roaming profile, the local profile is no longer used. It remains on the system, but the user account is now associated with the roaming profile.

By default, each time a user logs out, all changes made to his or her profile during that logon session (no matter which workstation he or she uses) are saved to the profile on the domain controller unless you specifically made this a mandatory profile. The next time the user logs on, the work environment is exactly the same as when he or she logged off. Local and roaming profiles should be used only by a single user. If multiple users need to use a single profile, you should employ a mandatory profile.

A *mandatory profile* doesn't save environmental changes when a user logs out. Instead, the profile retains the same configuration at all times. This type of profile is used mainly when groups of users using this profile are involved. You create a mandatory profile by simply renaming the NTUSER.DAT file to NTUSER.MAN in either a local or roaming profile. After this change is made, the profile remains consistent no matter who uses it. You can always reverse this process by renaming the NTUSER.MAN file back to NTUSER.DAT.

Where You Find Profiles, Policies Are Never Far Away

Group policies are the collections of rules governing, controlling, or watching over the activities of users. You can set group policies based on sites, domains, or organizational units. In Windows NT Server 4.0, this was known as the System Policy Editor. In Windows 2000, you set all these policies using the Group Policy and its extensions.

To administer the Group Policy from Active Directory Users and Computers, do the following:

1. **Start Active Directory Users and Computers (if you haven't already done so). Right-click the domain or organizational unit for which you want to set a policy and choose Properties from the pop-up menu.**

2. **Select the Group Policy tab.**

3. **If you want to modify an existing group policy, select it in the Group Policy Object Links portion of the Window and choose the appropriate option.**

The following options are available on the Group Policy tab (we've listed them in alphabetical order):

- ✔ **Add:** This opens the Add Group Policy Object Link dialog box. If you want to add an existing group policy object to the domain or organizational unit you're viewing, you would do so under this option.

- ✔ **Block Policy Inheritance:** Mark this option to prevent the directory object you chose from inheriting the Group Policy from the parent directory.

- ✔ **Delete:** Use this option if you want to remove the group policy object.

- ✔ **Edit:** Allows you to make changes to the selected Group Policy.

- ✔ **New:** Allows you to create a new group policy object.

- ✔ **Properties:** Opens the Group Policy Properties dialog box. This option allows you to find all sites, organizational units, and domains using the selected policy. In addition, it allows you to set permissions on a user or group basis to this object.

In addition, there's an Options button. When you click it, these are the options available:

- ✔ **Disabled:** This does not delete the Group Policy, but only temporarily disables it from the directory object.

- ✔ **No Override:** This is similar to a veto. If this is selected, the child directories must inherit the Group Policy from their parent directory.

If more than one group policy object is listed, you can use the UP and DOWN buttons to change the order of the group policies. Policies are enforced from the top to bottom, with the policy on top being enforced first.

Okay, so you're asking, "What does all that mean?" I create an example policy to guide you through the setup.

Creating a new group policy

You want to set a group policy that will apply to all users in the domain that will prevent the users from changing their passwords. Follow these steps to implement this new group policy:

1. **Start Active Directory Users and Computers (if you haven't already done so) and then right-click on the domain where you want to implement the policy.**

2. **Select Properties.**

3. **Click the Group Policy tab.**

4. **Click the New button, type a name for this policy, and then press the Enter key.**

5. **In the Group Policy Object Links section of the dialog box, highlight the new policy and click the Edit button.**

6. **Navigate your way down through the left window pane to User Configuration⇨Administrative Templates⇨System⇨Logon/Logoff. (See Figure 15-7.)**

7. **Double-click on the Disable Change Password object in the right pane.**

8. **Under the Policy tab, select Enabled, click the Apply button, and then click OK.**

This new policy affects all current and future user accounts in the domain or organizational unit in which you created the policy. However, it does not affect those accounts that are logged in. The effect takes place after they log out, then log back into the system.

Notice when you went into the Group Policy tab and clicked the Edit button, you saw information relating to computer configuration and also to user configuration. If there's a conflict between the two, you should note that in Windows 2000, the computer configuration takes precedence.

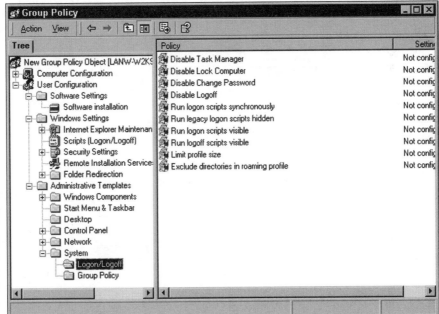

Figure 15-7: The Logon/ Logoff Policy options for User Configuration.

The previous eight steps that we went through allowed us to add a group policy and then edit the policy using the Administrative Templates that were visible to us. However, there are other templates that are available, but are simply not loaded. To add another template for use, go back to the left window pane under User Configuration and right-click on Administrative Templates. Next, select Add/Remove Templates to bring up a list of policies. Click the Add button to view other available templates.

You'll find a lot of useful policies that are already templated for you in Computer Configuration⇨Windows Settings⇨Security Settings. For example, there's a template for setting a policy for forcing unique passwords on accounts.

Figure 15-8 shows you an expanded view of the policies from which you can choose.

If you're concerned about security, you should employ an accounts policy that requires regular password changes (a new password every 30 days or so) and locks out accounts that fail to log on successfully after three tries.

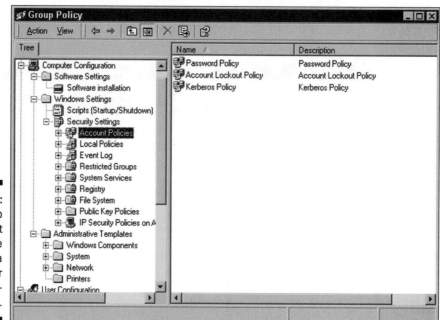

Figure 15-8:
List of Group Policies that can be applied on a computer configuration basis.

Auditing for trouble

To look at the Access Control Information for this Group Policy, you can look at which locations are associated with this policy, who has permissions within this policy, and how it is audited (which is what we cover in this section). All this is accomplished by clicking on the Properties button within the Group Policy dialog box.

Auditing information on the network allows you to track the activities throughout your network. Auditing the goings on within your network can help you locate configuration problems, security breaches, improper activity, and misuse of the system. To enable auditing on your network, do the following:

1. **Open Local Security Policy from the Administrative Tools area.**

2. **Navigate through the left pane to Security Settings⇨Local Policies, and then click Audit Policy.**

3. **Double-click the option you want to audit to bring up the Security Policy Setting dialog box for that option. From this dialog box, you can choose to audit either successful attempts or failed attempts. (This dialog box is brought up for each option.) After making your selection, click the OK button.**

It's beneficial to audit failed attempts for certain objects, such as logon attempts and object access. This can warn you of an impending intruder.

The information obtained through auditing is recorded in the Event Viewer's Security Log. Launch the Event Viewer from the Administrative Tools menu and select Security Log. In the right pane, you'll find a listing of the items you chose to audit. It's probably a good idea to check this log regularly, then clear the log so it doesn't fill up.

When Access Problems Loom. . . .

User accounts govern who can access a computer system and what level of access that person enjoys. However, users sometimes run into problems that prevent the normal operation of the logon process.

Most logon problems center around an incorrectly typed password. Therefore, users should take the time to type their passwords correctly. This is good advice only if their accounts haven't been locked out because of failed logon attempts. If your user's account is locked out, it must be re-enabled. This occurs in one of two ways. If the lockout policy is set with a duration, you only need to wait until the time expires and try again. However, if the lockout policy requires administrative intervention, you have to reset that user's account.

When a user can't log on or communication with the network seems weird, here are some things to check:

- ✔ Make sure that the network interface card (NIC) and other physical network connections are solid.

- ✔ If on a Windows 2000 or Windows NT Workstation computer, ensure that the computer is a member of the domain.

- ✔ If using the Internet Protocol (IP), check the IP protocol settings to ensure that the computer is using the correct IP address and subnet mask.

- ✔ If your network employs Dynamic Host Configuration Protocol (DHCP) to assign IP settings from a small pool to a larger group of computers, you may be stuck as the last person standing when the music stops and all available connection addresses are in use.

If users can log on but not access all the resources they think they should be able to access, you need to verify several items:

- ✔ Group memberships

- ✔ Physical network connections to resource hosts (that is, check to see that a server's network cable isn't disconnected)

- ✔ Presence of group policies restricting the user's action

If everything we mention checks out, you may have a fairly esoteric problem. Consult a Microsoft resource (online or via TechNet) to search for a solution. Yeah, that's a bit of weak advice, but it's the most valuable thing we can tell you. The Microsoft information database is expansive, and most often, someone else has had the same problem, and you can find information posted about its resolution.

Chapter 16

Managing Shares, Permissions, and More

● ●

In This Chapter

▶ Understanding how permissions apply to NTFS objects

▶ Understanding how permissions apply to file shares

▶ Exploring special access rights

▶ Distinguishing between creation and inheritance

▶ Determining actual permissions

▶ Undoing the NTFS and share defaults

▶ Making access controls work

● ●

*T*o a large extent, working with Windows 2000 Server means using the *Windows NT File System,* usually known as NTFS. This file system's advanced features include attribute-level *Access Control Lists* (ACLs) for objects, so you can control not only which users or groups can access a volume, directory, or file, but also which operations users or groups can perform against a volume, directory, or file.

Windows 2000 also supports the *FAT* and *FAT32 file systems* (FAT stands for *File Allocation Table),* which don't include object-level access controls. However, FAT and FAT32 do support so-called *file shares* (shared directories with the files they contain) that do support access controls. Understanding how shares work and how NTFS permissions combine with share permissions is a major focus of this chapter. We show you how to figure out what a user can (and can't) do to your files based on his or her account permissions, the groups to which he or she belongs, and the underlying defaults that apply to Windows 2000 Server itself.

Chapter 12 discusses this information as it applies to Active Directory.

More About Objects, Rights, and Permissions

Before you can revel in the details of the rights and permissions that apply to Windows 2000, you should ponder some technical terminology. That's why we take a brief detour to dictionary-ville — right here, right now.

An object lesson . . .

Windows 2000 treats all user-accessible system resources — including users, groups, files, directories, printers, processes, and lots more — as objects. The term *object* has special meaning to programmers and tech-heads: This term refers to a named collection of *attributes* and *values,* plus a named collection of *methods,* which Microsoft calls *services.*

For example, a file object has a variety of attributes that you already know about if you've spent any time at all around computers: Files have names, types, lengths, owners, plus creation and modification dates. For an object, each attribute also has an associated value; therefore, the attributes and values of an object that is a file might be:

- **Name:** BOOT.INI
- **Type:** Configuration settings
- **Contents:** Information on how to boot Windows 2000 (Windows 2000 can locate and read the contents using the drive's file directory.)
- **Size:** About 1KB

Attributes identify individual objects of some specific type — in this case, a type of file — and define what they contain, where they're located, and so on.

On the other hand, it may not be so readily apparent why methods or services are important for objects. If you examine a file object, you can see that the methods that apply to it describe operations that you would want to apply to a file. Therefore, the methods or services that apply to file objects include things such as read, write, execute, delete, rename, and other typical file operations. In short, methods define the operations that can be applied to a particular object. Among other things, this makes objects pretty much self-defining, because they not only include complete descriptions of themselves in their attributes, but they also contain complete descriptions of what you can do to them in their methods or services. Other object types have different associated methods or services that reflect the objects' capabilities and the data the objects contain.

When you examine the attributes for specific objects in Windows 2000, things start getting pretty interesting. Every single attribute of every single object has an ACL (this is sometimes pronounced *ackle,* to rhyme with *cackle*). ACLs identify those individual user accounts or groups that may access a particular object (or one of its attributes), and also indicate which services each user or group may apply to that object (or one of its attributes). How's that for granularity? Administrators use ACLs to control access to objects (and, logically, their attributes), giving themselves free rein to troubleshoot objects while limiting ordinary users' abilities to accidentally (or purposefully) harm the system.

When is a file NOT an object?

Windows 2000 uses objects for just about anything in its operating environment that users can access. In fact, NTFS volumes, directories, and files are Windows 2000 objects with associated attributes and a set of well-defined services that may be applied to those objects. However, because the older FAT file systems (and the newer Windows 98 FAT32) do not include built-in support for ACLs, FAT/FAT32 files are *not* objects. Therefore, even though FAT/FAT32 volumes, directories, and files still have attributes similar to those for NTFS files (namely, name, type, creation date, modification date, and so forth), FAT/FAT32 volumes, directories, and files are not Windows 2000 objects, per se. This explains why FAT volumes and their contents are inherently insecure (because normal permissions don't apply to them).

More importantly, this also explains why the default logon behavior for Windows 2000 Server is to deny everyone but administrators, server operators, backup operators, and printer operators the "right to log on locally." That's because anyone who can access a FAT/FAT32 volume can do anything they want to it. By denying ordinary users the right to log on to a Windows 2000 server at its keyboard and requiring them to log on only through the network, Windows 2000 can control access to FAT/FAT32 volumes through shares. Shares function as Windows 2000 objects, and therefore have built-in access controls.

Users have rights; objects have permissions

In Windows 2000, the standard terminology is to refer to *user rights* and *object permissions*. Because object permissions is rather vague, you usually hear permissions used in reference to a specific object, such as *file permissions, printer permissions,* and so on.

A user's rights define what he or she can do to objects (or its attributes) in the Windows 2000 environment. A user obtains rights to objects in one of three ways:

✔ The rights are explicitly assigned to an individual user account.

✔ The rights are assigned to the groups to which the user belongs. This is where users can be granted *privileges* to perform specific tasks, such as backing up files and directories.

✔ The rights are assigned via the Group Policy window. To access that window, right-click on a site organizational unit, domain, or local computer. Choose Properties, select the Group Policy tab, and click Edit. You edit the user rights in the Group Policy window under the Computer Configuration⇨Windows Settings⇨Security Settings⇨Local Policies⇨ User Rights Assignment.

When a user logs on to a Windows 2000 domain (or a stand-alone system), a special key called an *access token* is generated. The access token represents the user's explicit individual rights and the groups to which the user belongs. It takes some time to generate an access token, which is one reason why logging on to Windows 2000 isn't instantaneous.

Every object (and its attributes) in the Windows 2000 environment includes an attribute called *permissions* (which is found on the Security tab of each object). This permissions attribute includes an ACL that identifies all the users and groups allowed to access the object's attributes as well as the services that each user or group may apply to the object's attributes. Each time a user requests an object, Windows 2000 uses a built-in facility called the *Security Reference Monitor* (SRM) to check the user's access token against the permissions for that object. If the SRM finds that the user has permission, Windows 2000 fulfills the request; otherwise, the user is out of luck. It's possible for users to have access to specific attributes of objects, but not other attributes. For example, Nancy may be granted access to view part of JoAnne's account information, such as her telephone number, but not JoAnne's street address.

Of Windows 2000 NTFS and Permissions

NTFS is a file system just like FAT and FAT32 (the 32-bit File Allocation Table used in Windows 98) are also file systems. The difference between NTFS and these other file systems is that NTFS is an *object-oriented file system*. Unlike FAT and FAT32, NTFS sees everything in NTFS partitions as objects of some specific type that have attributes and to which methods and services can be applied. The benefit of using NTFS is that you can set permissions for the volumes, files, and directories that use NTFS.

In fact, NTFS recognizes three types of objects:

- ✔ **Volumes:** The NTFS-formatted drive partitions that show up as disk drive icons. A volume object may contain files and directories.

- ✔ **Directories:** Named containers for files that occur in a volume or within some other directory. In fact, Windows 2000 allows you to nest directories however deep you want, which means that you can put as many directories within directories within directories as you like (although nested directories reach a point of diminishing returns fairly quickly).

- ✔ **Files:** Named containers for data that include type, size, dates, and content among their attributes. Files are where information actually resides in NTFS.

To examine the permissions for any object in NTFS, right-click that object in Windows Explorer, My Computer, or Active Directory Sites and Services. In the pop-up menu, select Properties and then select the Security tab. At the bottom of the Security dialog box, you see the Permissions section (as shown in Figure 16-1). From here, you can investigate the list of available permissions for this object (volume C on our hard drive in this case) through the list that appears in the Permissions section in the lower half of the screen.

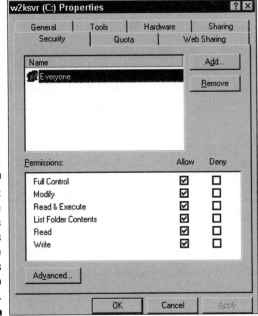

Figure 16-1:
The
Permissions
list shows
you all the
permissions
that apply to
the object.

NTFS permissions

The Permissions list shows permissions for files, volumes, and directory objects in NTFS. NTFS file, volume, and directory permissions are extremely similar. The only real difference is that the container objects offer child inheritance options and a few obvious permissions that apply only to containers. We use the generic term *container* to refer to volumes and directories — in other words, objects that act as parents to child objects.

Windows 2000 has a slightly different method of permission assignments and permission restrictions than what was used in Windows NT. First and foremost, there's no longer a No Access permission. Instead, all permissions are either granted or restricted using an Allow or Deny setting. Selecting Deny for all possible permissions for an NTFS object under Windows 2000 is the same as the No Access setting from Windows NT.

The standard or normal NTFS permissions are:

- **Read** grants users the ability to view and access the contents of the folder or file.

- **Write** (folders) grants users the ability to create new folders and files within the folder.

- **Write** (files) grants users the ability to change the contents of a file and to alter its attributes.

- **List Folder Contents** (folders only) grants users the ability to see the names of the contents of a folder.

- **Read & Execute** (folders) grants users the ability to view and access the contents of the folder or file and to execute files.

- **Read & Execute** (files) grants users the ability to view and execute files.

- **Modify** (folders) grants users the ability to delete a folder and its contents, to create new files and folders within a folder, and to view and access the contents of a folder.

- **Modify** (files) grants users the ability to delete a file, change the contents of a file, alter a file's attributes, and to view and access a file.

- **Full Control** (folders) grants users the ability to access all of the functions of files and folders completely unrestricted.

- **Full Control** (files) grants users the ability to access all of the functions of files completely unrestricted.

Taking ownership of objects in NTFS

An owner of an object can always modify its permissions, no matter which permissions are already set for that object. This permission exists, at least in part, to sidestep the "Deny" trap that can occur when an object's owner mistakenly sets permissions for a general group, such as Everyone or Authenticated Users. (These two default groups are discussed further in Chapter 18.)

If the Everyone group is assigned Deny for all permissions of an object, that group includes anyone who may want to access that object. Unless an administrator or the object's creator (its owner by default) can reset permissions to be a little less restrictive, nobody can access that object — or any objects it contains.

Full Control is important because it grants the object's owner the power to change access to that object and to change services that apply to the object. In essence, full control is your get-out-of-jail-free card!

Advanced permissions

Advanced permissions are detailed controls that can be used to create special access rights when the standard compliment of permissions don't properly apply. The Advanced controls are accessed by pressing the Advanced button on the Permissions tab of an NTFS object. This reveals the Access Control Settings dialog box, which has three tabs: Permissions, Auditing, and Owner. The Permissions tab is used to define special-detail permissions. The Auditing tab is used to define the auditing scheme. The Owner tab is used to view the current owner or take ownership of an object.

On the Permissions tab, users or groups can be added and their specific permissions defined. The possible selections are:

- ✔ Traverse Folder / Execute File
- ✔ List Folder / Read Data
- ✔ Read Attributes
- ✔ Read Extended Attributes
- ✔ Create Files / Write Data

- Create Folders / Append Data
- Write Attributes
- Write Extended Attributes
- Delete Subfolders and Files
- Delete
- Read Permissions
- Change Permissions
- Take Ownership

If you really must dig up all the details on special access rights, please consult Microsoft's TechNet CD and the Windows 2000 Resource Kit.

FAT and FAT32 Have No Permissions

Because the FAT and FAT32 file systems that Windows 2000 supports along with NTFS include no object mechanisms for associating attributes with files and directories, files stored in a FAT/FAT32 formatted volume have no associated permissions. Anybody who's allowed to log on to a Windows 2000 server with a FAT/FAT32 partition can access any of the files in that partition. This helps explain why you may want to restrict who's allowed to work on your servers, as well as why you should physically lock up your servers.

The reason why FAT partitions are still around is that a dual-boot machine that runs Windows 9x and Windows 2000 together must include a FAT partition from which the other operating system can boot. This might be a FAT32 partition for Windows 98, but we recommend FAT because Windows 2000 can read that partition when it's running and more operating systems can read FAT partitions than any other kind of file system.

Only Windows 2000 and Windows NT can read NTFS partitions, so be careful when reformatting partitions on dual- or multi-boot machines!

Share Permissions

When users access files on a Windows 2000 Server, they usually do so across the network, especially if you restrict who's allowed to log on to the server and limit physical access to the machine. Therefore, most users who access files on a Windows 2000 Server do so through a network share, which is a directory on a Windows 2000 Server that you've shared to the network for public access.

Shares are also objects for Windows 2000, so permissions do apply. The list of applicable permissions consists of the following three entries which are managed in the same Allow/Deny method as the direct NTFS object permissions:

- ✔ **Read** permits viewing of files in the share, loading of files across the network, and program execution.

- ✔ **Change** includes all Read permissions, plus creating, deleting, or changing directories and files within the share.

- ✔ **Full Control** includes all Change permissions plus changing permissions for and taking ownership of the share.

No Special Access exists for shares. Table 16-1 summarizes the basic permissions for shares.

Table 16-1	Share Permissions and Basic Permissions				
File	*Read*	*Write*	*Execute*	*Delete*	*Change*
Read	X		X		
Change	X	X	X	X	
Full Control	X	X	X	X	X

If you want to expose contents of a FAT partition on a Windows 2000 Server to network users, doing so through a share automatically gives you some degree of access control, which is yet another advantage to using a network!

To create a share, select a directory in My Computer or Windows 2000 Explorer, then right-click on it. Select the Sharing entry in the resulting pop-up menu. The Properties window for that directory appears with the Sharing tab selected. This is shown in Figure 16-2.

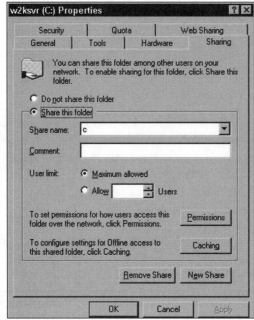

Figure 16-2:
The Sharing tab in the Properties window provides easy access to a share's name, user limits, and permissions information.

There are four important areas in this window that relate to creating and managing shares:

- ✓ **Share this folder:** You must click the "Share this folder" radio button to enable sharing on a directory.

- ✓ **Share name:** By default, a share's name is the same as the directory from which it comes. When creating shares, remember that DOS and Windows 3.*x* users can only access shares with names that are a maximum of eight characters long.

- ✓ **User limit:** The User limit pane lets you limit how many users can access a share simultaneously. This will usually be a concern only on heavily loaded Windows 2000 servers; in most cases, you can leave it set to the "Maximum allowed" default.

- ✓ **Permissions button:** You control share permissions through the Permissions button at the bottom right of the Sharing tab. These work the same way as NTFS permissions. If you click the Permissions button, you see that, by default, the Everyone group has the Full Control, Change, and Read rights.

Calculating Actual Permissions

Users have rights not only as a result of the NTFS permissions explicitly assigned to specific files or directories for their accounts, but also by virtue of the groups to which they belong. Because NTFS shares exist, figuring out permissions can get pretty interesting when you have to combine NTFS and share permissions for a particular file or directory while also taking user settings and group memberships into account. To help you figure out what's what, we give you a recipe for calculation, plus a few rules to use, and then walk you through an example to show you how things work.

The rules of calculation

To figure out which permissions apply to a share on an NTFS object, you must first determine which permissions apply to the NTFS object by itself. This could include inheritance features from parent to child object. (See Chapter 12 for a refresher on inheritance.) Next, you must determine the permissions that apply to the share. (The rules for this process appear in the following section.) Whichever of the two results is more restrictive wins and defines the actual permissions that apply to the file or directory in question. This process isn't difficult, but it may produce some counterintuitive results. You must apply these rules exactly as they're stated, or we can't guarantee the results. Here goes:

1. **Determine the permissions on the object.**

2. **Determine the permissions on the share.**

3. **Compare the permissions between the share and the object. The *more restrictive* permission is the permission that applies.**

Whenever you or your users can't obtain access to a particular file-system object through a share (or NTFS by itself, for that matter), always check group memberships and their associated permissions.

Figure this!

This formal explanation may not completely illuminate the process of figuring permissions, so we give you a couple of examples to show you how it's done.

Betty belongs to the Marketing Dept, Domain Users, and Film Critics groups. She wants to delete the file in an NTFS share named Rosebud.doc. Can she do it? Table 16-2 shows her individual and group permissions.

Table 16-2	Betty's NTFS and Share Permissions		
Type	*Membership*	*Name*	*Permissions*
NTFS	User Account	BettyB	Read
Group	Marketing Dept		Read
Group	Domain Users		Change
Group	Film Critics		Change
Share	User Account	BettyB	Read
Group	Marketing Dept		Read
Group	Domain Users		Read
Group	Film Critics		Read

On the NTFS side, Read plus Change equals Change; on the share side, Read is the only game in town. The most restrictive of Read and Change is Read. Read won't allow Betty to delete a file, so Betty's out of luck! Maybe next time. . . .

Undo the Default!

We'd like to warn you about a gaping hole in Windows 2000 file security: The default is to grant Full Control access to files and directories to a default group named Everyone (to which every user in the domain belongs). This means that anyone and everyone can read, write, execute, delete, change permissions, and take ownership of anything and everything in any new directory or volume that you create on your server. Delete the entire drive? Sure, no problem. Read any file you like? Whatever you say. Most workplace networks can't tolerate such lax security.

This is not the case on the %systemroot% and other Program File areas, which have more restrictive settings if installed on NTFS. If you convert to NTFS from FAT, this does not apply unless you use a Resource Kit utility to tighten the security.

To fix this problem, you can reset the permissions for Everyone to Read each time you create a new volume. Setting the permission for Everyone to Read is a safe, base-level permission for NTFS volumes.

When you reset base-level permissions, make sure you also grant the Domain Administrators or Administrators group Full Control. That way, you can always take ownership and reset permissions if something funky happens.

But What about Access Control with Active Directory Objects?

We've talked about objects and access control, but with Active Directory, there are two additional features of which you need to be aware: *delegated access control* and *property-based inheritance*. The following describes these two in general, but turn to Chapter 12 for the gory details.

Delegation of access control

You can enable others to manage portions of your network for you — otherwise, you'd be working 24/7! You can slice up the management by way of the domain, or you can give someone else rights to manage the organizational unit for you, depending on the functions you want them to perform. This is done through the Delegate Administration wizard found in the Active Directory Users and Computers snap-in. (Choose Start⇨Programs⇨Administrative Tools⇨Active Directory Users and Computers, and then choose Delegate Control from the Action menu.) As you may have guessed, there are some things to note before diving into this endeavor.

An organizational unit is an Active Directory container that holds other organizational units, computers, users, and/or groups. For more information on organizational units, see Chapter 11.

Before you can give others access to manage Active Directory objects, you must first have the proper permissions to delegate that object authority. In addition, you must give the proper permissions to others to manage that object. For more information on this, see Chapter 12.

Property-based inheritance

Just as you might inherit money from a relative, the lower levels of your network structure can "inherit" access control information set at a higher level of the structure. Inheritance, as its name suggests, always flows in a downward direction. We want to touch briefly on two methods of property-based inheritance. (For more information and detail on how this inheritance works, see Chapter 12.)

The first method is called *dynamic inheritance*. As the word *dynamic* suggests, the access control information for this type of inheritance is calculated on the fly every time a read/write to the object is requested. This results in some performance overhead (i.e., extra traffic) that should be considered on a busy network. (Extra traffic on a busy network can slow things down significantly.)

The second method is called the *static model*, also referred to as *Create Time Inheritance*. This means that the access control information for an object is set when the object is created by looking at the parent object permissions and combining those permissions with the new object permissions. Unless the new permissions are set at a higher level, the access control does not change for the object. Therefore, when a request is made to read or write to the object, no recalculation is necessary to determine the permissions. However, if permissions are changed at a higher level, these changes are propagated downward to change permissions or reset combined permissions at lower levels — similar to dominoes toppling over. The only time there's a recalculation is when the permissions at higher levels are set and the propagation is in progress.

Chapter 17

Backing Up for a Rainy Day

. . . .

In This Chapter

▶ Understanding why backing up data is important

▶ Looking at Windows 2000 Server backup methods

▶ Discovering third-party alternatives

▶ Getting familiar with the terminology

▶ Making backup a habit

▶ Using the Backup Operators group

. . . .

*H*aving a backup recovery scheme for your organization's data is very important because of the critical business applications and functions that reside on networks. Without a plan in place to protect data, disruptions to an entire organization's data and workflow process can occur, resulting in loss of revenue. Unfortunately, many organizations place little emphasis on protecting their data until an actual loss occurs. In this chapter, you find out about different methods for protecting your organization's data to prevent losses.

Why Bother Backing Up?

Backing up is the process of copying data from one location to another — either manually or unattended. Copying data from one directory on a hard disk to another directory on that same hard disk is effective until the hard disk crashes and both copies of the data are inaccessible. In addition, by copying the data to the same drive, you neglect to copy any of the security or account information. This means you have to re-enter that information manually. Don't you think it's a better idea to back up all files, such as system, application, and user data, to another physical medium, such as a tape or other backup device, and then rotate that device off-site periodically?

Many organizations today place critical business functions and data on a network, for example e-mail, accounting information, payroll, personnel records, and operations. Loss of just one segment of that information hinders an organization's operations, even if it's just for a short time. Imagine if the payroll information disappeared from the system, and all or some of the employees did not receive their checks on time. We wouldn't want to be there!

Organizations can avoid data loss problems almost entirely by backing up their networks on a regular basis. Data loss occurrences can be as simple as one corrupt file, or as complex as the entire contents of a server's hard disk becoming unreadable.

All types of threats pose danger to data. Everything from fires to computer viruses can obliterate data on a network. Planning for each type of possible disaster can help you completely secure and restore your organization's data should that disaster occur.

Data loss on a network can occur in many ways. If you know what the potential threats are and plan for them, you can prevent both serious damage to your network and loss of data. We want to urge you to always back up your network and to rotate a recent copy off-site.

The following are some of the potential threats you and your network can encounter:

- ✔ **Hard disk crash:** Even if you've built fault tolerance into your server, such as mirroring or duplexing, don't expect those methods to always work and recover everything 100 percent. We've seen mirrored drives going out of synch without notice until the hard disk crashes. Without backups, you can lose all of your data or segments of it. It's a good idea to complement mirroring and duplexing with regular backups.

- ✔ **Ungraceful shutdown:** Every once in a while, you get a smart-aleck employee who hits the on/off switch to the server, causing it to shut down improperly. Most servers today come right back up — but not always. Shutting the server down in this manner can render the hard disks unreadable. You should put your servers in a secure location away from end users. And don't forget to back up on a regular basis!

- ✔ **Viruses:** Many organizations connect to the Internet, allowing employees to download all types of data to the local area network (LAN) that could introduce viruses. Viruses pose a real threat to organizations. One virus can ruin an entire computer and render it useless in a very short amount of time. If this computer happens to be a server on your network, someone's going to be reading the employment classifieds. Installing virus protection software on the server allows you to check for viruses before they're stored on the server. Put a backup plan in place that allows you to restore the data on your network as it was prior to the introduction of the virus.

- ✔ **Environmental disasters:** We've seen many organizations lose data during environmental disturbances, such as a bad storm. If lightning can zap the electronics in your home, imagine what it can do to the data on a network.

Some environmental disasters you should plan for include

- *Fire:* One fire in a building or on a floor can annihilate an entire organization. If your organization loses everything in a fire, you'll be the savior if you produce a recent tape of the network that was sitting safely off-site somewhere. However, if you store your backup tapes on top of your server in the computer room, you'll be the one pounding the pavement.

- *Floods:* Placing a computer room, server, or backup equipment in the basement or first floor of a building is a bad idea, particularly in flood-prone areas. One flood can obliterate an entire organization. Even if a flood does occur, you're safe with your backup tapes off-site — away from the flood zone.

- *Hurricanes:* Hurricanes bring high winds and rain with them. Don't put your server or backup equipment in a computer room with outside windows. You could just come back and find everything strewn around the computer room and sopping wet and have no backup tapes to restore.

- *Temperature:* Something as simple as placing a server or backup machine in an enclosed room without proper air conditioning and ventilation can cause problems. Don't put a server or backup equipment in a small room with other heavy heat equipment, such as a copier, without cool air flowing through it. Buildings do shut down their air systems on weekends and holidays, and the heat can kill servers.

Some viruses have a gestation period; therefore, they can be inserted into your network but go unnoticed until after a set number of days. We've seen disgruntled employees place viruses on networks and then leave a company — 30 days later, a virus appears. Incorporate this thought into your backup plan by always backing up on a 30-day rotation scheme. If a virus like this is introduced onto your network, you can go back at least 30 days in your backup tapes to try to restore the network prior to the virus's introduction. If you only have a week's worth of backup, then all the backups you have contain the virus. Virus software from Norton (www.symantec.com/) and McAfee (www.mcafeemall.com/) tend to have fewer conflicts with Windows 2000 than other brands of virus software.

Just how many types of backups are there?

There are really only five types of backup methods in the computer world. The same is true with the Windows 2000 backup facility. The five types of backups available in Windows 2000 Server are:

- ✔ Normal
- ✔ Copy
- ✔ Daily
- ✔ Differential
- ✔ Incremental

Before you can truly understand these backup methods, you have to understand a little attribute called the *archive bit*. Files have what are known as attributes, which are the properties of a file. One of the attributes found in Windows 2000 is the archive bit. After a file is created or modified, its archive bit is automatically reset by the operating system. This archive bit indicates that the file needs to be backed up, even if backup software is not installed or configured on the computer. Of course, backup software looks for this bit to identify the status of files. Think of this as a seal on every file on your system. When the operating system, a user, or an application modifies the file, the seal is broken. The backup software then goes through the files and "re-seals" them by backing them up.

Normal

The *normal backup* copies all selected files and sets the archive bit, which informs the backup software that the files have been backed up. This is the type of backup that is performed the first time the computer data is backed up. Also, with this type of backup, only the last tape is required to restore all the files. (See the section titled "Local backup" later in this chapter for more information on tape backups.)

Copy

The *copy backup* is useful because it does not set the archive bit and, therefore, doesn't affect the normal and the incremental backups. It can be used to copy selected files between the scheduled normal or incremental backups. (See the "Incremental" section later in this section for more information on incremental backups.)

Daily

The *daily backup* copies selected files that were changed the day the backup job started. A daily backup does not set the archive bit. This backup can be used to copy only those files that were changed on that day, and, because the archive bit is not set, the regular backup would go on as usual.

Differential

Like the copy and daily backups, the *differential backup* also doesn't set the archive bit. It copies all files that were created or modified since the last normal or incremental backup. One practice is to use a combination of normal and differential backups to configure the backup job for the computer. In this combination, a normal backup is performed weekly, and differential backups are performed on a daily basis. If this is the backup job used and a restore is being performed, only the last normal and the last differential tapes are required.

Incremental

The *incremental backup* is similar to the differential backup in that it backs up only those files that have been created or modified since the last normal or incremental backup. Unlike differential backups, however, incremental backups do set the archive bit, which indicates that the files have been backed up. A combination of normal and incremental backups can be used to configure a backup job. In this combination, a normal backup is used once a week and incremental backups are done on a daily basis. To restore the files using this type of backup combination, the last normal and all incremental sets are required.

Configuring a backup job to use this combination is fast and efficiently utilizes storage space, because only those files that were modified get backed up. However, it's important to note that a restoration is more difficult and takes longer compared to the combination of differential and normal backups, simply because you have to use a whole set of incremental tapes. This type of backup combination or configuration is ideal for an enterprise in which an *Automated Tape Library* (ATL) can be used. Using an ATL, the backup software controls the entire restore operation, including the decision to load the correct tape sequence via its robotic arm.

An ATL is basically a software-controlled backup system in which it's not necessary to load or change tapes. A typical ATL system is usually designed around a container/library, which can hold from just a few tapes to several hundred, with each tape identified by a unique bar code. Inside the library, there could be one or several tape drives to read and write to tape. An ATL system also includes a mechanism responsible for moving the tape to and from the tape drive. This mechanism can be a robotic arm (in the case of the large ATLs) or it could be a simple system similar to those found in a cassette tape recorder. The backup software would control the entire operation by instructing the robotic arm to load a specific tape in a specific tape drive and start the backup or restore job.

Network versus local backup

When backing up information on a network, you have a choice between performing a network backup or a local backup. In the following two sections, we cover the particulars of each option.

Network backup

Network backups are used in large network environments. When you use a network backup, a *host computer* is configured to backup remote computers that are attached to the host computer via the LAN. In this scenario, data travels from the remote computer over the network to reach the host computer — the one configured with the tape drive. After data is off-loaded from the network interface card (NIC) onto the computer's bus, the data is treated as if it were a local backup. (See the "The Windows 2000 Backup Facility" section, later in this chapter, for information on how to configure your server to back up a remote computer.)

The transfer rate can be a problem with this type of backup, because data must traverse and share the LAN with the regular traffic. It's more than likely that the LAN is designed around a 10 Mbps Ethernet or a 100 Mbps Fast Ethernet. In either case, data speed would be greatly reduced compared to the local backup. To deal with this problem and to accommodate the needs of an enterprise in which a large amount of data must be backed up each night, the industry has developed the *Storage Area Network* (SAN). In this architecture, all computers and storage device(s) are attached directly to the loop using a *Fibre Channel Arbitrated Loop (FC-AL)*, which has a bandwidth of 100 Mbps. Furthermore, only computers and the backup device(s) share this bandwidth. Such architecture is expensive; however, its benefits for the enterprise more than justify its high cost.

Local backup

The local backup configuration consists of a local tape drive attached to or installed in the computer by means of an *Integrated Drive Electronics* (IDE) or a *Small Computer System Interface* (SCSI) interface. Local backup is fast because when you use these interfaces, the tape drive is directly attached to the computer bus. On some of the new SCSI interfaces, such as the Ultra2 Wide SCSI, the transfer rate can reach 80 Mbps. However, it's more likely that this transfer rate won't be met because the tape drive can only achieve anywhere from 4 to 10 Mbps, depending on the drive type. With today's advances in hardware, it's possible to get close to 15GB per hour.

Local backup is relatively inexpensive because it only involves the price of the tape drive, the tapes, and the price of a SCSI or an IDE interface, if required. Most computers are already configured with an extra IDE or a SCSI interface that can be used for this purpose. One additional cost would be the price of a license for the backup software, if a third party software is required; however, Windows 2000 comes with powerful backup software that is free of charge!

The backup tapes we use (Hewlett Packard DDS 3) hold up to 24GB of data. Depending how much data you have to back up and the type of tape you're using, you may need more than one tape to hold all your data.

Understanding the technology

Regardless of whether you choose a network or local backup, and regardless of how often you decide to back up, you need to understand some terminology and technology about the equipment used in backup systems and different methods.

Online, nearline, offline

You hear a lot of buzz about online, nearline, and offline storage options. Of these three backup types, choose the method that suits your organization's retrieval time and effort, depending on how often you find yourself restoring data and how fast you want data retrieved.

✔ **Online:** This type of backup is done typically on your server, usually in the form of a second hard disk purchased that is mirrored or duplexed. Data is readily available to users through their desktops with no intervention from you except that you must regularly check the status of this fault tolerance. Drives can go out of synch without notice unless you monitor the drives manually or through software.

✔ **Nearline:** These backups are performed on a device attached to the network. This type of backup requires some work on your part because it usually uses some method unknown to the user when backing up files, such as compression techniques. The data is there, but your users won't know how to perform functions, such as decompressing the files, to access the data.

✔ **Offline:** This type of backup involves separate devices from the server that include their own software and hardware. You need to know how to operate these devices because the users won't know how or might not have the security access to do so. These devices are typically the slowest because data must go from the server to another device. Many organizations place these devices on the network backbone and connect them via fiber-optic cable for higher transmission rates.

As you progress downward in the preceding bulleted list, options become more expensive, it takes longer for you to retrieve information, and more interaction on your part is required.

What's in the hardware?

Backup systems are composed of backup units, backup media, and software components (oh, and you, the operator). The systems come in all sizes, shapes, and dollar signs, depending on your needs. In the following sections, we describe the most common ones you encounter so you can talk with your vendor about meeting your network needs.

Backup units

A *backup unit* is hardware that can be as simple as a tape device with one slot, or as complex as a jukebox platter system that has mechanical arms. If you have small data-storage requirements, a simple tape backup unit that has more capacity than your server will suffice. These units are not that expensive and are available at local computer stores. Some of these units can be daisy-chained together if you need more space and don't want to be present to change the tapes.

If your organization has lots of data to back up, then you might consider one of the jukebox approaches. A *jukebox* is a device that looks like a little computer tower with a door. Inside, it has several slots plus a mechanical arm that can insert and move around tapes or CDs. With this type of system, you typically can insert a week's worth of backup tapes and let the system back up unattended.

Another option is *magneto-optical (MO) drives*. These units use a combination of magnetic and optical technologies for rewritable backups. The advantage of this technology is that it performs random access retrievals, which are faster than sequential retrievals. The units are not expensive, but the medium is. If you have large data requirements and need fast retrieval, look into this technology.

Each type of backup unit will have some sort of slot where the medium is placed. The size of this slot depends on the unit. Some come in 4mm, 8mm, ¼ inch, ½ inch, and more. You must purchase the correct size medium for the backup unit because you can't fit a ½-inch tape in a ¼-inch drive!

Backup media

Backup media mean tapes, cartridges, CD-WORMs (write once read many), erasable CD-ROMs, diskettes, and more. Any device on which the backup unit stores data becomes the medium. Backup media come in many shapes, sizes, and thicknesses. You want to make sure that you follow the manufacturer's recommendation for purchasing the right medium for your unit.

Don't buy video-grade tape cartridges at your local discount store for your backup purposes. Purchase data-grade tapes, which cost more but are designed for more rugged use.

Backup media come not only in different physical sizes, but also in capacity. Some tapes store as much as 24GB of data. Erasable CD-ROMs store as much as 650MB in uncompressed mode and GBs in compressed mode. Regardless of which unit and medium you select for your needs, get plenty of them so you can work on a rotational scheme without continually using the same medium. We've seen folks who buy just one tape and use that tape over and over until it's time to restore from that tape. And guess what, the tape was defective; therefore, there was no backup! Spread out your backups over multiple tapes to minimize putting all your eggs in one tape basket!

Software

You can use the Windows 2000 built-in backup software on a third-party backup device or you can use the software that comes with the device. We prefer to use third-party software because it's designed to work with certain manufactured devices and the drivers are always readily available. Installation of the devices goes much smoother when you use the recommended software. Always keep a copy of the backup software off-site in case of a fire or other disaster. If you lose all of your equipment, you'll need to reload this software on another machine before you can restore data.

Beep! Beep! Planning Backups

One of the most important tasks that you can perform is to plan your backup. Some of the best backup systems and methods can still fail, so it's smart to always test them first.

Store backup tapes off-site

It's not uncommon for companies to store their backup tapes in a fire-proof safe — usually stored in the computer room where the fire might occur. These safes are great for one thing, and one thing only: paper. They are designed to withstand enough heat so paper does not burn. This heat, however, is more than sufficient to melt any tapes that may be stored in them. For this reason, smarter companies store their tapes off-site on a daily, weekly or monthly basis, depending on how often data changes. Storing data off-site ensures data availability in case of a disaster, such as a fire or a flood. If such a disaster were to take place, a new system could be installed and data could be restored.

There are companies that provide off-site data vaulting for a fee. The tapes are picked up periodically and transferred to an off-site safe facility for vaulting. If needed, customers can call to get the required tapes for a restore. Such companies might have different service contracts. Although it's more costly to have this service 24 hours and 7 days a week, depending on the operation and how critical the data might be, spending the extra funds to ensure access to tapes might be justifiable.

Document your hardware and its settings

It's especially important to document your hardware and its setting because it saves time that would be spent guessing and trying different configurations to get the system back up and ready for data to be restored from tape. Document all of the important settings, such as the size of volumes or drives, the type of file system used, and whether the file systems are file allocation table (FAT) or NT File System (NTFS). If you've been using any kind of fault tolerance on your disk subsystem, such as mirroring or some type of Redundant Array of Inexpensive Disks (RAID), it would be important to note these details. Generally, accurate and comprehensive documentation ensures fast and reliable recovery in unforeseen situations.

You should also have a list of the part numbers of all the components that are installed in your systems. Include a list of all the vendors and your contacts as well. If the components in your system (and hence your system) are from one of the large server manufacturers, such as Compaq or Hewlett Packard, you may find that it can loan you a system to recover your data. Finally, have all your device drivers readily available.

Practice disaster recovery for your system

It's wise to practice disaster recovery periodically to ensure its success whenever it's required after a real disaster. In large companies, it's normal practice and, in fact, mandated by management. Whereas it's easy to make this statement, actually implementing this practice is harder than you might think. The problem is that you cannot attempt to recover your data on a production system (which is a system already used for another function). If you do, and the backup is corrupt, your live data will become corrupt as well. Many organizations will purchase a second system with the same specifications as the production system as a backup. These systems tend to get "borrowed" for other pilot projects and come into production.

Windows 2000 Server does have a new feature that makes disaster recovery much easier. This feature is similar to a third-party solution in which a total system recovery is possible with a few diskettes. Search for "disaster recovery" in Windows 2000 Help for more information.

The Windows 2000 Backup Facility

Microsoft has always included a backup program called NTBACKUP with its Windows NT operating systems. Windows 2000 continues the tradition. In the past, NTBACKUP has lacked in several major areas, including the inability to backup to non-tape media, no access to network resources, and no built-in scheduling capabilities. All of these shortfalls have been addressed in Windows 2000 Server.

The big picture

Windows 2000 Server ships with a new version of NTBACKUP, which includes two methods for backing up your server: a GUI interface (Start⇨Programs⇨ Accessories⇨System Tools⇨Backup) and a command line execution (\WINNT\system32\ntbackup). We prefer the GUI interface (shown in Figure 17-1) for quick manual backups, and the command line interface for batched and scheduled backups.

These methods are not exactly unattended because you have to start them to run manually — unless you set them up with a scheduler task to run automatically at a preset time. Although somewhat crude and not so fancy, NTBACKUP is better than nothing. If your budget is low and you can't afford to purchase a third-party vendor that specializes in backup software, this is the way to go. And, the best part is that it's free (it's included in the price of Windows 2000 Server)!

Before purchasing a third-party backup product or using the Windows 2000 Server built-in backup program, search Microsoft Knowledgebase (www.microsoft.com/support/) for known bugs and problems regarding backup issues. Be specific in the search (for example, **Windows 2000 Server NTBACKUP**). Also, always install the latest Service Pack on your Windows 2000 Server, which fixes most minor bugs known to Microsoft.

Before backing up, run the repair disk utility. In the past, this utility was a separate application from the backup utility. In Windows 2000, however, the repair disk option has been added to the NTBACKUP application (Start⇨Programs⇨Accessories⇨System Tools⇨Backup). There are two ways to create the *Emergency Repair Disk* (ERD). You can click on the Emergency Repair Disk button in the Welcome tab of the NTBACKUP program, or you can choose the Create an Emergency Repair Disk option from the Tools menu.

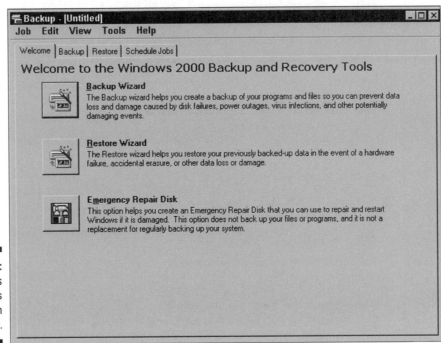

Figure 17-1:
Windows 2000's built-in GUI backup.

What's new in Windows 2000 Server NTBACKUP

One of the most frustrating things about the old Windows NT Server NTBACKUP program is that it can only back up information to a tape drive. It's not uncommon for you to need to back up information from a system with a tape drive and restore it on one that does not have a tape drive. The new NTBACKUP program that ships with Windows 2000 allows you to back up your information to any media that is available to you. These can include floppy drives, Zip drives, Jaz drives, a shared drive on a server, or a second hard drive.

Removable Storage Manager (RSM) is an integrated part of the Windows 2000 operating system. This service is responsible for managing tasks such as the mounting and dismounting of storage devices on behalf of Windows 2000 backup software. Relieving the backup software of these tasks and making them a part of the operating system, unlike previous versions of Windows NT, makes the software much more reliable and robust.

Also new to the NTBACKUP utility is built-in scheduling. You can finally schedule a job right in the backup program, what a concept! Now you don't have to struggle to get the AT command to function properly (although it's still available for you die-hard fans).

One of the most amazing new features of the Windows 2000 Backup is known as *Automated System Recovery* (ASR). ASR is a feature that allows you to restore your entire system in the event that your hard drive fails. This feature creates a bootable floppy disk that will initiate the restore process off your backup media. Before you can use this feature, you must run the ASR Wizard.

Finally, you can back up (and restore) using a Backup Wizard. The wizard will ask you all the questions that you need to answer for a backup to be completed properly. See the "Scheduling backup jobs" section later in this chapter for more details on the Backup Wizard.

Command line backups

You execute NTBACKUP from the command prompt using the following syntax:

```
ntbackup backup [systemstate] "bks filename" [/a][/d "backup
        set description"][/DS "servername"][/f
        "filename"][/g "guidname"][/hc:{on|off}][/IS
        "servername"]/j "jobname"[/l:{f|s|n}][/m type][/n
        "medianame"][/p "poolname"][/r:{yes|no}]
        [/rs:{yes|no}][/t "tapename"][/v:{yes|no}]
```

The / parameters (also called options or switches) in the previous syntax are defined as follows:

✓ **Systemstate:** The systemstate is a collection of information about the system that can be backed up or restored. These include: the Registry, the class registration database, the system boot files, the Active Directory, the SYSVOL, and the Certificate Services database.

✔ **bks filename:** This file is created using the GUI interface in NTBACKUP and simply lists all of the directories and files that will be backed up. This file has a .bks extension.

✔ **/a:** Appends the current backup data to the end of the tape. Omitting the **/a** means you want to overwrite the previous data on the tape. Either the **/g** or **/t** must be used with this switch. Please note that this switch should not be used with the **/p** switch.

✔ **/d:** Allows you to identify the backup set.

✔ **/ds:** This switch, in conjunction with the **/is** switch, is used to back up the directory database on a Microsoft Exchange Server.

✔ **/f:** The pathname and filename for the backup.

✔ **/g:** Causes the backup operation to overwrite or append to this tape.

✔ **/hc:** Turns the hardware compression on or off for the backup, assuming that the tape drive can handle it.

✔ **/is:** This switch, in conjunction with the **/ds** switch, is used to back up the Information Store database on a Microsoft Exchange Server.

✔ **/j:** When this switch is selected, the backup program uses this name whenever logging information about the operation.

✔ **/l:** Allows you to select the type of logging that is enabled: f=full, s=summary, and n=none.

✔ **/m:** Allows you to set the backup type: normal, copy, daily, incremental, or differential.

✔ **/n:** Allows you to specify a new tape name to use during the backup operation.

✔ **/p:** Assigns the backup to a media pool. A *media pool* is a group of backup media that have the same policies assigned to them.

✔ **/r:** Restricts access to the backed up data to either the owner or the members of the Administrators group.

✔ **/rs:** Backs up the Removable Storage database.

✔ **/t:** Overwrites or appends to this tape.

✔ **/v:** Performs a complete verification after the backup operation is completed.

Given the number of commands involved, it's obvious that this task can become tedious to perform by hand. You can try to automate some of your backups using batch files, but a few exceptions do exist:

✔ **User input:** Some of the commands, such as /nopoll and /missingtape, require you to input keystrokes. Therefore, if your backups don't require those specific commands, you can run batch files to perform unattended backups.

✔ **Backup scope:** You may back up directories using batch files only, but not files by themselves.

✔ **Backup syntax:** You may not use wildcards in batch files.

Some files that are hard-coded into NTBACKUP don't get backed up, and you can't change or alter this.

Some of the files and other things that don't get backed up are:

✔ **Open files:** Users can't have files open while the backup is running. Those files won't be backed up. Have the users log off the system and disconnect them from any shares.

✔ **Temporary files:** No temporary files, such as PAGEFILE.SYS, are backed up.

✔ **Permissions:** The account used to perform the backup must have permission to read files.

✔ **Registry:** Only the local Registry is backed up. Registries on other servers are not backed up.

Selecting files and folders

In the previous version of NTBACKUP, you could pick and choose the files you want to back up only through the GUI. The command line interface in previous versions of Windows NT Server only lets you back up from a starting point — either a drive root or a directory. This has changed in the Windows 2000 Backup application. You can now choose folders and/or drives to back up and back them up from the command line and the GUI. To back them up from the command line, you have to create a Backup Selection file (a .bks file) for the folder and/or drive you want to back up. To create a .bks file:

1. **Open the Backup Wizard (Start⇨Programs⇨Accessories⇨System Tools⇨Backup), click the Backup tab, and choose the desired folders and/or drives you want to back up. (See Figure 17-2.)**

2. **After all the desired folders and/or drives have been selected, choose the Job⇨Save Selections and name your .bks file.**

3. **Use the bks filename parameter as described in the previous "Command line backups" section.**

If you prefer to use the GUI version of NTBACKUP, just omit Step 3 and read the "Specifying backup destination, media settings" next for more information on using the GUI version.

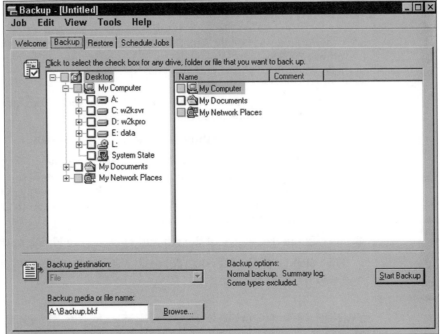

Figure 17-2:
Selecting
files and
folders to be
backed up.

Specifying backup destination, media settings

Now that you have selected the files you want to back up, you can choose the backup destination. If you do not have a tape drive installed on your system, the NTBACKUP program defaults to a file as its backup destination. Otherwise, simply select the backup device to which you would like to back up the information. Go to Start⇨Programs⇨Accessories⇨System Tools⇨ Backup and select the Backup tab. If you chose to back up the data to a file, in the Backup Destination field, simply enter the full path and filename in the Backup Media or File Name field (or click on the Browse button to explore to it) and click on the Start Backup button. For backups to a tape, choose a tape from the Backup Destination field and click on the Start Backup button.

Scheduling backup jobs

As we mentioned previously, scheduling backup jobs is now a built-in feature of Windows 2000 Server. Scheduling backup jobs is now as simple as following these steps:

1. **Go to Start⇨Programs⇨Accessories⇨System Tools⇨Backup and choose the Schedule Jobs tab.**

2. **Click on the Add Job button in the lower-right corner.**

   This starts the Backup Wizard. Simply answer the questions presented to you by the wizard. You'll notice that you're prompted for a username and password. The user performing the backup (probably you) must be either an administrator, a member of the Backup Operators group, or have equivalent rights of these groups.

3. **Specify the frequency of the job and click on the Finish button.**

   The calendar in the Schedule Jobs tab changes to reflect the jobs. (See Figure 17-3.)

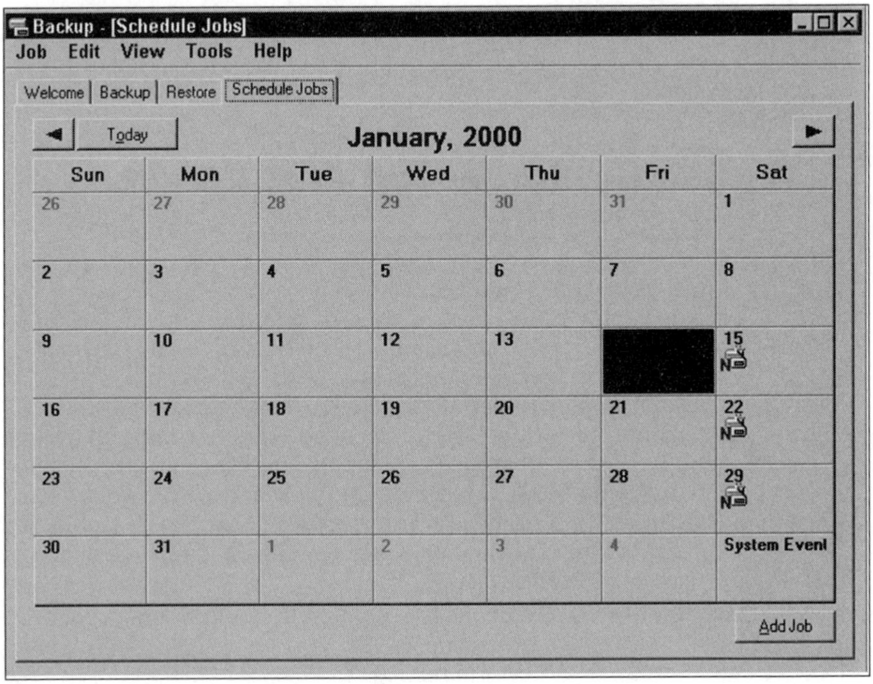

Figure 17-3:
Windows
2000 backup
scheduling
option.

Running NTBACKUP in the background

Hopefully, you're not backing up during the daytime when users are most likely to be on the system and have files open. However, if you need to, there's a way to run NTBACKUP in background mode:

1. **Create a shortcut to NTBACKUP.EXE by choosing Start⇨Programs⇨ Accessories⇨Windows Explorer. Find NTBACKUP.EXE in the \winnt\system32 directory and right-click on the file. Choose Create Shortcut.**

   You have created a shortcut icon.

2. **Drag the shortcut icon to your desktop.**

3. **Right-click on the NTBACKUP.EXE shortcut icon and select Properties.**

4. **Choose the Shortcut tab and, in the Target box, type your backup information using syntax you would use from the command line.**

5. **Click on the arrow next to the Run List box and choose Minimized. Click on the OK button to close.**

To start the backup in background mode, insert a tape and double-click on the NTBACKUP shortcut icon you created.

Restoring from a Backup

Backing up your data is only half the picture. The other half involves restoring files on the network. We hope that you have to restore only a few files for users from time to time. Making regular backups along the way makes this task friendly and easy. You can run into occasions, however, when you lose your data and computer equipment, including the server you need to restore to. We really hope this never happens, but in a fire or other disaster, it's entirely possible. Hopefully, you heed our advice when we say to rotate tapes off-site each week to plan for this catastrophe. If you also lose the server, we hope that you have a good working relationship with your local vendors so you can get equipment in a hurry.

The most important thing to remember when restoring your network is to practice the restoration process when you are not under the gun. This not only gives you confidence in performing the task but also periodically tests the integrity of your backup. Although you can examine log files each morning, it's better to perform real restore tests — just like a dress rehearsal. When disaster does strike and you need to perform a real restore, there are typically all sorts of people looking over your shoulder asking you when things will be up and running. If you confidently know your backup system, you can perform this task under extreme pressure. Don't wait until the last minute to test and learn the system.

Always restore the system files (\SYSTEM32\CONFIG and Registry files) first, reboot, and then take a peek at the system to make sure everything looks like it's in place. Then restore the data files. If you plan your network directory and volume structure to segment the system and data files, this task is much easier. Know ahead of time if certain business departments require that their data be restored first. Sometimes this is not necessary, but in instances where a customer service department exists, they usually want the network back up right away with immediate access to their data. Why? Because they are servicing the external customers that generate the revenue for your organization! Before restores become necessary, try to devise a restoration order plan for your network and practice it.

Note that sometimes you can't restore Windows 2000 system files and you may have to reinstall Windows 2000, then restore the system files.

Third-Party Backup Options

Because Windows 2000 is such a new operating system (and it's so different from Windows NT), there are currently no third-party options. Rest assured, however, that this will not remain so for long.

We always recommend going with the well-recognized, name-brand, third-party companies to ensure good compatibility with Windows 2000 and other network operating systems. Most of the popular packages support the ability to back up several different network operating systems at one time, plus contain easy-to-use interfaces for backup and restore options.

One easy way to find other third-party backup software is to visit popular search engines on the Internet, such as http://search.cnet.com/, and enter the keywords **Windows 2000 Server Backup**. Discount Internet shops, such as CDW (www.cdw.com/), provide information about various backup devices in one handy location where fact sheets and information are at your fingertips. On the CDW Web site, go to the Hardware section, click the Data Storage option, and look at how much information you have.

Two types of vendors are in the backup market: small-business backup solutions and enterprise backup solutions. We list the top several in each category to get your search started:

✔ **Small business:**

- Arcada (the original developers of NTBACKUP, now Seagate, now Veritas Software), www.arcada.com/
- Exabyte, www.exabyte.com/
- ADIC (Advanced Digital Information Corporation), www.adic.com/
- Hewlett-Packard, www.hp.com/storage/prodinfo.html

✔ **Enterprise business:**

- Veritas, `www.veritas.com/`

- Legato, `www.legato.com/`

 Search some of the backup vendors' Web sites for white papers and cost of ownership documents. This information is free, and a lot of research has been compiled. You can use this information to convince management of your backup requirements.

Regardless of which vendor you choose, the following checklist provides some helpful criteria in evaluating tape systems. Choose the requirements for your organization and query the vendor as to whether their product has the features you desire, or if you have to pay extra for some add-on modules.

You may not need all of the following criteria, but this list should give you a good idea of what you need when choosing a tape backup system:

✔ **Critical System Files:** An essential feature in any tape system that you purchase is that it can back up the Windows 2000 system files, such as the Registry and event logs, security information, user accounts, and access control lists, in addition to the actual data.

✔ **Fast tape index:** When backing up large amounts of data, it's critical that during the restore process you're able to obtain a catalog of the tape's contents within a minute or two. You don't want to wait 30 minutes each time you need to see the contents of a particular tape.

✔ **Multiplatform support:** Networks that support multiple networks, such as Novell, Microsoft, UNIX, and others, are easier to back up if one backup system can support more than one platform.

✔ **Client backups:** Some users simply refuse to store files on the network. In this case, look for a package that automates client workstation backups across the network to your tape backup system. Some popular systems already include this option. Ask which client operating systems it supports — for example, Macintosh, UNIX, Windows 98, and OS/2.

✔ **Unattended operation:** Some tape systems work like jukeboxes and have a mechanical arm that inserts and removes tapes, so you can go home while the backup runs. These systems are expensive, but if you have a lot of data to back up and don't wish to insert tapes all night, look for this feature.

✔ **Scheduling features:** If you want to perform incremental and full backups on different days, look for a system that is flexible and allows you to automate the scheduling features based on the day of the week.

✔ **Open files:** Open files are files that are in use during the backup operation. Not all backup systems are designed to back up open files, and some even halt when they get to one that's open. Most systems skip over the file and write an exception to a log file. More than likely, you want a backup system that backs up open files. If that's the case, you want to make sure that the system will do this for you.

✔ **Security and encryption:** For small operations, this feature might not be as critical, but for larger environments, ask the vendor how its system handles passing information through the network, such as passwords and account information.

✔ **Hierarchical Storage Management (HSM):** You want to make sure the vendor's product supports online, nearline, and offline storage and can manage using all three at one time.

✔ **Data storage size:** You want to find out how much data you can back up to the system (MB or GB), the size of the tapes the system uses (4mm, 8mm, DLT, or others), and if it compresses data.

✔ **Remote management:** Getting to monitor backup status and progress remotely instead of being in front of the console is a handy feature.

✔ **Scalability:** Find out if this system is one that can be scaled to a larger environment should your network grow.

✔ **Year 2000 compliant:** We're not far from the year 2000, so you probably aren't going to find a vendor that isn't compliant, but it's always best to check.

✔ **Security access:** Running an unattended backup means that a device must either log in to the network while you're gone or remain logged in with the keyboard locked. Check with the vendor as to how the product logs in to the network and maintains security.

The Backup Operator

Before a user is allowed to backup or restore the system, he or she must be a member of the Backup Operators group. This group is the same as the Backup Operators group in Windows NT, but Windows 2000 has changed the procedures for adding users to the group and changing the group's policies. Depending on whether you're running Windows 2000 with Active Directory, the steps involved in adding a user to the Backup Operator group will be slightly different.

By default, the Backup Operators group does not have any members. It's simply an empty container or a placeholder for when you need to assign users backup and restore rights.

To modify the membership of the Backup Operators group when Active Directory is not installed (in other words, your server's configured as a normal server instead of a domain controller), follow these steps:

1. **Choose Start⇨Programs⇨Administrative Tools⇨Computer Management to open the Computer Management window.**

2. **In the left pane, expand the System Tools icon and highlight the Local Users and Groups icon.**

3. **In the right pane, double-click on the Groups option.**

   At this point, all the groups that currently exist on your system are displayed in the right pane.

4. **Highlight the Backup Operators group, right-click on it, and choose the Add to Group option from the drop-down menu.**

5. **Click on the Add button and choose the user or users that you would like to become members of the Backup Operators group. After you've selected the desired users, click the Add button again. Then click the OK button to close the window.**

6. **Click the OK button to close the Backup Operators Properties dialog box.**

To modify the membership of the Backup Operators group when Active Directory is installed, follow these steps:

1. **Choose Start⇨Programs⇨Administrative Tools⇨Active Directory Users and Computers to open Active Directory Users and Computers.**

2. **Double-click on the tree in the left pane to expand it.**

3. **Double-click on the Builtin folder in the right pane.**

4. **Right-click on the Backup Operators group in the right pane and choose Properties from the pop-up menu.**

5. **Select the Members tab and click the Add button to add users.**

Chapter 18

Network Security Management

*I*n the advancing world of information technology, protecting private data from prying eyes is becoming more and more important. Maintaining security to prevent access to internal information is often critical to sustaining a competitive edge. In this chapter, we discuss how to impose tight security on Windows 2000 Server.

They Are Always Out to Get You

When you install Windows 2000 Server right out of the box, it does not provide you with a totally secure environment. You must impose security on Windows 2000 Server. This process involves executing many steps, careful planning, double-checking your settings, and a few non-computer activities. If you don't care about the security of your data, you can skip this discussion entirely.

The goal of security is not to create a system that is impossible for a hacker or misguided user to compromise. Instead, the goal is to maintain a sufficient barrier against intruders so the difficulty they encounter while attempting to access your system is significantly more than someone else's system. It's kind of like building a brick wall around your yard so tall that it discourages someone from climbing your wall — so they go climb your neighbor's instead. Your goal is to convince the hacker to attack an easier target. By following the prescriptions in this chapter, you can deploy a Windows 2000 Server system that is not only harder to crack than your neighbors' but also nearly watertight!

Protecting proprietary and private electronic property is not only a defense against outside attackers, but it also involves erecting a barrier against inside assaults and taking precautions against other threats to your data.

Network Security Basics

The basics of network security are to keep unauthorized people out of your network, to keep unwanted data out, and to keep wanted data in. Leave it to us to point out the obvious.

Creating a secure environment requires you to pay attention to three key areas:

- ✔ Understanding the operating system (or systems)
- ✔ Controlling physical access to the computer
- ✔ Educating the human users

These three areas are like legs on a bar stool. If any one of the legs is weak, the person on the stool will hit the floor.

In the following two subsections, we briefly discuss the issues involved with maintaining physical control and education of users. The third leg, the operating system itself, is the subject of the remainder of the chapter.

Getting physical

Controlling physical access means preventing unauthorized people from coming into close proximity of your computers, network devices, communication pathways, peripherals, and even power sources. A computer system can be compromised in several ways. Physical access is always the first step in breaking into a system. Remember that physical access does not always mean a person must be physically present in your office building. If your network has dial-up access, someone can gain access remotely.

Controlling physical access means not only preventing access to keyboards or other input devices, but also blocking all other means of transmitting to or extracting signals from your computer system.

Some physical access controls are obvious to everyone:

- ✔ Locking doors
- ✔ Using security badges

✔ Employing armed guards

✔ Using locking cases and racks

If you address just these items, you leave several other access methods wide open. You need to think about the architecture, structure, and construction of your building. Can ceiling or floor tiles be removed so access can be gained over or under walls? Do ventilation shafts or windows allow entrance into locked rooms? Paranoid yet?

A person getting into your computer room is not the only concern you should have. You also need to think about the environment in which the computers operate. Most computers have a limited range of temperatures within which they operate properly. Therefore, if intruders can gain access to thermostat controls, your system is compromised. What is the one thing that all computers need? Electricity. Is your power supply secure? Can it be switched off outside of your security barriers? Do you have an *uninterruptible power supply* (UPS) attached to each critical system?

Even after preventing entrance into the computer room and protecting the operating environment, you still have not fully secured your computers physically. You need to think about your trash — yes, the trash! You would be amazed at what private investigators and criminals can learn about you and your network from the information discarded in your trash. If you don't shred or incinerate all printouts and handwritten materials, you may be offering passwords, usernames, computer names, configuration settings, drive paths, and other key information.

Do you think we've covered everything now? *Wrong!* Ponder the following issues:

✔ Does the nightly cleaning crew vacuum and dust your computer closet?

✔ Is that crew bonded?

✔ How often do they unplug computer systems to plug in cleaning machines?

✔ Is the same key that unlocks your front door also the key that unlocks the computer room?

✔ How do you know that the cleaning crew is not playing with your computer system?

✔ How do you know that the members of the cleaning crew are who you think they are?

✔ Are floppy drives installed on servers and other critical systems?

✔ Can systems be rebooted without passwords or other authentication controls (i.e., smart cards)?

✔ Do servers have extra ports ready to accept new attachments?

✔ Are your backup tapes stacked beside the tape drive?

✔ Are your backup tapes protected by encryption and passwords?

✔ Are all of your backup tapes accounted for? Where are the missing ones? What information was stored on them?

✔ What really happens in your office building after business hours? Are the doors actually locked every night?

If you can still sleep at night, you probably have most of these items under control. If you can't answer some of these questions with a solid and reassuring response, you have some work to do.

So far, the physical access issues we've discussed have dealt with stationary computer systems. But what about mobile workstations? Remember that expensive notebook system you purchased for the boss, that manager, and that system administrator so they could work while traveling and connect to the network over the phone line? Well, if one of those notebooks were to fall into the wrong hands, someone would have an open door to walk right into your network and take or destroy whatever he or she pleased.

Notebook theft is becoming the number one method of gaining access to a company's network. Most notebooks are stolen at the airport. (We bet you could have guessed that one!) Although most travelers are smart enough not to check their notebooks in as luggage, there's a common location where a notebook and its owner are often separated — the metal detector. All it takes is a few moments of delay while waiting to walk through the metal detector after you've placed the notebook on the x-ray treadmill, and *poof* — the note-book is gone by the time you reach the other end.

Controlling physical access is important because without interaction with a computer system, a hacker can't break in. Just like you can't swim if you can't get to the water. If you fail to prevent physical access to your network, you'll be relying on your operating system-supported software security to protect your data. However, there is one problem — if you've failed to prop-erly educate the network users, your security may already be compromised.

Informing the masses

The most secure network environment is completely useless if the human users don't respect the need for security. In fact, if left to their own druthers, most humans will find the easiest path of least resistance when performing regular activities. In other words, your users will do anything to make tra-versing the security simple — such as automating the entry of passwords, writing down passwords in plain view, mapping unauthorized drives, installing unapproved software, transferring data to and from work and home on floppies, attaching modems to bypass the firewall or proxy servers, and more. If you put a software/operating system-based security measure in place, a human can often find a way to get around it, or at least reduce its effectiveness.

User education is a two-fold process. First, the users of your network must be thoroughly taught what security is, why it's important, and what security measures are in place on your network. Second, violations of the security system must be dealt with swiftly and strictly.

In most cases, educating your network users requires that an official organization document detailing the security restrictions, requirements, and punishments be created. This document, called a *security policy,* serves as your network's constitution. It's the governing body of regulations. This document allows your network security to remain intact while violators of the law are terminated.

So, what does a user need to know about the security imposed on the organization's network? Here's a brief list of the highlights:

- ✔ Use passwords properly and choose them wisely. (Don't use an obvious name or number such as a pet's name or birth date.)
- ✔ Never write down or share passwords.
- ✔ Never share security badges and smart cards or leave them unattended.
- ✔ Restrict network access to authorized employees only.
- ✔ Do not share user accounts with other employees or with anyone outside of the organization.
- ✔ Do not distribute data from the network in any form outside of the organization.
- ✔ Users should not step away from their workstations while they are logged in to the system.
- ✔ Understand the various levels of security in place on the network and the purpose of the stratification.
- ✔ Do not install unapproved software.
- ✔ Make it clear to all employees that tampering, subverting, or bypassing security measures is grounds for termination of employment.
- ✔ Respect the privacy of the organization and other users.
- ✔ Deal with violations of the security policy in a swift and severe manner without reservation or exemption.

This brings up the issue of punishment. If a user violates a significant issue in the security policy, a severe punishment must be applied. In most cases, firing the individual is the only form of punishment that will effectively control the situation and prevent other users from making the same mistake. The repercussions of violating the security policy must be detailed in the policy itself. But, if you spell out the punishment, you must follow through. Even if your top programmer is the culprit, he or she must receive the same severity of punishment as the temporary mail person.

Most analysts have discovered that the deployment of a severe security policy results in a common occurrence — a short-term improvement in security, followed by a brief period of laxness, which results in violations, causing several users to be fired, which immediately results in an overall sustained improvement in security. Companies have reported that the loss of man-power because of violations was negligible in comparison to the prevention of security breaches.

You should create your own security policy that includes details about physical control, user education, and operating system-level security measures. Remember the old adage about the ounce of prevention . . . ?

Windows 2000 and Security

Windows 2000 security centers around access control. Access control is dependant on user identity. A user's identity is his or her user account. To gain access to a Windows 2000 Server computer or network, you must provide a user with a user account that has a valid username and password. Anyone who knows a valid username and password combination can gain access. Therefore, both the usernames and passwords of user accounts need to be protected.

Usernames are more than just names

Protecting usernames is not always simple, but a little effort can subvert several "easy" attacks. First, don't create usernames that employ just the first or last name of a person. Combine two or more elements to create the name, such as first name, last name, initials, department code, or division name. You should also avoid using the same name for logon that is used as a user's e-mail address. This makes guessing usernames a bit more difficult. Even if a hacker knows your naming convention, making usernames complicated can make brute force attacks more difficult. (See Chapter 15 for more information on naming conventions.)

You should also rename the common accounts. These include the administrator, guest, and the IUSR_<servername> (created by *Internet Information Services,* or IIS) accounts. Rename these to something descriptive but not easily guessed. Then, create new dummy accounts with the original name that have absolutely no access, which provides a decoy for hackers, effectively wasting their time and giving you more opportunity to discover who they are.

In your security policy, you should include a restriction to prevent users from employing their network logon username as a logon name anywhere else. In other words, a user's network logon name should not be used as a logon name for Web sites, File Transfer Protocol (FTP) sites, or other external systems. If users don't use the same logon names everywhere, they'll be less tempted to use the same passwords everywhere as well.

Even with these precautions, usernames are often discoverable. The important issue here is to make obtaining any data item needed to log in to your network as difficult to get as possible. After a username is known, the responsibility of protecting your network rests on the strength of the account's password.

Passwords and security

Passwords are the primary method by which unauthorized access to a system is prevented. The stronger the password, the more likely security will remain intact. As part of your security policy, you need to require that strong passwords be used by each and every user. (See the end of this section for guidelines that lead to strong passwords.) A single account compromised can result in the entire system being accessed.

Strong passwords can be enforced using the built-in controls of Windows 2000. By employing all of the system-level controls that force strong passwords, little additional effort is required to ensure that users comply with the security policy.

Account policies define the restrictions, requirements, and parameters of the Password, Account Lockout, and Kerberos policies. To access the Accounts Policies, follow these steps:

1. **Open Start⇨Programs⇨Administrative Tools⇨Local Security Policy.**

2. **Expand the Account Policies selection.**

   Now you can see the Password, Account Lockout, and Kerberos policies in the right pane of the Local Security Settings window.

The Password Policy

After you've found the Account Policies option, you can access the Password Policy, shown in Figure 18-1 (choose Account Policies⇨Password Policy). The seven options in the Password Policy allow you to control the requirements for user passwords. The higher you raise the bar in each of the seven options, the stronger the password requirements, thus making it less and less likely that a brute force attack will succeed against your system. In the following list, we briefly explain each option, spell out the default setting, and recommend the most appropriate settings for general use:

- ✔ **Store Password Using Reversible Encryption For All Users in the Domain:** The default setting is "Disabled." By enabling this attribute, you can use Shiva Password Authentication Protocol (SPAP), which is a security authentication mechanism for PPP developed by Shiva Corporation. Leave this disabled unless SPAP is required by a client.

- ✔ **Enforce Password History:** The default setting is "1." We recommend a setting of 5 or greater, which means the system will remember the last 5 passwords used by a user so he or she can't reuse any of those passwords.

- ✔ **Maximum Password Age:** The default setting is "42 Days." Use this option to define when passwords expire and must be replaced. We recommend settings of 30, 45, or 60 days.

- ✔ **Minimum Password Age:** The default setting is "0 Days." Use this option to define how long a user must wait before changing his or her password. We recommend settings of 1, 3, or 5 days

- ✔ **Minimum Password Length:** The default setting is " 0 Characters." Use this option to define the smallest number of characters that must be present in a password. We recommend at least 6 characters.

- ✔ **Passwords Must Meet Complexity Requirements:** The default setting is "Disabled." Complexity requirements are rules such as requiring both capital and lowercase letters, requiring the use of numerals, requiring non-alphanumeric characters, and so on. If the native password requirements are not sufficient for you, we recommend that you research the complexity requirements further by using the Windows 2000 Help feature or the Windows 2000 Resource Kit.

Note that each of the previous attributes has a setting of Local Policy and Effective Policy and because the Effective Policy will vary, only the Local Policy default is listed. The Effective Policy is the cumulative effect of a legacy Windows NT 4.0 NTCONFIG.POL file, a unique Local group policy, site group policies, domain group policies, and organizational unit (OU) group policies. These policy objects are applied former to latter. If they define inconsistent settings, the latter object's settings take precedent by overwriting the settings of the former. Therefore, all policy objects contribute to the Effective Policy.

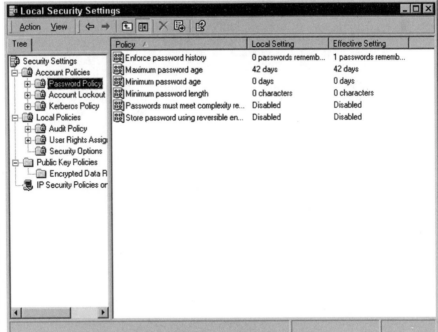

Figure 18-1:
The Group
Policy
editing tool,
Password
Policy.

The Account Lockout Policy

The next policy in Account Policies is the Account Lockout Policy, which governs when user accounts are locked out because of repeated failed logon attempts (choose Account Policies⇨Account Lockout Policy). Lockout prevents brute force logon attacks by turning off user accounts. The options are as follows:

- **Account Lockout Threshold:** The default setting is "0 Invalid logon attempts." Use this option to define how many failed logon attempts result in lockout. We recommend a setting of 3 to 5 invalid logon attempts.

- **Account Lockout Duration:** The default setting is "Not Defined." Use this option to define how long to lockout an account. A setting of Forever requires an administrator to un-lockout an account. We recommend a setting of 30 minutes or more.

- **Reset account lockout counter after:** The default setting is "Not Defined." Use this option to define the time period after which the count of failed logons for a single account is reset. We recommend a setting of 15 minutes.

The Kerberos Policy

The last policy in Account Policies is the Kerberos Policy, which governs the activity of secured communication sessions (choose Account Policies⇨ Kerberos Policy). Kerberos is an advanced network authentication protocol. Using Kerberos, clients can authenticate once at the beginning of a communication session and then perform multiple tasks during that session without having to authenticate again. In other words, Kerberos is used to prove the identity of a client and a server to each other. After this identity verification occurs, communications can commence without requiring this process again (or at least not until the communication link is broken). The options for this policy are:

- ✔ **Enforce User Logon Restrictions: Not Defined**
- ✔ **Maximum lifetime for user ticket renewal: Not Defined**
- ✔ **Maximum lifetime for service ticket: Not Defined**
- ✔ **Maximum tolerance for computer clock synchronization: Not Defined**
- ✔ **Maximum lifetime for user ticket: Not Defined**

For more information on Kerberos in Windows 2000, please see the Microsoft Windows 2000 Web site (www.Microsoft.com/windows/server/) and the Microsoft Security Web site (www.Microsoft.com/security/).

Two or three things we know about passwords

Whether or not you enable software controls to restrict passwords, we recommend that you include the following elements in your organization's security policy regarding passwords:

- ✔ Apply a minimum of six characters.
- ✔ Prevent the e-mail address, account name, or real name from being part of the password.
- ✔ Don't use common words, slang, terms from the dictionary, or other real words.
- ✔ Don't write passwords down, except to place them in a vault or safety deposit box.

✔ Don't use words, names, or phrases that can be associated with you, such as family, friends, hobbies, pets, interests, books, movies, car, or workspace.

✔ If real words are used, split them with capitalization, numbers, and/or non-alphanumeric characters, for example, Go7Ril-la.

✔ Use numbers or non-alphanumeric characters to replace letters, for example, 13TT3r (letters with a one and three's).

✔ Use at least three out of four types of characters: uppercase, lowercase, numerals, non-alphanumeric (symbols, punctuation).

✔ Create acronyms to use as passwords from sentences, for example, Fifty-five dollars will pay a parking ticket = 55DwPaPt.

Through the combination of Windows 2000-enforced password restrictions and strong recommendations in a company security policy, you can improve the security of your system through the use of strong passwords.

A Look into the Future: Service Packs

Microsoft regularly releases updates and fixes for its products, called *patch releases*. It did so for Windows NT 4.0 and will do so for Windows 2000. You should expect to see the first patch release for Windows 2000 around the middle part of 2000. (Maybe W2K is the Y2K bug!) Because the patches released by Microsoft correct all kinds of bugs, problems, and other issues, you should assume that some of the patches address problems related to security. Therefore, it's important to keep yourself informed about the release and content of these patches.

Microsoft releases patches in two forms: service packs and hotfixes. A *hotfix* is a patch for a single problem. A *service pack* is many hotfixes combined into a single "Band-Aid." There are more significant differences as well. Hotfixes are not fully tested nor are they supported by Microsoft. A hotfix should only be applied if you're actually experiencing the problem it fixes, because they sometimes cause other problems. Service packs are thoroughly tested and therefore safer for deployment. However, we recommend that you delay application of a new service pack until it's about two months old. This gives the rest of the Windows 2000 community the time to install and test the patch for you. It's always better to learn from the mistakes of others than to fall into the pit yourself.

Service packs are cumulative, meaning that each new release of a service pack includes the previous service pack plus all hotfixes and other improvements since that time. You only need to apply the most current service pack and any required hotfixes.

Before you apply any patch to Windows 2000, you should read the documentation included with the patches. Then make the following preparations:

- ✔ Back up the system, or at least your data and the Registry.
- ✔ Reboot the system.
- ✔ Close all applications and stop any unnecessary services.

Be careful about installing items from the original distribution CD after a service pack has been applied. Windows NT 4.0 had several problems with this, but Microsoft claims that Windows 2000 will not succumb to the same problems. Generally, you want to plan ahead. Try to install everything off the CD before you apply a service pack. If you install new applications after installing a service pack, it's a good idea to reapply the service pack. If the new application fails to operate afterwards, contact the application's vendor for a solution.

If you don't know which level of a service pack you applied, you can check by looking at the Help⇨About page from any native Windows 2000 application (such as Windows Explorer, Control Panel, or My Computer).

The Microsoft Web site can be secretive about the location of service packs and hotfixes, but you should always check there first. You can attempt to locate the patches from `www.microsoft.com/ntserver/`, or you can jump directly to the FTP site at `ftp://ftp.microsoft.com/bussys/winnt/winnt-public/fixes/usa/`. From the FTP site, select the appropriate operating system type — because there were not any patches for Windows 2000 at the time of this writing, there's not a directory. However, expect it to be something like "win2000", "2000", "w2k", or "w2000" and they may even separate the versions of Windows 2000 with "pro", "svr", and "adv" as part of the directory names. The service packs are in a subdirectory labeled "ussp#" (where # is the number of the service pack). The hotfixes are found in the "hotfixes-presp1" and "hotfixes-postsp#" directories.

Although Microsoft is still too quiet about service pack issues, there are several other online repositories of excellent information. We recommend keeping an eye on the following sites:

- ✔ **NT Bug Traq Web site:** `www.ntbugtraq.com`
- ✔ **Paperbits Web site:** `www.paperbits.com`

Cop an Attitude

To maintain a secure networking environment, you must be a pessimist. View every user as a potential security leak. With this attitude, you're more likely to deploy a meaningful security structure than if you're too trusting. The key to this philosophy is to grant only the exact level of access that users or groups need to perform their work tasks and absolutely nothing more.

To take this to its logical end, you need to deal with the Everyone group and user rights.

The Everyone group

The Everyone group is a default group created by the system that includes all defined users and all anonymous users. Although it's not the catchall group it was in Windows NT 4.0, the expansive nature of the Everyone group can still cause a security problem, especially because Windows 2000 defaults to grant Full Control to the Everyone group on new volumes and new shares. This means that you need to keep an eye on where this group appears in your system. You may be granting blanket access where you really don't want any snuggling going on.

The Everyone group can seem hard to track down. It doesn't appear in the list of Builtin groups as viewed through Active Directory Users and Computers, for example. However, it does appear in the list of groups when setting security on objects. The Everyone group cannot be removed from the system, but it can be effectively managed with a little effort. See Chapter 15 for more information on the Everyone group.

The Authenticated Users group is a standard feature of Windows 2000. It contains all defined users but does not contain anonymous users. Generally, you want to use the Authenticated Users group instead of the Everyone group when you need to grant blanket access. The Everyone group must remain on your system for backward compatibility and system level requirements (such as allowing your system to boot).

Don't set the Everyone group to No Access because you'll prevent anyone from accessing a resource. Instead, just remove the Everyone group from the list of users/groups granted access.

Each time you create a new drive or a share, remove the Everyone group, and then add in only those users or groups that need access to the resource. Just like you don't want everyone gaining access to your computer, you don't want "everyone" to be allowed access to areas where it's not required by the system.

User rights

User rights are system-level privileges that control what types of activities can occur or can be performed. The default setting of user rights is reasonably secure, but there are a few improvements you can make. The User

Rights management interface is accessed using the Local Security Policy editor (see the "Passwords and security" section earlier this chapter). The User Rights Assignment is located under Security Settings⇨Local Policies⇨User Rights Assignments. Through this interface, user rights are granted or revoked. Here are several changes you should consider making:

- ✔ **Remove the Guests group from the "Log on Locally" right:** Making this change inhibits non-authenticated users from gaining unauthorized access.

- ✔ **Remove the Everyone group from the "Access This Computer from the Network" right:** Making this change inhibits non-authenticated users from gaining access to hosted resources over the network.

- ✔ **Remove the Everyone group from the "Bypass Traverse Checking" right:** Making this change inhibits non-authenticated users from jumping into subdirectories for which they do not have access to parent directories.

- ✔ **Remove the Backup operators group from the "Restore Files and Directories" right:** Making this change inhibits non-administrators from restoring files from backup tapes. Because files can be restored to *file allocation table* (FAT) partitions where *Access Control Lists* (ACLs) are lost, this is an important security modification.

After you make these changes, double-check that regular users still have the capabilities they need to perform their required tasks. If not, you may need to grant a few users or groups these user rights. For example, if you want users to access resources on a server from across the network, you should add a group, such as the Users group, to the Access This Computer From the Network User Right.

Common Mouse Holes

Windows 2000 has a handful of common security holes that you need to look for and fill. Fortunately, we have crawled around on our hands and knees so you don't have to. Just follow our friendly advice, and you'll be all snug and secure.

Unseen administrative shares

Each time Windows 2000 boots, a hidden administrative share is created for every drive. These shares are backup paths for the system just in case direct access to system files is somehow interrupted. In other words, it's a redundancy you don't need! The administrative shares are disabled by adding AutoShareServer to the following Registry key:

```
HKEY_LOCAL_MACHINE\System\CurrentControlSet\Services\LanMan
          Server\Parameters
```

A value of 0 turns the administrative shares off, and a value of 1 turns them back on.

A hidden share is just like any other share, except it has a dollar sign as the last character in its name. This tells the system not to display the hidden share in standard browser listings of shares. You can use the System Manager to view hidden shares. You can create your own hidden shares just by adding a dollar sign to the end of the share name.

The problem with administrative shares is that they offer unrestricted access to every file on a drive. If the username and password of an administrator account are ever compromised, this share can be used by anyone to map to any administrative share on the network. Therefore, it's a good idea to turn these off just as a precaution.

Decoy accounts

Everyone knows the name of the most important user account on your system. Because Windows 2000 creates the Administrator account when Windows 2000 is installed, everyone already knows that you have such an account and exactly what its name is. Therefore, you need to change it!

Don't just change the name. Do one better and create a new dummy account that has absolutely no access or privileges at all and give it the name "administrator." This dummy account will serve as a decoy to lure hackers away from real access.

Creating decoys for other common accounts, such as the Guest and IUSR (the one created by IIS) accounts, is also a good idea.

Broadcasting internal information

Microsoft chose to employ NetBIOS communications to support system activity. Most system-level functions and network activities use NetBIOS for naming conventions, instructions, commands, and more. Microsoft conveniently added NetBIOS to all of its network protocols — NBT (NetBIOS over TCP/IP), NWLink (NetBIOS over IPX/SPX), and NBF (NetBIOS Frame). We think this is a bit sloppy and adds to network overhead. In addition, it can pose a security problem if this information is transmitted over external links.

You can seal off most of the problem by unbinding the NetBIOS interface on each external network adapter. (Choose Start➪Settings➪Network and Dial-up Connections; select Advanced➪Advanced Settings from the menu; and then select the Adapters and Bindings tab in the Advanced Settings dialog box.) If you're really paranoid about it, you can deploy a firewall or proxy server that supports port filtering. Then you can block all communications over Transmission Control Protocol (TCP) ports 135–139. That's one way to shut Microsoft up.

Last logged on username

By default, when Ctrl+Alt+Del is pressed, the logon dialog box displays the username of the last person to successfully log on. This is not the most secure setting. To prevent the dialog box from appearing, change the DontDisplayLastUserName value to 1. This value appears in the `HKEY_LOCAL_MACHINE\Software\Microsoft\WindowsNT\CurrentVersion\WinLogon` Registry key.

When floppies go bad

A nifty tool from System Internals (`www.sysinternals.com`) enables anyone to read NTFS files after booting from a DOS floppy. The NTFSDOS drivers make possible what Microsoft claimed was impossible. Now, anyone who has physical access to your system can reboot with a floppy and copy files right off of your NTFS protected drives. If you value your data (and your job), remove the floppy drives from critical systems.

Polly want a cracker?

Password cracking is the art of extracting passwords from a protected security database. If someone can obtain a copy of your *Security Accounts Manager* (SAM) database, either directly from the system's %systemroot%\repair\ directory or from backup media, he or she can use a password cracker against it. There are plenty of crackers out that are used against Windows NT 4.0, and we're sure someone will create one for Windows 2000 before long.

Before a hacker gets the chance to use a password cracker against you, use the cracker yourself to improve your own security. Any discovered passwords should be changed immediately.

Most of the password-cracking tools use a dictionary attack. A long list of words is generated, which the tool uses to compare hash results (the hash code results after the password encryption function is applied to a password) to the contents of the SAM. If matches are found, passwords are known. Other tools sequentially work through all possible characters. This second type of tool is more thorough, but requires significantly more time to execute. A dictionary crack is typically complete within a day or so; a brute force attack can last hundreds of years or longer.

The following are a few popular password-cracking tool sources, Windows 2000 versions should be appearing on these sites soon:

- **L0phtCrack:** www.l0pht.com/ (Note that the second "letter" is actually a zero.)
- **ScanPro:** www.ntsecurity.com/Products/ScanPro/index.html

Security Equals Vigilance

Maintaining a secure environment is an ongoing process. Keeping up with security fixes, system changes, user activity, and a security policy is often a timely task. In your efforts to maintain a protected deployment of Windows 2000, take the time to review the contents of the following Web sites, newsgroups, and other resources:

- **Microsoft Security Advisor & Notification Service:** www.microsoft.com/security/
- **Microsoft Security Partners:** http://backoffice.microsoft.com/securitypartners/
- **Windows NT Magazine:** www.winntmag.com/
- **Windows NT Enterprise Computing:** www.entmag.com/
- **NT Shop, NT Security News:** www.ntshop.net/
- **Security Bugware:** http://oliver.efri.hr/~crv/security/bugs/
- **Robert Malmgren's NT Security FAQ:** www.it.kth.se/~rom/ntsec.html
- **Bill Stout's Known NT Exploits:** www.emf.net/~ddonahue/NThacks/ntexploits.htm
- **TISC Security Web site:** http://tisc.corecom.com/
- **Somarsoft:** www.somarsoft.com/
- **Security Mailing lists:** http://oliver.efri.hr/~crv/security/mlist/mlist.html
- **10pht:** www.l0pht.com/
- **NTBugTraq:** www.ntbugtraq.com/
- **BHS Software:** www.bhs.com/
- **SERVERxtras, Inc.:** www.serverxtras.com/
- **Microsoft KnowledgeBase:** www.support.microsoft.com/search/

- ✔ **Microsoft Security reporting e-mail:** secure@microsoft.com
- ✔ **NTSecurity mailing list:** Majordomo@iss.net - subscribe ntsecurity

Here are some books you might find helpful too:

- ✔ *Microsoft Windows 2000 Security Handbook,* by Jeff Schmidt. Que, 1999. ISBN: 0789719991.

- ✔ *Configuring Windows 2000 Server Security.* Snygress Media. Publishers' Group West, 1999. ISBN: 1-928994-02-4.

- ✔ *Windows 2000 Server Security Little Black Book*, Austin, Edward (ed.). Coriolis Group, 1999. ISBN: 1-57610-387-0.

- ✔ *Maximum Security,* anonymous. Sams.net, 1997. ISBN: 1575212684.

- ✔ *Firewalls and Internet Security: Repelling the Wily Hacker,* Cheswick, William R., and Steven M. Bellovin. Addison-Wesley, 1994. ISBN: 0-201-63357-4. New edition announced for 1999.

- ✔ *Building Internet Firewalls,* Chapman, Brent D., and Elizabeth D. Zwicky. O'Reilly & Associates, 1995. ISBN: 1-56592-124-0.

Part V
Troubleshooting Server Snafus

"Before installing Windows 2000 Server, be sure to fog the users to keep them calm during the procedure."

In this part . . .

Despite your best intentions and all the prevention in the world, networks occasionally get weird. Sometimes, they even stop working altogether. That's when troubleshooting is required — when there's trouble to shoot! What you should discover in Part V is that troubleshooting is as much a state of mind as it is any particular set of tried and tested tools, tricks, and techniques for solving problems when they affect your systems or networks.

Part V kicks off with a review of key Windows 2000 utilities or troubleshooting system problems and continues with similar coverage of tools to help you handle network problems. After that, you learn how to tackle troubles arising from an inactive or wacky Active Directory.

Part V consciously covers the important bases when it comes to troubleshooting a Windows 2000 Server machine and the networks to which it is attached. Although we don't address every conceivable problem you might ever encounter, we do our best to steer you clear of the best-known (or at least the most-often-encountered) bumps in the road to networking success.

Troubleshooting is something everybody must do from time to time. Remember not to panic and to perform a systematic survey of the symptoms. You must try to identify what kinds of problems are manifesting themselves before you can figure out what might be amiss. Keep a record of problems and their solutions as you encounter and fix them. That way, you'll not only be able to solve most problems yourself, but you also build a knowledge base that will help you out for the rest of your networking career!

Chapter 19

Using Windows 2000 Troubleshooting Utilities

● ●

In This Chapter

▶ Using Event Viewer

▶ Dealing with crash dumps

▶ Working with Windows 2000 Computer Management

▶ Plotting performance with Performance Monitor

▶ Investigating the Resource Kit utilities

● ●

*A*lthough it's not necessarily the case that "where there's 2000, there's trouble," trouble with a Windows 2000 Server system is certainly not unimaginable. As you survey the contents of this chapter, you have a chance to delve into some of the better known — and more obscure — troubleshooting tools that Windows 2000 offers to savvy users.

And if that's not enough to satisfy your appetite, we mention some worthwhile Resource Kit troubleshooting utilities at the end of this chapter.

Event Viewer Reveals

Event Viewer is an essential troubleshooting tool for Windows 2000 Server. One of the most valuable characteristics of this tool is that you can always count on Event Viewer to give you the messy details about what's going on when drivers or services fail to load during system startup. Event Viewer is also your entry point into analyzing what's going on with your system, whether you're auditing specific events by design or trying to figure out where problems and errors may be coming from.

To launch Event Viewer, follow this menu sequence: Start⇨Programs⇨ Administrative Tools⇨Event Viewer. This produces the Event Viewer window shown in Figure 19-1.

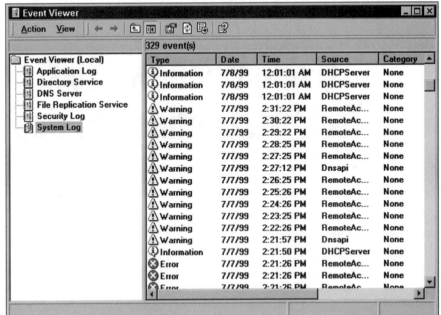

Figure 19-1:
The Event
Viewer,
System Log.

The small icons in the right column of the Event Viewer's various logs represent the following:

- ✔ **Small red circle with an X in it:** Known as the error icon, it identifies an error report that may be worth investigating.

- ✔ **Blue quote bubble with a lowercase *i* in it:** Called the information icon, it indicates an event that describes successful operation of a major server service.

- ✔ **Yellow triangle with exclamation point in it:** Known as the warning icon, it indicates that an event occurred that wasn't necessarily serious, but might indicate that potential problems lie ahead. This may be worth investigating, too.

To investigate any log entry, double-click the line where it appears. When we double-clicked one of the red circles in Figure 19-1, it produced the Event Detail report shown in Figure 19-2.

The System Log is what shows up in Event Viewer, by default. The utility also includes three main log files (in addition to the System Log) and may include service/application-specific logs, depending on what applications and services you have installed. Here's a rundown of what appears on our test system:

✔ **Application Log:** This log records events logged by some applications or services. When developers build applications, they can instruct those applications to send event information to the Event Viewer as part of their installation. The icons that appear in the Application Log are the same as those for the System Log.

✔ **Directory Service:** This log records events related to the Directory Service.

✔ **DNS Server:** This log records events related to the Domain Name Service (DNS) server.

✔ **File Replication Service:** This log records events related to the File Replication Service.

✔ **Security Log:** This log records security-related events, such as changes to a machine's security policy, failed attempts to log on or access files or directories, and so on. This is where security audit information is recorded. The Security Log uses two special icons: A yellow key indicates an audited security event completed successfully, and a gray lock indicates that an audited security event failed.

✔ **System Log:** This log records all events logged by Windows 2000 system components and appears by default the first time you run Event Viewer. By default, the System Log records all system-related hardware and operating system errors, warnings, and information messages.

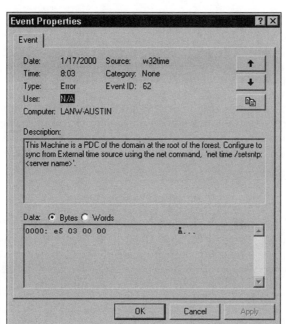

Figure 19-2:
An Event
Detail.

Working with Event Viewer should become part of your regular system maintenance routine. Check the System and Application Logs at least once a week to see if anything untoward has happened. If you audit security events, check the Security Log as often as makes sense.

Whenever you troubleshoot, the Event Viewer should be an early stop along your path. Count on this tool to keep you informed about most system problems, and any application or service problems that know how to use this facility to report warnings and errors. Unfortunately, this does not include all applications, but does include most server services and important applications, such as database managers, e-mail packages, and the like.

Taking a Dump

Should you ever be unfortunate enough to uncover a bug in Windows 2000 itself — a painful process that begins with mysterious server failures and progresses to long, arduous calls to Microsoft's technical support staff — you will probably have to create a crash dump for their use.

Reading crash dumps is well beyond the ken of ordinary system or network administrators. You just need to recognize the term and know how to create a crash dump for some expert to peruse at his or her leisure.

Therefore, we begin with a definition: A *crash dump* is a snapshot of everything in memory when a Windows 2000 system configured to capture a crash dump actually crashes. It includes information about the operating system, the hardware, applications, and all types of other information that Windows 2000 usually keeps hidden from view that it uses to manage its own operations.

Experts can pick through a crash dump to pinpoint causes of a crash, and use their knowledge to start formulating fixes or workarounds. This is one of the things that drives the creation of the patches and fixes that eventually show up in the service packs — in case you were wondering where that stuff comes from.

To enable a crash dump, your computer must first meet the following criteria:

✔ Your paging file must reside on the same partition where the Windows 2000 system files reside. (This is called the *boot partition* in Windows 2000-speak. The paging file contributes to the bulk of the crash dump and must be accessible after the system quits working — that means it must be on the same drive where the crash dump utility resides.)

✔ You must have sufficient free space on the boot partition to capture everything in RAM plus everything in the paging file. This means that the free space must equal the sum of those values (RAM and the paging file). To determine the amount of free space you need, open the Task Manager, choose the Performance tab, and look at the number reported in the Limit field in the Commit Charge pane. (To launch Task Manager, right-click on any open area on the taskbar, and then select Task Manager from the resulting pop-up menu.) This represents the number of kilobytes of free space you'll need (to convert to MB, divide this number by 1,024).

After you meet these criteria, you can enable crash dumps in the Startup and Recovery dialog box. To access this dialog box, choose Control Panel⇨System, choose the Advanced tab, and click the Startup and Recovery button. The Write Debugging Information section contains a pull-down list where you can select to write a small dump file, a kernel only dump file, a complete dump file, or none at all. The default filename (`%systemroot%\MEMORY.DMP`) is defined in the Dump File field. You don't need to change this default. The Startup and Recovery dialog box is shown in Figure 19-3.

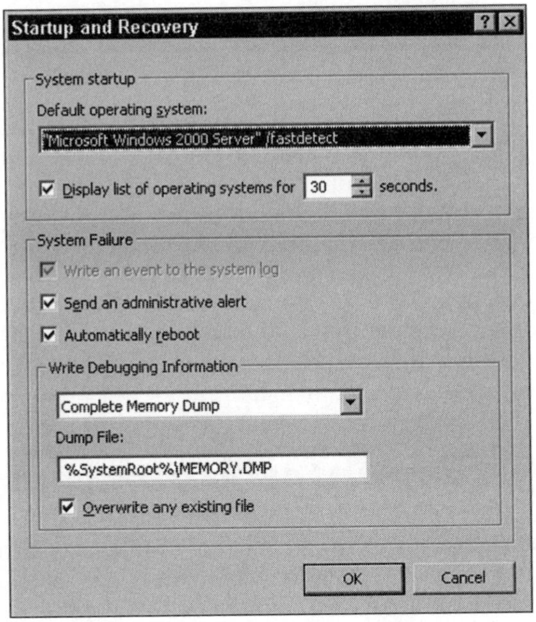

Figure 19-3:
Selections
to capture a
crash dump.

After you select the dump file settings, the next time your system experiences a STOP error, it writes the MEMORY.DMP file to your Windows 2000 system directory. By default, the value of the symbol `%systemroot%` equals C:\WINNT, assuming you installed Windows 2000 Server on the C: drive with the default system root directory name.

Sick applications? Call Dr. Watson!

Throughout this book, you encounter loads of tools and utilities for troubleshooting Windows 2000 Server hardware, networks, and the operating system itself. But what do you do when the applications go awry?

The answer to this question is "nothing!" Not because you can't *do* anything about application problems, but because such problems in the Windows 2000 environment automatically provoke error reports from the Dr. Watson utility. In fact, Dr. Watson's job is to report application difficulties whenever they occur.

Although you probably won't know what to make of Dr. Watson's content — unless you've got extensive Windows programming experience

and are familiar with debuggers — rest assured that there are plenty of people out there for whom this is old hat. Your entire involvement with Dr. Watson will be to check where the crash dump resides, to make a copy of that dump, and e-mail it to someone who can make heads or tails of this stuff! You can find the crash dump in the "Crash Dump" text box at the top of the Dr. Watson application window that you can produce by entering "drwtsn32" in the text entry box of the Run command.

However, when applications get weird, Dr. Watson can be good for the tech support folks who will try to cure what ails your system.

A crash dump creates two interesting problems. First, because the sum of RAM and the paging file is probably 200MB or more, you must find a way to get a copy to technical support. (You'd better have a fast Internet link.) Second, you must remember to delete that file after you copy it, or your server is likely to run out of space on the boot partition.

We've learned that compressing crash dumps usually reduces them by 70 percent or more, so we recommend that you zip them up (using a utility such as WinZip, which can be found at www.winzip.com) before you send them out.

Windows 2000 Computer Management

With the introduction of Plug and Play and the Microsoft Management Console (MMC), several functions and applications found in Windows NT 4.0 and Windows 9x have been combined to create a versatile inspection tool for Windows 2000. The Computer Management tool (see Figure 19-4) gives you access to troubleshooting tools such as System Information and Device Manager.

You may recall the Windows NT Diagnostics tool from Windows NT 4.0. It has been transformed into the System Information subsection of the Computer Management tool. By expanding the five subsections (System Summary,

Hardware Resources, Components, Software Environment, and Applications) you can obtain detailed information about the status, settings, configuration, and operations of the system. This is a great place to look before adding new hardware or when trying to find out why a device is failing.

The Device Manager (see Figure 19-5) is a component borrowed from Windows 9x. This nifty tool maintains a complete list of installed devices. After expanding the device type headings to reveal the list of individual devices, you can double-click on any device to reveal a Properties dialog box. From these Properties dialog boxes you can:

✔ Obtain device status

✔ Launch troubleshooting help

✔ Remove or replace drivers

✔ Change configuration settings

✔ Alter device-specific operational settings

The Device Manager is the tool that Windows NT users have been begging for, now it's available for you in Windows 2000. From now on, you'll be able to reconfigure devices on the fly and, in many cases, you don't even need to reboot for the changes to take effect.

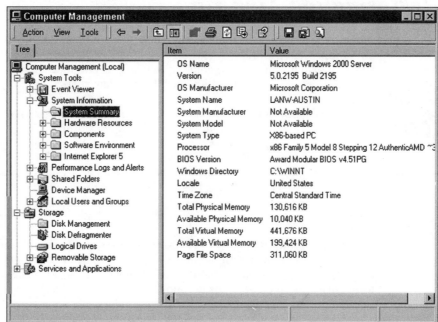

Figure 19-4:
The
Computer
Management
tool.

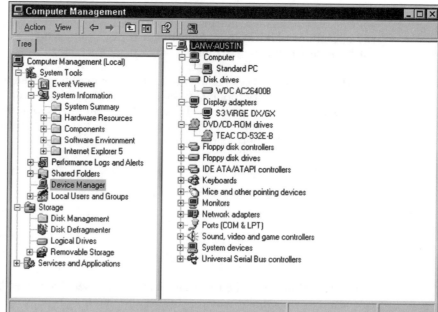

Figure 19-5:
The Device
Manager
tool.

Performance Monitor

Windows 2000's Performance Monitor utility (called PerfMon for short) is an underappreciated work of inspired genius. We say that not only because it's true, but also because we've come to rely on this outstanding tool to help us with all types of troubleshooting over the past few years.

PerfMon is another utility you can launch from the Administrative Tools menu (Start➪Programs➪Administrative Tools➪Performance).

When you first launch PerfMon, it defaults to the System Monitor option and presents an entirely bland exterior, as Figure 19-6 indicates. It takes some work to get PerfMon to do anything, but the results make the effort worthwhile.

See Chapter 20 for additional information on PerfMon.

You use the primary display of PerfMon to monitor either real-time or recorded measurements. Depending upon which button you select, the display area can show measurements in chart form (like an EKG), in histogram form (like a thermometer), or in report form (like a budget).

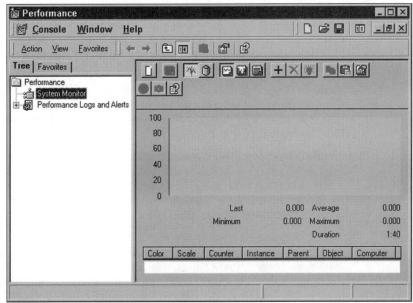

Figure 19-6:
Performance
Monitor.

Counting yer objects

Performance is measured on a counter and object basis. (Chapter 16 goes into some detail about Windows 2000 objects.) For this chapter, all you need to know is that everything in the Windows 2000 environment is an object, and each object has its own specific counters that measure certain aspects of the performance or activities of that object. The full context of performance is based on:

- ✔ **Computer:** The source system of the object
- ✔ **Object:** The sub-system of interest
- ✔ **Counter:** The aspect of performance of interest
- ✔ **Instance:** The specific object to be measured when multiple objects of the same type exist on a single system

Counters are added to the display area by clicking the big plus sign button on the PerfMon toolbar. This reveals the Add Counters dialog box, where you can select the context of the counters you want displayed. If you click the Explain button on this dialog box, details about the selected counter are revealed.

Some of the most important object/counter pairs to watch include the following (in the following list, the object name appears to the left, followed by a backward slash, followed by the counter name):

✔ **Server\Bytes Total/sec:** Shows how much data your server is handling over time (for a basic measurement of how busy your system is). Other counters for the server object, such as Sessions Errored Out, Work Item Shortages, Errors System, and Blocking Requests Rejected can all indicate potential system bottlenecks.

✔ **Memory\Pages/sec:** Shows how frequently the server is moving data from memory to disk, and vice versa. If this number gets large (more than 2,500 pages per second on an average server), it can indicate a shortage of RAM on your server.

✔ **PhysicalDisk\Avg. Disk Queue Length:** Indicates how many disk requests are pending service. If this number stays over 2.0 for long, it can indicate a disk drive that's too slow to handle its load, or one that's overwhelmed by current disk activity. Sometimes, this indicates a need for a faster drive or disk controller, or even a faster disk subsystem altogether.

The objects used to monitor disk activity can cause performance problems even when PerfMon is not recording them. Therefore, Windows 2000 does not automatically enable the disk counters (according to the documentation). However, we discovered that the PhysicalDisk object does in fact function, but that the LogicalDisk object does not. There's no longer a DISKPERF tool to enable or disable these objects. Plus, the documentation completely fails to explain how these objects should be enabled or disabled. Sorry, we are as clueless about this one as you are.

✔ **Network segment\%Network utilization:** Indicates the level of usage on the network segment to which a server network interface card (NIC) is attached. (In machines with multiple NICs, you must choose which NIC to monitor.)

To enable counters for the network object, you must install the Network Monitor Tools on your server. To install this component, follow these steps:

1. **Open the Network and Dial-up Connections window (Start➪Settings➪ Network and Dial-up Connections).**

2. **Select Optional Networking Components from the Advanced menu.**

3. **Highlight Management and Monitoring Tools and click Details.**

4. **Select the checkbox beside Network Monitor Tools.**

5. **Click OK, and then click Next. Follow any further prompts.**

Of logs and alerts

A major benefit of PerfMon is obtained through its logging capabilities. Through logs, you're able to capture performance data that you can review later. This not only allows you to collect data over extended periods of time without having to sit and watch, but it also creates a historical paper trail for baselining, troubleshooting, and capacity planning.

Log files are created using the Counter Logs and Trace Logs selections of the PerfMon main window. The Counter Logs are used to record the measurements of specific counters (not just entire objects). The Trace Logs are used to record memory and resource events. Log files are created by right-clicking in the right pane (after you've highlighted either Counter Logs or Trace Logs in the left pane) and selecting New Log Setting from the pop-up menu. You need to name the log file and define the items it will record. For example, you might name the file "server1-9-9-99-cpu.log" and record measurements from the CPU object. After you record a log file, you can view its content via the PerfMon display by selecting the View Log Data File option from the button menu. (It's the cylinder.)

Another benefit (perhaps not so major) stems from PerfMon's ability to let you define alerts. Alerts allow administrators to instruct PerfMon to watch certain counters and to send a message when preset values are reached. Administrators use the Alert view to issue warnings when disk space is running low, or when network or CPU utilization becomes dangerously high. Think of the Alert view as a type of "system alarm" capability. Generated whenever a counter's measurement crosses its defined threshold, an Alert event can record an item in the Application log of the Event Viewer, send a network message, execute a batch file, and/or start logging performance data. You can define alerts in the Alerts area of the PerfMon main window. Just select the Alert component in the left pane, right-click in the right pane, and select New Alert Setting from the pop-up menu.

Some light summer reading

There are lots of books about performance monitoring and tuning for Windows NT 4.0, and we are sure there will be many for Windows 2000 out soon. Most of the tips for Windows NT 4.0 should apply to Windows 2000, but your mileage may vary. Here are a few books we usually recommend for Windows NT 4.0 performance monitoring. Keep an eye on these authors for Windows 2000 versions of similar titles:

- Gardinier, Kenton. *Windows NT Performance Tuning & Optimization.* Osborne/McGraw-Hill, Berkeley, CA, 1998. ISBN: 0-07-882496-6. This book includes a great overview of Windows NT architecture and performance, and terrific coverage of PerfMon.

- Hilley, Valda. *Windows NT Server 4.0 Secrets.* IDG Books Worldwide, Inc., Foster City, CA, 1996. ISBN: 1-5688-4717-3. Although it's not as in-depth as Gardinier's book, Hilley's book includes the best discussion of key PerfMon objects and counters (and how to use them for handling bottlenecks) that we've ever seen in print.

Windows 2000 Resource Kit Utilities

Many of the programmers and engineers who helped design Windows 2000 created tools and accessories that never made it into the official product release of Windows 2000. Therefore, many of these time-saving and headache-relieving tools are included in the Windows 2000 Resource Kit, along with lots of technical details and how to's that the manuals and online help files simply don't contain.

The Windows 2000 Resource Kit was on the distribution CD with the main operating system in prerelease. We don't know whether it will ship on the CD in the final form of the operating system, but even if it doesn't, you should be able to find it from an online bookstore or via TechNet (`http://technet.microsoft.com`). No matter what, you'll want to find and exploit this resource.

Whichever way you gain access to the Resource Kit, you'll find that it contains tons of troubleshooting utilities. Here, we provide a brief list of the categories, and encourage you to explore this resource further for yourself:

- ✔ **Computer Management tools:** Includes a wide range of inspection, control, and profiling utilities.

- ✔ **Deployment tools:** Includes utilities for the Windows 2000 operating system and general software deployment, including specialty tools such as a *Security Identifier* (SID) monitoring tool and a system preparation tool.

- ✔ **Diagnostic tools:** Includes utilities for monitoring or inspecting applications, hardware, the network operating system, and the network.

- ✔ **Network Management tools:** Includes utilities for directory services, interoperability, network administration, performance, remote computing, security, and storage management.

- ✔ **Registry tools:** Includes a plethora of Registry tools that can be used to perform command-line actions, such as unique queries for values; add, change, or delete values; copy subsections; and backup and restore.

- ✔ **Win32 Debugger tools:** Includes programmer-level utilities for troubleshooting and debugging custom code and software designed for the Windows 2000 platform.

To find out more about these utilities, search for the file named RKTOOLS.CHM on either the Resource Kit Utilities CD or in the installed folder (\Program Files\Resource Kit\). It includes an explanation for each of them!

Chapter 20

Nixing Network Problems

· ·

In This Chapter

▶ Knowing what happens when networks go bad

▶ Understanding the symptoms

▶ Nosing about with NetMon

▶ Double-checking network settings

▶ Finding a missing server

▶ Dealing with a slow network

▶ Fixing intermittent problems

· ·

*E*ven with the best planning and equipment, even the best network administrators' networks crash from time to time. Spotting trouble before it happens is best, but knowing how to quickly remedy trouble after it happens can be a lifesaver. Because of today's heterogeneous networking environments, so many things can go wrong. In this chapter, we discuss some of the common network problems you may encounter and we tell you how to solve them.

When Good Networks Go Bad

Believe us when we say that you'll know when something goes wrong on your network! Your pager beeps (or vibrates), your phones ring, and people stand in your doorway tapping their feet. To help you lessen the chance of network problems, you should learn the warning signs associated with network problems and add preventative measures to your network.

Because networks consist of so many resources, when the network goes down, so could the Internet connection, or e-mail, fax, or printing service. Whoops, that sounds like the business could come to a crashing halt! That's right, a broken network can cause lots of problems for an organization.

What's healthy? Creating a baseline

One way to watch and monitor your network for trouble is to create a baseline report of what your network looks like on a day when it's healthy (that is, working properly). When you think the network is functioning poorly, you can compare the snapshot of the network on a good day with a snapshot of your network on a bad day. Some administrators like to take a baseline snapshot and then take weekly snapshots so they can keep a continuous eye on the network. You should monitor the network's memory, processor, logins, and utilization, because these areas usually contain the warning signs that show up when something goes wrong.

You can monitor these functions using the Performance Monitor tool (Start⇨Programs⇨Administrative Tools⇨Performance) that comes with Windows 2000 Server. After Performance Monitor (affectionately called PerfMon) is started, you tell it what you want to look at by selecting various objects and counters. When you first open PerfMon, you'll notice that it has two functions: One is called the *System Monitor,* and the other is called the *Performance Logs and Alerts.*

In the System Monitor, you can view real-time information, or you can load information from a previous capture of data that you made. If you're in author mode, you can load snap-ins to this console. However, you may want users to view this console, but not allow them to make changes to the configuration. You can set this information as well.

In Performance Logs and Alerts, you can look at the various logs in textual format to examine each individual alert. It's not really plain-old ASCII format; it's still a graphical user interface (GUI), but the alerts are listed as line items that you can view or filter.

To add counters and objects, right-click on the Counters button at the bottom of the System Monitor and select Add Counters to call up the Add Counters dialog box. (You can also click the Add button, which is the plus sign (+) in the right pane.) By default, your computer is automatically selected as the one to be monitored. However, you can monitor any computer in your domain. Next, you need to select the Performance Object that you want to measure, such as Processor (which is selected by default), Print Queue, Paging File, and so on. When you select the Performance Object you want to measure, the Performance Counters for that object are displayed. After you select the counter, you may need to select an instance for those cases when you have more than one object on your system. For example, if you have more than one hard drive on your computer, you can choose which one you want to monitor.

Figure 20-1 shows some sample information we obtained. You can check the server, processor, and memory for issues such as the total number of logons, how many logons your system is experiencing per second, how much memory is being used, and how much of the available sever bandwidth is being used. If you don't understand a particular object or counter, you can click Explain for more information.

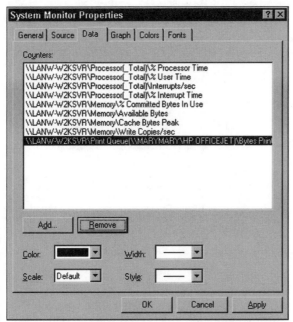

Figure 20-1:
Sample settings in PerfMon.

While you have the Add Counters dialog box open, you can add as many Performance Counters as you want. As you add each counter, it takes on a color that appears on the graph and in the legend at the bottom of the chart. Continue to click Add and choose the counters for the object until you're done, and then click Close. Figure 20-2 shows PerfMon in action after we added several counters and began monitoring. Notice the real-time (one-second intervals) lines on the graph.

You should establish a baseline when you first begin using Windows 2000. Then, set your alerts and counters to monitor performance during certain intervals of peak usage and other time frames. This allows you to analyze your network and server load after it's been used for a while. Make adjustments to your server and then look at the logs again to see if the adjustments helped. For example, if you determined that more memory was needed in the server, add memory and then go back and view the logs again to make sure that this actually improves performance. You may need to tweak some other setting besides the memory.

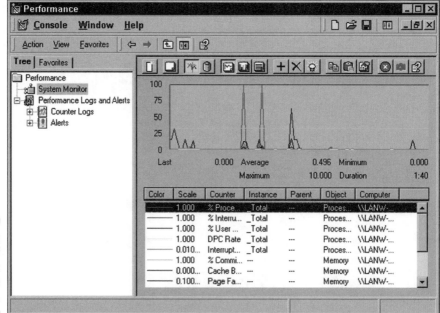

Figure 20-2:
A graph of
PerfMon
doing its
thing.

Because you want to monitor your server on a regular basis, save the configuration settings (Console➪Save As) and give it a filename such as Perfset.
msc. Then, each time you monitor the server, you can pull up your configured settings. If you save the settings to your desktop, Windows 2000 creates
an icon for you that you can double-click the next time you want to monitor
the server with these settings.

Documenting problems

We recommend that you grab a notebook and begin to document all network
problems as they occur or immediately thereafter. You should record the
symptoms, the items you changed to fix the problem, and the date and time.
Documenting what you changed can give you a leg up if, a week later, something else breaks that's related to a change you made. For example, you may
need to give User A the permission to get to a spreadsheet application, and
then a week later, you notice the master template file has been altered by that
user and everyone on your network is complaining that their spreadsheet
application has new defaults. You may have given that user too many rights.

You should include a drawing of your network (called a *network map*) in this
documentation. Seeing your network at-a-glance helps with troubleshooting
efforts because you can look at the various segments and their information.
See Chapter 5 for more information on network maps.

If you have a computer room, you should lock the door and require visitors to sign in on a visitor log notebook — even the person who comes to change the lightbulb in the ceiling, because the ladder could bump into some wires in your computer room and bring a segment of your network down.

What we've seen in organizations that have several network administrators is that while one administrator works on one problem, another lets the maintenance person into the computer room. When something on the network goes down, network administrators start looking for the problem, but didn't know there was someone in the computer room. If you keep access to all of your equipment as restricted as possible, know exactly who goes near that equipment, and log all changes, you stand a better chance of troubleshooting problems quickly.

If you have more than one network administrator and a problem occurs, gather everyone and ask these questions:

- ✔ Has anyone made any changes to the network today that don't appear on the log?
- ✔ Has anyone outside our group been inside the computer room?

Then, check your network change log to see if any changes to the network over the past week could be related to the current problem.

30,000-foot view

When your network breaks, try to step back and look at it from a distance. Ignore the panic that sets in because it won't help you keep your wits about you. Divide your network into segments so you can analyze which parts of the network are broken. Is it just one workstation, one segment, one server, one application, or one service? After you begin to isolate the problem, you can start to fix it.

If this network is connected to a *wide area network* (WAN), you have more work to do. Someone could have made changes on the WAN that affect your network. If you're connected to a WAN, be sure to use unique naming and addressing schemes. If everyone names their Windows 2000 Servers and domains the same (for example, Server1, Server2, Server 3, and so on), things stop working well. For example, you can install a Windows 2000 Server in an isolated manner (not connected to any network) and then later connect it to a WAN. If no naming scheme is in place, other servers on the WAN may have the same names and/or addresses, which can really foul up the network.

In addition to using unique naming and addressing schemes, you need to build redundant paths or links in your WAN in case links go down. If you don't, you may find that remote offices are not available until the link is restored. Links can go down because of carrier problems or faulty equipment on your end. In some cases, you may want to disconnect your WAN connection to see if the immediate problem goes away.

If you're using Active Directory Services and the directory isn't being administered properly, you may have some other LAN connected to yours via the WAN that's interfering with your network. Again, disconnect your WAN connection to see if the problem goes away.

Flowcharts can help diagnose problems because they force you to think in a logical pattern (if the flowchart is logical). Draw a flowchart of your troubleshooting technique and have it handy so when trouble arises, you can look at your flowchart for quick determination.

Open Up and Say Ahhhhh!

Just as a runny nose can tell you that you're coming down with a cold, symptoms on a network can indicate when problems are about to occur. Not only do you want to monitor your server and network for its general health, but you should also walk around the building and talk to your users. We find that a lot of users don't report problems as often as we would like. Sometimes you bump into a user who casually tells you about a problem he or she has that forces him or her to reboot three times a day. The user just accepts this instead of reporting it. We like to consider "walking the floors" as part of our general network-monitoring scheme.

The network's getting sleepy . . . very sleepy

Anytime the network begins to slow down, suspect trouble right away and start poking around at the disk space and memory on the Windows 2000 Server. Bad network interface cards (NICs) in workstations can cause a real slowdown because the network tries to work around the malfunctioning board. You can use PerfMon and Network Monitor (NetMon) to poke around and gather information about what's messing up. If you have intelligent hubs on your network that are collecting *Simple Network Management Protocol* (SNMP)-type statistics to a centralized management console, look at those logs also. Often, they graphically depict a workstation NIC that is acting up.

Yeah man, it's NetMon

NetMon is a Windows 2000 Server utility that enables you to poke around the data on the network in a fashion similar to the way a protocol analyzer works. You can set up your Windows 2000 Server computer to capture frames from the network and analyze what's going on at an error level, protocol level, and more. It's not that fancy because you can't view your entire network. You can only view the incoming frames to your Windows 2000 Server computer on which you install the agent and tools. If you want to view frames within an entire network segment, you have to go with *NetMon for Systems Management Server* (SMS), simply because it's more robust and includes more features.

Network Monitor has two parts associated with it: the administrative tool (Network Monitor) and the network protocol (Network Monitor driver). You have to install both of these before you can begin to analyze the frames. Convenience then dictates that when you install the Network Monitor, the driver is automatically installed along with it. That was nice of Microsoft.

The Windows 2000 Server installation doesn't install NetMon automatically. It's a service that you install separately and access via the Control Panel. Follow these steps to install NetMon on your server:

1. **Select Start➪Settings➪Control Panel➪Add/Remove Programs.**

   The Add/Remove Programs window appears.

2. **Click Add/Remove Windows Components in the left pane to bring up the Windows Components Wizard.**

3. **Choose Management and Monitoring Tools in the Windows Components Wizard, and then click Details.**

4. **In the Management and Monitoring Tools window, mark the Network Monitor checkbox, and click OK.**

   You may be prompted for more files to complete the installation. If you copied your Windows 2000 Server CD to the network, tell the wizard the path of the files. Otherwise, insert your Windows 2000 Server CD.

5. **Click Next.**

After you have everything running, you can start NetMon through the Administrative Tools area (Start➪Programs➪Administrative Tools➪Network Monitor). Your screen should look similar to Figure 20-3.

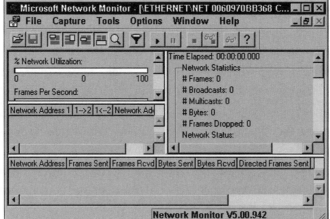

Figure 20-3:
The
Windows
2000 Server
NetMon
screen.

After you've launched NetMon, you can set up filters so you only capture certain information. For example, you may not want to monitor NetBIOS multicast information, but you may want to hone in on Internet Protocol (IP) information. You set filters to separate what's captured and what's not.

You can set triggers on events so "when this happens, take this action." For example, you may not want to capture all the data coming and going on the server. You may be looking for a certain pattern and when that pattern occurs, you want to begin the capture. This helps you further define what you're looking at in the capture trace.

Microsoft has a wealth of information about NetMon that you should become familiar with (Start⇨Help⇨Monitoring and Diagnostic Tools⇨Network Monitor). Always start with the Best Practices section first to learn what Microsoft feels is the best way to set up a particular function on your network. (You can also access the Windows 2000 Server online help at windowsupdate.microsoft. com/nt5help/Server/en/nt_frame.htm.)

Check Those Network Settings: Again!

A host of things can be configured improperly or changed that will affect network operation. The following list of questions can help you sleuth about and find things that may have changed:

✔ **Is proper addressing set (no duplicate addresses)?** Each node on the network (including servers) must have a unique address and computer name. If you can't ping (ping is an IP utility discussed in Chapter 14) or see the computer in the browser or Active Directory, check to make sure its identifiers are correct.

✔ **Are the proper IP ranges set?** If you're using an in-house IP numbering scheme and then connect to the Internet, your scheme may conflict with another registered set of numbers. Before connecting to the Internet, check with your Internet Service Provider (ISP) to make sure that you don't set up your network using someone else's IP numbers.

✔ **Are the services on server running?** Sometimes the service you need stops running on the server. Check the Start⇨Programs⇨Administrative Tools⇨Computer Management⇨Services and Applications⇨Services to make sure that the service is installed and running. Sometimes you need to start and stop a service.

✔ **Are any errors logged in Event Viewer?** Look in the Event Viewer to see if any errors have been logged (Start⇨Programs⇨Administrative Tools⇨Viewer).

✔ **Are there any conflicting devices?** Use the Windows 2000 Conflicts/ Sharing Manager to see if any devices are conflicting with interrupt requests (IRQs) or memory. (Choose Start⇨Programs⇨Administrative Tools⇨Computer Management and expand the folders to System Tools⇨ System Information⇨HardwareResources⇨Conflicts/Sharing.) You can also look in the Device Manager in that same area for more information.

✔ **Are the proper domains available?** Be sure that the proper domain controller for the server is up and running and Active Directory is available.

✔ **Are access rights assigned correctly?** Be sure users have the proper rights to the groups and resources they need to access.

✔ **Are the proper shares set?** Make sure that the resource in question is shared on the server and listed in Active Directory for all or some to see. Sometimes devices don't appear because they haven't been told to.

What Do You Mean the Server's Unavailable?

When users can't find the server from their workstations, they get antsy. Check to see if only one user has the problem, or several. If just one user can't find the server, the problem is probably at his or her workstation. If several users can't find the server, you probably have a segment problem, such as a downed bridge or router. (For more information on bridges and routers, see Chapter 4.)

If one user has the problem, ask the following questions:

✔ **Is the user logged in?** Don't laugh, but sometimes users call you about not getting services on a network and they haven't logged in yet.

✔ **Has the user ever accessed the network before?** If this is a new user logging in for the first time, the account may not be set up yet. However, if the user recently transferred from another department, you may need to reassign the user to another group or alter his or her account policies.

✔ **Has the user tried to reboot the workstation?** Sometimes, if the user reboots his or her workstation, the one-time glitch disappears.

✔ **Does the user have the proper rights?** Check the user's account policies and permissions to make sure he or she has the proper access rights on the network or directory to access the needed resource.

✔ **Has anyone made changes to the workstation?** If any new devices were added to this workstation, the new device may have a conflicting IRQ or memory address problem. Look at the root directory on the workstation and sort the files by date and time to see when the latest changes were made. Then, check the Windows directory and search for *.ini files to see whether changes have been made to any of those files. If a new NIC was added, check to see whether it was set to the proper speed of the network.

✔ **Can you ping the user's workstation?** If the Transmission Control Protocol/Internet Protocol (TCP/IP) is installed on the workstation, try pinging the workstation from your desktop, try pinging the server from the user's workstation, and try to find the server in the browser or directory listing. For more information on how to ping, see Chapter 14. If you can ping the server but can't see the server in the browser, you can force a browser election on the network to reset the master browser.

✔ **Does the user have a bad satin cable?** Satin cable is the silver-colored cable sometimes used for the network connection between the user's NIC and the wall plate. Sometimes housekeeping vacuums over the cables on a network and damages them. You can easily change out a cable to see whether it's bad. If the cable isn't the problem, try the NIC. (Of course, if this is a wireless workstation, the cable won't be the culprit!)

✔ **Does the user have a bad NIC?** NICs go bad sometimes. Replace the card with a card that you know works to see whether that solves the problem.

You may also want to check the following:

✔ **Login time restrictions:** If the user can log in to the network at specific times only, check the user's configuration to make sure no restrictions apply.

✔ **Remote Access Service (RAS):** If the unavailable server is a RAS server, you must grant users a dial-in privilege in their accounts to connect to it.

✔ **Dynamic Host Configuration Protocol (DHCP):** If the unavailable server is a DHCP server, make sure that the DHCP service is installed and running. (Open Start➪Programs➪Administrative Tools➪Computer Management and then expand Services and Applications.) If users who depend on DHCP services can't see the DHCP server, they can't obtain an IP address.

Slow Networking Services

When services on a network start to slow down, trouble is surely just around the corner. When this happens, it's possible that disk space on the server is running low, memory needs to be reconfigured, or a token ring board has gone bad and broken the ring. Hopefully, the NICs in the server are capable of handling a lot of traffic. If not, think about upgrading to higher performance NICs. Don't use old 8-bit NICs for your server; use 32-bit NICs at the very minimum.

Hark! I hear a board beaconing

Token ring is a funny creature because it forms a ring, and the data travels around the ring in a circular fashion. When a break in the ring occurs, data travels in a "U" shape instead. People located at the bottom of the "U" don't notice the slowdown as much, but those located at the tops see a tremendous slowdown. A token ring break typically happens when wiring gets out of whack or when one NIC starts beaconing. (This means the NIC is sending a signal that something is wrong with it.) If you use hubs that aren't intelligent, or Multistation Access Units (MAUs), you have to isolate the bad token ring board or port on the MAU by process of elimination. We've had to take an entire ring and unplug one MAU at a time, then unplug one port at a time. The older MAUs are actually relays, and you have to use a MAU tool to reset the relay. Other times, you need to replace the faulty NIC.

Oh where, oh where has the bandwidth gone?

You should check to see whether an application is running on the network that's consuming a lot of bandwidth. Applications consuming a lot of bandwidth occur frequently in 10 Mbps (10MB per second) Ethernet environments in which you have a lot of network activity and database applications. Some database applications aren't designed well, and therefore, when a user makes a database query, the entire contents of the database are downloaded to the user's workstation for processing. This creates a lot of extraneous traffic. To help alleviate this problem, you can upgrade to database software that has a database engine to do the record crunching; therefore, the user gets only the results. Another solution to this problem is to upgrade to a faster network-wiring scheme, such as 100 Mbps Ethernet.

High-volume printing can also cause this problem. If certain users or groups of users are printing volumes of data during the day, think about switching them to print at night (if possible) to alleviate the network congestion. You can set up a print definition for those users that only allows their information to be printed during certain hours.

Some organizations elect to upgrade their existing network backbone to help relieve bandwidth congestion problems, but this has a high cost associated with it. Organizations that have remote offices sometimes place an extra Windows 2000 Server in the remote office and install it as a domain controller. This allows user authentication to be performed locally at the remote office, which conserves WAN bandwidths. Other organizations elect to upgrade their current network backbone to 100 Mbps while leaving the users connected to the hubs at 10 Mbps. This involves upgrading the devices connected to the backbone to include 100 Mbps NICs and cables, plus adding a switch capable of changing between the workstation speed of 10 Mbps to the backbone speed of 100 Mbps. With this arrangement, even if users are going full throttle, the server still has 90 percent bandwidth available for other clients.

Congestion on the network: Pass the Kleenex please

If you have an Ethernet network that's experiencing lots of collisions and errors, there could be a problem with the Carrier Sense Multiple Access/Collision Detection (CSMA/CD) media access method. If you have intelligent hubs on the network, you can view information about the network either through a graphical interface or by looking at the LEDs on the hubs. A high collision rate is usually an indication of faulty wiring or bad boards. It can also mean that the bandwidth utilization is high. Ethernet has a lower utilization than token ring. Sometimes you need to segment off high-volume users.

Where did all the disk space go?

This problem should be obvious, but it never is! If your server's disk space is low, you're in for a fair amount of trouble, because servers can contain print queues, as well as user's data and applications. When disk space begins to run low, all sorts of strange problems appear. You should buy a lot of RAM up front, because Windows 2000 uses much more than its predecessor Windows NT does. You must have at least the minimum RAM required by Microsoft. Even then, you'll run into problems trying to do more than one task, so add lots more on top of the minimum.

Windows 2000 uses disk space to swap recently used information back and forth from RAM. Therefore, if you have more RAM, you'll be able to access files faster. You can look at your memory information and how it's being used by checking Start⇨Programs⇨Administrative Tools⇨Computer Management and expanding System Tools⇨System Information⇨System Summary.

Low disk space causes Windows 2000 to encounter difficulties when trying to write to the `Pagefile.sys` file. To view and change the minimum and maximum size of this file, go into Control Panel⇨System, and click the Advanced tab. Select Performance Options, and then click the Change button. You see a screen similar to the one shown in Figure 20-4.

You should have at least the same minimum and maximum numbers that Windows 2000 recommends or you may encounter problems. You can also move the `Pagefile.sys` to a location other than the Windows 2000 boot partition. This provides the boot partition with more disk space.

Also, note the size of the Registry, which is shown at the bottom of the screen in Figure 20-4. Keep an eye on this number so when your Registry begins to grow, you can allocate more memory space for it. Remember that the Registry contains settings for applications, hardware, and more. As you add items to the server, the Registry grows.

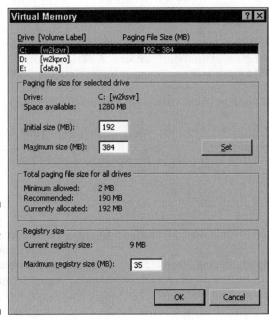

Figure 20-4:
The memory paging file information in Windows 2000 Server.

Do it after hours

Is someone performing a network task that's transferring a large amount of data, such as restoring a lot of files? Or is someone performing a function such as remirroring drives? If a network has large storage drives that are mirrored, and the mirroring breaks, you can remirror the drives, but doing it during working hours isn't a good idea. Check to see whether anyone is performing some sort of maintenance — either on the network or the server. If a large restoration of files is required across the network, try to do it during nonpeak hours — if possible.

If you check in PerfMon and see a heavy resource load, you can get a better handle on who's placing that load by going to Start⇨Programs⇨Administrative Tools⇨Computer Management, expanding System Tools⇨Shared Folders, and checking the resource usage per share, per person.

Can't Get "There" from "Here"

When a segment of your network is down, getting "there" is impossible. Several factors can cause this, depending on how you configure your network. Try to ping different nodes of the network to pinpoint what's down. For example, if you can ping one interface of a router, but not the other interface, chances are the problem is inside the router. You can also perform a TRACERT (as discussed in Chapter 14) on TCP/IP to determine the time intervals between the current and final destinations. A slow response between two destinations could point you to the exact location of the problem. Try using ping and TRACERT from different locations on your network to further define what can be seen and from where.

Use more than one utility to determine where your network failure may be. For example, ping works with the TCP/IP protocol only: Try using another utility, such as NBTSTAT, which works with NetBIOS and TCP/IP.

Also, the following problems could prevent you from accessing portions of the network:

- ✓ **Router problem:** Routers connect different networks. If you've defined it improperly, you can't see what's on the other side. Routers can also experience congestion and drop packets. Sometimes more memory in the router is required in these cases. Routers also require chip upgrades for older routers, but for newer routers, upgrades can be written to the current chips. Check which software version your router is using and contact the manufacturer.

✔ **Bridge problem:** If your network contains bridges, sometimes you need to reboot the bridge. Depending on the software and hardware used, this may occur frequently. Remember that bridges need high-end NICs because they pass a lot of packets between them. (See Chapter 4 for more information on bridges.)

✔ **WAN link problem:** If a T1 or 56 KB line goes down, you don't see anything on the other side. Sometimes, you may have to call a telecom company to resolve this problem. You need to have circuit information and the customer support number handy.

✔ **Hub problem:** If you lose an entire segment of the network, check the hub that connects that segment. Hubs usually have power supplies and ports that can go bad. Sometimes, just plugging a node into a different port on the hub fixes a problem. Make sure you mark the port as bad so someone else doesn't plug a device into that port. Putting a circle around the port is often a good way to denote a bad port.

✔ **Wiring problem:** Wiring can degrade over time or can be moved around enough that the wires can go bad. Use a *Time Domain Reflectometer* (TDR) tool to check the cable for breaks. You may have to pull a new cable to the desktop or server. If you suspect that housekeeping has vacuumed over one of your satin cables and damaged it, replace that cable!

✔ **Server problem:** Check that the server in question is up and running. This seems obvious, but check it anyway.

✔ **Name resolution problem:** You may need to install Windows Internet Naming Service (WINS), DHCP, or a host file, depending on the protocols used on your network. (See Chapter 14 on TCP/IP for more information.)

Tracking Down Intermittent Problems

Intermittent problems are by far the most difficult to solve because they don't happen when you want them to. Because you can't always reproduce intermittent problems, you often have a difficult time figuring them out. These types of problems occur after a sequence of events, usually in a particular order unbeknownst to you. Your work is to figure out the sequence of events. Impossible you say — not really!

If you started your system log, record the following items to help you eliminate possible causes of the problem:

✔ **Note the time and day of the problem:** For example, does the problem only seem to occur at 10 a.m. on Wednesdays? Perhaps a particular activity in one of the departments happens every week, such as right before a departmental meeting when everyone is trying to access or print reports. This extra activity could place a load on the server or network depending on the nature of the activity. Look for trends in dates and time. Use PerfMon if you suspect this.

✔ **Note the equipment in use:** Does the problem occur only on a particular workstation or server? Does the problem occur only when a particular user logs in to the network? Check the user's account information, plus his or her desktop configuration files.

✔ **Note the application in use:** Does the problem occur only when a certain application is used? Reinstall the application. An application file can become corrupt, and the corruption can go unnoticed until a user performs a particular function of that application.

✔ **Note the environment in use:** Does the problem occur only on a certain floor, near a certain area like an elevator? If so, you may get some wiring conflicts near heavy motors or fluorescent lighting.

✔ **Check the visitor's log:** Does the problem occur every time the maintenance person enters a wiring closet or the computer room? If so, follow this person in the next time and see what he or she is doing. (Don't forget the overcoat and sunglasses!)

✔ **Viruses:** Always an obvious possibility, viruses are often the last things checked. Viruses introduce random oddities onto networks. If you suspect one, immediately disconnect the server from the rest of the network and WAN, and scan it. Until recently, this would have been enough. However, it's important to instruct your users not to send any e-mail if you suspect a virus. You may have to disable the company post office to ensure no e-mail is distributed at this time.

✔ **Known bugs:** Sometimes, you pound your head into the wall trying to solve a problem that is really a known bug. Check the Microsoft Web site regularly and check for new service packs. Remember to check other organizations' Web sites as well. For example, if you use Microsoft Office, check Microsoft's site for service packs for that suite. If you use all 3Com Ethernet cards, check the 3Com Web site for driver updates that fix bugs. Staying on top of known problems can save you oodles of time.

Chapter 21

Reactivating Active Directory

Active Directory is a vital part of Windows 2000 Server. As described in Chapters 11 and 12, Active Directory contains and controls all the important objects in a network. Which important objects might those be? Well, they include user accounts, shared resources, computer membership, group policy controls, and more. In other words, Active Directory contains the items that enable and support a Windows 2000 domain.

When Microsoft designed Active Directory, it rightly perceived that any problems with this core service would cause network-wide problems. Therefore, it built powerful fault tolerance into the Active Directory service and provided several mechanisms that help Windows 2000 perform and maintain its regular functions. In this chapter we look into these recovery and restoration features of Windows 2000 Active Directory.

A fault tolerant system is one that can keep running during a software or hardware error. In addition, fault tolerance should prevent the loss of data.

Domain Controller, Heal Thyself

Active Directory is dynamically self-healing, or at least self-maintaining. It regularly checks itself for internal consistency, missing data, and expired entries. By default, a housecleaning operation is automatically performed every 12 hours. This housecleaning consists of deleting logs, removing expired entries, and defragmenting the database file. The logs deleted by the housecleaning operation are change or transaction logs that temporarily store operations. After the system verifies that all actions listed in these logs have been performed successfully, the logs are deleted because they are no longer needed.

When you use a computer, the data on the hard disk naturally becomes fragmented (or split), which results in slower access of data. The process of reorganizing this data back into the proper order to maximize performance is called defragmentation.

As Active Directory changes and adapts to the network environment, relationship and other object-related data becomes outdated or expires. This data, along with deleted items that still remain in the database, is removed. Defragmenting the database file compacts the data and reorganizes the file to maximize performance.

When defragmentation is performed by the system, it's called Online Defragmentation. Online Defragmentation creates space within the existing database file for new Active Directory entries, but it does not release the space back to the file system for use by other files. Only Offline Defragmentation releases unused database space back to the file system. Microsoft recommends that Offline Defragmentation be performed only when absolutely necessary (such as when not enough drive space is available to perform normal system operations). To initiate an Offline Defragmentation, you must reboot and press the F8 key to access the boot menu. Then select the Directory Services Repair Mode, which performs the Offline Defragmentation and boots the system into Safe Mode. You'll have to reboot again to return to a fully operational network-supporting boot.

When All Is Not Quiet on the Western Front

Things go wrong. Sometimes, administrators' mistakes cause problems, a failed network connection prevents resource access, or a stray neutrino corrupts a data point in the database file. In any case, things need to be fixed to restore the normal productive activity of Active Directory.

The Help system of Windows 2000 includes an Active Directory troubleshooter. This little tool asks you questions and offers specific advice based on your responses. We've found this tool to be immensely helpful in nearly every Active Directory-related problem we've encountered. To access the troubleshooter, follow these steps:

1. **Open the Help system (Start⇨Help).**

   The Windows 2000 Help window appears.

2. **Select the Index tab of the Help window to bring the Index forward.**

3. **Scroll down the list to locate the Active Directory topic and the troubleshooter subtopic.**

4. **Double-click on troubleshooter.**

   The troubleshooter information appears in the right pane of the help window.

5. **In the right pane, click on the Group Policy and Active Directory link.**

This takes you to the Directory Services Troubleshooter. From here, just answer the questions and follow the instructions given. You'll probably find that your system is restored quickly with a simple fix.

Common Issues

The Directory Services troubleshooter walks you through problem resolution one step at a time. In most cases, the troubleshooter leads you down the most direct path to the Promised Land of problem resolution. If you're an independent spirit, however, you may want to try to troubleshoot problems without any aid from the Help system. Luckily for you, the most common problems, which result from a failed or misbehaved Active Directory, are relatively easy to diagnose.

Communication interruption

The most common Active Directory problem is a communication interruption. Simply put, a communication interruption is anything that prevents clear and complete packet transactions between two hosts. These interruptions can result from something as simple as a broken network cable or an offline computer. More complex problems, such as a router with a corrupt routing table or a DNS server with wrongly defined entries, can also cause interruptions. When the problem is physical, you may need to replace the cables or reboot the system to restore functionality. When the problem is more complex, you need to investigate troubleshooting options specific to the ailing service.

If you suspect that a communication interruption is occurring, you can use common networking tools to help you obtain more specific information. For example, if your network uses the *Transmission Control Protocol/Internet Protocol* (TCP/IP), you can use tools designed for troubleshooting this protocol. The two most useful tools for this protocol are PING and TRACERT. (See Chapter 14 for more information on PING and TRACERT.) PING informs you whether packets can traverse the network between your system and any other host. TRACERT informs you of each router jump between you and another host, and specifically, if transmission is not possible past a specific route point.

If the results of both PING and TRACERT show that packets may not even be leaving your computer, use IPCONFIG /ALL to verify that the TCP/IP protocol is properly installed and that its settings (IP address, subnet mask, default gateway, etc.) are correct. If any settings are incorrect, change them via the Network and Dial-up Connections interface (Start⇨Settings⇨Network and Dial-up Connections) and reboot.

Group Policy problems

Another common problem arises from Group Policies that either restrict access too much or contradict or overlap each other, which causes inconsistencies in the way the system functions. You'll need to examine the Group Policies for each domain, user, group, and organizational unit to determine where the problem lies.

Domain controller communication

If Windows NT 4.0 and Windows 2000 domain controllers are unable to communicate, you've probably enabled Native Mode on a Windows 2000 Server system. The Active Directory of Windows 2000 can operate in two modes: Mixed and Native. *Mixed Mode* is the default mode that allows both Windows 2000 and Windows NT 4.0 Servers to act as domain controllers interactively. *Native Mode* prevents Windows NT 4.0 Servers from participating in domain controlling.

The *big* problem with the mode setting is that after it's set to Native Mode, it cannot be reversed without a complete system reinstallation. Therefore, don't switch your network over to Native Mode until you're *absolutely* sure that Windows NT 4.0 Servers are not required. The mode setting is made via the Active Directory Domains and Trusts tool (Start⇨Programs⇨ Administrative Tools⇨Active Directory Domains and Trusts). Select the domain you want to switch over, right-click and select Properties. Then, on the General tab, click the Change Mode button. You'll be prompted to verify the mode change.

If the combination of automated housecleaning, the instructions found via the Directory Services Troubleshooter, and your own troubleshooting efforts fail to resolve your Active Directory problem, there's only one solution left — restoration from backup.

Backing Up and Restoring Directory Data

Restoring Active Directory from a backup requires one important item: a timely backup of the system. Without a recent backup of the system when it was functioning normally, you can't restore Active Directory — just as you can't build a brick wall if you don't have any bricks. The only way this solution can be employed is to proactively prepare for it.

Preparing to restore Active Directory from a backup requires that you have a complete backup of your entire system. That means using the Backup tool (see Chapter 17) to create a backup using the Backup Wizard and selecting Back Up Everything on My Computer.

When you have a backup, restoring the system is not all that difficult. Just follow these steps:

1. **Reinstall Windows 2000 Server. Be sure to install the system using the same partition and root directory names as before.**

2. **Use the Backup tool to restore all data from the backup set back to its original locations.**

3. **After restoration is complete, reboot the system. Windows 2000 will automatically realize that it's been restored from backup and will rebuild the Active Directory database.**

That's it. As you can see, your only real tool for repairing a severely damaged system is a recent and complete backup. As we stress in Chapter 17, you need to implement a regular, regimented backup procedure to protect your data (and your job).

If you would like more information on dealing with Active Directory problems, please consult the Windows 2000 Directory Services Troubleshooter (as described earlier in this chapter), the Windows 2000 Resource Kit, and TechNet (http://technet.microsoft.com/).

Part VI
The Part of Tens

In this part . . .

When Moses came down from the mountain, how many commandments did he carry? Ten. How many fingers do most people have? Ten. On a scale of 1 to 10, what's a perfect score? Ten. We're not entirely sure that all these things are necessarily connected, but that number shows up everywhere, even on the *Late Show with David Letterman*. Perhaps that's why The Part of Tens is a key ingredient in this and all other *For Dummies* books. Then again, it could just be a coincidence . . .

Each chapter in this part includes a list of tips, tricks, techniques, reminders, and resources for inspired information about your Windows 2000 Server system and its network. We'd like to claim the same source of inspiration that Moses had for his commandments, but our Part of Tens comes only from the "School of Hard Knocks" next door.

These chapters have been constructed to save you time, steer you around common networking potholes, and get you safely past common sources of chaos and confusion. The best part of tens, however, is one that doesn't appear directly in this part of the book — that's the part where you hold your breath and *count to ten* as you begin to lose your cool. If you try that part first, the other parts of ten will probably do you a lot more good!

Chapter 22

Ten Top Tips for Windows 2000 Server Installation and Configuration

· ·

In This Chapter

▶ Beating the minimum Windows 2000 Server requirements

▶ Checking your hardware beforehand avoids aggravation afterward

▶ Installing Windows 2000 — the network way

▶ Automating installation

▶ Healing installation woes

▶ Using VGA mode when video drivers get weird

▶ Returning to the Last Known Good Configuration

▶ Building (and using) Startup floppies

▶ Undertaking emergency repairs

▶ Planning a successful server installation

· ·

1 f you spend enough time working with Windows 2000 Server, you undoubt-edly will be required to install this software on multiple systems. This job can be more "interesting" than it has to be — not to mention that it can take more time than you may want it to.

This chapter provides you with some fact-filled sources of information, some tried-and-true guidelines, and some great repair tools and techniques to help you successfully survive the Windows 2000 Server installation process. Knowing these ten tips and not needing them is better than not knowing and needing them anyway.

Minimum Requirements and Recommendations

Table 22-1 offers a quick rundown of the minimum requirements to run Windows 2000 Server (and bonus realistic recommendations).

Table 22-1	Windows NT Server Minimum Requirements (Plus Realistic Recommendations)	
Item	*Minimum Requirement*	*Recommended*
CD-ROM	None	CD-ROM or DVD player
CPU	Pentium 166	Pentium II 300 MHz or better
Disk space	685MB free	At least 1GB free
Display	VGA	VGA or better
Floppy drive	3.5 inch (optional)	3.5 inch
NIC	At least one	PCI bus mastering NIC
Pointing device	MS-Mouse or compatible (optional)	MS-Mouse or compatible
RAM	128MB or more	256MB or more

To configure a production server to simply meet the minimum requirements is a recipe for disaster. The performance (or lack thereof) you'd be able to squeeze out from such a machine would have a mob of users at your heels in no time at all.

When building a Windows 2000 Server computer, more of just about every-thing is better: This applies to more powerful (and more) CPUs, more RAM, and more powerful network interface cards (NICs). Servers do their things in quiet obscurity in most cases, so you don't have to install a 16MB graphics adapter, a fancy monitor, or a top-dollar mouse or touchpad. You can opt to skip the CD-ROM or DVD player on the Windows 2000 Server computer as long as you can access the server across the network from another machine where the contents of the CD-ROM have been copied to a hard drive.

If you install Windows 2000 Server on a machine that doesn't include a NIC, you won't be able to install or configure any of its network-related aspects. We're convinced that there's no point to installing a server that's not attached to a network, so don't install Windows 2000 Server on a machine unless it has a NIC inside (even better, a NIC connected to a real, live network).

Qualifying Server Hardware

Before you even think about installing Windows 2000 Server on a machine, you'd best be sure that the hardware you're considering will make a good home for that software. Nevertheless, without a formal seal of approval or a guarantee from a vendor, how can you be sure that the software will work with your hardware?

Fortunately, you *can* be sure by checking the Windows 2000 Hardware Compatibility List (HCL). This is a comprehensive list of hardware that's been tested and certified to be compatible with Windows 2000. The HCL is available in several forms from Microsoft:

- ✔ **The CD-ROM method:** For previous releases, Microsoft included a copy of the HCL on the Windows CDs; to find out if it's on your Windows 2000 CDs, use the Search button in the Windows Explorer, and enter **HCL.*** in the "Search for files or folders named:" input area in the Search window. Also, on the monthly TechNet CD distribution, if you search the Windows 2000 documentation using the string "Hardware Compatibility List," you should be able to find the many hardware components (audio, CPU, display adapter, input/keyboard, and so forth) that make up this collection. These components have been tested to certify that they work with Windows 2000.

- ✔ **The online search method:** You can find HCL online at `www.microsoft.com/hwtest/hcl/default.asp`. This HCL is in a form that you can search interactively by component category or by the name of a component's manufacturer.

Of the two methods, the online search method is easier, but more time consuming (depending on the speed of your Internet connection). Either way, using the HCL is the only way to be absolutely sure that what you have will work with Windows 2000 Server.

Many hardware vendors offer server machines with Windows 2000 Server preinstalled. If Windows 2000 Server is the network operating system of your choice, when you're buying new servers, price one that includes the operating system versus one that doesn't. You may be pleasantly surprised by the price breaks you can get when buying a preinstalled system.

Installing from Your Network

The following may seem counterintuitive, but here goes: Copying files from a hard drive elsewhere on a network is faster than copying files from a local CD-ROM player (even a 36x or 40x player). Why? Because hard disks are still as much as 100 times faster than CD-ROM drives.

Savvy network administrators create a set of directories on a network drive and install Windows 2000 (Server, Workstation, and so forth) across the network when they can. This tactic is fast, easy, and requires only that you load a CD once, no matter how many times you install from it. In fact, network installation is what makes the next topic feasible — namely, automated installations.

Let the Software Do the Work: Automating Installation

Normally, user input drives the Windows 2000 installation program: from character-based prompts during the initial load phase, and by user navigation of menus and input items during the later phases. As an alternative, text files called "answer files" may drive Windows 2000 installation instead, making it possible to automate installation more or less completely. Script-driven installation can be especially handy when you must install more than two or three copies of Windows 2000 at any given time.

In fact, Windows 2000 supports more methods for automating installation than previous implementations (such as Windows NT 4.0), including:

- A new [GuiRunOnce] section in the answer file that contains a list of commands to execute when a user logs onto the system the first time after the Graphical User Interface (GUI) mode portion of the installation completes.

- You can create a set of automated commands to complete the Setup process without requiring human intervention (at least, as long as no errors are encountered).

- You can even automate the first logon after Windows 2000's setup completes to install and configure selected applications, then shut down the system thereafter — all from the magic answer files!

How do you get a piece of this magic? Well, you can search for and edit a predefined answer file, called unattend.txt, in the Windows 2000 Resource Kit. Or you can work with a utility called the Setup Manager, which you must install on your system after Window 2000 Server's base installation completes, to create an answer file for you from scratch.

Windows 2000's Setup Manager is quite similar to the Windows 98 utility of the same name. If you're not familiar with this outstanding tool, it provides buttons that map to various sections of the install process and guides you through interactive dialogs to specify a script for a single system installation, or one that will work for multiple systems at the same time.

Windows 2000 also includes two utilities that are somewhat "Ghost"-like in their capabilities. (*Ghost* is a popular system imaging utility for Windows NT 4.0 that allows administrators to set up a single installation, take a snapshot, and then customize that same snapshot to install one, two, or many machines at the same time.) The two utilities are:

✔ **Sysprep:** A utility designed to duplicate disk contents when installing multiple, identically configured machines at the same time. First, you create a normal installation on a single machine, and then install the applications you wish to distribute. Next, you use Sysprep to distribute copies of this configuration to other identical systems elsewhere on the network. It doesn't get much easier than this!

✔ **Syspart:** A utility designed to clone installations across multiple machines where the hardware is dissimilar. It works as an extension of the unattended install facility with a default `unattend.txt` answer file.

Consult the *Windows 2000 Server Resource Kit* (Microsoft Press) or the TechNet CD to find out all you can about the various installation files before starting any big jobs. You'd also be well advised to try a couple of trial runs using these tools before attempting to automate the installation of one or more production servers.

When Installation Gets Weird

Despite your best efforts, and even if you've taken all the proper precautions, the occasional Windows 2000 installation will fail. We've seen causes of failure that range from defective media, to network congestion (trying to copy files onto too many machines at once), to boot sector viruses. (We hate when that happens!)

When an installation fails, take a deep breath, and try any or all of the following potential fixes:

✔ **Restart the installation:** If you get past the initial parts of the character mode portion of the installation, the software is often smart enough to pick up where it left off and carry on from there. If you're that lucky, count your blessings, then go out and buy a lottery ticket!

✔ **If installation won't pick up where it left off, look for a directory named WIN_NT.~LS:** (If you're doing a floppyless install with the /B parameter, also look for WIN_NT.~BT.) Delete one (or both) of these directories and their contents. The Windows 2000 installation program looks for these directories and attempts to save time by picking up where it left off. This behavior works fine when copies are correct and pristine, but can get in the way when problems surface. We include the DOS DELTREE command in our emergency install disk tool kit, because it lets us dispatch these directories and their contents quickly and easily.

> ✔ **If all else fails, repartition and reformat the boot drive to remove all prior vestiges of your failed attempt:** You'll start over with a clean slate! Our emergency install disk tool kit also includes DOS Fdisk and a handy utility called Delpart.exe, which can remove even non-DOS partitions (like NTFS) from a PC hard drive. Delpart.exe is available for free download from several web sites. Search your favorite search engine for **Delpart.exe**.

If the final technique doesn't work, recheck the Windows 2000 HCL for potential sources of difficulty (see the "Qualifying Server Hardware" section earlier in this chapter for the details on the HCL). Otherwise, look for guidance on your problems on Microsoft's TechNet CD or the Windows 2000-related newsgroups on the msnews.microsoft.com news server.

[VGA Mode] to the Rescue!

You'll find out that Windows 2000 doesn't care a bit if the display on your Windows 2000 Server or Professional machine is working or not. Windows 2000 continues to chug along quite happily — even if you can't see what the system is doing because the screen is totally "confuzled" or if nothing is showing at all. The leading cause of display problems is loading a display driver that doesn't work with either your graphics adapter or your monitor, or perhaps both of them!

When this problem happens (and it's a common post-installation problem), don't panic. Simply reboot the machine. When the boot menu shows up, press F8 to access the Advanced Options, then select Enable VGA Mode.

Doing so boots Windows 2000 with a plain-vanilla VGA driver. Then, you can try a different driver (or troubleshoot the hardware). This time, use the test button to make sure the driver works before you change your display!

When "Last Known Good" Does Good!

After installation is complete, you must continue to configure your Windows 2000 Server to install additional software, add all types of information about system and user policies, account and group names, and so forth. Every time you make a change to Windows 2000, those changes are recorded in the Windows 2000 Registry. Sometimes, those changes can have unforeseen side effects — especially if you've been editing the Registry directly — and can make your machine falter, or even fail to boot.

When your machine does falter or fails to boot, always try reverting to the last working version of the Registry. When the boot menu shows up, press F8 to access the Advanced Options, then select Last Known Good Configuration.

You roll back to the version of the Registry that was in use the last time your machine booted successfully. The good news is that your machine will probably boot; the bad news is that you will lose all the changes you've made since the last time you rebooted the machine. Bummer!

When you make lots of changes, either back up the Registry frequently or reboot frequently. This keeps the amount of work you can lose — from an ill-advised Registry change, a bad driver selection, and so on — to a minimum.

Using the Windows 2000 Startup Disks

When the Windows 2000 Server machine won't boot, use your Startup disks to boot that machine. These disks often give you access to the hard drive where the operating system and boot files live, so you can attempt repairs before worrying about restoring a backup or rebuilding the machine.

You do have a set of Windows 2000 Startup disks, don't you? If not, build yourself a set by running the Makeboot or Makebt32 utility from the Bootdisk directory on the Windows 2000 Server CD right now.

When in Doubt, Back Up!

Windows 2000 does not offer the same collection of repair tools that Windows NT did — not yet. Perhaps it's a matter of software maturity, or a plan to provide some whizbang functionality later down the road.

In the meantime, make sure you back up your Windows 2000 Server before you make *any* significant changes to that machine. Significant changes include adding beaucoups of new users or groups, making Active Directory changes, adding services or applications, or anything else that makes major changes to the Registry. This way, if the server goes down after the changes are applied, you can always restore the backup after booting from your startup disks and reactivating the backup software to get back to where you started. Don't leave home without it!

A generic boot floppy saves systems!

The problem with the Startup disks is that it takes four of them to boot Windows 2000. Using these disks also takes you through a time-consuming set of steps to get a machine running. Even worse, each set of boot floppies is specific to the machine on which it was created. This can be frustrating, and led creative minds to develop a generic Windows 2000 boot floppy. It works on any system and kick-starts just about any balky Windows 2000 machine. Here's how to build one:

1. Format a floppy using the Windows Explorer (right-click on the floppy drive icon in the left-hand panel and select Format from the pop-up menu).

   You MUST format this floppy inside Windows 2000. A DOS-formatted floppy won't work as a generic Windows 2000 boot floppy!

2. Check your Windows Explorer settings to make sure you can see hidden files by selecting Tools➪Folder Options, selecting the View tab, and then clicking the Show Hidden Files and Folders radio button in the Advanced Setting section of the View tab.

3. Copy the following files from your server's root directory to the Windows 2000-formatted floppy disk:

   - NTDLR
   - NTDETECT.COM
   - BOOT.INI
   - NTBOOTDD.SYS (only if it appears)

This creates a boot floppy that can bring up a Windows 2000 System without using all four startup disks. Make this part of your standard Windows 2000 toolkit.

If this generic boot floppy won't boot the system, try the Startup floppies and attempt a full-fledged system repair!

Now for the Real Work!

Although installing Windows 2000 Server by itself is no mean feat, the real work begins when that job is over: You must translate your plans for domain and directory structures, machine names, usernames, group names, and disk structures from concept into reality. This is the real work that makes Windows 2000 Server usable to your audience and able to deal with the demands they will put on your system. Remember to back up your system on a regular basis!

Chapter 23

Ten Steps to Networking Nirvana with Windows 2000 Server

*W*indows 2000 Server without a network is like a bicycle without wheels or chips without salsa (our apologies in advance to the unicyclist and fat-free members of our audience).

Because Windows 2000 Server and networking go together like gangbusters, your gang (of users) may try to bust you when the network stops working. Try as you may to avoid it, but it does happen from time to time. When the network goes on vacation, but you're still in the office, read over these tips and tricks to get things shipshape once again.

Never Overlook the Obvious

The number one cause for failed networks is — you guessed it — loose connections. Always check a server's *network interface cards* (NICs) to make sure that the cables are still plugged in or otherwise attached. Also, be sure to check all hubs, the routers, the Integrated Services Digital Network (ISDN) box, the modem, and anywhere else the cables go (like the client machines).

Networking experts often talk about a troubleshooting pyramid that follows the progression of network capabilities up from the hardware and cables, through the protocol stack, to the applications that request network services. In this analogy, the base of the pyramid is far bigger than the top. This pyramid illustrates that problems are most likely to occur at the physical level of networking. Why? Because that's where the cables and connections are. Go ahead — check them again.

When Windows 2000 Must Route Packets

Windows 2000 happily enables you to insert two or more NICs or other devices that can carry network traffic — such as modems, ISDN boxes, or even *Channel Service Unit/Data Service Units* (CSU/DSUs) for high-speed digital networking. Doubling up on NICs (or the other network traffic devices listed) allows Windows 2000 to move traffic from one connection to another. This capability, known as *routing,* enables Windows 2000 to tie separate pieces of a network together.

The most exposed and important part of many networks is the link that ties a local network to the Internet (or at least, to your local Internet Service Provider, or ISP). If Windows 2000 fills that role on your network, be prepared to perform regular troubleshooting rituals to keep this all-important link to the outside world running.

If you can, you should isolate this function on a separate computer. This is a good idea for two reasons: First, adding the burden of routing traffic and managing an Internet interface requires additional software and services that can tax a (possibly overburdened) Windows 2000 Server. Second, you should limit the impact of system failure to as few services as possible. Chances are that your users will be less unhappy if they lose only Internet access or access to shared files and applications, rather than losing both at the same time.

If you do use a Windows 2000 system as a router, especially if an Internet link is involved, think about installing some type of firewall software on that machine, such as Microsoft's Proxy Server or Ositis Software's WinProxy. A firewall protects your network from interlopers and allows you to monitor and filter incoming (and outgoing) content and information.

Tools for Handling TCP/IP Trouble

If you're going to attach to the Internet (and who isn't, these days?), you want to build a TCP/IP toolkit to help with the inevitable troubleshooting chores involved in keeping a TCP/IP network working properly.

Fortunately, Windows 2000 includes a fine collection of TCP/IP tools and utilities that you can use immediately. Table 23-1 includes some prime candidates for your IP troubleshooting toolbox.

Table 23-1	TCP/IP Diagnostic Utilities
Utility	*Description*
ARP	Displays the address translation tables used by the IP *Address Resolution Protocol* (ARP). Helps detect invalid entries and ensure proper resolution of numeric IP addresses to *Media Access Control* (MAC) addresses.
HOSTNAME	Displays your IP host name on-screen; use this to check your machine's current name.
IPCONFIG	Displays all current network configuration values for all interfaces; use this to check address assignments for your machine, the default gateway, and the subnet mask.
NBTSTAT	Shows protocol statistics and active connections using NetBIOS over TCP/IP; use this to troubleshoot Microsoft naming issues.
NETSTAT	Shows active TCP and *User Datagram Protocol* (UDP) connections; use this to check TCP/IP network connections and statistics.
NSLOOKUP	Displays information about known DNS servers.
PING	Verifies basic connectivity to network computers; type PING loopback to check internal capabilities first, and then check local and remote machines to check overall connectivity.
ROUTE	Displays network routing tables and enables you to edit entries; useful primarily when static routing is in effect.
TRACERT	Determines the route from the sender to a destination by sending *Internet Control Message Protocol* (ICMP) echo packets that cause all stations between sender and receiver to announce themselves.

Given this arsenal of tools, you should be well prepared to shoot TCP/IP troubles before they shoot you!

Fast Server NICs Make Fast Networks

On a Windows 2000 Server, performance is the name of the game. In networking, because network traffic tends to congregate at the server, spending extra bucks on a fast, powerful NIC makes sense. At a bare minimum, you want a *Peripheral Component Interconnect* (PCI)-based NIC because it offers the best bus connection to the rest of the system. Other hardware enhancements worth purchasing for Windows 2000 Server NICs include the following:

- ✔ **Direct Memory Access (DMA):** Enables the NIC to transfer data directly from its on-board memory to the computer's memory without requiring the CPU to mediate.

- ✔ **Shared adapter memory:** Enables a NIC's on-board RAM to map into the computer's RAM. When the computer thinks it's writing *to* its own RAM, it's writing straight *to* the NIC; and when it thinks it's reading *from* its own RAM, it's reading straight *from* the NIC. Shared system memory works the same way, except the NIC reads from and writes from the computer's RAM instead of its own on-board RAM. Extra memory for NICs is almost as good as more RAM on Windows 2000 PCs!

- ✔ **Bus mastering:** Lets the NIC manage the computer's bus to coordinate data transfers to and from the computer's memory. Bus mastering enables the CPU to concentrate on other activities and can improve performance by 20 to 70 percent. This is the most worthwhile of all the enhancements mentioned here.

- ✔ **On-board coprocessor:** Puts an additional CPU on a NIC and allows the NIC to process data that the CPU would otherwise have to handle. Many NICs today use such processors to speed operations.

The idea is to put the processing power and speed where it does the most good: on the NIC that all the users must interact with to obtain data from (or move packets through) a server. In fact, if you've got the money, you may want to investigate building backbones that use alternate or high-speed connections, such as FireWire (which is defined by IEEE 1394), Fibre Channel, Asynchronous Transfer Mode (ATM), or Gigabit Ethernet!

When to Divide, and When to Conquer

When traffic reaches high levels on a network segment, traffic jams occur just like they do at rush hour on the highway. When this happens, you either need to improve the existing roads (switch to a faster network technology) or add more roads (break up the existing network and put one subset of users on one new piece, another subset on another piece, and so on).

How can you figure out when traffic is starting to choke your network? Easy! Windows 2000 Server includes a service called the *Network Monitor* (affectionately called NetMon) that you can install on your server to monitor the traffic moving into and out of your server (and on the cable segment or segments to which that server is attached).

NetMon doesn't install on Windows 2000 Server by default, but it's easy to add. From the Start⇨Settings⇨Network and Dial-up Connections⇨ Advanced⇨Optional Networking Components⇨Management and Monitoring Tools, click the Details button, check the Network Monitoring Tools checkbox, and then click OK. After you follow the instructions from there, NetMon shows up in the Administrative Tools folder (Start⇨Settings⇨Administrative Tools⇨Network Monitor).

Get to know NetMon, and you get to know your network much better!

When in Doubt, Check Your Services

What do network servers do? They provide network services. When things get weird on a Windows 2000 Server and you can't find anything wrong with the network, visit the Services folder in Services and Applications, as shown in Figure 23-1.

To view this display, follow this menu sequence: Start⇨Programs⇨ Administrative Tools⇨Computer Management, and click on the plus ("+") sign to the left of the Services and Applications icon to expand its components. Then click on the Services entry to view the list of services currently installed on Windows 2000 Server.

Be sure to check the entries for key services like the Computer Browser, the Server service, and the Workstation service. Make sure the Status field says "Started" and the Startup field is properly set. (It should read "Automatic" for services that are supposed to launch upon startup.)

Many times, when the network shows no obvious problems, you may find a key service has been paused or stopped or has simply quit for some reason. If the service has stopped, you should refer back to Event Viewer to find out why; a stopped service usually indicates a serious problem that will recur.

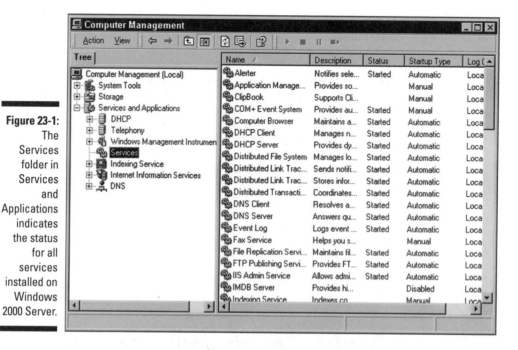

Figure 23-1:
The
Services
folder in
Services
and
Applications
indicates
the status
for all
services
installed on
Windows
2000 Server.

Handling Names and Addresses

The only way to find things on a network is to know their addresses. But alas, human beings are much better at remembering symbolic names than numeric addresses (or worse still, the arcane bit patterns that computers use to address one another).

This means many things when you operate a working network, but two primary concerns from a troubleshooting perspective exist:

- ✔ The services that provide name to address translation must be properly configured and working correctly for users to make effective use of a network.

- ✔ Network addresses, subnet masks, and related information (such as default gateways, router addresses, and so on) must be unique, properly specified, and in substantial agreement for computers to use a network properly.

Symptoms of trouble in this area are many and varied. Duplicate addresses usually cause all holders of the same address to lose their ability to access the network. Invalid names or addresses simply can't be reached and may require serious troubleshooting to fix. Active Directory may be unavailable, or not working, for some reason or another. (In general, check the spelling of names carefully and the numeric values for addresses equally carefully.)

Fortunately, problems in this arena usually make themselves known during initial configuration or when settings change. If you can simply check your settings and assumptions against a known, working set of values, you can usually fix these troubles quickly and painlessly.

What's New or Different?

When troubleshooting a network, what's new or what's changed is often a source of trouble. Therefore, when you investigate network woes, be sure to ask yourself this question right away, and then answer it in as much detail as possible. While digging up the details, you often uncover the source of the trouble and can determine its solution, all in one swift maneuver.

Savvy network administrators keep a log of changes and additions to the servers on their networks, so when those key questions ("What's new?" and "What's different?") are asked, answers are immediately forthcoming. You could do worse than to emulate these professionals!

If You Need It, Ask for Help

Occasionally, when troubleshooting a system, you run into problems that are so mysterious or baffling that you won't have a clue about how to fix them. When that happens, don't tear out your hair — ask for help instead.

If you're having a problem with Windows 2000 Server, paying $195 for a "Technical Support Incident" with Microsoft may be worth it. You can also check the TechNet CD (you can order it from www.microsoft.com/technet) or the Microsoft Developer Network (which you can join at www.msdn.microsoft.com/developer/).

If the problem's with a piece of hardware, check the manufacturer's Web site or bulletin board for a driver update. If that leads to no joy, you may have to pay that vendor's tech support operation for some advice, too. If you can determine a problem's root cause, you can often get help from those who know that root the best. Even if it costs you, think of the valuable time (and aggravation) you'll save. Better to light a candle than curse the darkness!

Outfits such as the Technical Support Alliance Network (www.tsanet.org) and even 1-900-787-7678, or the easy to remember version 1-900-SUPPORT (the phone number's also the name of the organization), can help with multi-vendor support issues. Don't be afraid to use them!

Prevention Beats Cure, Every Time!

The best way to shoot network trouble, and other types of system problems, is to stop them before they ever happen. The only way to prevent problems and keep your network running is to study your network environment closely and carefully and figure out where its weak points are. Do this before your network demonstrates its weaknesses to the world at large by breaking.

If you keep an eye on potential trouble spots and perform regular maintenance and upkeep activities (such as scheduled backups, file system cleanups, upgrades, service packs, and hotfixes), you can prevent problems. And believe us, preventing problems isn't just less work, it's also the cause of far less unwanted notoriety than fixing things after they break. Don't feel compelled to learn this the hard way!

Index